D0081581

TOURISM AND CULTURAL CONFLICTS

Tourism and Cultural Conflicts

Edited by

Mike Robinson

and

Priscilla Boniface
Centre for Travel and Tourism
University of Northumbria at Newcastle
UK

CABI *Publishing*

CABI *Publishing* – a division of CAB INTERNATIONAL

CABI *Publishing*
CAB INTERNATIONAL
Wallingford
Oxon OX10 8DE
UK

Tel: +44 (0)1491 832111
Fax: +44 (0)1491 833508
Email: cabi©cabi.org

CABI *Publishing*
10 E 40th Street
Suite 3203
New York, NY 10016
USA

Tel: +1 212 481 7018
Fax: +1 212 686 7993
Email: cabi-nao©cabi.org

A catalogue record for this book is available from the British Library, London, UK.

Library of Congress Cataloging-in-Publication Data
Tourism and cutural conflicts/edited by Mike Robinson and
Priscilla Boniface.
p. cm.
Includes bibliographical references and index.
ISBN 0–85199–272–2 (alk. paper)
1. Tourist trade. I. Robinson, Mike (Michael David)
II. Boniface, Priscilla.
G155.A1T58934 1998
338.4'791–dc21 98–8604
CIP

ISBN 0 85199 272 2

Typeset in Optima by York House Typographic Ltd, London
Printed and bound in the UK by Biddles Ltd, Guildford and King's Lynn

Contents

Contributors

Michael Barke, *Division of Geography and Environmental Management, Lipman Building, University of Northumbria, Newcastle upon Tyne NE1 8ST, UK.*

Sue Bleasdale, *School of Geography and Environmental Management, University of Middlesex, Queensway, Enfield EN3 4SF, UK.*

Priscilla Boniface, *Centre for Travel and Tourism, University of Northumbria, Longhirst Hall, Longhirst, Morpeth, Northumberland NE61 3LL, UK.*

Jane Henrici, *Huntington Art Gallery, University of Texas at Austin, Austin, Texas 78712, USA.*

Keith Hollinshead, *The Luton Business School, The University of Luton, Park Square, Luton, Bedfordshire LU1 3JU, UK.*

Michael Ireland, *The University College of St Mark & St John, Derriford Road, Plymouth, Devon PL6 8BH, UK.*

Effie Karpodini-Dimitriadi, *Institute of Cultural Studies of Europe and the Mediterranean, Chronpoulou 80, Paleo Faliro, 17563 Athens, Greece.*

Mike Robinson, *Centre for Travel and Tourism, University of Northumbria, Longhirst Hall, Longhirst, Morpeth, Northumberland NE61 3LL, UK.*

Chris Ryan, *Tourism Programme, Centre for Interdisciplinary Management Studies, Waikato Management School, The University of Waikato, Private Bag 3105, Hamilton, New Zealand.*

Myra Shackley, *Nottingham Business School, The Nottingham Trent University, Burton Street, Nottingham NG1 4BU, UK.*

Sue Tapsell, *School of Geography and Environmental Management, University of Middlesex, Queensway, Enfield EN3 4SF, UK.*

Geoffrey Wall, *Department of Geography, University of Waterloo, Ontario*

N2L 3G1, Canada.

Elvi Whittaker, *Department of Anthropology and Sociology, University of British Columbia, 6303 N.W. Marine Drive, Vancouver, British Columbia V6T 1Z1, Canada.*

Preface

Raymond Williams noted that 'culture' is one of the most complex words in language. But its myriad meanings, its use and mis-use merely reflect the diversity and complexity of a shrinking world which is struggling to find its own identity. What we do know is that there are the layers of culture, together with inter- and intra-cultural relationships based upon both difference and unity.

The expansion of tourism continues to reveal and thrive upon cultural diversity and difference. Not only are we able to explore cultures of place, we are increasingly able to explore cultures through time. Whether we define culture in artefactual and achievement terms, or in the sense of the ordinary, it shares an intimate, complex and compelling relationship with tourism. If any global phenomenon has the potential for liberating the spirit and unifying peoples it is tourism. The potential for deep and meaningful enrichment of our culture, and opportunities for greater understanding of other cultures, is implicit in tourism. But there is, as one would expect, a down side.

The impact of tourism upon cultures and sub-cultures has emerged as a key theme in the expansive literature which signals both academic maturity and the reality of tourism as a central feature of economic, social and political life. As one would expect, attention is frequently focused on those occasions where tourism and aspects of culture conflict; where the impacts of tourism are severe and highly visible. Moreover, the relations between tourism and culture are fraught with a host of ethical dilemmas, focusing on the extent to which tourism-induced change is for better or worse, or merely inevitable. Invariably issues of identity, ownership, economic equity, social justice and legal rights spill over into any discussion on tourism's impacts on society –

issues which are frequently opaque and often intractable.

It is conflict, and the potential for conflict when tourism brings cultures together, whether freely or through economic necessity, which is the underlying theme of this book. Each of the contributors to this volume offers his or her own views on the relationship which exists between culture(s) and tourism. The chapters include cases and examples drawn from a variety of countries and cultural contexts, which reflect the ever increasing pervasiveness of the tourism phenomenon and highlight the diverse ways in which tourism has impacted upon culture. They identify varying degrees of conflict, various routes of its expression through different cultural levels, and the ways in which it is managed, attenuated, avoided or ignored.

One of the more enjoyable features of editing a book which deals with such a wide ranging theme as tourism and culture is the variety of perspectives which are brought to it by our contributors. Tourism is truly a rich vein for inter-disciplinary study and we hope this shows through in this endeavour. Our thanks go first and foremost, to the authors of the chapters. We thank them for their thoughtful contributions on our theme, their patience, and their open and willing responses to our suggestions and reminders. The reality of the technological revolution really does hit home for a project such as this. With contributors in Canada, USA, Australia and Greece the wonders of Email are endorsed.

Thanks must also go to staff of the Centre for Travel and Tourism at the University of Northumbria for their assistance, particularly to Richard Sharpley and Nigel Evans. David Toney and Helen Watson are also to be thanked for their help in bringing this book together. Finally, we thank Tim Hardwick of CABI *Publishing* for his patience and attention.

Mike Robinson
Priscilla Boniface

Cultural Conflicts in Tourism: Inevitability and Inequality

1

Mike Robinson

Introduction

Tourism is arguably the largest of multinational activities. In 1996 some 592 million international trips were made (World Tourism Organization, 1997) and, according to WTO forecasts, by the year 2020 this will almost have trebled to some 1.6 billion international trips, worth some $2 trillion annually. The economic dimensions of this global systemic phenomenon and its attendant global structures are willingly recognized as being significant. The ability of tourism to generate foreign exchange revenue, create employment and absorb unemployment has provided it with a political and social legitimacy in the developed and developing world. The economic benefits of tourism are, however, the result of a fundamental process by which expressions and forms of environmental and cultural capital are traded. Environmental capital, in terms of natural resources and the more intangible and aesthetic constructs of landscape and built heritage, is clearly recognized as a platform for tourism development. Conflicts over the exploitation, over-usage and contested use of the environment for touristic purposes have over recent years attracted a great deal of attention and have paralleled wider public and political environmental debate. Cultural capital too, in its artefactual form, together with its 'way of life' and tradition dimensions, is also increasingly recognized to be at the root of the tourism phenomenon. The desire to make contact with one's own culture(s), in all its forms, and the search for experiences of other cultures is very much at the heart of tourism. But the processes by which tourists experience culture, and the way culture is utilized by the tourism industry and host communities, are increasingly characterized by conflict. Even if we consider tourists solely as hedonistic sun seekers safe in their environmental bubble (Cohen, 1972), we cannot avoid consideration of the conflicts which can and do occur between cultures at the interpersonal and structural level.

This chapter explores the dimensions of cultural conflicts in tourism. It begins by discussing the claims made about the the tourism–culture relationship and then considers the increased blurring of the distinctions which once marked out tourism and culture as separate spheres of activity. It goes on to examine various layers of conflict ranging from the direct tourist–host encounter, to the ways that conflicts exogenous to tourism activity and outside the control of tourists can nonetheless influence tourism. The context for cultural conflicts in tourism is then explored with reference to the implicit, if not explicit, search for difference. This search for difference is interpreted widely. It is not that conflict situations arise solely from inherent cultural differences; they also derive from the processes involved in the construction, accentuation and promotion of cultural identities. Discussion draws upon the changing discourse surrounding globalization, as both a process and a theoretical framework which can be utilized for greater understanding of cultural conflicts in tourism.

The underlying theme of the chapter is that conflicts between cultures in tourism are shaped and driven by the wider context of global intercultural power relations, of which tourism is one mechanism of cultural exchange (albeit one of growing importance). Given the current dominant cultural context for tourism, the structures which exist to support it, and the increasing economic importance attached to it, conflict appears as inevitable. Indeed, this inevitability is emphasized by an apparent indifference to cultural conflict on the part of both the tourism industry and tourists.

Tourism as a 'Passport to Peace'?

Reducing international tourism to economic patterns and flows, costs and benefits, neglects its formidable role as a vector of cultural exchange (UNESCO, 1997). Following Hannerz's (1990, p. 238) description of the world as a network of social relationships between which there is a 'flow of meanings as well as of people and goods', it is easy to see that the magnitude of world tourism, its apparent unbounded geographical reach and global inevitability provides significant opportunities for cultural encounters. This can lead one to a position of optimistic reflection. Tourism is imbued with potential to draw peoples and cultures together in a state of understanding and *communitas*.

The notion that tourism possesses the ability to generate cultural harmony is largely a residual attitude derived from the romantic (and élitist) traditions of travel in the 18th and 19th centuries. Craik (1997, p. 119), drawing upon historical perspectives of tourism, highlights that 'travel served as a means to facilitate national and international relations by making contacts, learning foreign languages, and engaging in debate with others'. This Eurocentric, moralistic tradition remains and has developed into political advocacy. Building upon the 'travel broadens the mind' school of thought, tourism has been cited as a potential means of contributing to world peace (Hunziker, 1961; Kaul, 1985; D'Amore, 1988; Var *et al.*, 1988).

The view is enshrined in the mission of the WTO: 'to develop tourism as a significant means of fostering international peace and understanding, economic development and international trade'. Leaving aside thorny issues of negative environmental impacts, social justice and resource equity, the role of tourism in fostering trade and economic development is difficult to contest. Host communities can enjoy cultural benefits associated with tourism (see for instance: de Kadt, 1979; Grahn, 1991), but on balance such benefits tend to be localized, temporary and heavily dependent upon neither tourist nor host being significantly disadvantaged economically. However, there is little or no evidence to indicate that tourism has played any role in fostering international peace. While not denying the nobility of such rhetoric and the *potential* that tourism could play in generating cultural harmony, claims that tourism is a 'vital force for peace' (WTO, 1980) are exaggerated and out of step with on-the-ground developments in world tourism – an activity increasingly characterized by conflict.

Before going on to consider the multidimensions of cultural conflicts in tourism it is useful to discuss the nature of the relationship between tourism and culture.

Tourism and Culture – Blurred Boundaries

The idea that we can consider the activity of tourism as somehow separate from the wider framework of culture has been overtaken by events. Rojek and Urry (1997, p. 3) point to the 'culturisation of society', and the post-modern process of de-differentiation, particularly de-differentiation of the cultural economy (Urry, 1990), whereby previously spatially and temporally distinct social and cultural practices are now merging, and distinctions between 'high' and 'low' culture are becoming lost (Wynne, 1992). Also, cultural hybridization in which conventional borders are increasingly crossed by both physical and 'virtual' means by peoples, products and cultures, now entails, in Rojek and Urry's words, that 'there is no simple sense of the spatially and temporally distinct "home" and "away"' (1997). Furthermore, as MacCannell (1992, p. 1) and others have argued, tourism itself can now be seen as a cultural experience: 'an ideological framing of history, nature, and tradition . . . a framing that has the power to reshape culture and nature to its own needs'.

Tourism has emerged as an important route towards cultural enrichment. Although no revelation in itself, the rapid diffusion of 'cultural tourism' emphasizes the process of disemblance between tourism and culture and, as Richards (1996a, p. 27) notes, is marked by the way 'culture is now primarily being promoted for economic, rather than cultural ends'. From a tourism industry perspective, cultural tourism is now considered as a distinct market segment (Stebbins, 1996), which Keller (1996) estimates to be as much as 50% of the tourism market. Craik (1997), following Silberberg's (1995) analysis, suggests that this is an over-estimate and that cultural tourism in its purest sense is engaged in by a relatively small number of visitors. The inference is that cultural tourists are drawn from the ranks of independent travellers rather than mass tourists. Richards (1996b, p. 57) argues that growth in the numbers of cultural tourists reflects an increase in the 'new service class and postmaterialistic forms of consumption'. A link is made to current tourism trends which point to the growth of short-break, city and niche holidays and a relative decline in popularity of short-haul, 'sun and sand' destinations in favour of more geographically and culturally distant locations.

But, the definition of cultural tourism (and by implication cultural tourists), particularly as used by the tourism industry, is unfortunately dogged by the dominant perspective of culture in the high-arts sense. Thus, cultural tourism is often reduced to a form in which the focus is upon an experience of museums, theatre, architecture and the like. This is a point exemplified by Richards' (1996c) useful edited volume *Cultural Tourism in Europe*. Although Richards himself notes the wider elements of the concept of culture, and the difficulties this raises, the majority of the chapters (which report on an European Union cultural tourism study) reflect this rather rarefied notion of culture.

The problem with addressing the tourism–culture relationship with an emphasis upon this narrow definition is that it can lead one to believe that cultural conflicts revolve chiefly around artefactual and heritage issues. Clearly, there are numerous conflicts arising out of the use and mis-use of heritage resources (Tunbridge and Ashworth, 1996), but we need to consider conflict as something more fundamental and resonant with the full pattern of world tourism. Despite growth in cultural tourism, the majority of tourists are not seeking the exotic, nor heritage attractions, but are 'culture-proof' (Craik, 1997). The forecasted percentage of long-haul travel in 2020 (often used as indicating the search for the exotic) is 24% of world tourism (WTO, 1997), and this includes business travel, made up of anti-cosmopolitans (Tyler, 1985). In the UK, the overlap between tourism and culture is recognized institutionally. In 1992 the tourism brief was picked up by the then newly created Department of National Heritage, and now resides in the follow-up Department of Culture, Media and Sport. Nevertheless, in 1996–97 a vast majority of approximately 22 million UK passengers were engaged in mass 'packaged' tourism to mainly the short-haul sun destinations of the Mediterranean basin (Civil Aviation Authority, 1998).

The central point being emphasized in this cursory foray into the dimensions and constituency of cultural tourism is that cultural conflicts are not restricted to so-called cultural tourists; the offspring of Boorstin's (1964) notion of the 'traveller'. Nor is it in any way automatic that conflicts are restricted to culturally uninterested masses. The idea of de-differentiation does not only refer to the entities of tourism and culture, but also to the elements which constitute our interpretations of culture. Indeed, though we should note the post-modernist merging which has occurred, we should not be restrictive in any analysis of the tourism phenomenon and the many ways in which culture and tourism touch and frequently collide.

Three interrelated reflections emerge from a recognition of this blurring of the boundaries between tourism and culture which have bearing on any attempt to understand the nature and form of cultural conflicts. First, as Urry (1995) indicates, if tourism is simply 'cultural', and if it is no longer a discrete event or series of events, but an extension of the cultural climate from which it emerges, examinations of cultural conflict need to extend beyond the immediate and the local to take in the socio-cultural context within which the tourist-encounter is framed. There is no Boorstin–MacCannell either/or about this context. It can be viewed in various ways: as a manifestation of programmed capitalist consumption or as an attempt to escape from it. But, there is a need to focus on both the immediate tourism/culture interface and the wider frame of understanding which involves recognition of the extensive cultural baggage which accompanies tourists and the tourism development process.

Second, as an extension of the above, cultural conflicts are no longer easily located in one place and at a particular instance in time. They can anticipate and succeed the moment of cultural interaction. Rojek and Urry (1997, p. 11) in the context of social and cultural 'mobility' note that 'cultures travel as well as people'. However, they do so at different rates. Tourists play a number of roles varying with their contact with host cultures. They can act as cultural prophets heralding subsequent changes which tourists may initiate, particularly in less culturally resilient destinations. They can work as catalysts (Kakazu, 1996) to speed up cultural changes, or act as inhibitors attempting to preserve cultures as objects of attention. These roles are culturally conditioned and cannot be turned on or off at a specific point of contact. All roles have different time and space dimensions and so too does the notion of conflict. It may be instantaneous and aggressive, or, much more common in the sphere of cultural change, rather take the form of a much extended process of erosion and attrition. During this process, the nature and type of tourists will also change, and the structures which support them will alter.

A further comment on the above perspective is the notion of conflict resulting from incommensurate world views on space and time. Whereas Urry (1995) goes some way in discussing the influence of time on the consumption of place, and Ryan (1991a, 1997a) examines the differences in the conceptions of the time construct between tourist and host, there remains a need for more empirical studies to examine the role of different time–space cultural paradigms, particularly in First and Third World encounters.

A third minor reflection follows on from the idea that tourism and its cultural effects can no longer be considered as apart from the cultural homelands from which they emerge. It relates to the idea of cultural 'feed-back', which is based on the idea that acculturation is a two-way process, i.e. hosts impacting upon tourists (Sharpley, 1994) and vice versa. This appears to have been forgotten in some studies of tourism's cultural impacts. While focusing on the value changes experienced by the host culture is important, tourists, whether touring the exotic or the mundane, experience changes in their own value systems as a result of their encounters. For instance, the experience of child beggars in Calcutta is at once a moving and disturbing by-product of a much larger 'exotic' cultural encounter. But it is interesting to countenance the extent to which this experience feeds back and diffuses into the culture and value systems of the touring individuals once they return home. Such an issue would seem to provide an intellectual greenfield site for further research.

Cultural Conflicts and Tourism

The arguments mobilized for the rather rosy view that tourism can be a vehicle for world peace can also be used to support a much less optimistic position that tourism is an agent of cultural conflict. The desire to tour the increasingly distant and exotic (although this may be over-emphasized) coupled with media developments which now allow experience of destinations prior to travel, in addition to the physical reality of visiting, has increased tourism's power to reach the majority of the world's 10,000 distinct societies living in over 200 states. But in doing so it has created the risk of intercultural conflicts, and has also created the potential for tourism to be caught up in intracultural conflicts.

It is important to remember not to place too great an emphasis on tourism as the sole mechanism for conflict. Worldwide interaction is now an established phenomenon (Gessner and Schade, 1990), and tourism is only one form of intercultural interaction. However, it is the most direct and it is increasingly linked with other 'modernizing' influences and exchanges. Multi- and transnational expansions in manufacturing production and in the consumptive industries have, for instance, generated increases in business motivated travel. In addition, the possibilities of 'armchair interfacing' via sophisticated global communication technologies have given substance to Anderson's (1983) ideas of 'imagined communities' and has direct links with improved marketing and distribution networks for the tourism industry.

Cultural conflict generally implies some degree of incompatibility between individuals, and between societies and cultures. Conflict itself generates dramatic images of battle and armed struggle; however, with

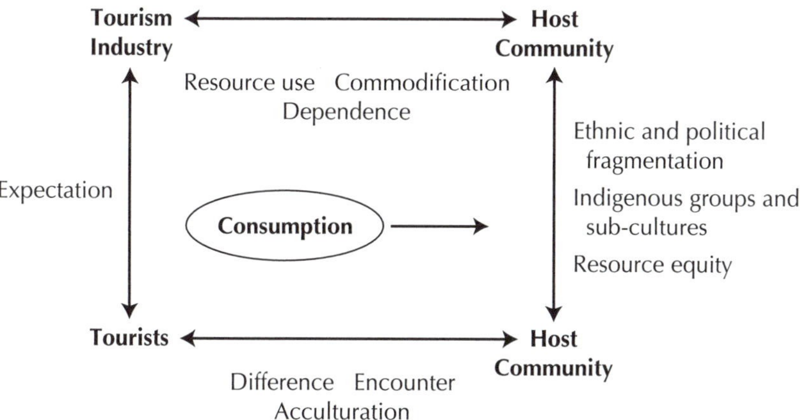

Fig. 1.1. Dimensions of cultural conflict.

regard to tourism it seldom results in violence or even aggressive behaviour. But cultural conflicts do occur on a regular basis on differing levels and between the different interest groups within tourism. Figure 1.1 illustrates four broad planes between which cultural conflicts occur. Perhaps the most obvious is that which exists between tourist and host, often characterized as a 'face-to-face' encounter, and a two-way process of communication (Swinglehurst, 1994). In a structuralist vein, the interface between the tourism industry (which would include the physical mix of accommodation, transport, attractions, support services, and the organizations behind these: tour operators, travel agents, hotel developers, government agencies as promoters and regulators) and the host community is also a rather obvious source of potential conflict. There is also room for cultural conflicts between the tourism industry and tourists, and even amongst the tourists themselves (Nash, 1996). Furthermore, a dimension of cultural conflict which is often overlooked in the literature is that which takes place within host communities and is largely independent of tourism.

These four dimensions of cultural conflict are discussed below in more detail. But at this point it is useful to note that the degree to which cultural conflicts extend along these dimensions is framed by the wider cultural context within which the touring and the toured interface. This links with the idea of what may loosely be termed 'cultural carrying capacity'. This is a rather ill-defined elaboration of the more substantive notion of 'tourism carrying capacity' (Mathieson and Wall, 1982) which theoretically identifies and measures a 'tipping-point' of the acceptability of tourism (Parris, 1996), in physical, perceptual, economic and social terms (O'Reilly, 1986). In cultural terms 'carrying capacity' is difficult to articulate, let alone measure. However, it is clear that the extent of cultural conflicts in tourism does vary in line with a myriad of 'culturally informed' variables within both toured and touring populations. Although it is difficult to generalize, essentially some host communities may be more passive and tolerant than others, at different times and within different spaces.

Tourist–Host Conflicts

Numerous studies have pointed to the mutuality of benefits experienced in cross-cultural, tourist–host encounters including the generation of positive attitudes on the part of tourist and host (Amir and Ben-Ari, 1985), increased cultural understanding, the reduction of ethnic prejudices and the development of pride, appreciation and tolerance (Reisinger, 1994, performs a valuable task in bringing together such studies). However, it would be true to say that by far the majority of researchers have focused upon those encounters which have resulted in negative socio-cultural impacts. This seems to bear out the idea that the focus of intercultural communication is on conflict (Gessner and Schade, 1990). Attention is also normally given over to the negative impacts experienced on the part of the host rather than the tourist, reflecting, in part, some ethnocentric bias in the research, but also an implicit recognition of an imbalance of power relations. Moreover, there has been (an understandable) concentration on the type and extent of the cultural impacts, as opposed to the follow-up reactions to the impacts by the host community. The result is that the cultural impacts of tourists can be perceived as somehow automatically index-linked to tourists' behaviour at specific points in time, whereas conflict will often remain when the tourists have gone.

Reisinger (1994) explores the tourist–host encounter in the context of the social contact hypothesis, which is heavily descriptive relating to the resultant changes in attitudes and relations from contact between different ethnic groups. Not surprisingly, in a tourism context, as with a wider context, changes have been identified as both positive and negative (see Table 1.1).

However, on balance it seems that the negative effects do outweigh the positive gains, in both number and depth. That this is the case would seem to echo Krippendorf's (1987) observation that there is an important distinction that while the tourist is engaged in leisure, the host is normally engaged in work. The possession of fundamentally different goals goes some way in explaining conflict, but this begs the question of where these goals originate and this brings us back to an analysis of the degree of imbalance and difference which exists between the two interacting cultures.

Gessner and Schade (1990, p. 258) see that in intercultural encounters 'an already complex situation is exacerbated by ambiguities, lack of awareness and/or the misunderstanding of cultural behaviour standards, of language or of relational dimensions such as confidentiality or status'. Following this we can note a hierarchy of cultural misunderstanding which broadly correlates with differing tourist types and destinations (Nash, 1996). Opportunities for cultural conflicts would, for instance, be low in the case of

Table 1.1 Cross-cultural tourist–host contact. Source: adapted from Reisinger (1994).

Positive Effects	Negative Effects
Developing positive attitudes about each other	Developing negative attitudes about each other
Learning about each other's culture and customs	Tension, hostility, suspicion and misunderstanding
Reducing negative perceptions and stereotypes	Isolation, segregation and separation
	Clashes of values
Developing friendships	Difficulties in forming friendships
Developing pride, appreciation, understanding, respect and tolerance for each other's culture	Feelings of inferiority and superiority
	Communication problems
	Ethnocentrism
Increasing self-esteem	Culture shock
Psychological satisfaction with interaction	Dissatisfaction with mutual interaction

someone from London visiting Manchester, increased in the case of someone from the UK visiting France, and substantially increased in a situation where someone from the USA was visiting China (Wei *et al.*, 1989).

This too is overlain with a mesh of variables representing degrees of distance between the value systems, social class, attitudes and patterns of behaviour which tourism individuals and groups possess, and those held by the host community; all points of potential misunderstandings and conflict. Expectation on both sides can accelerate or slow down the collision of such variables. Gessner and Schade (1990, p. 258) observe that 'intercultural tensions and mis-understandings occur if any of the participants in intercultural communication implicitly or explicitly acts in violation of others' expectations'. However, expectations are frequently utilized more for maintaining inequalities rather than reducing them. By definition, the tourist experience is sold on the back of expectation and anticipation. On the other hand, those parts of host communities which are not directly involved in tourism businesses and are passive stakeholders, seldom know what to expect from tourists and are unlikely to have been consulted as to their views.

Nettekoven (1979) sought to correct three misconceptions about intercultural tourist encounters; first that contact between tourists and residents of the host community is usually over-emphasized; second, the desire for close intercultural encounters amongst tourists is also over-emphasized; and third, in the context of developing nations, interaction with tourists is seldom the most important influence upon the host cultures.

On the first point Nettekoven may well be correct, although the massive increase in tourist numbers since 1979 has undoubtedly weakened the point.

Paradoxically, though more areas of the world are open to tourists than ever before, the majority of tourists seldom travel far, still preferring to congregate around the major resort areas. The major points of contact are thus between tourist and hotel employee, tourist and restaurant staff, tourist and local shopkeepers, tourist and local tour guide. These encounters are characterized by relatively short and *ad hoc* periods of contact (which itself supports Nettekoven's second point), a form of acting by both parties in which they conform to their respective roles in leisure and work, and an implicit, if not explicit, moment of power on the part of the tourist.

In line with Nettekoven's points, the acculturation process through the influence of tourists would be relatively limited within a host community. Given that local tour guides, shopkeepers and hotel staff, will probably already partly share, or at least be in touch with, the value systems of tourists, the extent to which cultural patterns are changed is likely to be limited. However, negative effects of acculturation via the 'demonstration effect' including deviant behaviour to support the imitation of touristic lifestyles, do occur, reflecting that although direct tourist–host encounters may be limited, indirect encounters are far greater and arguably more pervasive. It is difficult to pinpoint cultural conflict to individual tourist–host encounters in some cause and effect way. Despite possible 'culture shock' (Furnham and Bochner, 1986), and opportunities for misunderstanding between tourist and host, conflict in the form of aggressive behaviour by either party is unlikely to manifest itself in any immediate sense. What is important is the effect of these contact situations *in toto*, and over a prolonged period of time. This draws us in to discussing the wider context of tourism development and the impacts of the tourism industry, which shape the ways in which tourists and hosts interact.

Tourism Industry–Host Conflicts

Tourism is a highly structured and organized form of human activity. It is referred to, and refers to itself, as an industry. In reality it is a collection of a number of different industries which both formally and informally are brought together to service the 'needs' of society to travel. Fragmentation of the tourism industry involving millions of individual businesses around the world, from small accommodation enterprises to international hotel chains, makes it difficult to speak of tourism as a single industrial sector (for the purposes of discussion the collective term of tourism industry is used here); a point which inhibits tourism researchers and arguably accounts for a strong focus upon the demand rather than supply end of the tourist system.

Despite distinctions with manufacturing industry for instance, with the end-product being intangible, and despite dealing with the complexities of social motivations and the caprice of human emotions in juxtapositions of work and leisure contexts, the tourism industry nevertheless, and with minor exceptions, shares basic business characteristics; it is driven by the search for profit, employs people, is managed in the functional areas of marketing, finance, personnel, etc., and is subject to similar economic, political and environmental externalities. In addition, as Sinclair *et al.* (1992, p. 47) reminds us, 'tourism takes place in an international context dominated by the actions of large foreign firms, whose headquarters are usually in industrialised countries'. When we speak in terms of cultural conflicts in tourism we are invariably speaking of conflicts between systems and structures, as well as between individuals. In this sense we are speaking of cultural conflicts in the context of the processes of capitalism (Britton, 1991; Roche, 1992), the organization of capitalism (Lash and Urry, 1994) and the differences existing between capitalist and pre-capitalist economies (Crick, 1989).

Three central themes which shape the relationships between the tourism industry and host communities and which can lead to conflict can be picked out as: (i) the nature and extent of the commodification of the host culture; (ii) the utilization of natural resources and its cultural resonances; and (iii) the degree of economic dependency of the host community on tourism.

Commodifying cultures

In recognizing the business motivations of the tourism industry and the capitalist ideologies they work to, it is useful to consider the reality of cultural commodification and commercialization. Commodification is generally taken to be the process whereby ways of life, traditions and the complex symbolism which supports these, are imaged and transformed into saleable products (Cohen, 1987). In part, this process is explained to varying degrees by reference to the overlapping collection of 'isms': post-industrialism, post-fordism, post-modernism and post-nationalism. In essence, culture becomes the servant of consumerism and as a consequence its deeper meanings, social functions and authenticity are lost to the superficial (Greenwood, 1989; MacCannell, 1992). Whereas the literature has tended to focus upon the commodification issue in relation to developing nations, minority ethnic groups and indigenous populations, it is also relevant, if not so pronounced, in developed Western societies.

It is worth considering two features of cultural commodification which relate to conflict situations. The first relates to a distinction regarding what aspects of culture are commodified. While it is difficult to generalize, taking an inclusive definition of culture, it is clear that the 'packaging' and commercialization of some aspects are more contentious than others. The presentation of cultural artefacts within a museum context can be non-contentious. Indeed, its educational function can be liberating for local cultures, allowing them to exhibit their history and culture to a wider audience. Macdonald (1997), for instance, discusses this with regard to the Isle of Skye Heritage Centre, and concludes, though not straightforwardly, that commodification can be a way of affirming identity and value. Moreover, the notion of charging tourists for access to such a centre or a museum exhibition – often equated with somehow weakening cultural integrity – is not in itself a source of cultural conflict.

In westernized developed societies, ideas of formal display and exhibition have their own tradition. Leaving aside interpretative issues, the presentation of history through collecting, museums and heritage centres, possesses its own culture convergent with a secular, ethnocentric society. This 'weak' form of commodification is largely emblematic and historistic, and although not without conflict, it nevertheless carries a large measure of social legitimacy.

Contrast this with a 'strong' form of commodification of ethnic groups and practices in non-westernized developing societies which have neither tradition nor need of outwardly directed cultural exhibitionism. Indigenous societies *en masse* are often 'showcased' by developing nations for economic purposes (Walle, 1996). Religious rituals, ethnic rites and festivals continue to be reduced and sanitized in order to conform to tourist expectations, resulting in what MacCannell (1984, p. 361) has termed 'reconstructed ethnicity'. Crystal (1989) and Adams (1990) for instance, have highlighted the way in which the sacred funeral ceremonies of the Toraja people of Sulawesi, Indonesia have increasingly become directed to meet the needs of the tourists and, in doing so, provoked community resentment. In 1987 this resulted in a number of Toraja communities temporarily refusing to accept tourists, but having to relent in order that they could sell tourist souvenirs upon which the community has become dependent. Similar examples of cultural and ethnic reconstructions with their consequential social tensions are, unfortunately, not hard to find (see for instance: Altman, 1989; Daltabuit and Pi-Sunyer, 1990; Goering, 1990).

The exchange value of ethnic resources remains a potent argument for governments of both developing and developed nations. Harp (1994, p. 6) points to the realization by the Canadian Government of the 'increased awareness of the potential benefits to be derived from using a community's ethnocultural resources as a vehicle for stimulating tourism'. In this case multiculturalism is viewed as being available to be harnessed for economic purposes directed by the needs of the market-place and driven in particular by the demands identified by the US market.

The second feature relates to the lack of time and space constraints in commodifying culture for tourists and emphasizes that we no longer need to travel to effect cultural change. Tourists, irrespective of their actual destination choice, momentarily buy into other cultures. Packaging culture in a manner which will appeal to growing numbers eager to consume both its physical and lived manifestations now begins well away from original cultural sites. Cultures are selectively dissembled and reduced to two-dimensional word and image combinations within brochures. The brochure is probably the most conspicuous element of the commodification process and recognized as vital in communicating the tourism product across geographical and cultural distances (Dann, 1996a). However, as Lea (1988) and Silver (1993) have shown, the brochure is able to reduce distinctive and unique cultures to superficial and readily substitutable narratives. As Classen and Howes put it:

> The simplistic and traditionalistic imagery of 'otherness' used in product promotions and travel advertisements hinders the inhabitants of the countries concerned in asserting an identity as modern, industrially developed or developing peoples with complex lifestyles.
>
> (Classen and Howes, 1996, p. 187)

In some cases the commodification of culture for touristic purposes, even in its strong form, is not always contested (see for instance McKean, 1989; Boissevain, 1996). Some indigenous cultures are not unaware of the economic advantages of packaging their cultures to meet new world demands. The Canadian National Aboriginal Tourism Association (CNATA) for example, estimates that over 15,000 people are employed in approximately 2100 aboriginal tourism businesses which are worth some $250 million annually (Alberta Aboriginal Tourism Alliance, 1996). However, such examples are often precariously positioned against a cultural agenda shaped by dominant First World capitalist principles. Thus, even within an apparently buoyant Canadian Aboriginal tourism industry there is vigilance and a residual antagonism towards the Canadian Tourism Commission (CTC). As CNATA president Barry Parker told the first ever Aboriginal Tourism Convention in Calgary 1996, the CTC 'must never, never forget that the major stakeholder in aboriginal tourism are aboriginal people, their cultures are the environment. These must never be put at risk.' (Alberta Aboriginal Tourism Alliance, 1996)

This hints at the crux of the matter. Over and above the 'how' of presentation, the determining issues from which Greenwood's (1989) 'conflictual arenas' are constructed, are those power-related concepts of rights, ownership, and consent. Conflicts arise over claims regarding the ownership and presentation of cultural property. Culture, in terms of ethnic traditions, language, religious beliefs and community traditions, together with its symbolic expression in the form of 'cultural capital' are open to political manipulation by the state for both economic and nationalistic reasons. It is not solely the fact that commodification of culture takes place, we need to analyse the political basis upon which it occurs, the degree of selectivity involved, whether cultural rights are being transgressed, whether the 'owners' of culture receive the revenues generated by the gazing tourists, and whether communities possess a veto by which they could prevent exploitation.

In the case of some groups such as the CNATA, there have been encouraging and significant moves towards more effective control of aboriginal cultural and environmental resources. But in some ways this is not a typical situation. Aboriginal culture in Canada is succeeding, albeit overdue, in reclaiming its political and economic powers. By the year 2000 approximately one-third of Canada's land mass will return to aboriginal control together with up to $15 billion in land claim settlements (Alberta Aboriginal Tourism Alliance, 1996). This provides Canada's aboriginal peoples with the power of choice they have previously lacked, and thus the increased ability to shape the commodification process. However, in other parts of the world, opportunities for control remain thwarted and veiled by the dominant ideology of consumerism. Watson and Kopachevsky effectively summarize:

> Tourism by its very nature, is shaped by a very complex pattern of symbolic valuation; and this takes place in a structured social context over which tourists themselves have no immediate control. The essence of modern capitalism is the remanufacture of images, many of which effectively obscure the injuries of class, race and sex.
>
> (Watson and Kopachevsky, 1994, p. 293)

Environment and natural resource use

The tourism industry utilizes, and to a varying extent is based upon, the natural environment and its resources. Although clearly related to the specific negative environmental impacts of tourists, the tourism industry in a collective sense produces varying degrees of environmental disturbance, degradation and natural resource needs which flow from resort, associated infrastructure development and day-to-day operations. Tourism in the context of the environmental *problematique* has long been a strong focus for academic study and is of course worthy of a compartmentalist study. But it is the intricate relationships and holistic resonances between the environment and culture which are of relevance to any consideration of conflict. Following the above discussion, the natural environment is also a marketable commodity. The tourism industry has long recognized the value of packaging not just the value-free aspects of a destination's environment – the sun, sea and sand elements – but also the value-laden constructs such as landscape and heritage. This draws us into the cultural realm and raises a number of interrelated issues including those of appropriation, sacredness and development.

The environmental intrusions of the tourism industry are frequently cultural intrusions. At the very least, tourism can precipitate antagonism between the host community and the agents of development as valued resources are used to serve the needs of the tourism industry. For instance, the abstraction of local water supplies for the maintenance of golf courses in southern Spain deprives the host community of a limited resource and has given rise to community resentment towards the golf-associated tourism developments that have taken place (Robinson, 1996).

Indeed, taking the golf example further, the Japanese in their fanaticism for the game and its importance as a networking agent in their corporate culture, have taken to colonizing Malaysia with golf courses (Chatterjee, 1993) and associated leisure and industrial developments (increasingly, it is cheaper for the Japanese to travel abroad to play golf than pay very high domestic green fees). Although the Malaysian government welcomes this inward investment, the resultant environmental destruction of rainforest, displacement of peasant farmers, abstraction of vital water supplies, increased risk of local pesticide poisoning, can be framed as a fundamental cultural clash, driven by the Japanese interpretation of ostensibly American values which accentuate the social standing of golf.

The appropriation of natural resources by (or on behalf of) the tourism industry, whilst imperialistic in character, is often done with the tacit support of the host state. The issue is then one of conflict between different cultural groups within a destination, or conflict between the governed and the governing, each not only with different claims to resources, but different interpretations of how they should be used. An International Union for the Conservation of Nature (1997) case study exemplifies this. In Kenya, where tourism is an increasingly important source of foreign revenue (Sinclair *et al.*, 1992), Narok County Council are seeking to turn one of the last native forests of East Africa, Naimina Enkyio, into a nature reserve in order to attract more tourists. The Council own the land rights to the forest but the Loita Maasai population live and worship there and are already under threat from the tourism pressures being exerted on the nearby Maasai Mara reserve. The Loita Maasai are challenging the Council's rights as an infringement of the 1992 Biodiversity Convention. However, whilst at one level the conflict is represented as a legal battle, its ultimate structure is one of incommensurable world views.

This failure to see that environment and culture mean something more than a manageable, tradable resource is a major stumbling block for the tourism industry. The First World capitalist ideologies which propel it are, in theory anyway, capable of dealing with issues of resource equity and distribution. The market allows for its own adjustments and some element of intervention. Significant players in the world tourism industry have joined with the wider business community in adopting the rhetoric of sustainable development. Driven by self-interest, the tourism industry (and, by implication, national governments) increasingly recognizes that the rates of natural resource depletion can be reduced by effective management, differential pricing and in some cases restrictions on visitor access. Such actions can prolong tourism capacity and help to ameliorate environmental and associated cultural conflicts. But this reductionist managerial approach misses the point. In the above case of the Loita Maasai, and as Hollinshead (1996) cogently argues, in relation to Aboriginal Australia, conflict is not reducible in terms of neo-classical economics and marketing theory; it relates to different meanings and intensively different ways of seeing the world, its resources, space and time. Indeed, apart from recognizing the 'value' of indigenous peoples (World Commission on Environment and Development, 1987), the discourse of sustainable development actually says very little on culture and the ways it shapes relationships with the environment.

Tourism dependency

The depth and extent of cultural conflicts between the tourism industry and host communities are strongly influenced by the politico-economic circumstances that such communities experience and the extent to which they are dependent upon tourism. Tourism dependency in this context is interpreted both wide and narrow. At the meta-level tourism fits rather neatly with neo-Marxian ideas of global economic imbalances, and structural dependency of the developing nations upon the developed nations (Britton, 1982; Erisman, 1983; Crick, 1989). By extension world tourism has been represented as a form of neo-colonialism and imperialism (Mathieson and Wall, 1982; Crick, 1989; Nash, 1989, 1996). Such interpretations help rationalize commodification of cultures by outsiders, and the exploitation of natural resources, both with and without cultural significance. It is not just that the flow of tourists is primarily from First to Third World which lends weight to the neo-colonial view, but that the location of ownership of tourism businesses is concentrated in the developed north, and subsequently, the flow of tourism receipts is largely in a south to north direction (Harrison, 1992; Cazes, 1996). Of course, economic imbalances in a tourism sense are only part of a much larger mosaic of the imbalances between developed and developing nations in terms of production, consumption, access to capital, credit and information (UNESCO, 1995). But this asymmetry of relations (Watson and Kopachevsky, 1994) also accentuates associated cultural differences and creates an apparent permanent backdrop for conflict.

In a narrower sense the extent to which a state is dependent upon tourism either as one of a limited number of development options, or as the only option, does have bearing upon cultural relationships between the tourism industry and the host population. Dependency can generate its own internal conflicts. These are multifaceted conflicts in which political, economic, environmental and cultural dimensions are often tightly fused together. Solfield (1996), in his examination of tourism development in Anuha in the Solomon Islands, points to a number of different levels of internal conflicts, but fundamentally locates the main reasons for these as deriving from external (in this case Australian) tourism development pressures, and more substantively, from two conflicting world views.

Cultural conflicts are not only between tourists and locals, but between locals and those who work within the tourism industry (sometimes seen to serve the needs of outsiders), between competing communities and ethnic groups, and between the masses and the local élite (Crick, 1989). Tourism is highly symbolic of economic power, particularly in developing countries and this is clearly a driver for acculturation. The supply of tourism provides access to employment and incomes, which may be significantly higher than those of local agricultural workers for instance (Cukier-Snow and Wall, 1993; Cukier, 1996). Access to tourism employment and, in a developing country context, relatively high wage levels, may be skewed towards certain social and ethnic groups rather than others, or labour may be imported from outside the community. Kakazu (1996) for instance, writing of the high tourism dependency of small islands in the Asia–Pacific region, notes that in Northern Mariana Island the bulk of the tourism industry workforce is imported mainly from the Philippines, and this has created economic tensions which have spilled over into social relations.

The inability of the host community to 'control' the tourism industry in political and economic terms exacerbates the potential for resentment and conflict along cultural lines at a micro and macro level. Whilst it would be overstretching a point to argue that cultural conflicts can be wholly compensated in economic terms, there is nevertheless a trade-off position by which aspects of cultural intrusion and degrees of acculturation can be tolerated in the name of economic development and modernization.

Three points emerge. First, the concept of compensation for loss of cultural capital, or the loss of control of that capital, is firmly anchored in the same 'traditional' First World view, which has rationalized the commodification of culture and has legitimized its trading. Second, the extent of dependency in developing economies does have bearing on the issue of compensation. As Richter (1992, p. 37) points out: 'Tourism is not one among many industries, but often the chief or leading industry. Because it was not built amidst a developed economy, tourism revenues are less likely to stay in the society. Capital for tourism development often comes from outside and thus tourism itself is less diversified.' Resentment at the lack of adequacy in terms of 'reward' can manifest itself in cultural tensions. Third, it is worth noting there is nothing wrong *per se* in the utilization of tourism as an agent of development; it could well be the least disturbing of development options, and host communities may be in a position to freely choose tourism as an agent of modernization amongst others (de Burlo, 1996). Nor can we assume that culture in developing countries is as vulnerable and incapable of adaptation as is sometimes made out (Harrison, 1992).

Tourism–Tourist Conflicts

An area which has received scant attention in the literature is the extent to which cultural conflicts may exist between groups of tourists themselves, and between tourists and the tourism industry. The received assumption tends to be that tourists represent homogeneous groupings, united by virtue of them 'being' tourists and engaging in tourist behaviour. To the host community they are united in being outsiders and strangers (Simmel, 1950). However, the collective term 'tourists' masks a plenitude of social and cultural distinctions. Paradoxically for marketing purposes, although tourist markets are increasingly segmented along socio-economic and geodemographic lines – a myriad of different consumer 'types' now abound – tourism impact studies generally fail to take these segmentations into account. Rather unfortunately, crude taxonomies are often applied which divide up tourists as either belonging to the masses or the independent travellers, with the implication that good behaviour tends to reside in the latter rather than the former.

Tourists in any one destination will represent a panoply of cultures. The host community may, or may not, recognize the often subtle differences amongst visiting groups. On one level the cultural diversity of tourists presents the host with a series of problems in coping with their different socio-cultural needs. On another level, cultural plurality of tourists can lead to friction between tourist and tourist. Competition between British and German tourists over access to sun beds in Spanish resorts has been absorbed into folklore, and while unlikely to be construed as anything more than friendly rivalry, nevertheless assists in maintaining Anglo–German stereotypes. Moreover, the 'lager lout' brawls in Spanish resorts, although somewhat hyped by the press, are chiefly between individuals and subgroups of UK tourists, reflecting a home-from-home translocation of behaviour. Ritchie's (1993) lively account of British holiday-makers on the Spanish Costa del Sol picks out the variations between the mass of UK tourists; sub-cultures designated by region of origin, and indicated by different football strips and pub-names. However, despite signs of tourist–tourist conflict (Ritchie refers to the colloquially named 'combat alley' in Torremolinos), the potential for conflict is generally outweighed by a wider sense of unity in being outsiders.

We have already noted the role of the tourism industry in the packaging and commodification of cultures, in terms of the potential for generating tourism–host conflicts. This process of representation through advertising and brochures creates a significant degree of expectation amongst potential tourists *de facto*. Parris (1996, p. 36) observes that the idealized images of cultures projected via advertising agencies and national tourist bureaux in the sending countries 'enter the decision-making situation of prospective tourists and in interaction with their own "culturally specific" values, are carried to the chosen destinations'. This involves a process of selectivity on the part of the generators and receivers of the image in which reformed and contrived expectations of culture emerge (Dann, 1996b). It is these expectations, and projected idealized images of culture (which need not reflect the real/authentic identity of the hosts), which if not sold, are bought by tourists and are carried to a destination. Failure on the part of the host culture to live up to these externally imposed expectations, or failure on the part of the tour operator to deliver their promises, can result in tourist dissatisfaction and resentment. In itself this may not be a source of conflict, but in its willingness to meet consumer needs and impose westernized models of service and quality, the tourism industry can pressurize host cultures to conform to tourist expectations.

Host–Host Conflicts

All tourism buys into a dynamic of cultural relations although the degree of exposure and contact between tourists and host cultures varies. We cannot avoid a brief consideration of cultural conflicts between different host groups, majority and minority populations and their impacts upon tourism. As mentioned above, competition for access to natural and cultural resources utilized by tourists can initiate or inflame disputes between different cultural groups. Tourism is seen as a way of communities achieving political recognition in a competitive world (Smith, 1990), but in drawing on their cultural resources to gain this recognition, cultures come into conflict with themselves and with other cultures. Similarly, the economic benefits of tourism may not be distributed evenly across social or ethnic groups; rights can be infringed and this can engender resentment and hostility. However, we must accept that cultural conflicts exist independently of tourism and that although peace may be a pre-condition for tourism, unwittingly tourists may find themselves in the midst of cultural clashes. The roots of such conflicts may be deep, combining a complex series of historical events with contemporary political and social realities.

Medrano (1996) distinguishes between different forms of ethnic conflicts within host communities. He differentiates between: (i) violent forms of conflict most notably exemplified in Bosnia; (ii) institutionalized conflicts such as that surrounding Quebec nationalism; (iii) conflict involving indigenous territorial claims, for example the struggles between the Tamils and Shinalese in Sri Lanka; and (iv) ethnic conflicts between groups which do not focus on territories and which may involve elements of confrontation between the host majority ethnic group and one or a number of immigrant minority groups. In practice, the tourist is unlikely to be able to clearly differentiate between such forms of conflict and its often obscured cultural roots. Culture(s) is/are invariably politicized in order to articulate the economic, social and environmental claims which are attached to it. When conflict is expressed through violence, its obvious consequence for the prospective tourist, or the tourism developer, is that touristic activity is suspended. In the case of war, or violent conflict situations there is unlikely to be much in the way of deliberate contact between tourist and host community. However, tourists and the tourism industry have been used as targets in conflict situations. Ryan (1991b), drawing on a number of examples of violent acts against tourism, identifies the reasons for this as: (i) the tourism industry is seen to symbolize capitalism; (ii) tourists from 'wealthy' countries are also seen to represent capitalism; and (iii) tourism supported by the state becomes symbolic of government and a target for terrorist groups.

Ironically, and oft times perversely, the physical remnants of conflict have become absorbed into tourism. Sites of previous cultural and political struggles can draw their own tourist gaze. For instance, the demilitarized zone of the 38th Parallel, which marks the boundary between North and South Korea is now a tourist attraction (at least for those visiting South Korea). As was the case with the Berlin Wall, effectively there is nothing much to see, but what tourists seem to feed from is the apprehension of conflict and numerous emotional responses brought out by the tangible recognition of difference. As Tunbridge and Ashworth (1996) point out in their thoughtful analysis of the conflicts inherent in heritage, many tourist attractions – temples, churches, historic houses, museums and landscapes – remain as symbols of past and present conflicts regarding race, religion, language, class and gender. The conferring of 'heritage' status, commodification, and the marketing of such symbols involves an inherent selectivity which promotes certain value systems over others and can result in the 'disinheritance' of non-participatory, marginalized groups.

The inevitable question is whether cultural conflicts between host communities would cease if tourism/tourists were removed from the situation. The answer is clearly no. However, tourism retains a capacity for catalysing host cultural disputes, in part for the reasons Ryan suggests, and more fundamentally because of its ability to contribute to the marginalization and trivialization of cultural groups, its innate selectivity, and its capability to shape the economic, environmental and political agendas of destinations.

Tourism and the Search for Difference

Discussion of the dimensions of cultural conflict and tourism only serves to highlight the issues of difference and diversity. A practical view of difference as being the absence of what is the same (Nicholas, 1994), informs our ideas of diversity. Cultural diversity carries significant value, intrinsically, in utilitarian terms, and a way of 'keeping alternatives alive' (Hannerz, 1996, p. 63). Hannerz quotes economist Stephen Marglin (p. 62) to assist in making the not uncontentious case for cultural diversity, who notes 'cultural diversity as a global asset'. Recognition of this value has been slow in coming. It runs through the still emergent sustainable development paradigm (World Commission on Environment and Development, 1987; United Nations, 1993; International Union for the Conservation of Nature, 1997) which has identified the role of cultural diversity as an integral part of the concept of biodiversity as enshrined in the Convention on Biological Diversity (United Nations, 1993). The links which are made, focus chiefly on the important role of indigenous peoples as marking diversity and their holding of valuable knowledge which can be utilized in the management of the environment (Indigenous Peoples Earth Charter, 1992).

Cultural differences are valuable in tourism (economic) terms. Whether we are speaking of domestic tourism, outbound 'mass' tourism, or specialist tours and day visits, the underlying premise is that the tourist is offered, and largely expects experience of something different (Graburn, 1989). Bauman (1996, p. 29) comments that 'the tourist is a conscious and systematic seeker of experience of difference and novelty – as the joys of the familiar wear off and cease to allure. The tourists want to immerse in the strange and bizarre element. . . .' At the most fundamental level, this 'element' may be physical, what Cohen (1995, p. 23) refers to as 'placeness' or the geographical distinctiveness of a destination (Burns and Holden, 1995). The presence of warmer weather, a sandy coast or a mountainous landscape are features of destination which the tourist identifies as different from those features of his or her home environment. The suggestion is that in such cases differences are desirable, indeed, if the climate of the Costa del Sol was similar to that of Manchester in December, an important motivation for travelling to Torremolinos is lost. This echoes the description by Paul Theroux (1986) of tourism being 'home-plus'. Although the physical world is imbued with a variety of cultural interpretations, physical differences are largely non-contestable and relatively straightforward to evaluate before, during and after travel.

But while physical differences are important, it is the more intangible and highly contested aspects of cultural difference which provide a central motivation in tourism. Cultural differences operate at a number of related levels reflecting the multifaceted interpretations of the term culture. Some tourists (as opposed to 'people') seek contact with different 'ways of life', as identified by a wide variety of cultural signifiers including social behaviour, language, dress, music, the arts and cuisine. Indeed, tourism is one form of human activity that thrives on the celebration and display of cultural differences; ranging from the exotic to the mundane, the meaningful to the menial and the immediate to the imagined. In other spheres of human activity cultural differences may be apparent but may be neither relevant nor emphasized, but in tourism cultural differences are packaged and supplied to provide emphasis, and this very process is so often at the root of conflict.

Relatively few prospective tourists seek total immersion in a different culture and few host societies seek not to adapt wholly to the needs of tourists. Instead, the tourist seeks safe glimpses of cultural differences, and this may or may not be accompanied by a desire to understand the culture of the other. In part tourist safety from over-exposure to host cultures is ensured by the short and infrequent duration of contact between themselves and their hosts. Host communities, however, do not go home, they are home and contact may be continuous.

Culture is about differences and cultural differences are obvious (Wallerstein, 1990). Tourism is plainly about the *experience* of cultural difference whether it is desired or not. The experience of difference carries the potential to be rewarding, but at the same time can induce fear often accompanied by desire and envy (Hall, 1987). Experience itself is culturally conditioned, subjective, and bound up with a range of time and space variables which dictate its form and content. But the range of tourist experiences of cultural differences draws us to deeper motivations as why experiences of difference are sought. For tourism is about the *search* for difference; difference meaning something far more substantive than 'authenticity', which though important for some is of little consequence for others. Ryan (1997b) provides a well structured discussion of tourist motivation and highlights the problems in seeking to explain the variety of tourist experiences by reference to a limited number of apparently rational motivations. He notes that (p. 46) 'motivations only have meaning with reference to the social environment within which they are formulated'. This is true, but it stops short of positioning tourism as a function of culture. The very notion of engaging in a search for difference resides in some cultural groups and not in others.

Morley and Robins (1995) optimistically suggest that tourism represents a new valuation of difference, and this would seem to underpin the notion of the 'cultural tourism' phenomenon. However, this valuation is wrought in the image of the culturally-dominant developed world and reflects not only a range of social and economic determinants which make the search for difference possible, but also a series of cultural constructs which makes searching for difference meaningful. So when tourism pundits point to the potential in the fact that the majority of the world's population does not yet engage in 'touring' (as though it is only a matter of time!), not only are they recognizing new market opportunities, they are inadvertently recognizing a fundamental gap in learning and conditioning between those cultures which actively search for difference and those which do not. Out of the world's 6000 cultures relatively few are seekers of difference through the tourism process.

Here we should note a caveat in the form of the distinction between travel in the mechanistic sense of moving to and from, and tourism as a 'being there' experience. Many cultures travel, increasingly for the wrong reasons. Displaced minorities, migrating groups and refugees make up the involuntary mobile which UNESCO (1995) estimates at some 40 million foreign workers and about 15 million refugees. In the literal sense such peoples fit well with the WTO definition of tourists. Unfortunately, they are often not welcomed in the same way as the spending tourist.

The Context of Globalization

Tourism, cultural differences and conflicts are locked within an ever-changing framework. For the purposes of this discussion this framework is aligned to the concept of globalization, which despite its amorphous definition and contestability, nonetheless provides us with the necessary backdrop to the tourism/culture/conflict focus. In a representative sense it is fitting that the 'world's largest industry' is considered at the global scale. It is also appropriate to consider the deterministic aspects inherent within globalization as they bear upon the development of cultural conflict at both micro and macro scale.

Our conceptions of a 'shrinking' world, the 'new world order' and the global ideal, are dominated by progressive, Western neo-modern ideologies in which economic relationships are central (Tomlinson, 1991). The 'world as a single place' (King, 1991), is conceived largely from an élitist position whereby an unified world without boundaries merely makes for a more readily penetrable market. The dissolution of national boundaries is advocated for financial and commercial reasons, and interdependence is accepted as a state of global liberation. Conquest, exploitation and imperialism have given way to subtler means of supporting the inevitability of capitalism. Globally penetrating technologies, now allow the peaceful creation of pseudo-colonial dependencies at a distance through the dispersion of advertising messages and MTV. But, the telling metaphor of the 'world market-place' still reflects a neo-classical capitalist belief system that has evolved little over two hundred years.

Globalization has developed its own intellectual momentum and an inevitabilism which although contrived, remains politically acceptable. It is proffered as a positive process by which all parts of society are seen to benefit via 'trickle-down' theory; that everything flows from economic growth. Particularly since the breakdown of communist Europe, the world is displayed as moving inexorably towards a state of economic and political harmony, unified in the desire, if not the means, to consume. Economic conceptions of international tourism dovetail rather neatly into this world view, and fuel the idea that consumption is both a ubiquitous and an inevitable cultural goal. However, the implicit optimism behind such conceptions is dramatically challenged by the very imbalances which drive globalization. Despite the promises suggested by 'trickle-down' theory, globalization occurs unequally, and reflects residual imperialist traits of the developed countries of the North. This point has been recognized in environmental terms, and a strong case has been made for global interdependence both as a description of ecological realities and of finding policy solutions to transnational problems. But, in an economic sense, interdependence is rather more contrived. As Sachs (1995, p. 23) points out, in the language of globalization 'the concept of interdependence is often pushed to the fore in order to avoid any analysis of the degree of asymmetry, even domination, that exists in the relationships between strong partners and weak partners'.

The pervasive criticism of globalization is centred upon a fear of cultural homogenization driven by the consumptive process (Tenbruck, 1990). But this is a fear of extent, not total immersion. Complete uniformity in cultural terms is remote and reflects interconnectedness rather than unity (Hannerz, 1990; Robertson, 1996). Tourism is involved with this interconnectedness as perpetrator, victim and victor. The march of international capital, transnational investment and technological linkages for information and control is developing standardized, McDonaldized tourism products (Ritzer and Liska, 1997), and so-called 'global' quality standards for tourism businesses are inevitably accompanied by attempts to imitate and assimilate uniform patterns of social behaviour, language, dress and cuisine. Depending on where one stands, this has both positive and negative cultural impacts for tourist and host. As Jafari (1996, p. 34) asks: 'is tourism a force to bring out native colours or to camouflage all across cultural lines into one?'

Against this we can view globalization as being driven by the search for difference; a process by which the more homogeneous the world becomes, the greater the desire to re-invent those values which delineate our culture (Naisbitt and Auberdene, 1990; Naisbitt, 1995; UNESCO, 1995). In this way tourists are being presented with an increasing array of cultural differences to choose from, and the tourism industry is faced with a greater variety of product opportunities to package and promote. But, as we have seen, scrambles for deeper contact with our cultural identity are themselves marked by conflicts as communities seek to preserve themselves and draw upon their cultural resources to this effect. The more that cultural differences are utilized to meet the demands of the tourist, the greater the potential for conflict. The perceived threat of cultural engulfment and immersion, as one of the edges of the globalization debate, increasingly entails that the cultural differences which tourism seeks to harness are not easily bargained over (McGarry and O'Leary, 1993).

Though the dangers of global homogenization and 'coca-colonization' (Hannerz, 1992) may be realized, the trend is to promote tourism itself as a transcultural product. The erosion of frontiers begins with their crossing and tourism, in its literal and theoretical form, is very much concerned with the crossing of physical and cultural frontiers. Processes of cultural exchanges and re-invention follow and in this sense, as Rojek and Urry (1997, p. 11) emphasize, 'all cultures get remade as a result of flows of peoples, objects and images across national borders, whether these involve colonialism, work-based migration, individual travel or mass tourism'. Tourism has now taken its place, along with manufacturing and other service sectors, in this remaking of cultures, and it is here that conflicts are generated. It may be problematic to disaggregate tourism's role from that of the other influences (a point accentuated by the interconnectedness at the heart of globalization), but that it has an influence is undeniable.

Conclusion: Reflections on Inequality and Indifference

The wide ranging nature of this chapter serves to emphasize the realities of how tourism interconnects with culture on a multitude of levels and at different scales. It also points to the vast complexities of societies and cultures, from local to global level, reminding us of Marx and Weber who saw conflict as inherent within complex societies. Difficulties encountered in attempting to bring understanding to the tourism–culture relationship serve only to highlight the need for further elaboration, and in particular, approaches which seek to connect multifaceted cultural studies with dynamic economic, environmental, political and social contexts. The idea of conflict is often marked by a dipolarity of discourse which can mask the complexities which bring it about. It is certainly not a straightforward causal relationship between tourist and host. Moreover, cultural conflicts through personal 'encounter' often echo more deep-seated cultural divergence at the structural level and within the globalizing context. Tourism is only one of a number of catalysts for cultural conflict (Rowe, 1993), albeit a significant and symbolic one. But its importance in this respect is more than a function of tourism being the 'world's largest industry'; the very processes which constitute tourism are marked by conflicts.

As one of the most penetrating, pervasive and visible activities of consumptive capitalism, world tourism both reflects and accentuates economic disparities, and is marked by fundamental imbalances in power. Tourism, and the culture of tourism, was forged in the developed nations of the North and here it remains. Cazes (1996) reminds us that the low income nations of the world receive less than 2% of global tourism receipts – a figure which drops to 0.6% if China is excluded. Although, the lesser developed countries are scheduled to experience a degree of expansion as 'sender' countries, they remain ostensibly as Turner and Ash's (1975) 'pleasure periphery', politically marginalized and economically pocketed by the North and West. Moreover, in a global sense the pleasure periphery has expanded dramatically taking in more than any notion of the Third World and indigenous populations. Even *within* developed nations pleasure peripheries can be identified; rural margins are increasingly dependent upon urban markets, city centres have developed as recreational centres for suburbanites, and business travellers with company accounts are served by 'peripheral labourers' earning £2.50 per hour.

The rootedness of world tourism in historical relations, the legacy of imperialism, concentrated ownership of tourism's structures, the tendency to assume a dominant–subordinate relationship (Nash, 1989), together with still growing expectations and opportunities amongst developed countries to engage in tourism, all points to fundamental inequality and a process (however unconsciously articulated) of First World hegemony, which is reflected in distant local tourist–host encounters. But it is not solely an economic process, it is cultural too. The cultural expansion of the North and West in terms of consumer goods, associated cultures and consumerist values which possess the capacity to challenge and change cultural identities (Howes, 1996), continues to invoke conflicts. But whereas the exportation and impacts of products such as Coca-Cola and designer jeans, and the contestability of the cultural values which surround them, have attracted considerable attention, the exportation of the more intangible tourism and its culture, its effects and limits, remains relatively unexplored territory. The majority of the world's population do not tour, or holiday. This is not a straightforward First/Third world issue. Whilst there is clearly an issue of economy here, in terms of possessing the resources which allow indulgence in leisure-based tourism, there is also a lack of a tourism culture. The example of the surprising, and relatively small, proportion of the population of USA who hold passports would seem to indicate that an absence of a cultural framework for tourism (as opposed to leisure) is not automatically linked to economic and social status. In 'learning' the culture of tourism we are learning something more than *how* to consume. We are accepting the desire to consume otherness and implicitly, the need to select, commodify, and package the world.

At all levels, the culture of tourism is ghosted by an uncomfortable feeling of imbalance; a point reflected in research, the majority of which examines the impacts of First World values and behaviour upon distant, developing, and (to us) exotic cultures, and not vice versa. It is not as if we are immune from cultural conflicts. We frequently recognize the conflicts brought about through disparity and the commodification process in Western culture. We complain of the commercialization of our heritage, the loss of rurality, the intrusion of tourist masses in our historic centres. Yet, we are generally indifferent to these processes as they affect others when we tour, lapsing into 'them and us' imperialistic stereotypes, or justifying tourism as a form of fair trade. Representations of tourism as a simplistic and value-neutral exchange in which cultural differences, and 'otherness' are traded for tangible economic gains and elusive social 'well-being' still persist. Tourism is not like this. It is usually unequal in cultural terms (Robins, 1991), does not always take place on the basis of consent (Craik, 1994), and frequently escapes any notion of mutual understanding.

In our search for difference we are accepting the conflicts it can produce, and although the eco-tourist classes may suffer more guilt than others, tourists and the vast tourism industry are largely accepting of the inequalities which exist. Börözc puts it thus:

> Because of the standardization, normalization and commercialization of experience, tourism rarely induces questioning of the status quo. Undeniable evidence of poverty, suffering, backwardness and oppression is represented as acceptable because these ills are experienced via osmosis through the only seemingly transparent walls of the environmental bubble of tourism.
>
> (Börözc, 1996, p. 194)

Furthermore, as Mowforth and Munt (1998, p. 74) identify, not only are inequalities accepted, they can also be 'called upon to both titillate and legitimate travel'. Conflict itself, within and between cultures, is thus actually absorbed into the tourist experience, and the portfolio of tourism products, helping to maintain the distinctiveness that we (some of us) seek to gaze upon.

References

Adams, K.M. (1990) Cultural commoditization in Tana Toraja, Indonesia. *Cultural Survival Quarterly* 14(1), pp. 31–34.

Alberta Aboriginal Tourism Alliance (1996) 'Natives claim Government and indifference hurdles to Aboriginal tourism', *Alberta Aboriginal Tourism Alliance News Report* 17 November, Calgary.

Altman, J.C. (1989) Tourism dilemmas for Aboriginal Australians. *Annals of Tourism Research*, 16, pp. 456–476.

Amir, Y. and Ben-Ari, R. (1985) International tourism, ethnic contact, and attitude change. *Journal of Social Issues*, 41(3), pp. 105–115.

Anderson, B. (1983) *Imagined Communities*. Verso Ltd, London.

Bauman, Z. (1996) From pilgrim to tourist – or a short history of identity. In: Hall, S. and DuGay, P. (eds) *Questions of Cultural Identity*. Sage Publications Ltd, London, pp. 18–36.

Boissevain, J. (1996) Ritual, tourism and cultural commoditization in Malta: culture by the pound? In: Selwyn, T. (ed.) *The Tourist Image – Myths and Myth Making in Tourism*. John Wiley, Chichester, pp. 105–121.

Boorstin, D. (1964) *The Image: A Guide to Pseudo Events in America*. Harper and Row, New York.

Böröcz, J. (1996) *Leisure Migration – A Sociological Study on Tourism*. Pergamon, Oxford.

Britton, S. (1982) The political economy in the Third World. *Annals of Tourism Research*, 9, pp. 331–329.

Britton, S. (1991) Tourism, capital and place: towards a critical geography of tourism. *Environment and Planning D: Society and Space*, 9, pp. 451–578.

Burns, P.M. and Holden, A. (1995) *Tourism – A New Perspective*. Prentice Hall, London.

Cazes, G.H. (1996) The growth of tourism in the developing countries. In: UNESCO/AIEST Proceedings of Round Table, *Culture, Tourism, Development: Critical Issues for the XXIst Century*. UNESCO/AIEST, Paris, pp. 15–18.

Chatterjee, P. (1993) Clubbing Southeast Asia: the impacts of golf development. *Multinational Monitor*, November, pp. 23–25.

Civil Aviation Authority (1998) *ATOL Business*, Issue 11, January, p. 4.

Classen, C. and Howes, D. (1996) Epilogue – the dynamics and ethics of cross-cultural consumption. In: Howes, D. (ed.) *Cross-Cultural Consumption – Global Markets Local Realities*, Routledge, London, pp. 178–194.

Cohen, E. (1972) Towards a sociology of international tourism, *Social Research*, 39 (1), pp. 64–82.

Cohen, E. (1987) Authenticity and commoditization in tourism, *Annals of Tourism Research*, 15, pp. 371–386.

Cohen, E. (1995) Contemporary tourism – trends and challenges: Sustainable authenticity or contrived post-modernity? In: Butler, R. and Pearce, D. (eds) *Change in Tourism – People, Places, Processes*, Routledge, London, pp. 12–29.

Craik, J. (1994) Peripheral pleasures: the peculiarities of post-colonial tourism, *Cultural Policy*, 6 (1), pp. 21–31.

Craik, J. (1997) The culture of tourism. In: Rojek, C. and Urry, J. (eds) *Touring Cultures – Transformations of Travel and Theory*, Routledge, London, pp. 113–137.

Crick, M. (1989) Representations of international tourism in the social sciences,

Annual Review of Anthropology, 18, pp. 307–344.

Crystal, E. (1989) Tourism in Toraja (Sulawesi, Indonesia). In: Smith, V.L. (ed.) *Hosts and Guests: The Anthropology of Tourism*, 2nd edn., University of Pennsylvania Press, Philadelphia, pp. 139–168.

Cukier, J. (1996) Tourism employment in Bali: trends and implications. In: Butler, R. and Hinch, T. (eds) *Tourism and Indigenous Peoples*, Routledge, London, pp. 49–75.

Cukier-Snow, J. and Wall, G. (1993) Tourism employment: perspectives from Bali, *Tourism Management*, 14 (3), pp. 195–201.

Daltabuit, M. and Pi-Sunyer, O. (1990) Tourism development in Quintana Roo, Mexico, *Cultural Survival Quarterly*, 14 (1), pp. 9–13.

D'Amore, L.J. (1988) Tourism the world's peace industry, *Journal of Recreation Research*, 27 (1), pp. 35–40.

Dann, G.M.S. (1996a) Images of destination people in travelogues. In: Butler, R. and Hinch, T. (eds) *Tourism and Indigenous Peoples*, Routledge, London, pp. 349–375.

Dann, G.M.S. (1996b) The people of tourist brochures. In: Selwyn, T. (ed.) *The Tourist Image – Myths and Myth Making in Tourism*, John Wiley, Chichester, pp. 61–83.

de Burlo, C. (1996) Cultural resistance and ethnic tourism on South Pentecost, Vanuatu. In: Butler, R. and Hinch, T. (eds) *Tourism and Indigenous Peoples*, Routledge, London, pp. 255–278.

de Kadt, E. (1979) Arts, crafts, and cultural manifestations. In: de Kadt, E. (ed.) *Tourism: Passport to Development?*, Oxford University Press, London. pp. 68–76.

Erisman, M.H. (1983) Tourism and cultural dependency in the West Indies, *Annals of Tourism Research*, 10, pp. 337–361.

Furnham, A. and Bochner, S. (1986) *Culture Shock: Psychological Reactions to Unfamiliar Environments*, Routledge, London.

Gessner, V. and Schade, A. (1990) Conflicts of culture in cross-border legal relations: the conception of a research topic in the sociology of law. In: Featherstone, M. (ed.) *Global Culture – Nationalism, Globalization and Modernity*, Sage Publications Ltd, London, pp. 253–279.

Goering, P.G. (1990) The response to tourism in Ladakh, *Cultural Survival Quarterly*, 14 (1), pp. 20–25.

Graburn, N.H.H. (1989) Tourism: the sacred journey. In: Smith, V.L. (ed.) *Hosts and Guests: The Anthropology of Tourism*, 2nd edn., University of Pennsylvania Press, Philadelphia, pp. 21–36.

Grahn, P. (1991) Using tourism to protect existing culture: a project in Swedish Lapland, *Leisure Studies*, 10, pp. 33–47.

Greenwood, D. (1989) Culture by the pound: an anthropological perspective on tourism as cultural commoditization. In: Smith, V. (ed.) *Hosts and Guests: The Anthropology of Tourism*, 2nd edn. University of Pennsylvania Press, Philadelphia, pp. 171–185.

Hall, S. (1987) *Minimal Selves in Identity: The Real Me*, ICA Documents 6, Institute of Contemporary Arts, London, pp. 44–46.

Hannerz, U. (1990) Cosmopolitans and locals in world culture. In: Featherstone, M. (ed.) *Global Culture – Nationalism, Globalization and Modernity*, Sage Publications Ltd, London, pp. 237–253.

Hannerz, U. (1992) *Cultural Complexity: Studies in the Social Organization of Meaning,* Columbia University Press, New York.
Hannerz, U. (1996) *Transnational Connections – Culture, People, Places.* Routledge, London.
Harp, J. (1994) Culture, the state, and tourism: state policy initiatives in Canada, 1984–1992, *Cultural Policy,* 6 (1), p. 6.
Harrison, D. (1992) Tourism to less developed countries: the social consequences. In: Harrison, D. (ed.) *Tourism and The Less Developed Countries,* Belhaven Press, London, pp. 19–34.
Hollinshead, K. (1996) Marketing and metaphysical realism: the disidentifications of aboriginal life and traditions through tourism. In: Butler, R. and Hinch, T. (eds) *Tourism and Indigenous Peoples,* Routledge, London, pp. 309–348.
Howes, D. (1996) Introduction: commodities and cultural borders. In: Howes, D. (ed.) *Cross-Cultural Consumption – Global Markets Local Realities,* Routledge, London, pp. 1–16.
Hunziker, W. (1961) Human relations in tourist development, *Revue de Tourisme,* 1 (3), p. 90.
Indigenous Peoples Earth Charter (1992) *World Conference of Indigenous Peoples – Territory, Environment and Development,* Brazil.
International Union for the Conservation of Nature (1997) *Indigeneous Peoples and Sustainability – Cases and Actions,* IUCN and Inter-Commission Task Force on Indigenous Peoples, International Books, London.
Jafari, J. (1996) Tourism and culture: an inquiry into paradoxes. In: UNESCO/AIEST Proceedings of Round Table, *Culture, Tourism, Development: Critical Issues for the XXIst Century,* UNESCO/AIEST, Paris, pp. 31–35.
Kakazu, H. (1996) Effects of tourism growth on development in the Asia–Pacific region: the case of small islands. In: UNESCO/AIEST Proceedings of Round Table, *Culture, Tourism, Development: Critical Issues for the XXIst Century,* UNESCO/AIEST, Paris, pp. 7–14.
Kaul, R.N. (1985) *Dynamics of Tourism: The Phenomenon,* Sterling Publishing Co., New Delhi.
Keller, P. (1996) General trends in tourism today. In: UNESCO/AIEST Proceedings of Round Table, *Culture, Tourism, Development: Critical Issues for the XXIst Century,* UNESCO/AIEST, Paris, pp. 3–6.
King, A.D. (ed.) (1991) *Culture, Globalization and the World-System,* Macmillan, London.
Krippendorf, J. (1987) *The Holiday Makers – Understanding the Impact of Leisure and Travel,* Heinemann, Oxford.
Lash, S. and Urry, J. (1994) *Economies of Signs and Spaces,* Sage Publications Ltd, London.
Lea, J. (1988) *Tourism and Development in the Third World,* Routledge, London.
MacCannell, D. (1984) Reconstructed ethnicity: tourism and cultural identity in Third World communities, *Annals of Tourism Research,* 11, pp. 361–377.
MacCannell, D. (1992) *Empty Meeting Grounds: The Tourist Papers,* Routledge, London.
Macdonald, S. (1997) A people's story: heritage, identity and authenticity. In: Rojek, C. and Urry, J. (eds) *Touring Cultures – Transformations of Travel and Theory,* Routledge, London, pp. 155–176.
McGarry, J. and O'Leary, B. (1993) Eliminating and managing ethnic differences. In:

Hutchinson, J. and Smith, A.D. (eds) *Ethnicity*, Oxford University Press, Oxford, pp. 333–341.

McKean, P.F. (1989) Towards a theoretical analysis of tourism: economic dualism and cultural involution in Bali. In: Smith, V.L. (ed.) *Hosts and Guests: The Anthropology of Tourism*, University of Pennsylvania Press, Philadelphia, pp. 119–139.

Mathieson, A. and Wall, G. (1982) *Tourism: Economic, Physical and Social Impacts*, Longman, London.

Medrano, J.D. (1996) Some thematic and strategic priorities for developing research on multi-ethnic and multi-cultural societies, *Management of Social Transformations, Discussion Paper Series*, No.13, UNESCO, Paris.

Morley, D. and Robins, K. (1995) *Spaces of Identity*, Routledge, London.

Mowforth, M. and Munt, I. (1998) *Tourism and Sustainability – New Tourism in the Third World*, Routledge, London.

Naisbitt, J. (1995) *Global Paradox*, Avon Books, New York.

Naisbitt, J. and Auburdene, P. (1990) *Megatrends*, Avon Books, New York.

Nash, D. (1989) Tourism as a form of imperialism. In: Smith, V. (ed.) *Hosts and Guests: The Anthropology of Tourism*, 2nd edn., The University of Pennsylvania Press, Philadelphia, pp. 37–52.

Nash, D. (1996) *Anthropology of Tourism*, Pergamon, Kidlington.

Nettekoven, L. (1979) Mechanisms of cultural interaction. In: de Kadt, E. (ed.) *Tourism: Passport to Development?*, Oxford University Press, London. pp. 135–145.

Nicholas, T. (1994) *Colonialism's Culture – Anthropology, Travel and Government*, Polity Press, Cambridge.

O'Reilly, A.M. (1986) Tourism carrying capacity: concepts and issues, *Tourism Management*, 7(4), pp. 254–258.

Parris, R. (1996) Tourism and cultural interaction: issues and prospects for sustainable development. In: UNESCO/AIEST Proceedings of Round Table, *Culture, Tourism, Development: Critical Issues for the XXIst Century*, UNESCO/AIEST, Paris, pp. 36–40.

Reisinger, Y. (1994) Social contact between tourists and hosts of different cultural backgrounds. In: Seaton, A.V. (ed.) *Tourism – The State of the Art*, John Wiley & Sons, Chichester, pp. 743–755.

Richards, G. (1996a) The scope and significance of cultural tourism. In: Richards, G. (ed.) *Cultural Tourism in Europe*, CAB International, Wallingford, pp. 19–45.

Richards, G. (1996b) The social context of cultural tourism. In: Richards, G. (ed.) *Cultural Tourism in Europe*, CAB International, Wallingford, pp. 47–70.

Richards, G. (ed.) (1996c) *Cultural Tourism in Europe*, CAB International, Wallingford.

Richter, L. (1992) Political instability and the Third World. In: Harrison, D. (ed.) *Tourism and The Less Developed Countries*, Belhaven Press, London, pp. 35–46.

Ritchie, H. (1993) *Here we Go – A Summer on the Costa del Sol*, Hamish Hamilton, London.

Ritzer, G. and Liska, A. (1997) 'McDisneyization' and 'post-tourism': complementary perspectives on contemporary tourism. In: Rojek, C. and Urry, J. (eds) *Touring Cultures – Transformations of Travel and Theory*, Routledge, London, pp. 96–109.

Robertson, R. (1996) *Globalization – Social Theory and Global Culture,* Sage Publications Ltd., London.

Robins, K. (1991) Tradition and translation – national culture in its global context. In: Corner, J. and Harvey, S. (eds) *Enterprise and Heritage: Crosscurrents of National Culture,* Routledge, London.

Robinson, M. (1996) Sustainable tourism for Spain: principles, prospects and problems. In: Barke, M., Towner, J. and Newton, M.T. (eds) *Tourism in Spain – Critical Issues,* CAB International, Wallingford, pp. 401–425.

Roche, M. (1992) Mega-events and micro-modernisation: on the sociology of the new urban tourism, *British Journal of Sociology,* 43 (4), pp. 563–600.

Rojek, C. and Urry, J. (1997) Transformations of travel and theory. In: *Touring Cultures – Transformations of Travel and Theory,* Routledge, London, pp. 1–19.

Rowe, D. (1993) Leisure, tourism and Australianness, *Media, Culture and Society,* 15, pp. 258–268.

Ryan, C. (1991a) *Recreational Tourism: A Social Science Perspective,* Routledge, London.

Ryan, C. (1991b) *Tourism, Terrorism and Violence: The Risks of Wider World Travel,* Conflict Study 244, Research Institute for the Study of Conflict and Terrorism, London.

Ryan, C. (1997a) 'The time of our lives' or time for our lives: an examination of time in holidaying. In: Ryan, C. (ed.) *The Tourist Experience – A New Introduction,* Cassell, London, pp. 194–205.

Ryan, C. (1997b) Similar motivations – diverse behaviours. In: Ryan, C. (ed.) *The Tourist Experience – A New Introduction,* Cassell, London, pp. 25–47.

Sachs, I. (1995) Searching for new development strategies – the challenges of the Social Summit, *Management of Social Transformations Policy Papers* 1, UNESCO, Paris.

Sharpley, R. (1994) *Tourism, Tourists and Society,* ELM Publications, Huntington.

Silberberg, T. (1995) Cultural tourism and business opportunities for museums and heritage sites, *Tourism Management,* 16, pp. 361–365.

Silver, I. (1993) Marketing authenticity in Third World countries, *Annals of Tourism Research,* 20, pp. 302–318.

Simmel, G. (1950) *The Sociology of Georg Simmel,* Wolffe, K.H. (ed.), The Free Press, Glencoe.

Sinclair, M.T., Alizadeh, P. and Onunga, E.A.A. (1992) The structure of international tourism and tourism development in Kenya. In: Harrison, D. (ed.) *Tourism and The Less Developed Countries,* Belhaven Press, London, pp. 47–63.

Smith, A.D (1990) Towards a global culture? In: Featherstone, M. (ed.) *Global Culture – Nationalism, Globalization and Modernity,* Sage Publications Ltd, London, pp. 171–193.

Solfield, T.H.B. (1996) Anuha Island resort: a case study of failure. In: Butler, R. and Hinch, T. (eds) *Tourism and Indigenous Peoples,* Routledge, London, pp. 176–202.

Stebbins, R. (1996) Cultural tourism as serious leisure, *Annals of Tourism Research,* 23, pp. 948–950.

Swinglehurst, E. (1994) Face to face: the socio-cultural impacts of tourism. In: Theobald, W. (ed.) *Global Tourism – The Next Decade,* Butterworth Heinemann, Oxford, pp. 92–102.

Tenbruck, F.H. (1990) The dream of a secular ecumene: the meaning and limits of

policies of development. In: Featherstone, M. (ed.) *Global Culture – Nationalism, Globalization and Modernity*, Sage Publications Ltd, London, pp. 193–206.
Theroux, P. (1986) *Sunrise with Seamonsters*, Penguin Books, Harmondsworth.
Tomlinson, J. (1991) *Cultural Imperialism*, Johns Hopkins University Press, Baltimore.
Tunbridge, J.E. and Ashworth, G.J. (1996) *Dissonant Heritage – The Management of the Past as a Resource in Conflict*, John Wiley & Sons, Chichester.
Turner, L. and Ash, J. (1975) *The Golden Hordes*, Constable, London.
Tyler, A. (1985) *The Accidental Tourist*, Knopf, New York.
UNESCO (1995) *Our Creative Diversity – Report of the World Commission on Culture and Development*, UNESCO, Paris.
UNESCO (1997) *Culture, Tourism, Development: Crucial Issues for the XXIst Century*, UNESCO, Paris.
United Nations (1993) *Report of the United Conference on Environment and Development, Rio de Janeiro, 3–14 June 1992*, Volume I, United Nations, New York.
Urry, J. (1990) *The Tourist Gaze: Leisure and Travel in Contemporary Society*, Sage Publications Ltd, London.
Urry, J. (1995) *Consuming Places*, Routledge, London.
Var, T., Ap, J. and Van Doren, C. (1988) Tourism and Peace, Paper presented at Tourism: A Vital Force for Peace Conference, Vancouver, Canada, 16–19 October.
Walle, A.H. (1996) Habits of thought and cultural tourism, *Annals of Tourism Research*, 23, pp. 874–890.
Wallerstein, I. (1990) Culture as the ideological battleground of the modern world-system. In: Featherstone, M. (ed.) *Global Culture – Nationalism, Globalization and Modernity*, Sage Publications Ltd, London, pp. 31–57.
Watson, G.L. and Kopachevsky, J.P. (1994) Interpretations of tourism as commodity, *Annals of Tourism Research*, 21, pp. 281–297.
Wei, L., Crompton, J.L. and Reid, L.M. (1989) Cultural conflicts – experiences of US visitors to China, *Tourism Management*, 10, pp. 322–332.
World Commission on Environment and Development (1987) *Our Common Future*, Oxford University Press, Oxford.
World Tourism Organization (WTO) (1980) *Manila Declaration on World Tourism*, World Tourism Organization, Madrid.
World Tourism Organization (WTO) (1997) *Tourism 2020 Vision*, World Tourism Organization, Madrid.
Wynne, D. (1992) *The Culture Industry*, Avebury, Aldershot.

2

Indigenous Tourism: Reclaiming Knowledge, Culture and Intellectual Property in Australia

Elvi Whittaker

> The 'real Aborigine' is a marketable product, and has no relationship to the actual cultures of Aboriginal people beyond appropriation and exploitation.
>
> (Birch, 1993)

Introduction

The post-colonial age ushered in the promise of independence and restitution for indigenous people. It also paved the way for new visions about indigenous cultures and, inevitably, new conflicts. Within colonial nations the relationship between the descendants of European settlers and the descendants of the people indigenous to the area entered into a long process of inventing and negotiating new moral parameters. The process highlighted the status of rights that many Westerners consistently treated as their unquestioned entitlements, and just as consistently viewed as privileges, magnanimously bestowed, upon all others. On the whole these are simple human rights – geographic property, social justice, self-determination, self-management and restitution of cultural integrity. Such seemingly obvious equalities received differing acknowledgements by governments. Yet the deeply infused culture of relationships between settlers and the colonized, first created in those distant days of 'discovery', lingers and casts its stereotyped understandings on the contemporary world.

It is the remnants of colonization, its imagery and assumed privileges, that find their way into tourism and are reproduced there. The image of indigenous people so familiar in advertising and on postcard racks is essentially a display of colonization: a captured portrait. It could be argued that indigenous people incorporated into colonial nations have merely changed their function. In past centuries they were seen as adversaries, heathens to be proselytized, savages to be civilized, but most importantly, they were cheap labour. Now they are performers on a tourism stage. Past and present national states and national economies have depended, and depend, upon their presence. In the early days of Western settlement, indigenous cultures were seen as elusive symbolic codes to be cracked in order to permit maximum colonial control. Now, however, they have become attractive mysteries, promises of spirituality, recipes for a better moral life and the harbingers of a new world, or perhaps a 'new age'. Encapsulating so much that is desirable, Aboriginal people have become the foci of promotion and marketing. They are presented as exotica, that cornerstone of global tourist expectation, and they are produced, one might even say 'manufactured', to fit the tourist gaze. Carefully positioned among promises of natural beauty, heady entertainment, historic landmarks, unique shopping opportunities, museums and galleries, Aboriginal people assume their positions to complete the diorama of enticements every proper traveller has learnt to expect. They beckon the tourist to come and discover.

It is clear that national tourist industries capitalize on these creations. Originally transformed into viable imagery at 'discovery' (Donaldson and Donaldson, 1985; Smith, 1985), indigenous people continue to fascinate long after the presumed 'death of colonialism'. For indigenous people themselves, however, labouring for settlers on appropriated lands – their lot in colonial times – has evolved to turning the wheels of national tourism. What is particularly irksome for them, however, is that the nations benefiting from the appropriation are not nations they call their own. They are still colonized beings within an all-powerful and foreign state. Thus, the accusations of exploitation often levied at colonialism have hardly changed. The same accusations are levied at government or private tourism. Moreover, the issue of race, although in one sense an unproblematic concept in past centuries when race itself was seen as the very justification for (and even duty of) acts of exploitation, becomes 'racist' in contemporary times. Undoubtedly this is particularly vexing for those governments that pride themselves on being liberated from the dark inhumanities of the past. Within the perspective that views tourist industry promotions as exploitative, it is not surprising that indigenous people often view tourism as another form of racism.

The intent of this chapter is to consider the moral claims activated by indigenous people (specifically Aboriginal Australians) and what political and social implications they have for the tourist industry and for knowledge industries generally. Central to ongoing debates in many parts of the world with indigenous populations, such as Australia, Hawaii, Canada, New Zealand and Norway, is the cherished notion of self-determination. Even a couple of decades ago, attempts to install self-determination would have been seen as indigenous revolutions, as political insurgencies or, at best, as evidence of a graceless disregard for the many acts of benevolence and restitution enacted by governments and well-meaning citizens. At present, moves towards self-determination crowd the contemporary international agenda as the following three recent examples suggest:

1. Indigenous Hawaiians, their images disseminated by the tourist industry as icons of the myth of 'racial paradise' and subtly suggestive of illicit sexual encounters and freedoms of all kinds (Whittaker, 1986), are now promoting sovereignty. For decades, as a lucrative tourist industry swirled around their cultures and persons, they have referred to themselves as members of the Fourth World, colonized and marginalized in their own country, victims of the arrival of Captain Cook in 1778, the overthrow of the Hawaiian monarchy and annexation by the United States in 1898 and, finally, the conferral of American statehood in 1959. Years of assertive action against these acts of aggression culminated in 1993 when the United States Congress passed a resolution, signed by President Clinton, apologizing for the overthrow of the Hawaiian monarchy. In 1996 the state government condoned a plebiscite on the viability of creating a native-Hawaiian government. It received support from 73% of those voting. The creation of a native-Hawaiian government could bring the possibility of secession and the rebirth of nationhood – 'decolonization in the last area of the world to colonize' (Goldberg, 1996).
2. In 1999, Inuit Canadians will assume a measure of self-determination when the Northern Territories will be divided into two territories, perhaps *en route* to provincial status – Nunavut in the east and the western portion of the Territories yet to be named. A recent plebiscite indicated that the first choice for a name was to retain 'Northwest Territories', the second – in a comic parody of colonialism, Euro-Canadian culture and the élitism of instituted power – is to call it Bob! Also proposed were Restavit, Alluvit and Fullavit.
3. Each year the elected Chief of the Assembly of First Nations of Canada demands to sit as a delegate at provincial premiers' conferences, claiming that these provincial leaders cannot speak for the indigenous people of the country. This request for equality of leadership has yet to be recognized.

Turning now to the drama as it is enacted on the Australian scene. Clearly, at least in the moral sense, the relationship with indigenous people, forged in colonial cultures, has come to an end. Just as clearly the status of Aboriginal people is altering with such rapidity that pressure is placed on all segments of society to respond to new initiatives. In March 1992, a new climate of moral priorities and expectations was created by a High Court decision, heralding a paradigmatic shift in Australian politics. The *Mabo and Others* v. *the State of Queensland* decision rewrote colonialism. It reinterpreted the long-cherished European morality of *terra nullius*, the principle which had condoned European annexation of land in the first place. This figment of the past offered the establishment some rationalized protection from a tide of colonial guilt and from the status of being deemed oppressors and land thieves. The decision clearly stated that the concept of *terra nullius* could not apply if the land to be appropriated was occupied by a 'political unit'. This was a victory for Aboriginal Australians confirming a previously existing state of self-government. Any rights awarded to Aboriginal people could no longer be seen as the liberal acts of advanced governments, but as the restitution of human rights and simple social justice (Bartlett, 1993; Rowse, 1993; Goot and Rowse, 1994; Stephenson, 1995).

Energized by the *Mabo* decision and the subsequent Native Title Act of 1993, Aboriginal people are producing a new sense of viable Aboriginality. New initiatives appear daily: the move to establish a First Nations University, the possibility of having self-government by the 21st century, many calls for restitution for past abuses of Aboriginal youth in educational custody, the assertions that academics steal knowledge to build their own careers, the argument that white film-makers do not have the rights to make films about Aboriginal people, the advent of the Aboriginal delegation demanding an apology from an American author and an open admission that her reported experiences with Aboriginal people (Morgan, 1994) were fabricated and untrue, the claim to Luna Park (a fun park on Sydney Harbour) for a cultural centre and the creation of a course on Aboriginal language and culture in a Cairns high school. There are numerous initiatives. They join earlier creations such as Magabala Books (the Aboriginal publishing house), Aboriginal radio stations in the Northern Territory and the Kimberleys, *Bran Nue Day* (the Aboriginal rock musical), rock bands and many internationally renowned Aboriginal artists (Whittaker, 1997).

Given this renaissance of Aboriginal culture and Aboriginal voices demanding appropriate recognition, the tourist industry faces a new kind of political confrontation. Obviously the question of the restitution of land remains as a daily agenda for Aboriginal people and the government. Yet there is also a knowledge revolution afoot. It is this revolution that confronts tourism. It demands new ways of gaining access to Aboriginal cultures, new perspectives towards ownership and possession, and obviously, appropriate forms of appeasement or compensation.

Knowledge and Authenticity: An Indigenous Right

The continual development of understandings about the justice of the proper moral rights of Aboriginal people to their own culture and to themselves as persons has introduced new sensitivities. In the light of recent developments the past offences committed by tourism and related industries have come to appear, at the very least, unthinking and insensitive, if not downright embarrassing and even illegal. The abuses that could be levelled at the tourist industry, let alone all of the knowledge industries, are often graphic and even offensive.

Postcards which sold in Queensland in the early 1990s presented a four-photograph arrangement with an emu, kookaburra, kangaroo – and, finally, a traditionally posed Aboriginal male, spear in hand. While obviously intent on proclaiming the uniqueness of the continent, the card also heralded the notion that in the natural kingdom the Aboriginal person belonged with the beasts. 'Well, what can you expect? They see us with the animals' was one irritated comment. Among other offences are the appropriations of views of Aboriginal territory, rendered as glossy photographs in tourist advertising. The Western alienation from the land makes it difficult for photographers to see anything beyond a scenic spot. They do not have access to the knowledge that locations and the stories that accompany them are a kind of property, often sacred and not to be disseminated or 'owned' in a photograph: 'I could tell it was our hill, even though the photograph was supposed to be of a different part of the country entirely.' Added to this is the unquestioned use of the Aboriginal image by Western entrepreneurs announcing tourist mementoes of all kinds and even advertising establishments which appear to have little to do with tourism. Sometimes the image is a mere abstraction, a logo, of an Aboriginal male with a spear and spear-thrower. A much clearer case can be made against the appropriation of the work of artists, whether internationally recognized or new practitioners in the world of Aboriginal art, into fabric design or onto T-shirts (Johnson, 1996).

Tourism, like other knowledge industries, finds itself in the midst of conflicting versions of what constitutes 'the authentic'; what is truthful, real or natural. It places much value on visual materials, on images and the production and reproduction of these. As tourism is usually possible only from the fruits of the promotion and marketing of such visible knowledge, it is shaped to satisfy Western tourist cultures. At the same time it needs to satisfy Aboriginal proprieties about the appropriations and the representations of their persons and their cultures. Needless to say these demands are hard to synchronize.

Objectification: At the Mercy of Racism

The industry, unaware of its own semiotic acts, resorts to its dominant mode of communication, creating stereotypes, cartoon-like representations, icons and idioms; a kind of internationally viable simulacra, what Baudrillard calls 'the discrete charm of second order simulacra' (1983, p. 1). In short, it produces what could be called Aboriginal kitsch, a kitsch that sells tickets in Germany, Japan, Britain, the United States and elsewhere.

> In the colonialist imagination there is no authentic indigenous body. What exists are images and categories which are fluid and ever-changing, in order to suit the contemporary dominant racial philosophy.
>
> (Birch, 1993, p. 16)

The Aboriginal response, on the other hand, is powerfully stated. They ask for representations that depict them 'as they are' in all their diversity. They note that Aboriginal people do not come naked with loin cloth for modesty, or as nomads holding a spear – the icon *par excellence* – but rather are found in the same multiple sets of social situations as white Australians, or as populations almost anywhere in the developed world – as inhabitants of cities, parents, professionals, yuppies, politicians and civil servants. They are themselves ethnically diversified, and not necessarily of Aboriginal physical appearance. They are not always the urban poor on the margins of big cities, or the rural poor on the outskirts of small towns. There are innumerable social designations occupied by Aboriginal people, designations which have received no visibility, unnoticed and marginal to the constructed kind of Aboriginality to which they are forcibly tied. Thus, they object to the encapsulation into traditional idioms, which crystallize for perpetuity, the image of the Aboriginal person. The obvious implication is that the Aboriginal past endures, unchanged, to represent them in the present. All of this is seen as the not-at-all subtle intention of a racist ideology at work to freeze every Aboriginal person into a category, a species, a racial type, an image acceptable to the West. This is not reality, they argue; this is a past, which may have only ever existed in the Western imagination. It is certainly not the present.

Aboriginal people in Australia and elsewhere are voicing disapproval of being inducted into other peoples' scripts, whether tourist industry scripts or academic ones. This kind of colonization of images and knowledges, it could be argued, negates Aboriginal culture in favour of a medium which the Western world considers as universal, namely 'objectivity'.

An image is defined, Susan Sontag suggests, as something predatory that is stolen from its owner (1977, p. 14). Indeed, in some cultures a person's soul as well as his/her privacy may be stolen. Once an image falls into another's possession, it is argued, he/she can do with it as he/she will (Carpenter, 1972, p. 167). A postcard, a tourist pamphlet is such an assault on privacy. 'How would you like it', one Aboriginal person asked, 'if your picture is captured and sent to millions of strangers around the world?'

Depicting people in tourism, as in academic papers and research findings, not only throws up problems of representation, but also wrests control from the hands of those depicted. The retention and display of collected images is not the romantic homage to indigenous people that many naive tourist entrepreneurs, film-makers and others assume. It is, instead, a kind of possession, colonial or otherwise. In the words of a Maori film-maker, Merata Mita, it perpetuates the experiences of those thus captured as:

> part of a colonized country that has imposed upon me its ideal and that has appropriated my culture . . . I must learn to stand back and look at myself and see myself as others see me and also understand how I see myself as my own people do and how I react and respond. I have walked the galleries, archives and museums of the world. I have seen much that has been recorded and preserved. I have participated myself, in the collecting of that material . . . that has always filled me with pain and anguish . . . I have gazed on the past and seen other lives and other worlds and my heart has filled with grief . . . Still

> grieving, I pay respect to the artist, the artisan, the craftsperson, and the labourer, those of my people whose images are thrown up constantly, not only before me but before the world.
>
> (Mita, 1992, p. 73)

One might indeed wonder about a culture that concentrates on such objectification practices, and query its ever-present colonizing agenda and its passion for ownership.

The Aboriginal portrait, the images of Aboriginal cultural practices, whether romantic or something that might be called 'real' (Peterson, 1985), embeds Aboriginality in a colonial language declaring Aboriginal people to be 'hunters and gatherers' and 'nomads' – surely an unwelcome fiction. No incorporation of Aboriginal voices is attempted. No remuneration is usually forthcoming. In being deemed worthy of photography, postcard exposure, pamphlet inset – or whatever the genre happens to be – declares one to be an outsider, in short, an 'other', to use the anthropological vernacular. Trinh Min-ha notes that such 'threatening otherness must therefore be transformed into figures that belong to a definite image repertoire' (quoted by Todd, 1992, p. 77).

Conflicting Notions of Knowledge and Intellectual Property Rights

Indigenous people everywhere are examining the boundaries of their knowledge and their rights to ownership. Specifically, they evoke the question of the nature of cultural knowledge itself. These issues of ownership of knowledges are becoming increasingly subsumed under the rubric of intellectual property. Aboriginal and academic explorations of the matter of intellectual property rights have been enthusiastically supported by international agencies such as the World Intellectual Property Organization, the Commission on Human Rights of the United Nations, and the Working Group on Indigenous Populations. The issue was a prominent feature in the United Nations' Year of the World's Indigenous Peoples in 1993.

Rights to material property, covered by copyright, patent and trademark, and the ownership of visible intellectual products have long had precedence in law. But only recently have such rights been activated to put a halt to years of pirating of Aboriginal designs, not only in the manufacture of T-shirts, but even in the design elements of promotions and communications by the tourist industry, by reputable museums and commercial outlets (Golvan, 1992; Johnson, 1996). In 1989, the matter of copyright of Aboriginal art on T-shirts came to the courts under the Copyright Act of 1968 and the Trade Practices Act of 1974. This unprecedented landmark court decision heralded the beginning of public education and constituted a public warning to the tourist industry. In short order, cases were instituted against the manufacture of fabrics and sarongs forged in Japan, India, Indonesia and Vietnam, and carpets counterfeited in India, all obviously indebted to Aboriginal artists. The implications for tourism are clear enough in these copyright matters.

Other intellectual property rights await clarification and the needed visibility of successful court cases. As they are claims to non-material knowledge, they present themselves more elusively, are not always recognizable and, most importantly, suffer from conflicting notions of what this thing called 'knowledge' actually means. The reference ranges from indigenous knowledge of culture and cultural resources, to indigenous ownership of images and styles of depiction. Such knowledge of resources has been referred to as the 'West's new "frontier"' in 'the latest, if not the last, great rush for resources' (*Cultural Survival*, 1991). It is also a frontier invaded daily by the tourist industry. In addition, Aboriginal people also direct their challenges to academics, scientists, journalists, the media generally and to the government. Obviously the Western notions of copyright, patent, trademark and trade secrets do not cover the matter of indigenous cultural knowledge (Greaves, 1994; Posey, 1994).

Undoubtedly, it is in this particular area that the newest struggles will position themselves and where the next paradigmatic revolution is liable to occur. The problem rests uneasily on two conflicting versions of the nature of knowledge. Western knowledge, safely embedded in the hegemony of Western science, is viewed as value-free, and most importantly freely available for dissemination. Indeed, issues of plagiarism aside, 'knowledge will out', the 'right to know' and 'the responsibility to inform' are dictums which proclaim the nature of ownership quite clearly. Attempts to control, to establish private fiefdoms of knowledge are viewed in the Western collective consciousness as infringements on social justice.

Aboriginal people point out that their knowledge is owned very differently (Fourmile, 1996). It belongs to cultural communities, individual families, tribal groups and to Aboriginal people more generally. Therefore the use of knowledge without appropriate permission, access and recognition is illegitimate knowledge. Knowledge held by academics, scientists, journalists and tourist organizations is especially aggravating in terms of these cultural understandings. Such knowledge, after all, leads to the building of careers and to financial compensation – important ends from which the owners of the knowledge are excluded. It is a 'living off our people' in the name of some Western myth about 'knowledge being public property', in short, it is stolen knowledge (Date, 1994; Osorio, 1994; *Sydney Morning Herald*, 1996; *Sydney Morning Herald*, Editorial, 1996). Culture, in Aboriginal eyes, is not a commercial venture. Moreover, in their experience, compensation for knowledge donated by them has been non-existent or minimal. The case of 'bush tucker' has been raised, with Aboriginal claims that this knowledge collected from Aboriginal people and used, lucratively, by a television personality in a popular programme called *Bush Tucker Man* is the illegitimate use of cultural resources belonging to indigenous Australians (Fourmile, 1996).

Such acts of appropriation immediately evoke the ever-present colonial sub-text. They become new acts of dispossession, and yet one more example of prevailing racist ideologies. 'Possessing Aboriginal knowledge may be the final step of colonization, the means by which settler Australians are transformed from aliens into indigenes' (Jacobs, 1994, p. 307).

Call for a New Theory for Tourism Relationships

The Aboriginal voice has now been raised in Australia. It is begging for new considerations, for a truly post-colonial presence. Frequent wry comments by Aboriginal people on the existing state of affairs are: 'What do you mean *post*-colonial? I don't see the *post*.' They proclaim that racism is too visible in policy, including tourist policy. 'Primitive art' is still too often the designation for artistic products; 'contemporary art' far too seldom evoked. Aboriginal voices seem to be asking that the tourist industry lift itself out of an outdated theoretical commitment, that is to evolutionary theory the obvious backbone of the whole colonial enterprise. The message is clear. The morally acceptable course is to rely on some version of interactive and phenomenological theory. Permit Aboriginal people a voice and a choice. Consult. Interact to understand. Seek permission. Learn to understand cultural contexts. Ask about 'ownership' of stories and seek permission to refer to such stories. Mediate the image of 'beautiful', 'natural' 'Aborigines'. Don't talk about 'gins' or 'bucks' or 'picaninnies'. Use tribal designations – Pitjantjatjara, Yawuru, Gagudju, and so on. Or community designations – Mititjulu or Pularumpi community. Don't talk about going 'walkabout'; it suggests aimlessness (Torres, 1994, p. 25). Include Aboriginal people in planning and recognize their self-management of resources. Pay consultancy fees.

Australian Tourism: Meeting the Post-colonial Challenge

In 1993 the Land Management Officer of the Central Land Council of Alice Springs noted: 'A problem within *Aboriginal tourism* is one of matching government policy with the needs and aspirations of Aboriginal people. Tourism policy is being developed with little understanding of the social and cultural aspects of Aboriginal tourism' (Law, 1993, p. 55). Clearly much needs to be accomplished. Much educating needs to go on, and, as a beginning, Aboriginal people need to be consulted.

Comparing the indigenous tourism of 1998 with that merely ten years before, reflects that considerable advances have been made by the industry in the Northern Territory and the Kimberleys in meeting the new frontiers. The development of the sites of Kakadu and Uluru under joint management – Aboriginal communities and the government – are widely known success stories (Uluru-Kata Tjuta Board of Management *et al.*, 1991; Whittaker, 1994). They are often cited by the industry and the government, and apparently are seen reasonably positively by indigenous people as well. Successful privatized Aboriginal ventures like Anangu Tours at Uluru, Manyallaluk Aboriginal Cultural Tours out of Darwin to Kakadu, Litchfield Park and Katherine, and the tours of Bathurst and Melville Island have gained national and international attention. Meanwhile other tourist sites develop without Aboriginal involvement (Whittaker, 1997), often abusing privilege and evading Aboriginal ownership. Moreover, unauthorized images continue to appear as does the appropriation of Aboriginal cultural resources using Western para-legalistic arguments about 'land for all Australians' (Whittaker, 1994).

There are other significant turning points in the new face of indigenous tourism. Two are worthy of mention. The first happened and passed by with little enduring notice from the tourist industry. It is a traveller's guide, entitled *Burnum Burnum's Aboriginal Australia* (1988) produced by Burnum Burnum, one of the Wurundjeri people. The second happened in June 1993 in Darwin with the Indigenous Australians and Tourism Conference. The conference brought together:

1. the Aboriginal and Torres Strait Islander Tourism Industry Advisory Committee;
2. the Chief Minister and Minister of Tourism for the Northern Territory;
3. the Northern Territory Tourist Commission Aboriginal Liaison;
4. Aboriginal Land Councils;
5. the Aboriginal Arts Unit of the Australia Council;
6. the Pacific Area Travel Association (PATA);
7. indigenous tour operators;
8. owners of Aboriginal communities;
9. the Aboriginal member of the Western Australian Department of Conservation and Land Management;
10. the director of Kakadu Tours;
11. Aboriginal dance theatres;
12. the Economic Division of the Aboriginal and Torres Strait Islanders Commission (ATSIC);
13. the Commonwealth Department of Tourism;
14. academics.

The decisions made at this conference involved the commitment to train Aboriginal people for employment in the tourist industry, to encourage small-scale family operated cultural tours, to develop joint ventures in tourism between indigenous and non-indigenous people with the strategy of exclusive contractual arrangements and to attract private venture capital from banks and other possible investors (Aboriginal and Torres Strait Islander Commission, 1993). The training of guides and coach drivers was advocated, marketing problems were aired and partnerships suggested.

Following this meeting a new Draft of the National Aboriginal and Torres Strait Islander Tourism Strategy, 1994, commits the industry to a target of an employment figure of 8500 for Aboriginal people. It talks of integrating indigenous people into a partnership, of bridging the gap, of the 'quality presentation of a unique, living culture', of providing a means for economic independence for indigenous participants and of bringing government pilot project funds and resources to bear on the issue.

Clearly, concerted efforts are underway between Aboriginal cultural commitments and ownerships and the tourist industry. On a related front, and one which may play an influential role in future negotiations between indigenous tourism advocates and the government industry, is the 'Proposal for the Recognition and Protection of Indigenous Cultural and Intellectual Property', prepared for the Indigenous Cultural and Intellectual Property Project (ICIP Project). Its aim is to solicit opinion 'for increasing the protection and recognition of Indigenous Cultural and Intellectual Property' and ultimately 'ATSIC will then make recommendations directly to the Government' (Janke, 1997). The arenas of concentration will be literary, performing and artistic works; scientific, agricultural, technical and ecological knowledge; all items of movable cultural property; human remains and tissues; immovable cultural property (sites and burial grounds); documentation of indigenous people's heritage in archives and all forms of media (Janke, 1997, p. 1). If successfully implemented, the far-reaching effects will temper the abuses now widespread and will bring not only new cooperation into the tourist industry, but also the burgeoning growth of the Aboriginal management of various knowledges, of material and non-material productions.

Acknowledgements

An earlier version of this paper was read at the International Conference on Tourism and Culture at the University of Northumbria at Newcastle, 13–19 September 1996. The research was made possible through a grant from the Social Science and Humanities Research Council of Canada. The information contained in this chapter reflects the fact that help came from many quarters and I wish to acknowledge Rachel Ben Salleh and Bruce Sims of Magabala Books, Andrea Martin of the Northern Territory Tourist Commission, Donna Browning of the Australian Nature Conservation Agency, Scott Butcher of Ayers Rock Resort, Michael Ames, Robin Hanigan, Kevin Puertollano, Lyn Riddett, Dot West, Hazel Wilson and many others over the years. Michael Robinson is to be thanked for generosity with his time.

References

Aboriginal and Torres Strait Islander Commission (1993) *Indigenous Australians and Tourism: A focus on Northern Australia*, ATSIC, Northern Territory Tourist Commission and the Office of Northern Development, Darwin.

Bartlett, R.H. (1993) *The Mabo Decision*. Butterworths, Sydney.

Baudrillard, J. (1983) *Simulations*, Columbia University Press, New York.

Birch, T. (1993) 'Real Aborigines' – colonial attempts to re-imagine and re-create the identities of Aboriginal people, *Ulitarra*, 4, pp. 13–21.

Burnum Burnum (1988) *Burnum Burnum's Aboriginal Australia: A Traveller's Guide*. Steward, D. (ed.), Angus & Robertson, Sydney.

Carpenter, E. (1972) *Oh, What a Blow That Phantom Gave Me*, Bantam Books, Toronto.

Cultural Survival (1991) Introduction to intellectual property rights, *Cultural Survival Quarterly*, Summer 1991.

Date, M. (1994) 'The hand that holds the camera'. *Sydney Morning Herald*, 17 May, p. 27.

Donaldson, I. and Donaldson, T. (eds) (1985) *Seeing the First Australians*, George Allen & Unwin, Sydney.

Fourmile, H. (1996) Intellectual property rights: the Aboriginal perspective. Keynote address to the inaugural National Aboriginal History and Heritage Forum, Sydney Institute of Technology, New South Wales, 9–10 July.

Goldberg, C. (1996) 'Native Hawaiians vote in ethnic referendum', *The New York Times*, 23 July, p. A6.

Golvan, C. (1992) Aboriginal art and the protection of indigenous cultural rights, *Aboriginal Law Bulletin*, 2, No. 56.

Goot, M. and Rowse, T. (eds) (1994) *Make a Better Offer: the Politics of Mabo*, Pluto Press, Leichardt.

Greaves, T. (ed.) (1994) *Intellectual Property Rights for Indigenous Peoples: A Sourcebook*, Society for Applied Anthropology, Oklahoma City.

Jacobs, J.M. (1994) Earth honouring: Western desires and indigenous knowledge, *Meanjin*, 53, pp. 305–314.

Janke, T. (1997) *Our Culture, Our Future: Proposals for the Recognition and Protection of Indigenous Cultural and Intellectual Property*, Michael Frankel & Company, Solicitors.

Johnson, V. (1996) *Copyrites: Aboriginal Art in the Age of Reproductive Technologies*, Touring Exhibition 1996 Catalogue. National Indigenous Arts Advocacy Association and Macquarie University, Sydney.

Law, A.P. (1993) Tourism: issues within Aboriginal Australia, *Issues*, 24, pp. 55–60.

Mita, M. (1992) The preserved image speaks out: objectification and reification of living image in archiving and preservation. In: National Archives of Canada (ed.) *Documents that Move and Speak: Audiovisual Archives in the New Information Age*, K.G. Saur, London, pp. 72–76.

Morgan, M. (1994) *Mutant Message Down Under*, Harper Collins Publisher, New York.

Osorio, J.K. (1994) Protecting our thoughts. In: van der Vlist, L. (ed.) *Indigenous Peoples, New Partners and the Right to Self-Determination in Practice*, Netherlands Centre for Indigenous Peoples, International Books, NCIP, Amsterdam. pp. 206–212.

Peterson, N. (1985) The popular image. In: Donaldson, I. and Donaldson, T. (eds) *Seeing the First Australians*, George Allen & Unwin, Sydney, pp. 164–180.

Posey, D.A. (1994) Traditional resource rights (TRR); de facto self-determination for indigenous peoples. In: van der Vlist, L. (ed.) *Voices of the Earth: Indigenous Peoples, New Partners and the Right to Self-Determination in Practice*, Netherlands Centre for Indigenous Peoples, International Books, NCIP, Amsterdam, pp. 217–235.

Rowse, T. (1993) *After Mabo: Interpreting Indigenous Traditions,* Melbourne University Press, Carlton, Victoria.

Smith, B. (1985) *European Vision and the South Pacific,* 2nd edn. Yale University Press, New Haven.

Sontag, S. (1977) *On Photography,* Dell, New York.

Stephenson, M.A. (ed.) (1995) *Mabo: The Native Title Legislation: A Legislative Response to the High Court's Decision,* University of Queensland Press, St Lucia.

Sydney Morning Herald (1996) 'Indigenous knowledge "stolen"'. *Sydney Morning Herald,* 21 February, p. 5.

Sydney Morning Herald, Editorial (1996) 'Stolen facts'. *Sydney Morning Herald,* 17 February, p. 12.

Todd, L. (1992) Naming ourselves. In: National Archives of Canada (ed.) *Documents that Move and Speak: Audiovisual Archives in the New Information Age,* K.G. Saur, London, pp. 77–81.

Torres, P.M. (1994) Interest in writing about Indigenous Australians, *Australian Author,* 26(3), pp. 24–30.

Uluru – Kata Tjuta Board of Management and Australian National Parks and Wildlife Service (1991) *Uluru (Ayers Rock – Mount Olga) National Park : Plan of Management,* Commonwealth of Australia, Canberra.

Whittaker, E. (1986) *The Mainland Haole: White Experience in Hawaii,* Columbia University Press, New York.

Whittaker, E. (1994) Public discourse on sacredness: the transfer of Ayers Rock to Aboriginal ownership, *American Ethnologist,* 21, pp. 310–334.

Whittaker, E. (1997) The town that debates tourism: community and tourism in Broome, Australia. In: Chambers, E. (ed.). *Tourism and Culture: An Applied Perspective,* State University of New York Press, Albany, pp. 13–30.

Myth and the Discourse of Texas: Heritage Tourism and the Suppression of Instinctual Life

3

Keith Hollinshead

Introduction

Recently, a growing body of social scientists have come to the same Socratic conclusion that a large part of tourism is very much concerned with the manufacture and maintenance of preferred visions and sought images of peoples, places, and pasts. To Hobsbawm and Ranger (1983), tourism is very much involved in the continuing invention and reinvention of claimed tradition. To Horne (1986, pp. 70–71) tourism is the modern orthopraxy (common practice) by which modern populations remain 'tribal', as it serves as the principal vehicle for those forms of pre-selected 'legends', 'icons', 'rituals', and 'festivals' which help a society constitute an approved 'public culture' for itself. To Hewison (1989, p. 102), tourism is the economic prime mover that selectively memorizes, then protects and conserves legitimated versions of itself. To Fjellman (1992, see also Hollinshead, in press a and b), tourism is a vast industrial world of commodified visions that helps a host population celebrate with hordes of visitors what its history and inheritances really ought to have been like. And to Tunbridge and Ashworth (1996), tourism is a vital ideological means by which certain elements within a population, state, or 'nation' are able to mainstream their own account of received heritage and peripheralize the alternative/competing narratives of others.

This chapter seeks to follow such insights into the inventive nature of so much cultural and heritage tourism by examining the meaning and value of tourism as an occasionally loud and an occasionally quiet – and so frequently an unsuspected – maker of peoples, places, and pasts as it trades in culture, heritage and history to privilege some manufactured versions of the past while it helps silence or disenfranchise others. Thus the chapter positions a given projection of heritage in tourism as a form of historical truth amongst a plurality of manifest, latent and subjugated alternative outlooks on the past; just as in society there are also multi-social possibilities of what the 'real' culture/cultural truth of a given population is, and also of what the 'appropriate' nature/natural truth is for that particular locale.

In this sense, the chapter is concerned with what Frend (1955) called the *Tragic Paradox* of the human story. Frend's tragic paradox constitutes the view that in order to be 'integrated' and 'successful' each complex or civilized/civilizing society necessitated the suppression of instinctual life: 'civilized man has exchanged some part of his chances for happiness for a measure of security' (Frend, 1955). Civilized/civilizing societies repress individuals' instincts to be free: that is the tragic cost of civilization, and it can be carried out via the repression of certain heritages or the subjugation of certain pasts, just as it can be more overt and direct forms of power and dominance.

The chapter starts by considering how visions of and about historical truth have matured in the last couple of decades, before generating a number of findings on the pervasive character of invented or manufactured historical truth anywhere and everywhere. The chapter then proceeds by noting, however, that treatments of historical truth are far from uniform, and indeed that many of the emergent, critical and post-modern modes of inspecting the mobilizations of forms of truth in heritage tourism are yet neither intuitive nor widespread.

In order to reveal heritage truth at work in a given geography, the state of Texas is then introduced as a fascinating part of the globe which can readily reveal the rise and fall of various versions of fabricated culture and manipulated history, and which can richly illustrate the power of heritage tourism to manufacture and/or maintain privileged versions of peoples, places and pasts. In order to show how heritage truth in the 'Lone Star' state (or indeed in any territory as nation) could fruitfully be explored, a research agenda is drawn up on plural or contested heritage, where the narratives, the story lines, and the versions of the peoples, places and pasts of Texas are seen to constitute 'the discourse' (or the talk) of and about Texas. This discourse is then briefly examined in terms of the emergent literature on Texas as cultural-cum-historical truth, and particular attention is paid to the way in which the received inheritances of the Lone Star state are treated and re-treated in these myth-making practices. From this examination of the meaning or value of myth in Texas, a number of important political functions of myth in general are drawn out. But research work as myth as it applies to the tourism/culture interface, and to heritage tourism in particular, in the Lone Star state and elsewhere is still a somewhat virginal affair. The chapter therefore closes by synthesizing a range of future prospects for inquiry into the multivocality of myth in various settings and scenarios around the globe.

Research into Historical Truth

Many problematics surround our knowledge of what history means for given populations. Ten of these problematics are now introduced in terms of the relevance to notions of historical truth. While there remains a considerable body of experts on history and heritage who maintain that the study of historical truth ought to remain fundamentally a matter of hard evidence and rational argument, an increasing proportion of historians now view historical truth as a sort of narrative literature that needs to be understood for its quiet but powerful didacticism as much as for its relevance to proven events in and of the past (Gungwu, 1997, p. 14).

A 'renaissance' for heritage itself?

Although, we are today supposed to be living in an age of historical deafness, certain aspects of history appear to be undergoing a revivification with regard to popular support in the Western world. Great Britain has seen new museums appear 'at the rate of one a fortnight' (Lumley, 1988, p. 1); France has a major nationwide public museum construction policy and, since 1979, a Commission for Ethnological Heritage; in North America, meanwhile, the landscape of the 1980s in the USA had become a vast site for 'creeping heritage' (Lowenthal, 1985, p. xv). Ironically, 'we moderns [in the West] have so devoted the resources of our science to taxidermy [in the widest sense of the word, meaning "the preservation, conservation and constant projection of certain of our esteemed material and symbolic inheritances"] that there is virtually nothing that is not considerably more lively after death than it was before' (Dennis, 1974, p. 165).

But is all this, in fact, symptomatic of a genuine regeneracy of history? Do citizens of post-modernity, post-industrialism, late capitalism, need their past revealed and their inheritances displayed more so than previous generations? Has history a larger place in our minds and in our miscellanies? As yet, of course, no thorough, hard longitudinal 'evidence' is yet known, to answer such a moot point; there is little consensus on the matter in the humanities.

An apostasy for nationalism?

The development of the research agenda on state/national truth-making must consider questions of nationalism. Even in Texas (nominally and conceptually a fiftieth part of the USA), the state is frequently deemed to be a separate or chosen 'nation' (Meinig, 1969).

At various times since the Second World War, currents of thought have surfaced around the world which have celebrated 'the ultimate downfall of nationalism' (Alter, 1985, p. 1), as hopes were raised that 'one world' citizenships would slowly replace identifications of acute nationalism. Frequently, since 1945, important questions have been asked as to whether nationalism was now becoming 'devoid of a function in the contemporary world'. Certainly, in the 1980s and 1990s, many of the impulses of post-modernity have fuelled this critique of nationalism, for many of the impulses which constitute the condition of post-modernity are 'anti-tendency' in mood or feeling and nationalism is perhaps one of the strongest received tendencies which any group can collectively have or desire.

But nationalism will not lie quiet. It repeatedly appears to resurrect itself as a generic political and historical force, and continues to be a universal historical principle decisively structuring international relations and the domestic order of (certain) states. The juxtaposition of nationalism to nations and to the global throes and throws of post-modernity is an involved and an ever-altering dialectic, therefore. 'Nationalism presupposes the image of the nation as a manifest, latent or desired form of collective identity and relates it to the nation-state as a co-evolving anticipated form of political organization' (Arnason, 1990, p. 209). These images change in focus and centrality in places over time. Moreover, a 'nation' (or, rather, the acceptability anywhere of a given claimed nationalism) is an inescapably selective and affiliative entity. Though territorially based, all nations are competitive and perspectival entities, constructed socio-politically as the 1997 devolution referendum in the United Kingdom over the creation of a distinct elected assembly for Wales (and, consonantly, the re-creation of Wales – or the *creation* of Wales, as some would have it) evidences (Osmond, 1997, p. 17). In the noted verdict of Marcel Mauss, there can be no objective criteria by which nations, nationhood or nationalism are universally 'approved' – they are each self-definitional (p. 211) phenomena.

Perhaps, in the last decades of the 20th century, however, affiliations to 'ethnie' are now beginning to supersede those of nationalism in many contexts of identity around the globe. As nations become territorialized – viz., centralized, politicized, legally bonded, economically united, and civic (but without the pungent assimilative force of the 19th century heyday of nationalism and nation-formation) – the myths, and the symbolic memory of 'ethnie' are now being rediscovered to frustrate the comprehensive and ubiquitous complete division of the world into national blocks of territories (Smith, 1986, p. 152).

But if nations and nationalism are now in a form of slow decline, relative to 'ethnie' and perhaps also to large blocks of continental identity, does this concept of nationalism only apply to what are deemed to be 'nations', *ipso facto*? Or can 'nationalism' apply to any large, centralized and politicized state or State? Hence, at the end of this chapter, we will inspect whether the term 'nationalism' indeed can apply to the Lone Star 'nation', viz., to the majestic state or State of Texas; a possible 'nation' within a 'Nation'.

The erosion of certainty in history?

Many historians and museum officials view themselves as being uniquely qualified to be just and fair in the assessment and communication of the past (Kirby, 1988, p. 99). They have been, one might suggest, inclined towards surety, proud in their judgements on yesteryear and assertive in articulating them. 'Professional historians [have often seen] their mission as the stripping away of myth and the exposure [underneath, thereby] of unvarnished truth' (Buenger and Calvert, 1991, p. xi). But the post-modern rejection of universal standards of value and of morality have hit hard at the infallibilisms of history as disciplined investigation and at positivistic/neopositivistic understanding of the real, raw, truth about the past. Post-modernity has brought an erosion of certainty to and about assumed things (Burgin, 1986, pp. 192–198), an agonistics of opposition towards received truth (Connor, 1989, p. 243) and an irreducible diversity of voices and interests about all human ideas (p. 244) in many places. Consequently, the human predispositions which enwrap historians in the quotidian and often under-recognized desire to *naturalize* their favoured narratives and make such story lines appear natural, axiomatic, and 'God-given' are nowadays a little more easily spotted than they used to be (Buenger and Calvert, 1991, p. xi) from the welter of different, alternative or competitive perspectives which now emerge, or which in many instances have been subdued all of the time. We are now better able to spot the mobility of bias in the telling of history, and better able to spot the preferentially-imposed fixities of narrative and story line.

But yet, from many other perspectives, historians are still unimpeachably eminent and the history they pontificate upon is given and gospel (Arnold, 1997; Evans, 1997). Conceivably, history is not deemed to be history until in the United Kingdom it is told by an E.P. Thompson or a Geoffrey Elton, in Australia by a Manning Clark or a Geoffrey Blainey, or in the USA by a Samuel Eliot or a Henry Steele Commager, and perhaps the entrenched lines of national, state or regional Great White Aged Male Historian's history as metered out in books, magazines, 'Discovery Channel' programmes and museums represents, to many individuals, the most unchallengeable source of proper and decent factuality they ever receive? 'It is still assumed in some quarters that [the great books of history are *neutral* documents, and that] museums are *neutral* environments, and that museum activities – collecting, recording, researching and exhibiting – can be carried out without bias' (Kirby, 1988, p. 99).

Perhaps, for some historical subjects certain mainstream populations do only want to hear or know *one* given and gospel mainstream past? In many instances it seems, ironically, that the bigger the mainstream story, the less the number of alternative story lines that are acceptable, even today.

The demise of history?

A few paragraphs ago, the problematic regeneracy of *heritage* was introduced. It is now necessary to balance it with something of a corollary – the problematic atavism of *history*! One of the fundamental consequences of modernity was the creation of an absolute gulf between the past and the future (Connor, 1989, p. 24). The past had little functional value for modernity. But what has happened 'since' modernity, if modernity can here be assumed to precede the problematic concept of post-modernity? Has, to some extent, post-modernity accentuated that consequence, that very relegation of history?

Jameson considers that post-modernity has brought about the abolition of historicity, *ipso facto*, and of historical depth (see Stephanson, 1988, p. 4). He suggests that under the claimed post-modern predicament 'historical consciousness' and 'the sense of the past' are becoming ever more frequently lost, so that historical time has become heavily distorted. Unable to guide and interpret for the present age, history is no longer the object-pole of our being in the West, and the meanings, weight, or received importances of things *dissolve*; there are less, fewer, and even 'no'(?) intensified experiences from the past which cognitively inform the present under the so-called post-modern age (Stephanson, 1988, pp. 4–7). David Donald (1977) had similarly recognized the bleakness of the contemporary era brought about by the deemed irrelevance of history; to him, people nowadays are no longer so keen to learn from the lessons of the mistakes of previous peoples and times.

Despairingly for the sanctity of received history and for factist historians, people are seen to increasingly live for the present moment. For Lasch (1979, p. 30), to live for oneself, not for one's predecessors or for posterity, is the prevailing passion particularly in narcissistic North America under the contemporary moment.

If such observers are correct, the key problematic, then, is how long does a given history last? How long will story lines of the past keep being relevant for the people of each new age or era? In terms of interpretations of history, Woodward (1986) reckons that scholarly writings on history currently have a shelf-life of about 20 years. But may that same concept be applied to oral, folk or common history? Does every person's past indeed have a shelf-life? Do myths have a predictable life cycle?

Hence, while the problematic on heritage presents the possible flowering of heritage, the proposition of above sees history, itself, as now conceivably ailing as a noble and unquestioned inheritance of people.

Which alternative histories really matter?

Under the Foucauldian vision (see Foucault, 1980), the emergent genealogists of history of the 1980s and 1990s do not just examine mainstream or surface history but channel their prospecting towards 'the darkground' where local, marginal and alternative histories may lurk. These alternative histories (and in aggregate human society, marginal story lines will always exist) are held to exist in slumber, variously opposed by the structures, the ways of living and the ways of thinking that surround them (Habermas, 1987, p. 280). They are seen by mainstream members of a given society to be naive truths, lowly positioned on the knowledge hierarchies beneath politically esteemed levels of social cognition and of accepted science (Foucault, 1980, p. 82). They are the disqualified truths of the given place or region.

But, for any given state or territory, what are these latent hidden histories (Lumley, 1988, p. 12)? Are they of women, of the environment, of oral culture (Horne, 1986), of blacks (Wolfe, 1987), or of what or whom? The hardest of all to know of, find or see are those truths disenfranchised by mainstream system, denied by embedded discourse and through entrenched iconological structure – viz., the structure of a society's dominant thought-processes. The ideology of 'the darkground' as embedded in process and in form is so difficult to spot (Williamson, 1978), however, since in history, as for all truths, a *fait accompli* is conceivably at work. For instance:

> European tourism is so patriarchal that to go on repeating the point would be tedious. With exceptions such as the Virgin Mary or Joan of Arc, women are simply not there [in the manuscripts and/or in the museum interpretations of dominant European historical tourism]. They make their appearances as dummies of sturdy peasant women in folk museum reconstructions of peasant kitchens, or in other useful supporting roles; they may be seen nude, or partly nude, created as an object for the male gaze.
>
> (Horne, 1984)

So, does male intolerance or ethnocentric ignorance *significantly* shape the truths in currency for the state or place in question and, if so, on what, and where, and when? How many *other gazes* beyond 'gender' (and distinct from the subtle but mighty discriminations of race and colour) are there unsuspectingly moulding the history of localities and enlarging or reducing the contours of the darkground of historical understanding? Accordingly, one may, for instance, have a book on or about the 'complete' set of histories on a contentious subject like the Dead Sea Scrolls, yet it would be most difficult to ever get a 'complete' range of alternative, adversarial or competing interpretations on that complete set of historical 'facts' (Collins, 1997, p. 25). The possible range of contesting interpretations are always infinitous, or at least potentially infinitous (if a tautology can be accepted to register a cardinal point?).

What will? Whose will?

If historical truth is not objectified by the unwitting but meticulous attentions of the anonymous gaze or the unprehensive and constant compositions of the nameless gaze, it may be tainted by large acts of in-group volition. History can be transformed by sheer acts of imaginative will (Connor, 1989, p. 227). Frequently the will to rewrite history will be accompanied by the use of military force. As such it can be unarguably spotted as was evidently the case at the time of the break-up of Yugoslavia during the early 1990s:

> By bombing Dubrovnik's medieval heart, Yugoslavia's federal generals have made plain that they are no longer waging war to protect Serbian minorities or to capture strategic positions but to assert a victory of Serbian culture over Croatian. In a war designed to rewrite history, churches, palaces and museums are 'legitimate' targets, not accidental casualties. The Zagreb national museum believes that 214 out of 224 registered Croatian monuments have come under fire. Half of these have been either badly damaged or destroyed . . .
>
> The co-ordinated attack on Dubrovnik's center, where the treasures include the baroque cathedral housing Titian's Assumption, the 14th century rector's palace and the Sponza palace and clock tower, indicates the target is now Croatia's cultural heritage.
>
> The Serbs say Dubrovnik, 'the pearl of the Adriatic,' was never Croatian, and does not belong to an independent Croatia . . . The main point is simply to take Dubrovnik away from the Croats.
>
> (Boyes, 1991, p. 12)

At other times, and in other places the imaginative will of in-groups is much more ethereal, a mysterious power 'starting from despotic centrality [which] becomes by the half-way point a "multiplicity of relations" . . . and it culminates, at the extreme pole, with resistances . . . so small and so tenuous that, literally speaking, atoms of power and atoms of resistance merge at this microscopic level' (Baudrillard, 1987, p. 37).

Baudrillard suggests that local and disenfranchised histories cannot often resist the force of the imaginative will of mainstream truths. Alternative histories are unable to tactically outflank the dominant foci of political and cultural power and *inevitably* end up mimicking them, unsuspectingly trapped within the entrenched identifications and the embedded prejudgements of that place (Pêcheux, 1982), unable to register their own corrective counter-identifications, or their own decidedly new/different/oppositional ideological disidentifications (Hollinshead, 1996, pp. 323–337). Thus, under the reign of embedded identifications 'the spread of power away from *conspicuous* centers of control [seemingly to accommodate marginal truths and lifespaces] . . . is not diffusion but a consolidation of control, *a spiralling of power into a system that can resist any resistance*' (Connor's translation of Baudrillard: Connor, 1989, p. 226; emphasis added). Consonantly, to Baudrillard, imaginative will is at its strongest in the hollow arenas of regulated simulation where each piece of historical resistance or cultural contradiction can be predicted, checked and absorbed into the dominant discourse. These simulated worlds, are 'metastable': they can claustralize opposing truths, proselyte them and reconstitute alternative history into sublimated and stable truth.

Is 'state significance' significant?

Nations and states are artificial human constructions, generally of an ephemeral nature in terms of the total history of mankind. At any given time during recent centuries (i.e., since there have been many universally recognized 'nations' as such), numerous populations or large subcultures have been denied their own nationhood, even though they deem themselves to be a distinct nation other or apart from those who have militarily, territorially or administratively enveloped them. In the present era, perhaps the Basques, the Armenians, the Kurds and the Tibetans are best known examples of such a collective 'people' who have been arbitrarily denied their own state (Alter, 1985, p. 119).

Nations and states are often difficult entities to work within with regard to longitudinal human history because they do not necessarily correspond neatly over time with the 'geophysical' and 'natural' regions in which society has existed. There will inevitably be a lack of fit between the way the modern nation or the emergent state of the day relates to that broad environment and the way nations of old, or precursor states, used to rule or administrate those tracts of land.

Moreover, established nations and consolidating states tend to have particularist historical predispositions about the evolution of their present society in relation to the geo-physicality of past populations resident in that region or territory, and are inclined to praise only the past deeds of selected ancestors. New Yorkers triumphalize the Labour of the Dutch Colonists, for instance; Californians heavily feature Spanish missionary work (King *et al.*, 1977, p. 101) and Catholic/Republican people of Eire/Northern Ireland define their 'Green' ancestors as 'Irish', while the 'Orange' forefolk of others long domiciled in Eire/Northern Ireland are projected as being 'alien/non-Irish'. Such interests can dominate the telling of history to the denial or the rejection of the histories of peoples who might indeed have wider and longer story lines in that region or in that geo-physical territory. And such particularist truths can become official nationally-held or state-held truths. 'National merit' and 'state significance' labels can and do certainly accrue to highly élitist or selectivist narrative.

One reason why wider and longer themes are often excluded is that the majority of historians are trained to deal with 'little questions about particular cases' (King *et al.*, 1977, p. 101) rather than being schooled to handle larger questions of macro-cultural change, mass population translocation or heritage diffusion. They are more commonly trained to observe the readily *notable* in history and as such, they privilege the hiccups of history, not the mundane health or ordinary matter-of-fact inheritances of past existence. Hence, these small and local issues so frequently tend to be inadequately screened against the ongoing universalisms and the broader, *globate* humanisms of the moment. Local middens, local battlegrounds and local high streets are not just local or state features of history; they can have a different or contrasting significance at the national, the extra-national and the continental levels. But which level is indeed truly significant in the telling of a given history? Can significance in fact ever be accorded a set of universal criteria for us all to deploy in the telling of history?

Patriotisms now purchasable?

An earlier problematic (above) introduced the possible eclipse of many nationalistic tendencies. But has the now pejorative (in many social groups and subcultures) been replaced to a limited extent by quieter and lower key forms of patriotism? Patriotism is the love of one's homeland (Alter, 1985, p. 6) or rather 'the will to maintain and defend what is one's own and [what is collectively] cherished' (Huizinga, 1959, p. 97). But should the term patriotism now be applied to all manner of contemporary group feelings which need not be territorially bounded or territorially inspired? Does patriotism no longer just relate to the hearth and to the homeland *per se*, but to the contents of the home and the transient identifications that go with it? Is patriotism now consumptive (Bourdieu, 1979) or rather, in this sense of the term, *only* consumptive under the contemporary phases of late capitalism (Fjellman, 1992, pp. 7–10 and 47–57; Hollinshead, 1998c)?

One is reminded, for instance, of the fact that 'from 1970 to 1980 the population of North American Indians increased from 700,000 to 1.4 million, including the creation of several new tribes' (Friedman, 1990, p. 311). Is that predominantly evidence of a genuine revitalization of indigenous cultural pride or is it testament to borrowed and commodified ethnicity? Is patriotism, in many of its forms, now reduced to being a temporary element in one's *fashionable* narcissism or in one's *conspicuous* present-moment culture-hood?

Is history not consumptive but consuming?

Myth is generally presented as something apart from, or in opposition to, 'proper' history; even though to the dismay of many unqualified, occasional or amateur 'proper' history-peddling historians, that distinction is an unhelpful and inaccurate one (Woodward and Vidal, 1988, pp. 56–58). To many factist diehards of this ilk in history, myth is seen to be always spurious, and history is seen to be always genuine. The former – untrustworthy and make-believe myth – is usually presented as being subjective and possessive, and the latter – actual and reliable history – as being objective and neutral.

However, as our understanding of the production of historical truth becomes fine-tuned, it is becoming hard to separate myth from history. Both myth *and* history are subjective accounts, and one could argue that certain peoples around the world are becoming increasingly possessive about their myth *and* their history. Oppressed peoples are becoming consumed by their myths and engrossed by their histories. Myth and history can solidify to become pillar features of cultural identity wherever nasty or unwanted foreign pressures threaten: myth and history have consequently become a political act where the new critiques of antifoundationalism and globalization of post-modernity knock loudly (Asad, 1990, p. 239). The perceived confrontationist threat to Islam by the post-modern/post-colonial texts of Salman Rushdie on Muslim past inheritances can be interpreted as evidence of this (Asad, 1990, pp. 239–269). Inherited selfhood and traditional custom is suddenly a desperate matter for many populations and thereby for authors such as Mr Rushdie 'The very consumption of modernist [sic!; post-modernist, perhaps?] literature is suddenly an highly dangerous act' (Friedman, 1990, p. 312) in some fundamentalizing or re-fundamentalizing parts of the world. Where a proud or desiring collective is intimidated externally (or internally), sacred symbols proliferate and revered customary meanings throb. Where external narratives invade and flower, the myth and the history of besieged places can suddenly rise in resistance, becoming enwrapped within loud and large restatements of that population's *whole-being,* richly involved in, and symbolic of, their entire affiliative importances.

Prisoners of one's past?

People in each and every age are prisoners of their past. Their views, lifestyles and places of habitation are moulded by their antecedents in an endless multitude of ways. Today, and indeed at any time, 'we are acting parts in a play that we have never read and never seen, whose plot we don't know, whose existence we can glimpse, but whose beginning and end are beyond our present imagination and conception' (Laing, 1971, p. 87).

People inherit a multiplicity of sociocentrisms and live within an edifice of ethnocentrisms which were borne in earlier attempts to explain the world in that place for that population (Hollinshead, 1993a, 1993b) The history of the 20th century has conceivably been dominated by the entelechic Western view to provide a single progressivist *tabula rasa* – a Western *tabula rasa* – for, over and across the world (Touraine, 1990, p. 139). Yet so many of the perpetrators of this ethnocentric, entelechic vision are not necessarily conscious of the part they are playing in its very existence and consolidation, nor necessarily conscious of the damage they are doing to other subdued cultures and to other subjugated truths (Sampson, 1993, pp. 13–16).

Touraine believes that the second half of the 20th century has gradually brought about the shattering of such progressivist Western modernistic and developmentalist spectres, with '[other] nationalisms liberating themselves from the colonial system, each searching for their proper vision of a modernity which is everywhere different' (Touraine, 1990, p. 139).

But is that so, in fact? Is the advance of the Western presence, with the Western present and the Western past in such ruins? Or are occidental ethnocentrisms becoming almost systemic, almost now universalizing reason, mobilizing economic and social resources and substantively constraining the future world's right to know the non-Occidental past (Sampson, 1993, pp. 142–143)? Is the world's grand play largely *always* going to be an entelechic North Atlantic drama (Mason, 1990, pp. 153–168)? Watch this space!

Findings on Historical Truth

The previous section on research into historical truth presented some major problematics on 'truth' in history and heritage – that is, of areas in need of considerable further research. This current section of the chapter now attempts to briefly draw out some of the findings that investigations into the production of truth have already begun to uncover. These findings help contribute to the public knowledge in history – such as myth, legend and sacred themes – as constructed here, there and everywhere.

Everything can be history

A first important finding in historical research is that whilst almost everything can be history, historians tend to have strong beliefs about what is worthwhile/authentic history. In North America, for instance, the term 'historic' is variously utilized by some historians and preservationists with reference to built structures and material objects stemming from both before and after the European migrations to the Americas (King *et al.*, 1977, p. 10). Such a problem exists because potentially all things have an historical significance. Sadly (though some would say thankfully) historians and preservationists frequently make such decisions all of the time without considered thought. They make axiomatic and immediate assessments about what would indeed qualify for state National Registers of Monuments/Sites, when in fact 'all buildings [and structures] are buildings of historic interest' (Summerson quoted in King *et al.*, 1977, p. 95). It is the learnings and the preferences of historians and preservationists, allied to the political process, which decides, after all, what is deemed to be significant and worthy of state registration or of national recognition.

The lower-order imperative of history

The view has just been stated that everything can potentially be history, and earlier in this chapter the view was offered that history can potentially be everything. But in many places around the world, history, pragmatically, cannot be anything, for circumstantial, operational or opportunity cost reasons:

> A ruin, which appears worthy of restoration to Western eyes may demand investment of national funds which the local [i.e., the country's] government feels would be better spent on programs to improve agriculture or village water supplied. Suakin, a romantic ruined city on the Sudanese Red Sea coast, might seem to the Americans to be a splendid candidate for restoration and development into an historic theme park. To the Sudanese national, however, programs for improving housing for the present population of this old seaport and for developing local industries must receive a higher priority, and even if foreign investment funds were available for the construction of an historic preserve at Suakin, they would not be able to underwrite the improvements in local infrastructure which are so much more pressing.
>
> (Newcomb, 1979, p. 224)

Thus history has its spell, but history must compete with other life-course realities and other contemporary domestic political actualities. The evaluation of historical merit is once more seen to be perspectival and time-bound.

The undulating contours and irregular temporal pulses of history

Historians reveal that different continental and now global exigencies drive human political and state activity in different eras. As has been mentioned already, a guiding tenet of 19th century *realpolitik* was the principle of the nation-state which established itself 'with remarkable speed and dynamism' (King *et al.*, 1977, p. 94) over city-state configurations around the West and in areas of Western influence. In 20th century capital city manoeuvres in diverse colonialized or externally administered 'states' and 'nations', the surge for independence from colonial or imperial overlordship has characterized much recent history. But a problem occurs when those rejuvenated histories are conveyed, for it is often so hard for historians and site interpreters to speak beyond or outside of the felt current realities. For instance, Prussia was a mighty component of Europe, yet scarcely anyone today wants to see Prussia of old, because there is no broad Prussian 'political' constituency reinforcing Prussian-hood everyday; the proud Prussian pulse is (momentarily?) dormant. Similarly the vast and steamy mysteries of the Congo were rather lost on youngsters of the 1980s and early 1990s around the world, unless they had been advised that the Congo of their school history books was and is again the Zaire and the Brazzaville of their own new age. The capricious 'Congo' cadence was, consequently, dormant during the 1980s and early 1990s, until a change of government resurrected it for its iconological worth in 1997.

The power of late cosmopolitan history

The history of the 20th century might principally become 'the story of independence gained' by various small states, but that is not the only vast story line tenable for these decades. There is now a world culture: ergo, there is now an immediate one-world or macro-scale history. That, as Hannerz warns (1990, p. 237) does not mean there is a replication of uniformity across the globe, it means the world now consists of a knitted diversity of increasingly internally-entwined 'block political cultures'. There is 'an increasing interconnectedness of varied local cultures' (p. 237) globally. Thus, in a new power-block like Europe, the history of Europe now *matters* so much more than it used to in proportion to, for example, the distinct history and power of the land/throne/kingdom of England *vis-à-vis* the land/throne/republic of France. Furthermore, in the new cosmopolitan and metropolitan realities of the melting-pot nations of the 20th century, the former 'alien' history of erstwhile enemies is now frequently taken to be part of the acknowledged and accepted past, rather than the oppositional and resisted past, by mainstream groups. It is now much safer and more widely acceptable, for instance, for the Hispanic communities of Los Angeles to be able to lobby loudly to develop the historic city Plaza there amongst the Anglo population of L.A.; Spanish and Mexican traditions are no longer pungently outlawed truths in 'the City of Angels', they are newly adult and participant 'truths' in the life of the city (Newcomb, 1979, pp. 223–224).

The soft and pleasant nature of much historical insight

The contemporary practice of historians, preservationists and interpreters is frequently criticized for being incomplete in other ways, too. So often, only 'decent', 'acceptable' or 'accordant' history is served up. Hard, nasty and unpalatable history is remoulded into soft and pleasing story lines. Bennett (1988, pp. 64–70) advises, for instance, that the Beamish Open Air Museum in the north of England exemplifies the British capacity 'to transform industrialism from a set of ruptural events into a moment in the unfolding of harmonious relations between rulers and ruled'.

In a similar vein, Reynolds (1981, p. 2) challenges the conventional ideas about the relatively harmonious takeover of the Australian outback from Aboriginal people. Past and recent historical accounts in Australia have been softened by the generalized search to find a single mode of black behaviour towards the advancing whites: the diversity, the contradictions and the play of competing objectives (and thereby the lack of inner harmony amongst Aboriginal groups) has been considerably understated. Then, too, the 'Australian' blacks were not necessarily the particularly peaceful and the passive people that orthodox history has been inclined to draw them as being: Reynolds (p. 123) finds an overwhelming ubiquity of conflict, banditry and duplicity against the encroaching Europeans as he lately and correctively offers insight into the darker facts of the frontier resistances. The blacks of Reynolds's account appear to be more fully human in contrast to caricature 'blacks' within the narratives of certain other history-cleansing historians.

Insular nature of much historical insight

It is the view of King *et al.* (1977, pp. 189–190) that the planning and management of historical preservation and conservation (in the USA in particular) is considerably hampered because of the limited range of disciplinary backgrounds that exist amongst senior decision makers in the interpretation and the display of 'public culture'. Whilst they currently regret the absence of effective standards and universal procedures which could guide such administrators of preservation and conservation schemes on historical truth and cultural authenticity, the long-term fear of King *et al.* is that over-regulation of this very sort may suddenly arise as a worse evil, something which could cement the insular views of the narrow pool of historians and preservationists on given topics in and of history. They believe that if agency policies are concretized in the 20th century along the lines of current agency orientations, the field of visitable and viewable history will become increasingly narrow, increasingly self-serving and increasingly of a sterile intellectuality (King *et al.*, 1977 p. 191). The absence of involvement of anthropologists in historic preservation is deemed by them to be a particularly grave disciplinary/interdisciplinary shortfall: '[If we are all not careful'] it is easy to envision a future of research . . . and preservation only of those properties that represent dominant Anglo-American conceptions of historicity, propriety, and aesthetics' (King *et al.*, 1977 p. 191).

The training of historians: impact making

King *et al.* suppose that, where it is prevalent, the often insular nature of historical insight in practice within heritage interpretation often stems substantively from the inadequate breadth of training that historians and preservationists have and the 'trained incapacity' which results from that limited state of affairs. They prefer to identify 'historic preservation' as a subfield of 'cultural resource management', and nominate both as divisionary aspects of the umbrella art of social impact assessment. Clearly there is some sense in their judgement, though others may quibble that the relationship between historic preservation and cultural resource management is

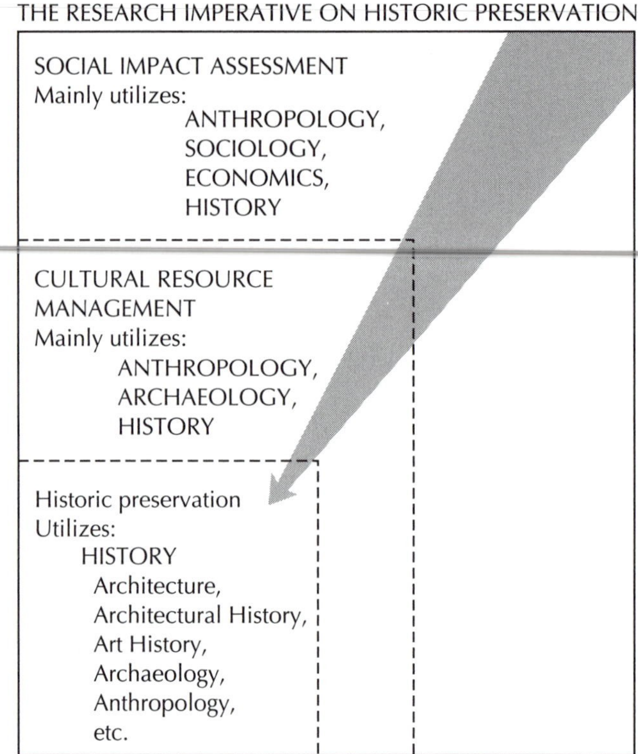

Fig. 3.1. The relationship of historic preservation to larger world issues: the place of historical truth *vis-à-vis* cultural and social truths.
Key: Main disciplines are shown in capitals, contributing ones in lower case.
Source: adapted from King *et al.* (1979, p. 9).

essentially led by 'administrative/developmental' imperatives, while that between historic preservation and social impact assessment is fundamentally led by 'research' imperatives. Nonetheless a slightly revised version of the King *et al.* relationship tier is now provided in Fig. 3.1. In it, they illustrate the view that a host of disciplines ought to contribute to historic preservation along with history itself, but that cultural resource management is chiefly the more restricted concern of anthropology and archaeology alongside history. Social impact assessment draws heaviest upon, perhaps, anthropology, sociology and economics, along with history.

Figure 3.1 illustrates the view that historic preservation tends to concern itself with tangible aspects of past cultural systems and historical activities. Insight into the interpretation and the projection of the preserved site need *not* just relate to the palpable, however. It is the strong view of King *et al.* that historians, conservationists, preservationists and interpreters of historic/heritage sites should also be widely schooled in the knowledge base of cultural resource management and in the broad issues and *realpolitik* of social impact assessment. Otherwise, practitioners in history/heritage are merely being trained in the *technical* matters and in the site specifics of each singular venerated historical case study. They maintain that historians (plus) are not normally or sufficiently schooled in the wider opaque and transcendent cultural, societal and political significance of 'veneration', 'identity' and 'affiliation'. The outlook of historians is generally too contained and purblind.

The training of historians: the making of multiple story lines

Too frequently, numerous observers of heritage conservation and interpretation inform us, the past is simply 'pillaged'. Too frequently, we are advised that the past is looted not only by fast-buck developers and urban-industrial magnates, but by unthinking maverick historians and carefree-to-irresponsible interpreters themselves. Meyer (1973) reminds that important site after important site has been ruthlessly exploited by narrow-minded, self-interested public museum officials or by private collectors who have carted off treasures, purloined antiquities and selfishly ensnared artefacts.

Yet it is not just in terms of the removal of the visible and the portable that such historians and interpreters (of various sorts) have transgressed. They have also erred by tending *not* to recognize the biases with which they themselves have viewed, sought, labelled and celebrated the past. To repeat, 'professional [and private/amateur] historians often see their mission as stripping away [the unwanted veneer of] myth and exposing some unvarnished truth. Yet cultural and sociocentric biases bind historians just as they do [individuals in] society at large' (Buenger and Calvert, 1991, p. xi).

Buenger and Calvert maintain that scholars are interpreters of history and must not be trained to just look at the past solely from dominant or favoured perspectives, but they ought to be trained to see how different groups and societies look at the past 'perspectively' *and* how different generations of previous decades and centuries have socially constructed, i.e., how they looked at and covered the past. This very question of bias in museums and in presentations of viewable history is one to which the profession has only recently turned with vigour (Tunbridge and Ashworth, 1996). Site interpreters, collectors and museum directors in heritage tourism are only just beginning to collectively recognize and acknowledge that they are continually disqualifying other/alternative and multiple truths (Selwyn, 1996). And such factist zealots are only just beginning to collectively recognize and acknowledge that the petty, the opaque and the ongoing limited width of the interpretations they routinely deal with in the *petits recits* (viz., in their quotidian actions (Morris and Patton, 1979), may be continuously wrecking havoc amongst the range of strong and pertinent truths that each and every site or historical presentation potentially (or rather 'actually') possesses. The aggregate field is only just beginning to perhaps recognize that it should be training itself and monitoring itself in the width and quality of its everyday conveyance of multiple truths and symbolic meanings of and about the past (Fees, 1996). It is only now beginning to identify the need for a more panoramic and constructive *interpretive* future for the metaphorical significances of, and within, the past (or rather, pasts) it holds within its tutelage, that is, of the need to understand how received symbolic structures can and do reify certain privileged culturally-formed images as observed realities, and then can and do harden them as 'objects' over time (Edwards, 1996).

The delivery of broader outlooks on social and temporal constructions of the past, and the provision of multiple accounts, will not be an easy matter for either public or private sector historians and interpreters to carry out. Heritage experts within the public domain are subject to local political pressures, and the spent past routinely has no active political constituency able to lobby for corrective or ameliorative interpretation (Hall, 1994). Then, heritage enthusiasts in the private sector have, in most Western countries, the constitutional or inherited right to do or say almost whatever they want with or about those elements or features of the past which they have been able to own or purchase. Modern urban-industrial/cosmopolitan societies (unlike many traditional or primal societies) simply do not tend to have the in-built protection with regard to the past, in comparison to many primal/traditional populations around the world. In such primal/traditional societies, indigenous, communal or inherited story lines are often held under relatively stable and consistent care (or should that be 'control'!) on behalf of the society by respected 'elders'. For the Pueblo people of the Rio Grande, for example, all phenomena – animate and inanimate, including history – were indeed knowable and controllable within specific esteemed myth cycles about which there was quite solid unanimity (Kupferer, 1988, p. 244). The uninitiated young who did not know the approved myths, legends and knowledges of that indigenous population were considered to be 'not-yet-fully-human' and were deemed to be 'raw' and 'uncooked' individuals. Yet by contrast, in cosmopolitan, Western society, the raw and the uncooked can actively own or purchase components of the past and can determinedly lead the new, the revived, or the fast hybrid interpretation of myth and legend.

One could argue that here, in the urban-industrial West, that the opportunity for multiple debasement of the past is just so much greater. Modern-day, contemporary society usually has little of the close respectful control of indigenous societies. Veneration is increasingly for sale in the urban-industrial West, and history is ripe for comparative annihilation (Fjellman, 1992, pp. 21–33). The not-yet-fully-human can immediately buy their way to the mastership of the past, and can retell it profitably through clever historicide and fictive employment (Fjellman, 1992, pp. 62–63). But other observers might say that even this account is an over-roseate reductionism, and that indigenous elders indulge in the manufacture and the reinvention of history just as much as occurs in the urban-industrial West. Such doubters would possibly state that all narrators of the past inescapably indulge in self-privileged, inventive storytelling in each place and every era.

Undeserved Approaches to Historical Truth

Michel Foucault (1972, p. 14) considered history to be predominantly 'a place of rest, certainty, reconciliation, a place of tranquilized sleep'. His archaeology of knowledge saw history as a place where the weight of the past and the majority of possible/potential truths were cast off into slumber; only select realities of the past and re-punctuated versions of yore earned the light of day in different succeeding ages.

Recently, approaches have emerged which are designed to help individuals and institutions identify and 'correct' some of the pitfalls of that very supposed selectiveness. Clearly, many of those responsible for these various attempts to 'lubricate', to 'level out' or to 'democratize' history will never have read continental litero-philosophies like Foucault (nor should they, necessarily!) and obviously, it will never ever be possible to completely smooth out history and render the past's past symmetrical with the present's past. New felt discriminations, new felt injustices and new felt reasons to disidentify history (i.e., to retell history in terms of the squashed realities or the disenfranchised frames of reference of subjugated populations) (Pêcheux, 1982; Hollinshead, 1996) will inevitably emerge as the decades and centuries roll on. During the 20th century, the antidotal and reformatory impulses in and on revisionist narratives are to realign towards *race*, to correct towards *colour* and to genuflect to *gender* in the retelling of the past. Inevitably, new ameliorative and counteractive impulses will emerge to join them and possibly take over from them as the major corrective and rehabilitative work upon heritage interpretation and historical truth. What will these reinterpretations be for the 21st century? In the late 1990s, this question tantalizes for the late 2010s, for the 2020s, and for the 2030s.

But what have these emergent mandatory 'curative' or 'remedial' approaches conceivably been in the present era? Two unfolding examples of the therapeutic treatment of history warrant explanation. They inherently attest to the political value of embroadened 'multiple interpretation' or 'melting pot' historical accounts.

With regard to truth in historical research, national/state governments are beginning to authorize 'comprehensive' approaches to the audit of items of viewable history. The California Department of Parks and Recreation has maintained since the 1970s an inventory of 'visible history' (State of California, Department of Parks and Recreation, 1976). Undoubtedly no such collation can ever be ultimately or absolutely comprehensive to suit everyone's standards of thoroughness and faithfulness to and about the past, but the principle and the endeavour has to be nominally applauded. Identified history is at least being rendered a little more 'open': the admission of the need to critique and update prevailing interpretations of history is indeed a large gain in and of itself.

Elsewhere, in terms of exhibited national or public culture, the Republic of Indonesia's 'Indonesia in Miniature' is a museum-cum-park of 120 hectares (300 acres) and has been conceived to explain the many subcultures and different ways-of-living that are supposedly comfortably enwrapped within the modern state. No doubt the function of the truth conveyance there is not only to inform visitors of the diversity of the archipelago cultures of Indonesia, but to catalyse patriotic feelings and integrative sentiments on the part of those very different long-standing and recent 'Indonesian' peoples themselves (Newcomb, 1979, p. 51). The discourse of such propagandist approaches in newly formed nation-states is rarely ever just externally pitched.

In many nations of the world it seems that the agencies responsible for the exhibition of 'public culture' or the institutions charged with the exhibiting of 'the national past' are not advanced in their intent or capacity to self-examine their own concepts and their own vogue themes of historical truth. One could argue that such agencies and institutions are always rather more politically-articulated than historically-articulated. The six aspects below are possibly some of the more critical approaches to inquiry and practice that nations and states could encourage should they indeed wish to pursue more plural and reflexive interpretations of the past of this sort.

Firstly, the assumptive base of historic preservation of heritage management can generally be more rigorously examined. Exhaustive analysis, according to King *et al.* (1977, p. 220) is required in terms of:

- *what* is conserved/preserved/interpreted?
- *for whom* that care/stewardship/projection is pitched at?
- *for which* purposes/functions/goals is that effort/endeavour/enterprise conducted?
- *around which* periods/places/personalities are the historical themes and story lines built?
- *who* takes charge of the research/monitoring/evaluation of the crucial consistency and continuity tasks necessitated?
- *with whose* monies/resources/services are the historical truths constructed?
- *which* of the interpretations will be singular/paired (alternatives)/multiple?
- *how* will ongoing audits be structured to check into the continuing rationalities represented – by permanent/limited duration/special exhibits and presentations, etc.

Secondly, the legitimacy of the actions of state ministries or departments for heritage/public culture merits fuller and sincere attention with particular reference to the rights and freedoms it ought acknowledge on behalf of its population in defining nationhood (Horne, 1986), in selecting viewable heritage (Horne, 1992), and in otherwise engendering 'politically correct' national consciousness (Alter, 1985 pp. 11–18).

Thirdly, approaches into the cultural concepts of *value* regularly warrant systematic and refreshing avenues of inquiry (Tunbridge and Ashworth, 1996). In the field of cultural resource management, contemporary conceptualizations of and about group perceptions of value are still inclined to be only emergent (King *et al.*, 1977, p. 103). Where cultural resource management researchers are indeed able to plumb and probe value attribution, the capacity of each and every society to sacralize precious things is newly seen to be significant (Horne, 1992). Appadurai (1986, p. 3) has recognized that places, events and commodities have traceable *social lives* and are differentially venerated, rationalized or secularized across cultures. Anthropologists, historians and political economists can gain considerably by working together with greater frequency and collective sense of purpose to uncover the myriad of meanings behind such macro-social human transactions and such macro-social attributions in order to trace the historical, geographic and temporal circulation of things (Hall, 1994, pp. 174–189 and 196–200).

Fourthly, while the separation of rhetoric from reality in the interpretation of history, and in historical preservation, appears to have been recognized for some time (King *et al.*, 1977, p. 187), the degree and manner by which skilled or petty/opaque rhetoric in historical interpretation actually creates reality (or rather forges new realities) is still imperfectly known and admitted (Golden, 1996). When the National Trust (Mulloy, 1976) (in the USA, or equivalent bodies elsewhere) talks about 'the rich ecletic diversity' of the peoples of North America, does that have a sizeable consequential effect upon the present-day integration of mainstream and subcultural populations in the USA? When promoters of heritage tourism in cotton-belt states talk of 'the old Southern ways of living' in their narratives on things historical, does that have strong resonance on the unification of contemporary styles of life across the South of today? These are questions about *the performative power* of the representation of history and culture which Bruner (1994, 1996) is beginning to inquire into with imagination and frequency, and which Bruner and Kirschenblatt-Gimblett (1994) have decided to attack on a transdisciplinary front.

Fifthly, approaches into the historic image of 'other', 'foreign' and 'overseas' places are so commonly under-served (Selwyn, 1996, pp. 9–14). Smith (1984) undertook a vast artefactual and literary inquiry into the perceptions Europeans have and hold of the history of the people of the South Pacific, but comprehensive categorical analyses utilizing statistical, discriminative or comparative techniques appear to have been rare and dialogic/interpretive/discursive 'soft science' accounts only available recently (Wetherall and Potter, 1992; Sampson, 1993). Accordingly, the geography of semiotic and iconological representations is in its infancy quantitatively and qualitatively (Dann, 1996). It is assumed that the Alamo is a world-recognized symbol of victory in defeat (King *et al.*, 1977, p. 197). It is assumed that Chief Sitting Bull is a world-renowned symbol of vanishing First Americans (Stedman, 1982, pp. 173–192). It is assumed that the Rhonda Valley is a world-received symbol of urban-industrialism (Urry, 1990, p. 105). Yet, such judgements on the power of the representation of in-group/out-group identifications have rarely been scientifically corroborated or discursively mapped in historical tourism/heritage tourism. Delving into the differential contexts of the semiotics or the semiology of 'myth' is just not yet commonplace in the social science of tourism (Selwyn, 1996, pp. 28–30).

Finally, the relationship between 'public' and 'private' history has rarely been approached in anything other than impoverished fashion (Hall, 1994, pp. 20–58). Can the views of Lasch (1979, pp. 31–32) on the rise of narcissism in contemporary North American society be reasonably translated to the use or deployment of history? Do macro-social cultural traits translate well to particular surface-level individual interpretations of history? Is there yet much examined awareness of the ways in which the past history of a given group of individuals is conceivably composed for 'private performance' or for 'transcendental self-attention' or for 'conspicuous consumption' – a subject which Golden (1996) has mused over in her critique of the difficulty which Hebrew associations and university authorities had in finding a singular all-inclusive story line for the New Museum of the Jewish Diaspora in Tel Aviv which would suit all sorts of Jews? Elsewhere, is there testing scrutiny of a claimed 'indigenous' ancestry, a claimed 'German-ness' in heritage, or a claimed 'African' antecedence of a given population, each of which are now being heavily projected by various groups in the late 1990s in cultural tourism? Are such nationalist representations now sometimes becoming merely an acceptable 'facet-of-fashion' over and above needing to be something of 'real' value in terms of a testimony-to-truth? Do we underappreciate the fact that so many individuals across the world nowadays do not live within well bordered states and within nicely fixed cultures with neat histories, but actually exist in difficult Third Space forms of uncertain hybridity (Bhabha, 1994), living locally in ambiguous zones of troublesome identification where their post-colonial or other inheritances tend to be confused and situated in contested identificatory terrain or in misconstrued iconological circumstance quite beyond the traditional historical polarities of 'self' and the 'other', and quite outside the traditional trajectories of 'Eastern' and 'Western' heritage (Hollinshead, 1998a,d)?

The critique of the power and force of invention in the telling of the past and the selling of history and heritage is, it seems, only just beginning to be understood in the domain of cultural tourism.

Historical Truth in the Discourse of Texas

Texas is now the screen for this study of the manufacture and maintenance of truth in representations of statist public culture and projections of this in touristic terms. Fundamentally, then, the subject of interest is whom does the state of Texas belong to, i.e., whom do state decision-makers in public culture, history and heritage appear to represent and privilege (if anyone?) when they make their large *and* small (particularly their small and recurrent) representational decisions. One could argue that the matter is, therefore, a political-economy of historical truth concern, that is, one in the Foucauldian mode, utilizing technical *and* critical *and* interpretative understanding to get a large purchase on the heritage issues and the manufacturing activities involved. Thus the study problem constitutes a rare inquiry into *both* procedural and substantive values in the making and the maintenance of peoples, places and pasts (Morgan and Rohr, 1986; Morgan, 1987) within Texas, that is, into the way projective processes in governmental promotion of heritage juxtapose with esteemed displays of sentiment. To that end, the following series of questions are pertinent.

To what degree is Texas a distinct entity?

To what degree do Texans think of themselves as different from 'others' (Meinig, 1969, p. 124)? To what extent do Texans have residual values different from the rest of the region/nation/continent? To what measure are Texans notably separate from the larger, enveloping US myth (O'Connor, 1986, p. 229)? To what compass are Texans part of or apart from the even grander, continuing European-Protestant (or just European) conquest of the New 'Western' Continent? Or in what fashion may one almost completely identify Texans not so much as distinct Lone Star citizens, but as Super Americans (the chronological culmination of what North American society has been able to produce over its many centuries [or few centuries, depending upon one's take is as to what properly constitutes 'society'!] of human habitation on the continent)? Or in what fashion may one locate Texans as Super Europeans who have had to deal in this part of the south and the west of North America with the fiercest(?), the longest(?), the most durable(?), the most recent(?) and the most difficult of the 'Western' frontiers (O'Connor, 1986, p. 139) as the fledgling-to-mighty United States of America expanded to manifestly fit the geography of North America?

In what fashion is Texas a doctored historical concept?

To what extent has eugeny been (and is being) practised in Texas where the quality of its population is not so much improved by the microscopic doctoring of genes but by the cosmological doctoring of received heritage? And if there has been selective breeding of this subtle iconological sort, which strains of humankind have been projectively reproduced and which have been summarily excised or performatively diminished?

Is there, in most regards, one Texas or are there many Texases?

Has culture triumphed over nature to produce one sort of rugged, geophysical Texas in the present and in the surviving accounts of the state's robust past? Or does nature take priority over culture in the shaping of the people within the state? Is Texas one integrated culturo-environmental or geographical morphological region, or is it more apposite to suggest it is indeed a mixed territory constituted of several distinct regions (Meinig, 1969, p. 121)?

Does Texas consist of one singular societal region?

Is there a distinct Texan way of living, with its own distinguished set of shared assumptions about life and lifestyle? Is there, in the Foucauldian sense, a well accepted order of things (Merquior, 1985, p. 54) in Texas lifestyles and lifespaces; a swag of unconscious meanings which are critical to, between and amongst fellow Texans? Or are there many distinct sub-societal or sub-cultural regions – as many as nine, even (Maxwell and Crain, 1990, p. 2) – where the 'internal' similarities have deeper distinct significance than the 'external' continuities across the whole state afford?

Is Texas a totalized state in terms of its cultural history where entrenched sectors/groups have been able to impose a hegemony over historical and heritage interpretations?

Is there a unified Texan myth to which all major legends and story lines adhere? Is what Foucault called 'the apparatus of historical truth' (see Rabinow, 1984 on Foucault) held in a relatively stable and consistent set of administrative, governmental and interpretive hands? Is the state indeed the least competitive of states, as is sometimes claimed (Maxwell and Crain, 1990, pp. 133–136), in terms of the degree of control held over history and heritage as well as over other more established issues of statist/nationalist intrigue? Or is the sheer geographical size of the state, and the great variety of peoples, groups and interests that occasions, nowadays producing a late legitimacy crisis for those who used to wield privileged control over the state image and identity?

Is Texas growing more homogeneous, or is it becoming more differentiated over time?

Do any significant barriers face new immigrants to Texas (there, one must suppose, can never be a barrier-free social and cultural world for newcomers, anywhere), brought about through definitions of history and heritage in currency? Do the received ethnocentrisms of myth, legend and fable translate or transfer themselves nowadays to present-day groups and populations who have perhaps been the butt of such grand and petty discriminations in the past? Do new immigrants adapt to, and largely adopt, the dominant, mainstream myths, legends and story lines of Texas, or are the changes in culture and the shifts in lifestyle which they occasion in fact of more significance in the shaping of the contemporary public face of Texas?

Is Texas remaining stable, as it was during its first century since its 1836 founding (if indeed it was then 'stable' at its time of foundation), or is it being substantively decentred (Owens, 1985, p. 57)?
Is Texas becoming schizophrenic in terms of its identifiable culture or represented heritage (Stephanson, 1988, p. 21) because post-war, sunbelt and cosmopolitan Texas is decidedly more eclectic than the received Texas of past 19th century patronage? Is there merely a hierarchy of decision-takers and identity-shakers on heritage matters in Texas, or is there nowadays an (emergent, growing and established) heteroglossia of such 'nation state'-moulders?

Has Texas recently, or is Texas suffering from any Foucauldian discontinuities (i.e. macro-generational breaks) regarding its held favoured and celebrated identifications (Rabinow, 1984, p. 9)?
Is the new-present of the later-immigrant-loaded Lone Star State out of harmony with the old-past of the state as was forged by the early trickle of immigrants? Texas and America have strong agrarian origins (Tocqueville, 1969), thereby, is Texas noticeably 'still-agrarian' (Bellah, 1985, p. 38) in its felt ideologies and cultural warrants, or has it been considerably softened and suburbanized? Do its strongest ethos and institutions still spring from autonomous, small-scale, face-to-face, rural-community doxa (i.e., tenets of living) or from its wealthy 'Plano' new Dallasian community style of bricked-up and easy-material living?

Do the traditional images of Texan history and heritage attract and arrest the modern population within the state(?) and/or beyond the state?
Or do the received myths, legends and story lines of Texas disturb, annoy or turn off sectors of the 1990s population within and outside the borders (sorry, the boundaries!) of the state? Are the famously 'tall-tale' images and the famously 'large-tale' identities and the famously 'grand-tale' cherished episodes of braggadocio Texan history as believable or as revered in the modern day age cum post-modern mood at 2001 as they are supposed to have been in 1901? Or are many of those gross tales and bloated pioneering triumphs entirely suspect and beyond popular support?

Hence, the state of play in the possible manufacture and maintenance of Texas-hood considerably intrigues. It is now the function of the following brief review of literature on the history and heritage of Texas to begin to provide background intelligence upon some of the above set of fascinating questions and problematics. Taken *in toto*, the brief and illustrative literature review conducted constitutes a state-of-the-art inspection into 'truth' formation for the state's projected heritage, culture and promoted public history – the core elements which confront the tourist. The insight has been obtained principally from the Texas Committee for the Humanities text on Texas Myths

(O'Connor, 1986) and from the eclectic Buenger and Calvert (1991) account of established and emergent interpretations of the state's manufacture of past history and heritage. This state-of-knowledge insight has been organized for this chapter into nine exemplary subject areas, synthesized from the lead classifications of these O'Connor and Buenger/Calvert manuscripts. These nine illustrative topics (but not comprehensive topics) are:

1. Texas Myth in General
2. The Frontier – People and Nature in the Myths of Texas
3. Race and Colour in the Myths of Texas
4. Women in the Myths of Texas
5. Individual Freedoms and the Good Life in the Myths of Texas
6. Texas in and as 'America' – Statehood in the Myths of the Lone Star State
7. Sunbelt Texas and the Lone Star Future in the Myths of Texas
8. Historians of Texas and the Myths of Texas
9. Political Versions of the Lone Star Story in the Myths of Texas

In this short and suggestive critique, the reader should again note that no strong attempt is made within this review of the literature to differentiate absolutely between *myth* and *history*. Both are deemed to be held versions of truth about the past. Myth is normally a 'folkloric' or 'fabulous' (in the older and 'proper' sense of the term rather than the contemporary and rather 'vacuous' application of the word) version of the truth about the past. But, to repeat, myth can become accepted history, and one may suppose that 'proper', authorized history can always retreat or metamorphose into dubious and unreliable myth. It is all a matter of audiencing. It considerably depends upon who is interpretively constructing the particular 'history' with what interpretive voice, and for which interpretation-receiving audience.

There is no single, widely approved definition for myth across all social science disciplines (Buenger and Calvert, 1991, p. x). In various contexts it functions as either mythology, or legend, or archetype, or imaginative poetry, or communal psychic response, or hero generator (Cowan, 1986 pp. 9–15). Principally, though, myth-making activity occurs within societies around those customs and institutions which require justification of some sort (Malinowski, 1954, p. 144). Myth is therefore a cultural force and an organizing force in a given society (Cowan, 1986, p. 9), as is suggested in Table 3.1. This helps construct and maintain the approved moral and social order of the given society. Myth tends to emphasize the unusual rather than the commonplace, and its explanations of phenomenon tend to be put forward in highly exaggerated terms (Myres, 1986, p. 133) of and about favoured inheritances from the past.

Under high positivism, myth tended to be disparaged in schools of social science as being unscientific understanding. Recently, however, myth has resurfaced in social science as a critical set of cultural, social, political and cosmological perspectives on and about the world (as is indicated in Fig. 3.2),

Table 3.1. Myth introduced: the state of research into myths in general.

Statement of needs

The statements	Related sample questions
(i) Myths can compete (1 > 1).	(i) Which group own/have which myths?
(ii) Myths can interpret history (1 > 2).	(ii) Which importances, perspectives and rationalities do myths reveal for the given population/groups?
(iii) Myths can vanquish history (1 > 3).	(iii) Which other historical truths do the myths at hand undo or threaten?
(iv) Myths can help a population settle into a new territory or geophysical region.	(iv) What do the extant myths say about the origin of the region or the special properties of the area?
(v) Myths can narrate the sacred history of a people (1 > 4).	(v) What do the extant myths say about the religion, the beliefs or the venerated traditions of the people?
(vi) Myths can enable a group or society to place themselves with a larger destiny than their own mundane existence.	(vi) Which cosmological, creative or provenant story lines does the particular myth point to?
(vii) Mythical reasoning can enable a group member to gain a whole belief or an entire worldview where parts are apprehended with a graspable totality (1 > 5).	(vii) Which are the larger, comprehensive, unifying myths a society has?
(viii) Myths can bind the natural and the supernatural into a coherent whole (1 > 6).	(viii) Which critical, life-sustaining or dangerous events and occurrences is the given myth attending to?
(ix) Myths evolve (1 > 7).	(ix) Which myths has a population recently dropped from its repertoire, and which ideas have been relegated from which prevailing myths?

Findings

A. Myths 'serve principally to establish a sociological character' (1 > 8).
B. Myths are 'a perennial force within both the human psyche and the social order' (1 > 9).
C. Myth patterns the social order by authenticating experience (1 > 10).

continued over

Table 3.1. *continued*

D. Myths are often magnified fears: anxieties and irresolutions are elevated into myth and (sometimes) thereby converted into an institution (1 > 11).
E. Myths are political (1 > 12).

Research approaches tried

Myths, during the Enlightenment, were fundamentally regarded as falsehoods – 'opposite to historical fact and counter to scientific evidence' (1 > 13).
Myths (being regarded as untruths) were regarded as evidencing immature rationalities.
Myths are now being studied as anthropomorphic projections of truth and value.

Research approaches underserved

Statements of generalized study problems	Related generalized study problem questions
(a) Myths transmit values across the generations (1 > 14).	(a) Which values are currently being transferred across to youngsters in overt or subtle fashion, for the given population?
(b) Myths instruct, authoritatively (1 > 15).	(b) Who are the exemplary heroes of the population, as revealed in didactic myth?
(c) Myths establish a charter for the present (1 > 16).	(c) Has a new myth recently emerged for the given population to legitimize the rise or the rights of its rulers/leaders/elders?
(d) Myths should not be judged by standards of historicity (1 > 17).	(d) Where do myth and history vehemently clash?
(e) Myths are not necessarily 'false' (1 > 18).	(e) Who insists/claims/demands that another group's myths are false and why do they need to be so.

Key	
1 > 1	O'Connor, 1986
1 > 2	Schorer, 1960:355
1 > 3	O'Connor, 1986
1 > 4	Eliade, 1968:5
1 > 5	Richards, 1969:172
1 > 6	Enstam, 1986:139
1 > 7	Buenger and Calvert, 1991:xi
1 > 8	Malinowski, 1954:144
1 > 9	Muller, Lang, Taylor, Frazer and Durkheim summarized by O'Connor, 1986:7
1 > 10	O'Connor, 1986:8
1 > 11	Cuthbertson, 1986:183
1 > 12	O'Connor, 1986:4
1 > 13	O'Connor, 1986:3
1 > 14	Enstam, 1986:139
1 > 15	Eliade, 1968
1 > 16	Bauman, 1986:25
1 > 17	Bauman, 1986:25
1 > 18	Buenger and Calvert, 1991:xi

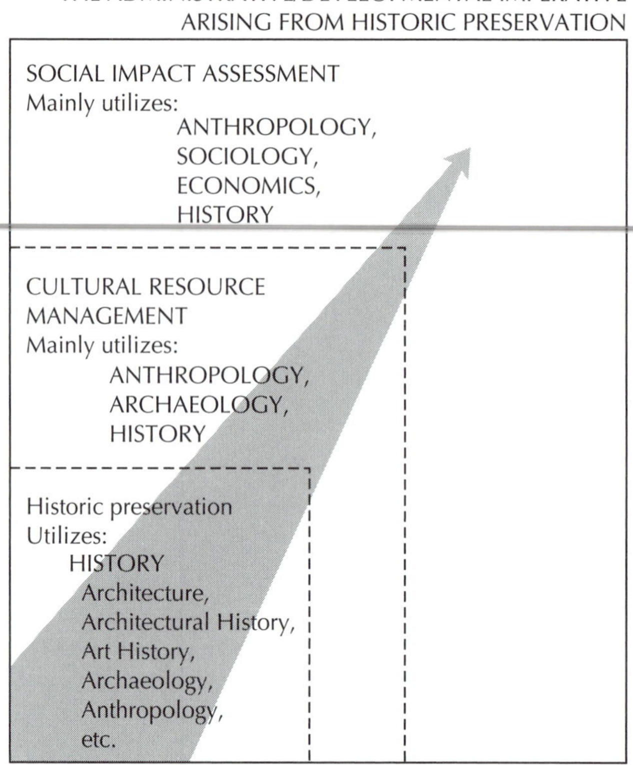

Fig. 3.2. The relationship of historic preservation to larger world issues: the place of historical truth *vis-à-vis* cultural and social truths.
Key: Main disciplines are shown in capitals, contributing ones in lower case.
Source: adapted from King *et al.* (1979, p. 9).

through the insight already gained by researchers into the social coherence of and within various shared imagined worlds. In the currently increasing mix of imaginative research agendas which pry into the nefarious and nebulous acts of history-making via tourism, it is now increasingly deemed to be important to learn *who* is, or endeavours, to legitimize *which* myths (and for which purposes?), and *who* is, or endeavours, to neutralize *which* myths (and for which reasons?) (Tunbridge and Ashworth, 1996).

Texas Myth in General

Myth is important because it helps dictate both what historians consider are worthy subjects for investigation and what the public regard as important about the roots, traditions and inheritances of a place. As Table 3.2 implies, the oral and other myths of Texas (as for other myths in other regions) may

Table 3.2. Texas myth in general: the state of research into the truth about the past.

Statement of needs

The statements	Related sample questions
(i) Texans are completely different individuals than other North Americans (in myth).	(i) Are Texans different in myth, or are they merely transplanted Americans (US Americans): are the Texas legends/storylines/impulses quite removed in type/style/form from anyone else (2 > 1)?
(ii) For certain episodes of the Texan past, the distinction between 'myth' and 'history' has collapsed – there is almost no history (for the Alamo, the border ballads, etc.)! (2 > 2).	(ii) Where has myth in Texas obliterated or cannibalized 'history' (assuming that 'history' is something separate from myth)?
(iii) Texan myths are fundamentally European (in civility), Puritan (in commitment), American (in confidence) and southern African (in courtesy) (2 > 3).	(iii) Which commonplace elements or features of Texan myths escape this simple taxonomy: what other strong strains persist in Texan legend?
(iv) The Texan myths are recent and composite, yet uncommonly virulent (2 > 4).	(iv) Have the Texan myths in currency changed substantively during the 20th century?
(v) North American myths frequently are arcadian and salute 'The Earthly Paradise', 'The New Eden', 'The Golden Age' (2 > 5).	(v) Are Texan myths festooned with the romantic pastoralism of arcadian images?
(vi) North American myths speak *natively* of the 'authentic American as a figure of heroic innocence and vast potentialities, posed at the start of a new history' (2 > 6).	(vi) Are Texan myths still loaded with visions of immense opportunity?
(vii) North American myths celebrate manifest destiny.	(vii) Do Texan myths not celebrate manifest destiny with particular vehemence (2 > 7)?
(viii) North American myths accentuate the American's brave and enriching confrontation with 'the Other' (2 > 8).	(viii) Do Texan myths heavily emphasize the Texan's brave and enriching confrontation with 'the Other'?
(ix) The inherited Texan choice of hero favours the 'tough', the 'resourceful' and the 'powerful': it is heavily, heavily male (2 > 9).	(ix) Do the new Texan myths of the 1980s and 1990s also reflect a strong viraginous bias?

continued over

Table 3.2. *continued*

Findings

A The oral myths of Texas have sustained the state's identity and given its society shared values and common goals (2 > 10).
B The myths of Texas are ambiguously located variously with and within 'Southern' and 'Western' US history (2 > 11).
C North American people are 'twice born'. Their culture is fundamentally a transplanted one from Europe, but they have to also re-identify with the lands and cultural imprint of the New World. There is an absence of sustained/continuous/rooted North American culture in site (2 > 12).
D The Texas myth and Texas written histories have a heavy 19th century orientation (2 > 13).
E The history of North America is essentially a *new* history loaded with a moral posture towards the future (2 > 14).
F Many of the present day public conceptions of Texan folklore stem from 'romantic' and 'nationalistic' writers (such as J. Frank Dobie) whose expressed aim was to *improve* history (2 > 15).
G Much Texan history and myth is late and new: many of its principal features/buildings/sites still stand (such as the Alamo) or are still available to regenerate the myth (2 > 16).

Research approaches tried

Gradual recognition has arisen of the need to study the nature and function of myth for the state's ethnic groups (2 > 17).
Gradual recognition has arisen of the need to submit the myths of Texas to rigorous ongoing examination (2 > 18).
Texan myth has begun to be identified in terms of (i) cosmological story lines (of 'Indian' peoples); (ii) hero legends (of border bandits and Alamo defenders, for example); (iii) folk tales (of cow camp and early settlements, for example); (iv) other fables and fictions (2 > 19).

Research approaches underserved

Statements of generalized study problems	Related generalized study problem questions
(a) Texas has been formed in *recorded* time.	(a) How does oral history, fictional literature and myth (i.e., the state's semi-sacred history) relate to the state's official history (i.e., the formal-sacred history)? (2 > 20).
(b) Texas historians have had difficulty rejecting and denying old truths (2 > 21).	(b) Which old understandings have been discarded (and why)?
(c) The Institute of Texan Cultures has recently begun to draw attention to imbalances in the telling of historical truth in the state – particularly with regard to the shortfall of treatment of ethnic men and women (2 > 22).	(c) Which possible/potential/manifest imbalances has the Institute of Texan Cultures 'uncovered' and which has it played no role in identifying?
(d) The historical demography of Texas largely excludes the Tejana (Mexican Texan). Indian and black story lines (2 > 23).	(d) Which story lines of which European countries/European immigrants are also strongly underserved in the historical demography of Texas?
(e) Do visitors to Texas (and inhabitants of the state) have a developed sense of how 'myth' differs from 'history'?	(e) What are the different expectations visitors from beyond Texas bring to the state before they have visited any preserved/conserved/interpreted sites/museums/heritage centres? How do their prior experiences and presuppositions vary (2 > 24)?
(f) The following socio-economic story lines appear to be *underserved* in the myths of Texas: oil and cotton (in comparison to ranching); cities and large towns (in comparison to rural settlements and small towns) (2 > 25).	(f) Which other socio-economic story lines are underserved in Texas?
(g) Folklife festivals and folklore events are presentations of the past, but they do help construct the present (2 > 26).	(g) Which 'themes' or 'truths' are celebrated and re-generated in Texas through current folklife festivals?
(h) Groups which are excluded from a state/regional/area myth will feel alienated from the state's history and from the state itself (2 > 27).	(h) Which groups or segments of the Texas population currently feel alienated from the state's history and/or from the state?

continued over

Table 3.2. *continued*

Key	
2 > 1	Cowan, 1986:20
2 > 2	O'Connor, 1986:vi
2 > 3	Cowan, 1986:19–20
2 > 4	Cowan, 1986:20–21
2 > 5	Marx, 1964:3, 229
2 > 6	Lewis, 1955:4–5
2 > 7	Veninga, 1986:230
2 > 8	Cowan, 1986:18–19
2 > 9	Myres, 1986:124
2 > 10	Buenger and Calvert, 1981:xiii
2 > 11	Buenger and Calvert, 1991:xxxiii
2 > 12	Cowan, 1986:16
2 > 13	Myres, 1986:122–123
2 > 14	Lewis, 1955:4–5
2 > 15	Wittlif, 1966:93
2 > 16	Cowan, 1986:14
2 > 17	O'Connor, 1986:7
2 > 18	Buenger and Calvert, 1991:backcover
2 > 19	O'Connor, 1986:vii
2 > 20	Fehrenbach, 1986:206
2 > 21	Buenger and Calvert, 1991:backcover
2 > 22	Myres, 1986:129
2 > 23	Enstam, 1986:143
2 > 24	Veninga, 1986:234
2 > 25	Enstam, 1986:142
2 > 26	MacCannell, 1976:8–9
2 > 27	Buenger and Calvert, 1991:xxxiii–xxxiv

preclude certain citizens within the state from reasonably identifying or fully identifying with the given state or nation. The skewed chronologies and reconceived accounts of Texan myth and history inevitably will advantage some groups/segments/élites over others within the state population. The 19th and 20th century newness of the myths of Texas clearly diminish, for example, the importance of the history and the inheritances of those largely indigenous, Indian, First American and Hispanic populations which lived prior to the 1800s in what is now present-day Texas.

Yet, as Table 3.2 also implies, tourists (along with citizens, scholars and interpreters) may not in fact be able to differentiate many of the myths and truths of Texas from the broader and larger southern and western US accounts of the past.

The Frontier: People and Nature in the Myths of Texas

A review of the literature sampled for this section of the chapter discloses the 'fact' that in the myths and legends of the state, the lands and tracts of Texas have, during the last two centuries, so frequently signified or stood for 'raw opportunity' for the myth-making group. In this regard, Texas has been solidly and consistently championed as a removed but expansive frontier wonderland; a torrid and testing 'country', but yet a 'rough and ready' accommodating one, once its teeming remote adversities and its seemingly alien perversities had been mastered. Table 3.2 intimates that this white, male, Anglo-American interpretation of Texas has almost become a 'mono-myth' for the state about the strong ties so many Texans have (or claim to have) with their hostile but conquered (or supposedly hostile and supposedly conquered) natural environment.

Race and Colour in the Myths of Texas

The implication of and within the literature reviewed is that in Texas the quality of life and the realms of opportunity and freedom available to non-Anglo-Americans have tended to dissolve in the face of the weight, magnitude and repetivity of the white, English-language and Christian master-discourse on the past. Blacks, Hispanics and 'Indians' have particularly been subjugated by the petty and opaque presence of the ruling Protestant and progressivist reverberations of the predominant Lone Star state truths. The fact that the first Anglo-Americans were at times quite loyal to Mexico is not heavily celebrated today, for instance, amongst their Anglo-American descendants. El Paso (which today is 60% Hispanic and 40% Anglo), is not generally projected as a heartland city in or of Texas, for instance (Miller, 1991, p. 299), but it is a different almost externalized city within the domination conception of the Lone Star constellation of settlements. And the contribution of blacks and 'Indians' to the projected might of the state is not eagerly cultivated within the most powerful of the myths amongst the perduring narratives. It appears, from the literature reviewed for this chapter, that the eclectic population of Texas does not have, in terms of race and ethnicity, an eclectic mythology about the state's creation, nor yet a decently multicultural stable of truths about the state's subsequent development over the changing decades.

Women in the Myths of Texas

The evidence of and about the manufacture of legend and of heritage in Texas, as accounted for in the literature examined (see Hollinshead, 1993c), teaches that the male grip on truth in Texan narratives on the past is so fixed that it almost suffocates (Myres, 1986, p. 130). As a group or as individuals, the women who have lived for, lived in, fought for and fought in Texas, and the women who have conquered, cultivated and 'cared for' Texas have yet to be mainstreamed with the state's history (Downs, 1991). Table 3.2 implies that by the somewhat fresher social standards and 'politically correct' dues of the present day, the bulk of the legends and truths of contemporary Texas are becoming rather anachronistic (Fehrenbach, 1986, p. 221) in their narrative treatment of women.

Individual Freedoms and the Good Life in the Myths of Texas

Some of the common qualities that are triumphalized amongst the leading myths of Texas are those of self-independence, pluck, penetrability and sanguinity (Veninga, 1986, p. 229). The truths of the Texan past reveal that, in Texas, a grand and profitable existence is indeed available amongst immense acres and vast resources to or for those who are particularly rugged and hardworking; assuming of course that one's gender, race, colour, religious disposition or other unfortunate traits have not already interfered to reduce such promissory possibilities!! (Sumner, 1978, p. 135).

Cuthbertson has done much work upon the cultural warrants which are held by Texans, whereby each cultural warrant (or doxa) acts as a metaphor for certain approved rational appeals within that society (Texas), or put another way, upon the manners by which myths and historical legend can constitute a model or a legitimating story line which leads the myth-holder towards an approved truth, or towards an appropriate future (Cuthbertson, 1986, p. 174). Table 3.3 identifies the way certain myths in Texas can thereby authorize, legalize and reinforce particular ways of living (e.g., the creed of individuality) and justify select economic or social activities over and above other reject or outlawed activities.

Table 3.3. Some political functions of the heritage myths in Texas.

Function	Description
Legitimizing	Texas was initially a 'state of nature'. It became a 'state of mind'. Noble savages had to be Christianized and the land conquered, for the devil had slipped into paradise. Legitimacy was found in the idea of Anglo-Saxon superiority, Manifest Destiny, the liberal ideas of the Mexican Constitution of 1824, and the need to destroy tyrants to protect natural rights.
Legalizing	Legal myths are reflected in the various constitutions of the state. Law and order is symbolized by the Texas Rangers; 'the gentlemen in the white hats', who appear as 'los Rinches' in the Mexican–American mythology.
Reinforcing	Education uses certain heroic models of virtue and patriotism to reinforce cultural values. A synthesis of models taken from classical history, the frontier and the American Revolution support the tradition of individualistic freedom and the government itself.
Justifying	Myths also support the social and economic establishment of the state, the economic power-holders based on oil, cattle, banking and cotton.

Source: Cuthbertson, 1986, p. 178

But the routes to freedom and to the good life are not absolute, and are not entirely immemorial. The prescribed path to liberty and to bliss can change in Texas, as elsewhere. Table 3.4 is Cuthbertson's assessment of how some of the *Tejan/Texian* conceptualizations of liberality and right have ripened over time into the known *Texan* ideas of freedom which are nowadays expected by many to lead contemporary Texans into further glories in the first half of the 21st century.

Texas in and as 'America' – Statehood in the Myths of the Lone Star State

According to O'Connor (1986) and to Buenger and Calvert (1991), the main myths of Texas celebrate Texans, themselves, as a chosen 'race'. A 'Saga Texana' is seen to exist as generally a notably pungent visualization of the wider and older 'Saga Americana' (Goetzman, 1986, p. 74). What O'Connor and Buenger and Calvert identify is an incipient nationalism within the Texan spirit which has survived long after the 1830–1840s decade of the formation of the separate identity of the 'state' or 'nation' of Texas as a distinct republic.

Table 3.4. The evolution of the idea of freedom in the myths of Texas.

Historical Period	Concept of Freedom
Frontier (1820s–1836)	The frontier is pre-political. Texas is a gateway to freedom that allows an escape from the past. Freedom is really limited to Anglos. In fact, Indian 'freedom' is a threat. Settlers discover the TANSTAFT principle, or 'There ain't no such thing as a free lunch in Texas'. Freedom is viewed as freedom from hardships.
Republic (1836–1845)	Freedom begins to be translated into political terms of constitutional and human rights, freedom from Mexican oppression, freedom to expand territorially and to take control of the community's own affairs. The struggle for freedom re-enacts that of the American Revolution, with the themes of the 'pursuit of happiness' and government by consent of the governed.
War between the States and reconstruction (1861–1876)	Freedom from the Union ironically means support of the institution of slavery as the war inverts and confuses fundamental values. The countermyth urges Texas to free itself from the Confederates. The reconstruction period marks Texas' efforts to free itself from carpetbaggers and the like. The cowboy enters with the 'freedom of the range'.
Democratic dominance: 'the old politics' (1870s–1970s)	There are several themes, which occasionally contradict. There is freedom from economic oppression in the form of the corporations and freedom from economic inequality. There is freedom from the national government, bureaucracy, regulation, and interference with the individual.
Two-party system: 'the new politics' (1980s–2050)	Freedom includes more meaningful political choices, removal of obstacles to political participation, and the broadening of the base of the electorate, so that Texas by the year 2050 stresses increasingly not only the toleration of eccentricity, which has always characterized its political culture, but toleration of diversity. Space and technology open up new frontiers for maximizing freedom and the democratic process. There is a continuing split between the liberal concept of freedom as moral permissiveness and the conservative concept of freedom as moral responsibility.

Source: Cuthbertson, 1986, p. 181

In historical and mythical accounts, Texas was and is still very much a country within a country (Fehrenbach, 1986, pp. 221–222), and that to be found out to be non-Texan while living within these borders (according to the weight of the aggregate truths) was certainly something inauspicious (Lack, 1991).

Sunbelt Texas and the Lone Star Future in the Myths of Texas

The myths of Texas reveal the continuing predominance of the inherited vision into the 1990s of Texas as an 'all cowboys and glorious revolution' territory (Buenger and Calvert, 1991, p. xxx). Yet contemporary Texas is found under other circumstances to be an intensively urban state, increasingly inhabited by immigrants from elsewhere in the USA and from abroad (Miller, 1991). Such a corrective realization strongly questions the fit of the frontier monomyth of the past with the sunbelt, multicultural Texas of the present. But one should recognize that there are some substantial similarities of emotive rationalization between the Texan frontier expressionism of the 19th century and the Texan sunbelt expressionism of recent decades: both vigorously and performatively proclaim the sheer readily available opportunism in life within the imagined past and present of Texas (Myres, 1986, p. 136; Veninga, 1986, pp. 231–233).

Historians of Texas and the Myths of Texas

The penultimate finding from study of the literature sampled and examined for this chapter draws attention to the fact that the very historians of prominence in Texas have been, themselves, immense conceptual barriers to the measured analysis of and scholarly investigation into the state's past (Stagner, 1981, pp. 165–181). Indeed, it seems that the evidentially shallow nativism of the self-belief by so many of the inhabitants of Texas has been well matched by the evidentially shallow nativism of the truths codified by so many of the historians of Texas (Buenger and Calvert, 1991, p. xiv). It appears that in Texas, the refreshing but scant insights of 'new social history' and of other novel approaches have generally not been able to replace the heavily biased and jingoistic interpretations of Garrison, of Ramsdell, of Webb, of Dobie and of like 'respected historians' (Stagner, 1981, pp. 180–181; Buenger and Calvert, 1991). Just as historical eras overlie each other in Texas, so are historical accounts built up layer on top of layer (Davis, 1991). The present may be a template on the past, but in this fashion, the written past of Texas is also a template for the written present of Texas. Old proud provincialisms and established uncatholicities are drawn into present-day consciousness through this characteristic of written historical interpretation in Texas (Veninga, 1986). The mobilization of the biases of historians has been extraordinarily capillary in its force in the Lone Star world.

Political Versions of the Lone Star Story in the Myths of Texas

Finally, examination of the literature of O'Connor (1986), of Buenger and Calvert (1991) and of recent others, suggests that Texas is an arena in which different people try and construct a past which bestows political or other advantages on themselves: individuals and groups in Texas have participated cohesively and restrictively in a game to manufacture a 'usable past' (Hollinshead, 1993c, pp. 202–204). Clearly those who feel they are held prisoner by a past which debilitates are prone to revising or re-emphasizing those truths. But the game is never played anywhere upon a level playing-field (Sills, 1990), as Maxwell and Crain convincingly suppose elsewhere, and here translated with regard to matters of public policy on and about heritage in the Lone Star state:

> Whether the great inequalities in impact of various parts of the Texas population can be reconciled with democracy depends on what one means by democracy. If democracy implies only equality of legal status (the right to organize), then democracy is substantially in existence already in Texas. If it implies equality of opportunity to influence the public policies that affect one's [and others] lives, then it is debatable whether democracy exists in Texas today. If it implies equality of benefits from the operation of those [practices] and policies, then such equality is obviously not to be found [in Texas].
>
> (Maxwell and Crain, 1990, p. 149)

Taken *in toto*, the above nine subject areas collectively argue that the past of Texas suffers a dual provincialism to a quite unusual degree. The largely patriarchal and Protestant patriotisms of the 19th century have conceivably been reflected back by an astonishingly insular and somewhat intolerant brotherhood of historians, during the 20th century. The truth about Texas has been and is considerably brutalized by a state (or rather a genuinely Lone Star 'nationalistic') chauvinism, and hardened in the past (but still also in the present) by the very prodigality and the very profligacy of unbalanced and anecdotal historical accountancy (Hollinshead, 1993c, pp. 797–800).

Given that judgement on the double-force of nativism in Texas, the principal research needs on and about the truth are now summarized in Table 3.5. The table calls for investigations into the progress of revisionist interpretations and projections of history and heritage in Texas in relation to the entrenched triumphalization of individualistic culture and of the 'epic' moments of the Anglo-American 19th century. Now is there anyone in North America (or elsewhere) who is trained liberally and sufficiently in a mix of

Table 3.5. The principal characterization of historical truth in Texas: some outstanding research needs as identified in the literature.

Area of discourse	Principal finding from the literature	Principal research needs in Texas on the manufacture of historical truth
Myth and history	Myth and history are exceedingly difficult to differentiate(?)	Who constructs the myths and who constructs the histories?
1 Texas myth in general	Texan history is fundamentally European Puritan, American and southern African myth(?)	Which current groups/segment(s) of the Texas population are alienated from the state's past?
2 The frontier – people and nature	Texan myth and history are inescapably frontier story lines: therefore, Texas is vigorously nationalistic(?)	Do contemporary interpretations of Texan history still triumphalize survivorship?
3 Race and colour	The Darwinian notion of 'the white man's burden' has driven accounts of the conquest of the development of Texas(?)	Do state sponsored tourism ventures and promotions in Texas still heavily promote Manifest Destiny themes – directly or indirectly?
4 Women	Women have been stereotyped out of the limelight of Texas myth and history(?)	Are any substantive sites/events/themes of Texan history nowadays mainstreaming women?
5 Individual freedoms and the good Life	The Texan past is largely a mix of traditionalistic culture in the East, and individualistic culture in the centre and West(?)	The great, great majority of magical/powerful/ inspirational sites and places projected in the state of Texas continue to be Anglo-American ones?
6 Texas in and as 'America' – statehood	The myths and history of Texas predominantly address the development of a chosen 'race'(?)	The great, great majority of themes projected about the Texan past speak to the conquest of the land and territory of what is now Texas?
7 Sunbelt Texas and the future	The myths and histories of contemporary Texas are predominantly rural myths set in a cosmopolitan/ urban state(?)	The projection of the Texan past continues to heavily stress its 19th century decades?
8 Historians of Texas	The myths and histories of Texas have predominantly been linear, epic and 'improved'(?)	Revisionist versions of Texan myth and history continue to flounder?
9 Political versions of the Texas story	The myths and histories of Texas have largely been one huge enthymeme in salute of the population's mythical synonymity?	Heterotopical accounts of Texan myth and history do not thrive in Texas?

Source: The above perspectives have been culled from several texts, chiefly O'Connor (1986) and Buenger and Calvert (1991).

social science disciplines and therefore able to mount such a wide-angled research study? We need a rarebird investigator indeed, or a transdisciplinary research team, to delve into the past and the present of the Lone Star world(s). It is important. Is there a liberally educated resident of Texas who is keen to pry into the time-honoured values of his or her own statist culture as 'it' conflicts with the history and the culture of 'other' peoples, as 'it' engages the life-ways of ethnic and racial minorities, and as 'it' encounters the experiences and achievements of women, et cetera?

But it is not only Texas that has such an imperative need. As Nussbaum (1997b, pp. 18–19) admonishes, in all locales there is indeed a whole range of 'close to home' subjects like heritage which nowadays 'need to be approached with broad historical and cross-cultural understanding. We [all and everywhere] make many mistakes [in the contemporary age, still] by thinking that our habitual ways of doing things are indeed *rooted in nature*, and could not be otherwise. [We all and everywhere need to find] intelligent participant[s] [for debates on these evolving characterizations and differences]'. Every social science field must have its appropriately imaginative Socratic thinkers about the complexities of longing, identity and affiliation (Nussbaum, 1997a). Each social science field needs to develop its means of knowing where the stereotyping starts and stops and where the propagandizing starts and stops. All social science fields need to continually refine their capacity to generate balanced judgements (i.e., taken in account of the differing multiple cultural warrants, the doxa, and the collective truths which are held and performatively participated in over a given territory) in terms of the decency and the authenticity of peoples, places and pasts.

Come on you budding Socratic thinkers on tourism, culture and heritage. Examine those sites, visions and conflictual scenarios where various, differential forms of *instinctual* life have possibly been, or are conceivably being suppressed, beneath the historical weight of the singular and the supposedly *natural* order of things as the mainstream populations of that particular heartland privilege their own proud narratives and mythologies over the alternative and othered story lines and 'out-terpretations'.

References

Alter, P. (1985) *Nationalism*, translated by S. McKinnan–Evans, Edward Arnold, London.

Appadurai, A. (1986) *The Social Life of Things: Commodities in Cultural Perspective*, Cambridge University Press, Cambridge.

Appadurai, A. (1990) Disjuncture and difference in the global cultural economy. In: M. Featherstone, M. (ed.) *Global Culture: Nationalism, Globalization and Modernity*, Sage Publications Ltd, London, pp. 295–310.

Arnason, J.P. (1990) Nationalism, globalization and modernity. In: Featherstone, M.

(ed.) *Global Culture: Nationalism, Globalization and Modernity*, Sage Publications Ltd, London, pp. 207–236.

Arnold, J. (1997) 'Truths and facts in history' (letter to Editor), *Times Higher Education Supplement*, 19th September. p. 15.

Asad, T. (1990) Ethnography, literature, and politics: some readings and uses of Salmon Rushdie's 'The Satanic Verses', *Cultural Anthropology* 5(3), (August), pp. 239–269.

Asad, T. (1964) *The Painter of Modern Life and Other Essays*, Phaidon Press, Oxford.

Baudrillard, J. (1987) *Forget Foucault*, translated by Nicola Dufresne, Semiotext (e), New York.

Bauman, R. (1986) The transmission of the Texas myth. In: O'Connor, R.F. (ed.) *Texas Myths*, Texas A & M University Press, College Station, Texas, pp. 23–44.

Bellah, R.N. *et al.* (1985) *Habits of the Heart: Individualism and Commitment in American Life*, University of California Press, Berkeley, California.

Bennett, T. (1988) Museums and 'the people.' In: Lumley, R. (ed.) *The Time-Machine: Putting Cultures on Display*, Comedia/Routledge, London, pp. 63–86.

Bhabha, H. (1994) *The Location of Culture*, Routledge, London.

Bourdieu, P. (1979) *Outline of a Theory of a Practice*, Cambridge University Press, Cambridge.

Boyes, R. (1991) 'Cultural riches a target in battle for borders', *The Weekend Australian*, 26/27 October, Sydney, Australia, p. 12.

Bruner, E.M. (1994) Abraham Lincoln as authentic reproduction: a critique of postmodernism. *American Anthropologist*, 96(2), pp. 397–415.

Bruner, E.M. (1996) Tourism in Ghana: The represention of slavery and the return of the black diaspora, *American Anthropologist*, 98(2), pp. 290–304.

Bruner, E.M. and Kirschenblatt–Gimblett, B. (1994) Maasai on the lawn: tourist realism in East Africa, *Cultural Anthropology*, 9(2), pp. 435–470.

Buenger, W.L. and Calvert, R.A. (eds) (1991) *Texas Through Time: Evolving Interpretations*, Texas A & M University Press, College Station, Texas.

Burgin, P. (1986) *The End of Art Theory: Criticism and Postmodernity*, Macmillan, London.

Collins, J.J. (1997) 'The scrolls unravelled. Review of the complete Dead Sea Scrolls in English'. G. Vermes (Penguin, 1997), *Times Higher Education Supplement*, 22 August, London, p. 25.

Connor, S. (1989) *Postmodernist Culture: An Introduction to Theories of the Contemporary*, Basil Blackwell, Oxford.

Cowan, L. (1986) Myth in the modern world. In: O'Connor, R.F. (ed.) *Texas Myths*, Texas A & M University Press, College Station, Texas, pp. 3–22.

Cuthbertson, G.M. (1986) Individual freedom: the evolution of a political ideal. In: O'Connor, R.F. (ed.) *Texas Myths*, Texas A & M University Press, College Station, Texas, pp. 174–184.

Dann, G. (1996) The people of tourist brochures. In: Selwyn, T. (ed.) *The Tourist Image: Myths and Myth Making in Tourism*, John Wiley, Chichester, pp. 61–82.

Davis, R.C. (1991) Modernization and distinctiveness: twentieth century cultural life in Texas. In: Buenger W.C. and Calvert, R.A. (eds) *Texas Through Time: Evolving Interpretations*, Texas A & M University, College Station, Texas, pp. 3–19.

Dennis, N. (1974) *Cards of Identity*, Weidenfeld and Nicholson, London.

Donald, D. (1977) 'The irrelevance of history', *New York Times*, 8 September, New York.

Downs, F. (1991) Texas women: history at the edges. In: Buenger W.C. and Calvert, R.A. (eds) *Texas Through Time: Evolving Interpretations*, Texas A & M University, College Station, Texas, pp. 81–101.

Edwards, M. (1996) Postcards: greetings from another world. In: Selwyn, T. (ed.) *The Tourist Image: Myths and Myth Making in Tourism*, John Wiley, Chichester, pp. 197–222.

Eliade, M. (1968) *Myth and Reality*, translated by W. Trask, Harper Torchbooks, New York.

Enstam, E.Y. (1986) The family. In: O'Connor, R.F. (ed.) *Texas Myths*, Texas A & M University Press, College Station, Texas, pp. 139–158.

Evans, R. (1997) 'Truth lost in vain views', *Times Higher Education Supplement*, 12 September, p. 18.

Fees, C. (1996) Tourism and the politics of authenticity in a north Cotswold town. In: Selwyn, T. (ed.) *The Tourist Image: Myths and Myth Making in Tourism*, John Wiley, Chichester, pp. 121–146.

Fehrenbach, T.R. (1986) Texas mythology: now and forever. In: O'Connor, R.F. (ed.) *Texas Myths*, Texas A & M University Press, College Station, Texas, pp. 204–226.

Feyerabend, P. (1962) Explanation, reduction and empiricism. In: Feigh, H. and Maxwell, G. (eds) *Minnesota Studies in the Philosophy of Science*, Volume 3, University of Minnesota Press, Minneapolis.

Fjellman, S.M. (1992) *Vinyl Leaves: Walt Disney World and America*, Westview Press, Boulder.

Foucault, M. (1972) *The Archaeology of Knowledge*, Tavistock, London.

Foucault, M. (1980) *Power/Knowledge: Selected Interviews and Other Writings: 1972–1977*. Translated by Colin Gordon *et al.*, Pantheon Books, New York.

Frend, S. (1955) *Civilization and Its Discontents*, Hogarth Press, New York.

Friedman, J.E. (1990) Being in the world: globalization and localization. In: Featherstone, M. (ed.) *Global Culture: Nationalism, Globalization and Modernity*, Sage Publications Ltd, London, pp. 311–328.

Goetzman, A. (1986) Keep the white lights shining. In: O'Connor, R.F. (ed.) *Texas Myths*, Texas A & M University Press, College Station, Texas, pp. 70–80.

Golden, D. (1996) The Museum of the Jewish Diaspara tells a story. In: Selwyn, T. (ed.) *The Tourist Image: Myths and Myth Making in Tourism*, John Wiley, Chichester, pp. 121–146.

Gungwu, W. (1997) 'Historic rewrite reguiled', *Times Higher Education Supplement*, 22 August, London, p. 14.

Habermas, J. (1987) *The Philosophical Discourse of Modernity: Twelve Lectures*, Translated by F. Lawrence, M.I.T. Press, Cambridge, Massachusetts.

Hall, C.M. (1994) *Tourism and Politics: Policy, Power and Place*, John Wiley, Chichester.

Hannerz, U. (1990) Cosmopolitans and locals in world culture. In: Featherstone, M. (ed.) *Global Culture: Nationalism, Globalization and Modernity*, Sage Publications Ltd, London, pp. 237–252.

Hewison, R. (1989) *The Heritage Industry: Britain in a Climate of Decline*, Methuen, London.

Hobsbawm, E. and Ranger, T. (eds) (1983) *The Invention of Tradition*, Cambridge University Press, Cambridge.

Hollinshead, K. (1993a) Encounter in tourism. In: Khan, M.A., Olsen, M.D. and Var, T. (eds) *Encyclopedia of Hospitality and Tourism,* Van Nostrand Reinhold, New York, pp. 636–651.

Hollinshead, K. (1993b) Ethnocentrism in tourism. In: Khan, M.A., Olsen, M.D. and Var, T. (eds), *Encyclopedia of Hospitality and Tourism,* Van Nostrand Reinhold, New York, pp. 652–661.

Hollinshead, K. (1993c) The Truth About Texas: A Naturalistic Study of the Construction of Heritage, Doctoral Dissertation, Dept. of Recreation, Park and Tourism Sciences, Texas A & M University, College Station, Texas.

Hollinshead, K. (1994) The unconscious realm of tourism [a counterstatement on Foucault in 'Rejoinders and Commentary'], *Annals of Tourism Research,* 21(2), pp. 387–391.

Hollinshead, K. (1996) Marketing and metaphysical realism: the disidentification of aboriginal life and traditions through tourism. In: Butler, R. and Hinch, T. (eds) *Tourism and Indigenous People,* International Thomson Business Press, London, pp. 308–309 and 323–337.

Hollinshead, K. (1998a) Tourism, hybridity and ambiguity: the relevance of Bhabha's 'Third Space' cultures, *Journal of Leisure Research,* 30(1) Special Issue on Race, Ethnicity and Leisure, 121–156.

Hollinshead, K. (1998b) Disney and commodity aesthetics: a critique of Fjellman, analysis of 'Distory' and the 'Historicide' of the past, *Current Issues in Tourism,* 1(1), 58–119.

Hollinshead, K. (1998c) Cross-referential marketing across Walt Disney's 'world': corporate power and the imagineering of nation and culture, *Tourism Analysis,* 2, 217–228.

Hollinshead, K. (1998d) Tourism and the restless peoples: a dialectical inspection of Bhabha's 'Halfway Populations', *Tourism, Culture and Communication,* 1(1).

Horne, D. (1984) *The Great Museum,* Pluto Press, London.

Horne, D. (1986) *The Public Culture: The Triumph of Industrialism,* Pluto Press, London.

Horne, D. (1992) *The Intelligent Tourist,* Margaret McGee Holdings, McMahans Point, New South Wales, Australia.

Huizinga, J. (1959) *Men and Ideas. Essays on History, the Middle Ages, the Renaissance,* New York.

King, T.F., Hickman, P.P. and Berg, G. (1977) *Anthropology in Historic Preservation: Caring for Culture's Clutter,* Academic Press. New York.

Kirby, S. (1988) Policy and politics: charges, sponsorship, and bias. In: Lumley, R. (ed.) *The Museum Time-Machine: Putting Cultures on Display,* Comedia/Routledge, London, pp. 89–101.

Kupferer, H.J. (1988) *Ancient Drums, Other Moccasins: Native North American Cultural Adaptation,* Prentice Hall, Englewood Cliffs, New Jersey.

Lack, A. (1991) In the long shadow of Eugene C. Baker: the revolution and the republic. In: Buenger W.C. and Calvert, R.A. (eds) *Texas Through Time: Evolving Interpretations,* Texas A & M University, College Station, Texas, pp. 134–164.

Laing, R.D. (1971) *The Politics of the Family,* Pantheon, New York.

Lasch, C. (1979) *The Culture of Narcissism: American Life in an Age of Diminishing Expectations,* Warner, New York.

Lewis, R.W.B. (1955) *The American Adam: Tragedy and Tradition in the Nineteenth Century,* Chicago.

Lowenthal, D. (1985) *The Past is a Foreign Country*, Cambridge University Press, Cambridge.

Lumley, R. (ed.) (1988) *The Museum Time-Machine: Putting Cultures on Display*, Comedia/Routledge, London.

MacCannell, D. (1976) *The Tourist: A New Theory of the Leisure Class*, Schocken Books, New York.

Malinowski, B. (1954) *Magic, Science and Religion*, Doubleday, New York.

Marx, L. (1964) *The Machine in the Garden*, Oxford University Press, New York.

Mason, P. (1990) *Deconstructing America: Representations of the Other*, Routledge, London.

Maxwell, W.E. and Crain, E. (1990) *Texas Politics Today*, West Publishing Co., St Paul, Minnesota.

Meinig, D.W. (1969) *Imperial Texas: An Interpretive Essay in Cultural Geography*, University of Texas Press, Austin.

Merquior, J.G. (1985) *Foucault*, Fontana, London.

Meyer, K. (1973) *The Plundered Past*, London.

Miller, C. (1991) Sunbelt Texas. In: Buenger W.C. and Calvert, R.A. (eds) *Texas Through Time: Evolving Interpretations*, Texas A & M University, College Station, Texas, pp. 279–309.

Morgan, D.F. (1987) Varieties of administrative abuse: some reflections on ethics and discretion, *Administration and Society*, November, 19, pp. 267–284.

Morgan, D.F. and Rohr, J.A. (1986) Traditional responses to administrative abuse. In: Hibbein, D. and Shumavon, D.H. (eds) *Administrative Discretion and Public Policy Implementation*, Praeger, New York, pp. 211–232.

Morris, M. and Patton, P. (1979) *Michel Foucault: Power, Truth, Strategy*, Feral Publications, Sydney.

Mulloy, E.D. (1976) *The History of the National Trust for Historic Preservation: 1963–1973*, Preservation Press, Washington.

Myres, S.L. (1986) Cowboys and southern belles. In: O'Connor, R.F. (ed.) *Texas Myths*, Texas A & M University Press, College Station, Texas, pp. 122–138.

Newcomb, R.M. (1979) *Planning the Past: Historical Landscape Resources and Recreation*, Dawson–Archon Books, Folkestone, Kent.

Nussbaum, M. (1997a) *Cultivating Humanity*, Harvard University Press, Cambridge, Massachusetts.

Nussbaum, M. (1997b) 'Democracy's wake-up call', *Times Higher Education Supplement*. 3 October, pp. 18–19.

O'Connor, R.F. (1986) *Texas Myths*. Texas A & M University Press, College Station, Texas.

Osmond, J. (1997) Return of the Welsh Nation, *Times Higher Education Supplement*, 12 September, p. 17.

Owens, C. (1985) The discourse of others: feminists and postmodernism. In: Foster, H. (ed.) *Postmodern Culture*, Pluto Press, London, pp. 57–82.

Pêcheux, M. (1982) *Language, Semantics and Ideology: Stating the Obvious*, Translated by H. Nagpal, Macmillan, London.

Rabinow, P. (1984) *The Foucault Reader*, Pantheon, New York.

Reynolds, H. (1981) *The Other Side of the Frontier: Aboriginal Resistance to the European Invasion of Australia*, Penguin Books, Ringwood, Victoria, Australia.

Richards, I.A. (1969) *Coleridge on Imagination*, Indiana University Press, Bloomington.

Sampson, E.E. (1993) *Celebration the Other: Theoretical Imagination in Psychology*, Harvester–Wheatsheaf, New York.
Schorer, M. (1960) The necessity of myth. In: Murray, H.A. (ed.) *Myth and Mythmaking*, Beacon Press, Boston.
Selwyn, T. (1996) *The Tourist Image: Myths and Myth Making in Tourism*, John Wiley, Chichester, England.
Sills, E.M. (1990) Minority hires and promotions targeted in state agencies. In: Maxwell, W.E. and Crain, E. (eds) *Texas Politics Today*, West Publishing Co., St Paul, Minnesota, pp. 245–247.
Smith, A. (1986) *The Ethnic Origins of Nations*, Blackwell, Oxford.
Smith, B. (1984) *European Vision and the South Pacific*, 2nd edn., Harper and Row, Sydney.
Stagner, S. (1981) Epics, science and the lost frontier: Texas historical writing, 1836–1936, *Western Historical Quarterly*, 23, April, pp. 165–181.
State of California, Department of Parks and Recreation (1976) *California Inventory of Historic Resources*, Sacramento, California.
Stedman, R.W. (1982) *Shadows of the Indian: Stereotypes in American Culture*, University of Oklahoma Press, Norman.
Stephanson, A. (1988) Regarding postmodernism: a conversation with Frederic Jameson. In: Ross, A. (ed.) *Universal Abandon?: The Politics of Postmodernity*, University of Minnesota Press, Minneapolis, pp. 3–30.
Sumner, A.R. (ed.) (1978) *Dallasights: An Anthology of Architecture and Open Spaces*, American Institute of Texas Architects (Dallas Chapter), Dallas, Texas.
Tocqueville, A. de (1969) *Democracy in America*, Translated by G. Lawrence. Editor J. P. Mayer. Doubleday Anchor, New York.
Touraine, A. (1990) The idea of revolution. In: Featherstone, M. (ed.) *Global Culture: Nationalism, Globalization and Modernity*, Sage Publications Ltd, London, pp. 121–142.
Tunbridge, J.E. and Ashworth, G.J. (1996) *Dissonant Heritage: The Management of the Past as a Resource in Conflict*, John Wiley, Chichester, UK.
Urry, J. (1990) *The Tourist Gaze*, Sage Publications Ltd., London.
Veninga, J.F. (1986) Epilogue: prospects for a shared culture. In: O'Connor, R.F. (ed.) *Texas Myths*, Texas A & M University Press, College Station, Texas, pp. 227–236.
Wetherell, M. and Potter, J. (1992) *Mapping the Language of Racism: Discourse and the Legitimation of Exploitation*, Harvester–Wheatsheaf, New York..
Williamson, A. (1978) *Decoding Advertisements*, Marion Boyars, London.
Wittlif, W. (1966) J. Frank Dobie in folklore. In: Hudson, W.M. and Maxwell, A. (eds) *The Sunny Slopes of Long Ago*, Publications of the Texas Folklore Society, No. 33, Southern Methodist University Press, Dallas.
Wolfe, G.C. (1987) *The Colored Museum*, London.
Woodward, C.V. (1986) *Thinking Back: The Perils of Writing History*, Louisiana State University Press, Baton Rouge.
Woodward, C.V. and Vidal, G. (1988) Exchange. In: *New York Review of Books*, New York, pp. 56–58.

Managing the Cultural Impacts of Religious Tourism in the Himalayas, Tibet and Nepal

4

Myra Shackley

Introduction

Few destination areas have experienced as many problems with the social and cultural impact of international tourism as the Himalayas, despite the fact that the equally grave environmental issues have, in general, received greater publicity. This is partly because the environmental impact of the first type of tourism to develop in the Himalayas (based around outdoor activities such as climbing and trekking) was so much easier to see. However, more recent tourism developments, which are increasingly focused around social and cultural products, are producing an equally serious portfolio of impacts, more difficult to disentangle from other developmental issues within Himalayan societies. Such problems frequently result from the conflicting aims of international visitors and host communities, and nowhere can these impacts be better observed than in the context of religious tourism involving international visitors to mainly Buddhist Himalayan monasteries, temples and festivals. Even the routine visiting of these sacred sites by tourists can create problems (Shackley, 1993, 1995), not helped by poor visitor behaviour and inadequate visitor education concerning appropriate etiquette and behaviour. Once a primary focus of social cohesion, monastic festivals, in particular, have now become cultural products for sale to visitors. These festivals, characterized by spectacular masked dances, are held annually throughout Nepal, Bhutan and north India constituting significant cultural and religious events. In recent years their popularity as visitor attractions has resulted in modification of traditional practices, decreased local interest and participation, and increased commercialization and economic exploitation.

Although the majority of visitors to the Himalayan kingdoms are still activity tourists (climbers, trekkers, wildlife watchers), increasing numbers have cultural interests. This is particularly the case in Tibet, whose tourism product is focused around the great temples and palace in Lhasa, but cultural tourism is increasingly significant in Nepal (to the World Heritage sites of the Kathmandu valley, for example) and to the fortress-monasteries of Bhutan. The rapid growth of trekking tourism in Nepal has introduced large numbers of activity tourists to monasteries and other religious sites and events in remote areas. This can work to the advantage of the monastery (as in the case of Tengboche in the Everest area where visitor donations rebuilt the structure after a fire) but visitor impacts are generally negative.

Increased interest in visiting Buddhist sites may be seen as part of a general cultural and spiritual realignment in the West, as well as reflecting easier access and constant media attention. The spectacular monasteries and colourful monastic dances have been shown in a number of recent documentary films and even featured in advertising commercials. This has resulted in greatly increased demand for access to Buddhist monastic sites and, in particular, for access to the masked dance festivals which are held annually at many locations throughout the Himalayas, generally on dates determined by the Tibetan lunar calendar.

Such festivals have primarily a religious basis (such as the Tenchi festival of Lo Manthang which celebrates the liberation of the community from a demon) but also create a social focus for scattered communities and maintain cultural continuity in remote and inaccessible areas. The festivals last for several days and typically include at least one day of ritual dances performed in the monastery courtyard by monks dressed in spectacular robes and masks, commemorating specific historico-religious events. These inevitably attract Western visitors and some tour companies offer treks carefully timed to coincide with the festivals.

The precise impact of Western visitors at religious sites is related to the volume of visitors, which is itself controlled by the location of the monastery and ease of access, as well as to their expectations and standards of behaviour. Isolated monasteries off trekking routes may see no more than a handful of visitors in the course of a year, whereas the Mani Rimdu festival held at monasteries in the Everest area is especially popular, with festival audiences at monasteries near the main trekking route composed of up to 80% visitors. Such large volumes of visitors change the character of the festival, exclude local people, decrease local participation and alter the function of the festival as a focus for social cohesion. However, monastic authorities often encourage these changes by practices such as selling tickets to tourists and ensuring that tourists get priority seating. There are many instances of local resentment, sometimes enhanced by culturally insensitive behaviour from visitors. Other results have included programme changes where dances are shortened to accommodate Western tastes.

Tourism Development in the Himalayas

Technically, the 2500 km length of the Himalayas includes territory owned by Afghanistan, Myanmar, Bangladesh, China, Bhutan, Nepal and Pakistan, but the first three countries have negligible volumes of international leisure tourism. Before the middle of the 19th century, few travellers visited the Himalayas except explorers, traders or pilgrims. This situation changed with the establishment of British rule in India and the development of summer resorts, such as Simla in the Himalayan foothills, to escape the heat of the Indian plains. It was not until after Indian Independence that the numbers of visitors to the Himalayas increased significantly (Jenner and Smith, 1992). The tremendous growth in mountaineering (and subsequently trekking) tourism dates from the 1950s, stimulated by the conquest of Everest by Sir Edmund Hillary and Sherpa Tenzing in 1953. Access to new areas is becoming steadily easier as a result of newly constructed roads (Singh and Kaur, 1986), better internal air services and more local airports. This has in some cases produced dramatic changes in potential tourism utilization. A wealthy traveller wishing to visit the Khumbu or Mustang areas of Nepal can now charter a helicopter to do so, reducing his travelling time from several weeks to a few hours.

Today's Himalayan tourism is concentrated into four core regions outlined on Fig. 4.1. In the central core area, tourists to Nepal most frequently trek or climb either within the Everest area and Khumbu Region or around Annapurna. Much smaller numbers of visitors reach Nepal's peripheral Buddhist kingdoms such as Mustang or Dolpo, or border areas such as the Langtang valley and Kachenjunga/Sikkim region. In the eastern Himalayan foothills the Indian hill stations around Darjeeling and wildlife sanctuaries of Assam attract visitors, as does the Buddhist kingdom of Bhutan. Tourism to the western Himalayas is concentrated in Ladakh and Zanskar with secondary foci in McLeod Ganj, Kulu, the Spiti valley and the Nanda Devi sanctuary. In the Pakistan Himalayas the Karakorums and Hindu Kush attract primarily climbers and trekkers.

Within these regions the pattern of tourism development has been varied but many environmental problems are common to all, including deforestation and overgrazing, rapid population growth and in-migration to urban centres associated with uncontrolled tourism expansion and population growth (Shackley, 1996). Throughout the Himalayas, tourism has acted as a catalyst for speeding up inexorable Westernization with concomitant changes in dress, food, family structure, language, community values and patterns of daily life. However, most studies of Himalayan tourism concentrate on environmental, rather than socio-cultural, impact. The intensity of problems produced by tourism development is related to three factors: the duration of tourism development, government and private-sector policies, and the type of tourism which has been encouraged. Environmental issues are felt particularly acutely in Nepal, for example, where high-volume low-cost tourism

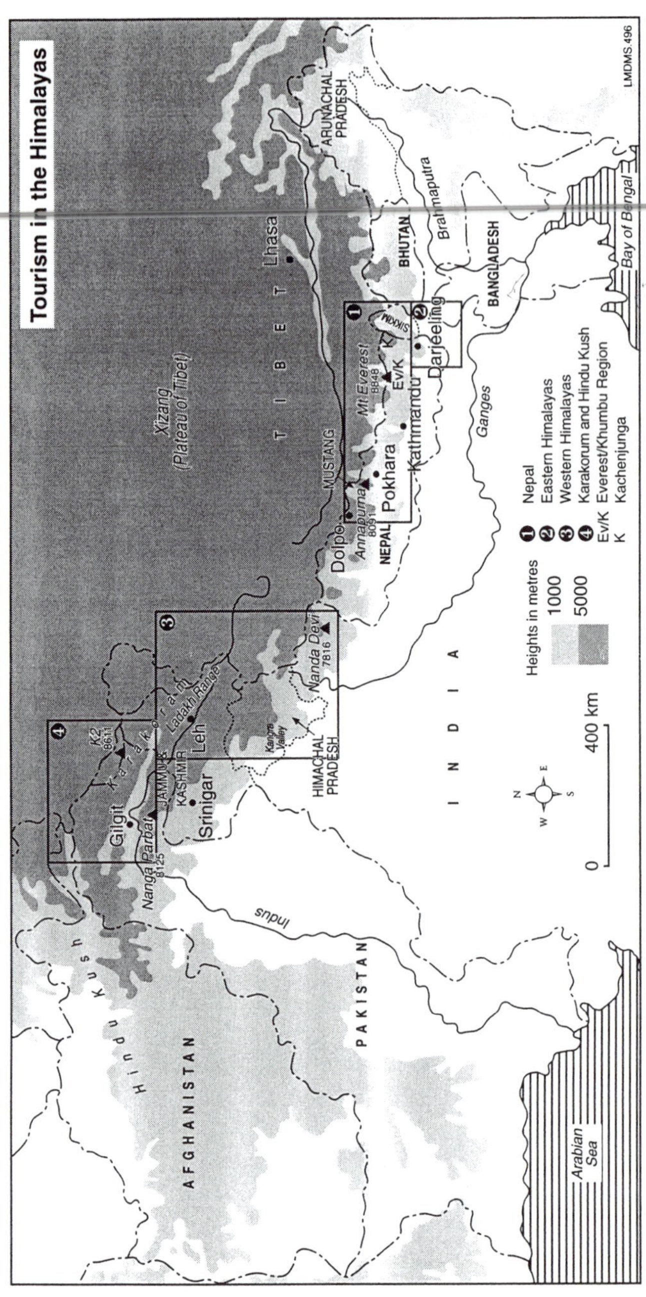

Fig. 4.1. Tourism in the Himalayas.

has been promoted. They are much less significant in neighbouring Bhutan which has maintained strict controls over tourism development and encouraged cultural tourism (WTO, 1994). Tourism impacts in Bhutan have been minimized by direct government control of tourism with minimum private sector involvement in accommodation and support services until the mid-1980s, although it has been argued that this and associated policies has caused cultural fossilization. In contrast the modification or destruction of the cultural heritage of Tibet over the last 30 years, has severely affected its tourism development opportunities and other Himalayan regions, such as Kashmir, are prevented from developing large-scale tourism because of political instability (Shackley, 1995).

Today's Himalayan visitor is likely to be a special interest traveller. Adventure and cultural tourism, major Himalayan motivators, are growing at 10–15% per year, twice the annual growth rate of leisure travel in general (Hall and Weiler, 1992). Himalayan visitors are often seeking 'life enhancing' travel experiences where contact with other cultures is used to gain a sense of personal achievement and satisfaction. Many visitors to the Himalayas are independent travellers wanting a cultural experience, but many travel with adventure tour companies which have a constant need for new regions and new tourism products to satisfy the demands of increasingly sophisticated and experienced consumers. However, Himalayan domestic tourism remains significant and religious tourism, primarily pilgrimage, still represents a major motivation (Kaur, 1995). All Himalayan governments are continuing to open new areas to tourism each year, generally without properly-developed management plans or any idea of carrying capacity. During 1994, for example, India opened Arunachal Pradesh and new areas of Himachal Pradesh and Nepal permitted cross-border trekking to Tibet on its northwest frontier and allowed freer access to its peripheral Buddhist kingdoms. Bhutan increased private-sector participation in the tourism industry and opened new trekking routes. By contrast, Kashmir and Ladakh experienced decreased numbers of visitors because of political instability. Despite having been established for more than 50 years, the tourism industry of Nepal attracts a relatively small number of visitors – currently 320,000 per year (KMTNC, 1992) – but they cause disproportionate environmental damage.

Religious Tourism in the Himalayas

Visiting important Buddhist sites is a minor but interesting motivator for both domestic and international tourism in the Himalayas. In the western Himalayas, for example, the Namgyal monastery at McCleod Ganj houses the centre of Tibetan studies known as Little Lhasa which attracts students, pilgrims and tourists all year round, as does the town of Dharamshala in Himachal Pradesh which is the seat of the Dalai Lama and Tibet's government in exile (Fig. 4.1). It is possible for visitors to gain an audience but problems with the inappropriate dress and behaviour of foreigners have compelled the monks to set up a committee to monitor the appearance of visitors and reject those unsuitably clad for visiting a head of state. However, the number of international visitors to such localities is only a small fraction of total Himalayan leisure tourism. The number of domestic tourists making such visits or undertaking pilgrimages is much greater (though as yet uncounted) but these individuals and groups have little impact (either negative, in the cultural sense, or positive in the economic sense) on the religious sites which they are visiting.

With the exception of those motivated to visit *gompas* (Buddhist temples/ monasteries) the everyday tourist to the Himalayas has few structured encounters with Buddhism. *Gompas* are often shut and when opened may be in poor repair. Quiet, fusty monasteries are often poorly lit and smell of rancid butterfat and it is only by luck that the visitor might see an ancillary ceremony such as a house blessing, rarely encountered and often not explained. Outside the monasteries, *mani* (prayer stone) walls, prayer wheels and occasional pilgrims are reminders of the regional religion, together with *stupas* (monuments) and wayside shrines or paintings. This means that the non-Buddhist tourist has few opportunities to understand the mundane aspects of local religious life. The masked dances and bright ceremonies seen at festivals represent only the extreme and exceptional. Tibetan Buddhism's colourful pantheon of gods and demons, its emphasis on death and its extraordinary iconography has created images which seem to fascinate Western visitors but are generally imperfectly understood.

Masked dances are a feature of major Buddhist monasteries in Himalayan regions. Here the people practise Tibetan-style Mahayana Buddhism and the local *gompa* forms a focus of community life. Because the inhabitants of these remote regions are distant from the national capital and frequently practise a different religion from the ruling political party (as in Nepal) they generally receive little aid money and are very poor. Monasteries are starved of their traditional charitable donations and are sometimes anxious to explore new sources of funding, including visitors. Political problems have sometimes meant that there are few *lamas* (Buddhist monks) in residence and the monastic school may have atrophied. However, some life including the celebration of major festivals will generally be maintained in even the most remote monastery by visiting *lamas*, and tourists are often welcome to see the inside of the *gompa* (generally on payment of a fee). In some areas this has been regularized to a standard admissions charge as in Lo (Mustang, northwest Nepal). Lo was among the latest of the Buddhist kingdoms to admit visitors who have been allowed there since 1993 (Shackley, 1993, 1995). Its *gompas* contain an as yet uncatalogued collection of artwork including statues, *thankas* (ritual paintings on silk) and wall paintings. Some of the latter are in very poor repair and one unfortunate by-product of tourism in Lo has been a spate of serious art thefts (Shackley, 1994). Among the first projects to be funded from tourism revenues was the installation of security screening at major *gompas*. Lo has a standard visitor fee for *gompas* (R100) which is paid directly to monastic authorities and goes towards the monastery school and restoration projects. The visitor receives a ticket with a brief history of the building. Not all the interest in visitors stems from a desire to generate revenue; Buddhism is traditionally a tolerant religion and the monks welcome the opportunity to meet Westerners and, where possible, to share a little Buddhist philosophy. Indeed, when it was realized in Lo that visitors to *gompas* might be stealing artwork the High Lama actively opposed any regulation of visitor activities on the grounds that this was against Buddhist principles of tolerance and free will.

Tourism and Dance

It seems probable that more visitors experience contact with Himalayan Buddhist traditions through attending monastic festivals than through the routine visiting of temples. This is not unusual – dance performances are popular tourist attractions in many developing world countries. Such events are often colourful and seen as exotic or mysterious by the visitor, able to transport him or her temporarily into a wilder and more primitive world. Almost anyone can respond at some level to dance, irrespective of the dance's intended meaning, but dance media presented to tourists run the danger of becoming merely a set of signs rather than a set of symbols, with most of the original depth of meaning being lost. In order for a such a cross-cultural transaction to be more effective there is likely to be a rearrangement of the component parts. The result may be an accommodation of supply (the elements of the dance) to take into account the expectations and wishes of the audience (demand). 'Ethnic' or 'tribal' dances staged for visitors are frequently simpler and shorter than the original forms since the visitor is appreciating the performance at a purely visual level. He/shě may be unwilling to sit through repetitious and complex dances which may be of great ritual significance to the performers but have little visual merit for the consumer. Tourist performances typically condense or amplify part of the ritual such as the complex ritual performances of healing and exorcism performed by the Berava or Drummer caste of southern Sri Lanka (Simpson, 1993). The majority of rituals were performed for a clientele of rural peasants but were being increasingly transformed into commodities appropriate for consumption by tourists. Such 'devil dances' have been described for over 300 years and have a similar appeal to the masked dances of the Himalayas, offering their audience a combination of mystical malevolence and primitive ritual.

Masked dances and festivals occur throughout the world and are especially attractive to visitors, with masks forming part of an archetypal continuum of dance, costume and magic for an expression of beliefs and ideas about deities and demons. The materials used for mask-making vary; in

African dance, for example, most masks are of wood whereas in the Himalayas masks are typically constructed of plaster. They may be of considerable antiquity and remain in the monastery treasury between performances. Some masks featured in the Himalayan dances are 300–500 years old, and if destroyed or damaged (by fire, theft or simply attrition) identical replacements are made (Shackley, 1994). The production of masks requires both cash and expertise; unfortunately many monasteries are rich in the latter but have none of the former. Charging visitors for admission to masked dances is therefore sometimes seen as a way of paying for essential replacement and repairs to costumes and masks, and thus of ensuring cultural continuity as well as a high standard of performance. Further cash can sometimes be earned by creating replicas of masks for sale to visitors, a practice that occurs wherever masked dances are held. Famous or particularly spectacular masks will be replicated for sale to tourists and the images made available on everything from T-shirts to *thankas*. However, not all masks are considered suitable for reproduction as some have religious significance which precludes their being made generally available.

Many writers have stressed the significance of cultural tourism in strengthening performing arts. It has been argued that tourism has led to the strengthening of the arts and crafts tradition in both Bali (McKean, 1989) and Indonesia (Crystal, 1989). Balinese dances performed traditionally in temples may also become forms of entertainment for visitors. This blurs the distinction between the sacred and profane, a distinction which becomes increasingly difficult to make in scenarios where dancers continue to wear consecrated masks and obtain religious benefits when dancing specially for tourist audiences. Nor is the popularity of masked dances as tourist attractions confined to Asia. The chance of seeing masked dances has been mainly responsible for the growth of tourism to the Dogon people of Mali whose enormous repertoire of masks are classified according to the roles played in sacred performances. Dogon dances are also staged in abbreviated forms for visitors, and masks are also used by neighbouring people such as the Mossi, Bobo and Yoruba in ceremonies taking place at a fixed date marked in ritual calendars. As in the Himalayas, West African tour operators target these dances (especially those of the Dogon) whose primary function is to create significant landmark dates and give a time structure to the group as well as to provide an opportunity for excess resource consumption. Dogon masks and costumes are thought to possess intrinsic energy, a concept tied up with ritual possession. This also occurs in the Himalayas where masked monks take on many of the attributes of the deity or demon that they are portraying, creating genuine fear among audience and performer alike.

Masked Dance Festivals of the Himalayas

Figure 4.2 shows the location of the major masked dance festivals of the Himalayas which attract visitors; an immediate overlap can be seen with the chief tourist destination regions shown in Fig. 4.1. These masked religious dances (*cham*) form an integral part of the festivals and can be didactic (with a moral) or purificatory (protecting against evil spirits and celebrating the victory of Buddhism). The theme is always the triumph of good over evil and the drama of the dances is punctuated by comic interludes, much in the manner of a Greek tragedy. Individual dances include the famous 'black hat' dance performed by monks wearing ornate hats, high boots and elaborate silk brocade costumes, accompanied by drummers. The 'dance of fearsome gods' utilizes terrifying masks of angry deities, the 'dance of heroes' features yellow skirts and skull masks. *Cham* dances form only one part of the festival which usually lasts several days. They are usually performed by the younger monks and watched by the High Lama of the monastery and senior monks and an extensive lay audience. A musical accompaniment is provided by traditional instruments including the long Tibetan trumpets, drums, pipes, gongs, cymbals and conch shells. The brilliant colours, exotic dances and the chance to see local people dressed in traditional costumes are an irresistible magnet for visitors, who are inevitably drawn to such events wherever they are held in the Himalayas.

The masked dance festivals of Nepal are held mostly in the Himalayan regions whose people are mainly Mahayana Buddhists. In lowland areas such as the Kathmandu valley (Fig. 4.2) Hindu festivals such as Holi (the colour festival held in March–April) are attractive but seldom the motivation for a tourist trip although the masked Hindu dances of Bhaktapur would be an exception. Some Buddhist masked dances are also performed in the Kathmandu valley, such as the Newari temple dances which date back to the 7th century, but these are generally performed in secret. The Mani Rimdu festival held in the Himalayan monasteries of the Sherpa country near Everest (Nepal) is particularly popular with visitors (Fig. 4.2). These festivals were first observed by Westerners in the 1950s at the start of the popularity of mountaineering. The Tengboche Mani Rimdu festival is the best known since it is held in late October, coinciding with the main trekking season. Equally vivid but less crowded Mani Rimdu are held in May at Thami *gompa* and at Chiwong *gompa* during November. The full Mani Rimdu festival lasts for 19 days of prayer and community ceremonies but it is the single day of masked dances that attracts visitors. The Sherpas also celebrate the Tibetan Losar festival and the Tibetan New Year, generally in February and always accompanied by much singing, dancing and consumption of *chang* (home brewed rice wine).

In the western Himalayan kingdom of Ladakh (Fig. 4.2) most people are also Mahayana Buddhists with beliefs consisting of a mixture of animistic pre-Buddhist Bon and Tantric influences. Their festivals take place in the

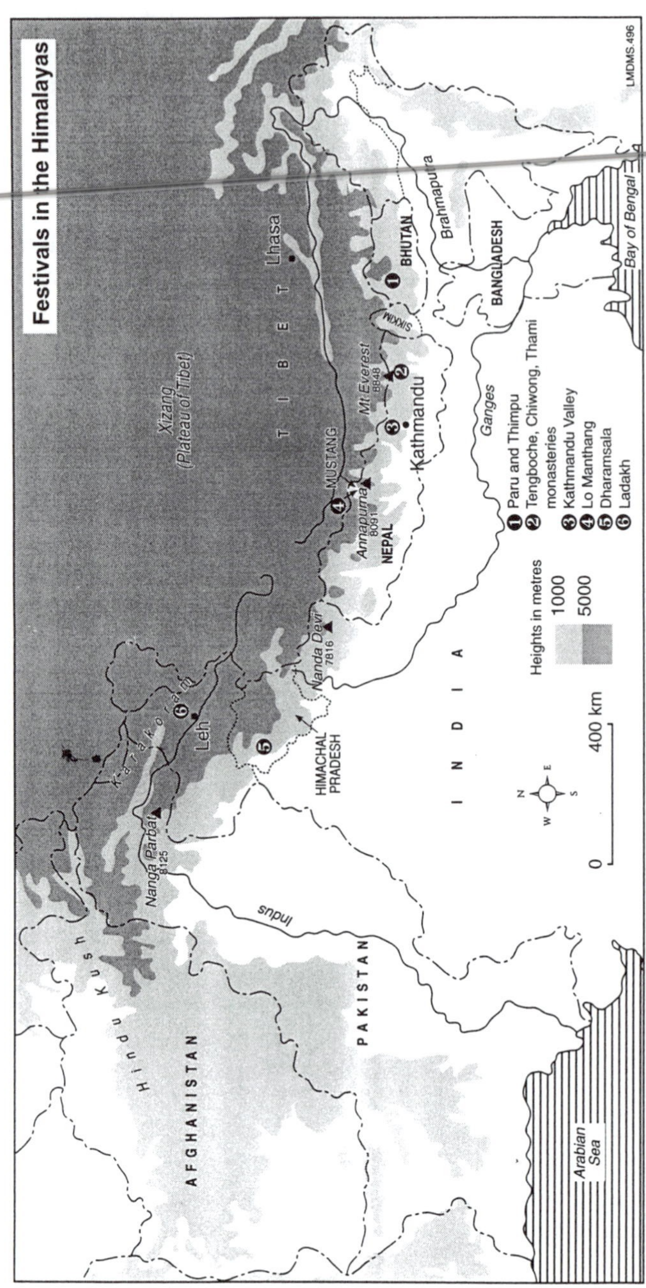

Fig. 4.2. Festivals in the Himalayas.

bleak winter months when villagers gather together, stalls and a market develop round the *gompas* and the associated festivals include *cham* dances. As with all these Himalayan festivals the musical instruments, weapons and religious objects used in the dances are brought out of secret monastic stores where they are kept concealed at all other times. Ladakhi festivals which have been visited by Westerners for many years (Goering, 1990; Norberg-Hodge, 1991) include that at the Lamayuru monastery on a crag overlooking the Indus valley which dates from the 11th century, and the Red Hat *lama* festival held at Phyang monastery since the 16th century. A more modern development is the 'Festival of Ladakh' held during the first week of August and organized by the tourist office rather than monastic authorities, purely to attract visitors.

The Bhutanese state religion is the Drukpa Kagyupa school of Tantric Buddhism with around 5000 monks accommodated in fortress-monasteries called *dzongs* which form the kingpin of all tourist itineraries. Their annual masked dance festivals (*tsechu*) are the only time visitors may enter many of the *dzongs*, some of which were placed off-limits after complaints of inappropriate visitor behaviour. The effect on the Bhutanese tourism industry was so severe that most have now re-opened. Larger *dzongs* (such as Paru and Thimpu – see Fig. 4.2) may house several hundred *lamas* who are highly respected, and who provide spiritual comfort and guidance to local people. Monks in Bhutan are state supported but also rely on charity. The Bhutanese religious festivals also include sacred dance and provide an occasion for people to get together for enjoyment, to renew faith and also to receive teaching by watching the sacred dances. Most Bhutanese festivals were started in the 17th century after the country had been unified by a Drukpa hierarchy who had fled from Tibet, and are dedicated to the spiritual leader who introduced Buddhism into Bhutan. At the *dzongs* of Paru, Wangdi, Mongar and Tashigang an enormous *thanka* (literally 'a banner which brings liberation by sight') is on show for a few hours on just one day, thronged by people coming to see it and be blessed. This practice is also common elsewhere and important monasteries may have more than one *thanka* as in Lo Manthang, Nepal, where two magnificent 15 m-high *thankas* are displayed on different days.

The masked dance festival of Lo Manthang, the capital of Lo (Mustang) a Tibetan-speaking Buddhist kingdom in north Nepal, was observed by the writer in 1994. The complete festival, known as Tenchi, lasts over five days in May–June, at a date determined by the Tibetan lunar calendar. The festival has many similarities to the Mani Rimdu events of the Everest area, and is held to celebrate the slaying, by a famous Buddhist *lama*, of a demon which was causing problems for Lo Manthang in the 13th century. The first two days of the festival involve rites carried out within the monastery confines but during the third and fourth days masked dances are held in the main square of the city. The dances, performed by monks, may last up to seven hours. On the fifth day the end of the festival is celebrated by ceremonies outside the city which involve the firing of volleys of arrows and ancient muskets. In the four years since Lo has been opened up to visitors, probably less than 30 tourists a year have had the opportunity to witness the Tenchi festival, whose precise date is not advertised. However, since the festival has now been photographed some tour companies are timing visits to Lo to coincide with the festival but the volume of visitors is unlikely to significantly increase due to the cost of the trip (around $5000–7000 from Europe) and the extreme difficulty of reaching Lo Manthang which involves at least a four-day walk over mountain passes.

Cultural Conflict at Masked Dance Festivals

The impact of visitors on Himalayan masked dance festivals is directly related to their number, which itself is controlled by the accessibility of the site and the way the festival has been promoted. The longer the festival has been known the more likely it is to receive large visitor numbers. The Tenchi festival of Lo Manthang represents one extreme where very small visitor numbers, difficult access and a short market availability (four years) have meant that the festival still preserves most of its original characteristics. The Mani Rimdu festivals of the better-frequented Everest region represent the opposite extreme where at the better-known monasteries (such as Tengboche) the festival audience may be composed of more than 80% visitors. In Lo Manthang the figure would be nearer 1%. No systematic survey work has been done on the visitors to such festivals but qualitative indications are that visitor concerns include:

- boredom due to incomprehension;
- lack of any interpretative or visitor facilities;
- too many visitors affecting the 'authenticity' of the experience;
- erratic scheduling and timing making key events impossible to predict.

Concerns expressed by local people and monastic authorities include:

- poor visitor behaviour lacking cultural sensitivity;
- inconsiderate taking of photographs;
- best seats (and best views) being taken by visitors;
- no revenue from visitors to help with the costumes, and expenses of staging the festival;
- visitors lacked reverence or interest in the festival's meaning.

The problem of interpretation is a serious one. These festivals are often staged in Tibetan-speaking areas yet tour parties usually have guides who do not speak Tibetan. Moreover, the meaning and plot of each festival and dance varies and few generalizations can be made. Therefore, in order to understand what is going on, a local guide or locally-produced leaflet is required. For religious reasons, any such publication must be sanctioned by the relevant High Lama but the monasteries themselves are unable to fund their production. The problem is not insuperable. During the 1980s a specialist tour company operating in the Everest area financed and wrote an explanatory leaflet for the Mani Rimdu festival at Chiwong *gompa*, providing the monastery with free copies which they could then sell to visitors to generate revenue for monastic funds. A similar leaflet is currently being prepared by the writer for Lo Manthang which will include both a script and instructions on appropriate behaviour.

The lack of interpretation is clearly related to a common visitor complaint at masked dances, that of boredom. Most visitors are initially entranced by the colourful dances but then bored by their length, a problem exacerbated by the fact that the dance locations may be high, dry and dusty and will certainly lack any visitor facilities. By the end of the first day at Lo Manthang many visitors, even those who had trekked to the area especially for the festival, had given up and resumed their journey, with the remainder paying less than perfect attention. Without interpretation the dances become repetitive, breaks and characters are incomprehensible and many visitors are unable to cope with the lack of a proper timetable. Poor visitor behaviour may stem from ignorance or thoughtlessness and is a great cause of local resentment. Isolated instances occur at almost every festival. Clough (1994) notes that two Europeans gatecrashed the High Lama's platform at a *tsechu* performance in Bhutan, but the monks were too courteous to remove them. The spectacular dances attract photographers who are intrusive in their quest for a perfect shot; flash photography is often frowned upon. Many local people feel that photographing religious ceremonial is inappropriate, yet for the visitor getting a good photograph may be the motivation for his visit. Local people often resent the fact that foreigners assume that they could get the best seat, and were indeed actively encouraged to do so by monastic authorities who try by this means to enforce a contribution to funds as the price of a decent view. Some of the Everest area monasteries have taken this idea to its logical conclusion by issuing tickets. However, it was observed at Lo Manthang that many visitors, including some who stated that the Tenchi festival was the express purpose of their visit, refused to make any contribution to festival expenses, claiming that the sum should have been included in the trek fee. The attitude of monastic authorities to visitors is also ambiguous. Many welcome increased foreign attendance principally for the chance of gaining cash contributions, claiming (rightly) that the visitor should help pay for replacement costumes, monk training and general festival expenses since the monasteries have declining fortunes. A secondary motive is religious since the festival presents an opportunity to display local traditions and promote Buddhist principles. However, better interpretation of the festival would clearly facilitate this second objective.

Conclusions

The Himalayas receive more than two and a half million visitors each year, with a further million visiting China, although in global terms this only represents about 0.3% of total world arrivals (Waters, 1995). Within the leisure tourism element of this volume, special interest and nature tourism, which bring visitors to the Himalayas, are likely to experience the fastest growth. Nature tourism generates around 7% of all international travel expenditure and is estimated to be growing at 20–25% between 1990 and 1995 with adventure travel growing between 10 and 15%. Assuming that these figures may be projected into the Himalayan region it is reasonable to assume that in areas where visitors are not controlled by a quota system, annual increases of 10–20% can be anticipated. It therefore seems inevitable that the numbers of visitors to religious sites will proportionally increase over the decade, especially those attending festivals. More specialist cultural tour operators to the Himalayas are providing opportunities for tourists to see ceremonies, including the ritual dances, which provide a unique window on the local religious life. The masked dance festivals provide the opportunity for visitors to experience both the religious and secular aspects of Himalayan Buddhist societies, since the festivals themselves have traditionally played so strong a role in social cohesion. It remains to be seen whether that role will be diminished by the presence of increasing numbers of visitors. Buddhism is a tolerant religion, emphasizing moderation, the welcoming of strangers and acceptance of different modes of behaviour. However, local complaints about the poor and ill-informed behaviour of visitors to sacred sites and resentment at being reduced to the status of spectators by being 'crowded out' of their own festivals would indicate that a tolerance threshold has been passed. Of course, the tolerance threshold of local people and of the festival providers may be very different since the latter frequently have a supplementary economic aim.

In most regions, tourists can see only the 'front regions' of their destinations and the spaces specially prepared for them (MacCannell, 1973). Religious activities, in particular, are difficult to explain to visitors from a different cultural background but are primary motivators of tourism activity. Himalayan masked dance festivals are not staged for visitors, thus providing an unusual opportunity to see the 'back space' (Goffman, 1959) where real living takes place. There are, however, some indications that the dance performances at some popular locations have been slightly shortened to accommodate visitors, although the level of variation from year to year is so great that it is difficult to see whether such changes are attributable to visitors or merely to religious or political factors. Boorstin (1975) noted that tourists often expect experiences to be arranged for their convenience and are frequently unwilling to except uncomfortable local conditions. This is clearly the case in the Himalayas where the masked dances are often long, puzzling and boring after first excitement has worn off. Start times are impossible to predict and the monks apparently break off when they feel like it for tea to be served. Many of the associated ceremonies are held behind closed doors. The visitor who has been attracted to the dances by the chance of seeing something authentic is often dismayed by the fact that he does not enjoy it, with the discomforts and irritations not compensated for by interest in the proceedings. Although some monasteries make efforts to provide for the needs of visitors (roped-off areas where they will not be jostled, chairs, access to good spots for photography), the festivals remain primarily local events at which visitors are tolerated but seldom really welcomed.

Religious tourism can have very powerful positive effects on local communities. The Solu area of the Sherpa country in Nepal, for example, has recently seen a religious revival and now has some of Nepal's finest and most active Buddhist monasteries. This is not unconnected to the increased prosperity of the area as a result of trekking and climbing tourism. Tengboche monastery is now one of Nepal's prime tourist destinations housing an active community of over 40 monks. Yet the monastery was almost deserted in the 1970s when the monks left to work in trekking tourism and was destroyed by fire in 1988. The Mani Rimdu dances were only introduced here in 1942 but are now seen annually by hundreds of tourists, producing revenue to keep the monastery going and expand its activities which now include a solar-heated lodge and helicopter landing pad. Both Ziffer (1989) and Walle (1993) have examined how cultural conservation has helped traditional people practise self-determinism and deal with the outside world. Such people tend to be regarded as quaint vestigial remains and utilized by governments as tourist resources. Religious tourism can have a role in preserving their dignity as people and thus transforming the viability of their cultural tradition. This is particularly significant in the Himalayas where the Buddhist kingdoms are peripheral, impoverished and inhabited by practitioners of a minority religion. It is difficult to see any cultural objections to charging visitors for admission either to monasteries or to masked dances, if such charges pay for essential replacement and repairs to costumes and masks as well as for monastic education programmes, thus ensuring cultural continuity as well as a high standard of performance for host and guest alike. The key to the successful management of conflicts caused by increasing levels of religious tourism in the Himalayas clearly lies in education of the visitor, thus aligning the expectation and behaviour of the tourist with the expectation of local communities. This may be far more significant than simply avoiding obvious adverse socio-cultural impacts, delving behind the observable social face of a community to examine the symbolism and rituals necessary to ensure its survival. It is not coincidental that elderly Lo-Ba people attribute the drought that has afflicted Lo for the past four years to the presence of foreign tourists (Shackley, 1994). Visiting temples and dance performances combine, for the Western visitors, a fascination with the exotic for its own sake with a search for the deeper meanings and connections which that 'exotic' implies. It is debatable whether most visitors to Himalayan temples or festivals are fully aware of the deeper meanings of the religious iconography or performances which they are witnessing. Himalayan Buddhism is not going to change to accommodate visitors, so visitors to sacred sites must harmonize their behaviour with accepted local social norms.

References

Boorstin, D.J. (1975) *The Image: A Guide to Pseudo-Events in America,* Harper and Row, New York.

Clough, J. (1994) 'Dzongs of Praize', *Guardian,* 9 April 1994, pp. 40–41.

Crystal, E. (1989) Tourism in Toraja (Sulawesi, Indonesia). In: Smith, V.L. (ed.) *Hosts and Guests: The Anthropology of Tourism,* University of Pennsylvania Press, Philadelphia, pp. 139–168.

Goering, P.G. (1990) The response to tourism in Ladakh, *Cultural Survival Quarterly,* 14(1), pp. 20–25.

Goffman, E. (1959) *The Presentation of Self in Everyday Life,* Doubleday, New York.

Hall, C.M. and Weiler, B. (1992) *Special Interest Tourism,* Belhaven Press, London.

Jenner, P. and Smith, C. (1992) *The Tourism Industry and the Environment,* Economist Intelligence Unit Special Report 2453.

Kaur, J. (1995) *Himalayan Pilgrimage and the New Tourism,* Himalayan Books, Delhi.

KMTNC (1992) *ACAP Two Year Evaluation Report 1990–1991,* KMTNC, Kathmandu.

MacCannell, D. (1973) Staged authenticity: on arrangements of social space in tourist settings, *American Journal of Sociology,* 79(3), pp. 589–603.

McKean, P.F. (1989) Towards a theoretical analysis of tourism: economic dualism and cultural involution in Bali. In: Smith, V.L. (ed.) *Hosts and Guests: The Anthropology of Tourism,* University of Pennsylvania Press, Philadelphia, pp. 119–138.

Norberg-Hodge, H. (1991) *Ancient Futures: Learning from Ladakh,* Rider, London.

Shackley, M. (1993) The land of Lo: the first eight months of tourism, *Tourism Management,* 15(1), pp. 17–26.

Shackley, M. (1994) Monastic rituals and extinct animals: the significance of a meh-teh mask at Ngon-qu Janghub Ling Monthang Choedhe Gompa, Nepal/Tibet, *Anthrozoos,* 8(2), pp. 82–84.

Shackley, M. (1995) Lo revisited: the next 18 months, *Tourism Management,* 16(2), pp. 150–151.

Shackley, M. (1996) Too much room at the inn?, *Annals of Tourism Research,* 23(2), pp. 449–463.

Simpson, B. (1993) Tourism and tradition: from healing to heritage, *Annals of Tourism Research,* 20, pp. 164–181.

Singh, T.V. and Kaur, J. (1986) The paradox of mountain tourism: case references from the Himalayas, *UNEP Industry and Environment,* 9(1), pp. 21–26.

Walle, A. (1993) Tourism and traditional people: forging equitable strategies, *Journal of Travel Research,* Winter, pp. 14–19.

Waters, S. (1995) *Travel Industry World Yearbook 1994–5,* Vol. 38.

World Tourism Organization (WTO) (1994) *Yearbook of Tourism Statistics,* World Tourism Organization, Madrid.
Ziffer, K. (1989) *Ecotourism; The Uneasy Alliance,* Ernst and Young, Washington.

Developing Cultural Tourism in Greece

5

Effie Karpodini-Dimitriadi

> Tourism would not exist without culture.
>
> (UNESCO, 1996)

Tourism Development and Cultural Interaction in Greece: Conflicts and Consensus

Cultural tourism – journeys made in order to familiarize oneself with a cultural area and its creations – has always aroused interest. Visits to Greece for tourist purposes have been made as early as the 2nd century AD, when the traveller Pausanias bowed to the spirit of the times and came in order to describe important cities and monuments and record myths and traditions. In Pausanias' day, tourism had reached a rare intensity; practised, of course, by the villa-owning 'well-to-do' classes, who were attracted by an emerging literature describing journeys of interest, and who acted as early 'role-models' for travellers. For instance, the travels of the Emperor Hadrian served as an example for many of his subjects (Derruau, 1987). Travellers interested in culture are to be found in every period. From the travellers of Hellenistic and Roman times to those of the Ottoman period, and later the Philhellenes, a journey to Greece was always an ideal.

The development of industrial society and the progress made after the 18th century in the spheres of communications and transportation in material culture in general, opened up new horizons for the use of leisure time and new prospects for 'the search for variety', frequently spiced with a quest for the exotic and the idealized – a search that travel was able to satisfy.

Indicative here is the way in which Mediterranean cruises, organized by Thomas Cook and Son and advertised in issues of the National Geographic Magazine in 1929, were dubbed 'Homeric Days' (O'Barr, 1994).

Major technological advances, the reduction in the number of hours worked, the rise in living standards and a series of advances in the sphere of access, combined to make it possible for previously less favoured population groups to turn to travel and make journeys. The result was an impressive increase, particularly after the 1950s which were favourable for this development, in mass tourism; a phenomenon discernible at international level, which had both positive and negative consequences. While tourism in Greece has a long history, its growth as an organized activity begins in the period after the Second World War. Moreover, in the form that developed after 1950, it exercised an influence on the formation of new models and had repercussions on both social and cultural evolution.

These repercussions vary from area to area, depending on when the area underwent tourist development, and the number and kind of tourists that visit it. The development of tourism in contemporary Greece had a series of consequences for the economic and social life of the country and in particular for those areas that in the beginning received the biggest waves of tourists: the coasts and the islands. It has to be stressed that the influence exerted was by both domestic and foreign tourism. The latter, better known as mass tourism, contributed to the formation of new models of behaviour since Greece, a mostly rural country, entered into new forms of development in a first phase after the 1950s and in a second phase after becoming a member of the European Community.

Tourism in Greece, as in other places, while accepted as an important economic measure, was also responsible for changes in the social structure, the reformation of rites and customs, the dominance of folklorism, the establishment of new types of living and the gradual standardization of life. To all these one should add the damage to (and attrition of) historic monuments, air and water pollution (especially on the coasts) and the destruction of the natural environment. As Marc Auge (1997) has written, tourism has been blamed for all the damage in the cultural landscape.

Different types of conflicts arose. Foreign tourists brought new ways of life. Moreover, they visited Greece influenced by images which they wished to see in reality; images of rurality and locals dressed in traditional costume. But Greece has changed with people adopting the modern way of life and the inventions of technology. Traditional habits have been abandoned, settlements have changed in character and structure, and conflict has emerged between those who are in favour of change without discrimination and those, especially the archaeologists, who wish to save the particular (architectural) character of each place. Tourists, on the other hand, brought their own values and codes of behaviour influenced by the countries where they lived and worked. In the meantime they wished to experience traditional customs and attitudes, partly abandoned by locals. Gradually they have changed the synthesis of local cultures, and folklorism has become dominant.

Mass tourism has been blamed for a variety of social changes many of which have their causes elsewhere. Tourists have generated mixed attitudes amongst locals, which have included jealousy and contempt (Burgel, 1981). Their positive impacts have either been ignored or have not been mentioned. Changes have occurred but some of these tensions still exist on a smaller scale. Tourists have become more familiar to locals, although they still have a great impact on their lives in a different way. The preservation of the cultural environment as a whole, the expression of identity, the return to tradition was partly influenced by the new type of tourists who search for difference, and wish to live new experiences. 'Tradition' and 'modernity', once antagonists, are now important for development (Karpodini-Dimitriadi, 1995), and it is the main problem of development to transform these contradictions into complementarities. This process needs to be explored in greater depth as there exists a rather limited role of academic anthropology and ethnography (with only a few exceptions) in Greece as regards the analysis of social phenomena and the contribution of tourism.

Mass tourism appeared in Greece as early as the 1920s, but it was after the 1950s that it developed at a rapid rate and became recognized as one of the basic sectors in economic development (in 1938 the number of tourists visiting the country was approximately 100,000, increasing to over 2 million by the end of the 1960s). The need to draw up a policy on tourism became clear at an early date, and was expressed at state level through the National Tourist Organization of Greece, a public body originally founded in 1929 and re-established in 1951 with the remit (under Law 2160/93) to organize, develop and promote Greek tourism.

Greece was from the beginning associated with certain specific images, frequently 'imaginary', which promoted the wealth of the natural environment, the good climatic conditions, as well as the historical and archaeological riches; emphasis was placed on the large, well-known monuments (the Acropolis, Delphi, Olympia, Epidauros, etc.), which could be visited on special excursions lasting a fixed time, with information supplied in a particular way. This created a complex situation, the repercussions of which are still felt in almost the whole of Greece. Regions that have a large concentration of historical monuments (e.g. the Peloponnese) or a special natural environment (e.g. the Cyclades) were preferred over other areas which, despite possessing important cultural monuments and making their contribution to the building of the Greek cultural identity, remain unknown and scarcely exploited (e.g. Epiros, West Central Greece, etc.).

It must be noted, however, that despite the expression of a desire to promote the image of Greece through its cultural riches, tourism has never been approached within the context of a broad policy for cultural tourism. It is mainly viewed in terms of its economic magnitude capable of contributing to the growth of the Greek economy, creating an increase in foreign currency reserves, employment and income, and assisting in the development of the periphery.

The result of this 'quantitative approach' is that there has been no attention paid to the environment, both natural and cultural, which is a necessary precondition for balanced and continuing development. At the same time, the concentration of tourists on particular places, the arrival of tourists with low cultural interests, and above all the seasonal nature of the phenomenon, have adversely affected many areas with predominantly negative consequences (damage to monuments of the cultural heritage, cultural standardization, commercialization of cultural goods, ecological anarchy, pollution, deterioration of biotopes, ecosystems and traditional settlements). The effects were more overt in the island societies, whose systems are of a fragile nature. The increase in tourism had consequences for the economy: incomes, cost of living, employment, change of orientation in the productive sector, often the intense working of the land and the reserves of the land, and an increase in employment in the services and supply sectors. These changes in turn affected the social structure and values, where the conflicts are often more fundamental, though more difficult to identify, than in the case of the effects on the natural environment and settlement patterns. Phenomena observed in other regions with a similar or analogous tourist development can also be traced in parts of Greece, amongst them the abandonment of traditional social values, the dissolving of the network of relations within the family, an increase in the frequency of divorce, an increase in the frequency of marriages between tourists and natives (cf. the case of Rhodes), and the practice of holding two jobs, particularly in areas that entertain tourists with high incomes or from specific groups. There were similar repercussions on the cultural image of some areas, and of course on the local identity. The frequent pursuit by tourists of as great a degree of authenticity as possible, or 'staged authenticity' (MacCannell, 1976) led to commercialization and standardization; one example of this is the creation of 'authentic' folk dances aimed exclusively at tourists (e.g. the *syrtaki*), or of what is considered to be authentic Greek cooking, in order to satisfy the desires of the tourists. To this same category belongs the production of local goods which are thought to be authentic, objects of folk or local art which are to be found in most places that attract large numbers of tourists; what Holloway (1989) refers to as 'airport art'. The development of large hotel complexes designed to satisfy the wishes of the tourists in line with their expectations and the facilities they have grown accustomed to expect, has resulted in a globalization that leads to new forms of standardization, and often restricts contacts and cultural exchange, since the tourists confine their movements and only visit predetermined sites.

Despite these negative consequences, it must be noted that thanks to tourism some sectors of the cultural heritage have benefited (restoration of monuments and buildings, revival of traditional techniques, etc.); villages and sites have been regenerated that would otherwise have been abandoned, and in certain cases, the local culture has been promoted (GNTO, 1990). In many regions women are now involved in economic and commercial activities, especially in areas where once only domestic activities were accepted for them (mountainous areas, etc.). Cultural exchanges, too, have benefited, as have communications, with the teaching of foreign languages experiencing unprecedented growth thanks to tourism. We should not forget that cultures are areas crossed by tourists (Karpodini-Dimitriadi, 1996). At the same time, the improvement in the standard of living has led to revenues being channelled not only into areas such as health and education, but also into the conservation and preservation of monuments and the wider cultural heritage.

The decline in tourism observed since 1992 has been a source of concern to many and has stimulated further investigation, resulting in special meetings and scientific publications aimed at mitigating the adverse effects arising from mass tourism, exploiting its positive aspects and developing benign forms of it (Technika Chronika, 1995). This fluid situation is to be seen against the background of the more general vigilance observable at international level, and above all of the increasing general awareness of issues relating to the protection of the cultural heritage, in which a leading role has been taken by the international organizations.

In an effort to minimize its negative effects, there has been a search for new, alternative forms of tourism, of which 'cultural tourism' is considered to be the most effective in creating *quality* tourism with an educated profile and high economic return. This follows the definition of 'cultural tourism' formulated by International Council of Sites and Monuments (ICOMOS), which refers to a specific form of tourism which as defined by the World Tourism Organization is considered as 'a movement of persons for essentially cultural motivations such as study tours, performing arts and cultural tours, travel to festivals and other cultural events, visits to sites and monuments, travel to study nature, folklore or art, and pilgrimages'. It is felt that the exploitation of the cultural heritage may be the answer for a sector of the economy that is otherwise threatened with decline, and may also have favourable repercussions on the general cultural life of Greek society (Drakatos, 1997). Cultural tourism, moreover, is thought to be more resilient in the face of international crises, is not constrained by the seasonal factor but may, on the contrary, be developed outside the main tourist seasons. It offers greater economic benefits, and may create new prospects for direct and indirect funding, since it can be included within European Community Programmes (Interreg, Leader, etc.) that support projects promoting ongoing development. It is for this reason, moreover, that tourism has been incorporated as part of the same measure as culture in the Second European Community Support Framework for Greece.

Actions Based on Cultural Criteria

The above is the context for a series of pilot programmes and actions aimed at exploiting the cultural heritage and establishing 'new cultural products'.

Many of these programmes have been drawn up in cooperation with the Greek National Tourist Office (GNTO) and other bodies, and are frequently supported by the European Commission. Outstanding among them is the programme for renewing and exploiting the traditional settlements of Greece. This was drawn up, studied and implemented in the period 1975–1992, and one of the benefits from this has been the way it has acted as a stimulus to the private sector to engage in renewal projects. It emerges clearly from the publications that this is a comprehensive programme that goes beyond the restoration and remodelling of buildings to house tourist and other activities, and includes other works on both the infrastructure (water supply, drainage, roads) and various other environmental improvements (squares, cobbled streets, fountains, consolidation of monuments, etc.). So far some 360 houses have been restored and handed over to the GNTO. The successful implementation of the programme, the positive response to it on the part of the local communities in the area in which it was implemented, and international recognition of it, have led to the mobilization of other communities to upgrade old buildings and bring them into use again, or to remodel open spaces. The programme has positive consequences both in the sphere of the protection, display and conservation of the cultural and architectural heritage, and in the development of a form of tourism (both internal and external) that has contributed to the economic growth of the areas in question and an improvement in the quality of life.

The endeavour to establish a new development policy that would favour benign, non-conflictual forms of tourism includes a series of projects involving the remodelling of areas that lie at vital points on tourist routes (e.g. Leivadia on the route from Athens to Delphi), the improvement of coasts with a historical past (e.g. Rhodes), and the restoration of stone school-buildings in declining villages that might otherwise be completely destroyed. These are community buildings that will continue to be owned by the communities, will house tourist and cultural activities and together will create a complex of projects that will assist visitors and, by extension, promote the growth of cultural tourism.

Projects (pilot programmes supported by European Community funds) involving the renewal of long-distance paths originally used as trade routes and modelled on similar paths that have been, or will be, exploited in other parts of Europe (used in earlier periods by merchants to facilitate contacts and exchanges) are being developed. This will allow the incorporation of historical monuments and natural landscapes, and will form a network of routes beginning at the northern borders of Greece, crossing the central and east Greek mainland and ending at Crete in the south. The renewal of old paths covers about 3000 km and extends beyond the Greek mainland to nine islands. We may note indicatively that on Santorini alone a network of eleven paths is being renewed, involving a series of interventions (repairs, paving, stonework, etc.) to facilitate visitors and encourage them to follow the new routes (N. Agriantonis, 1998, personal communication).

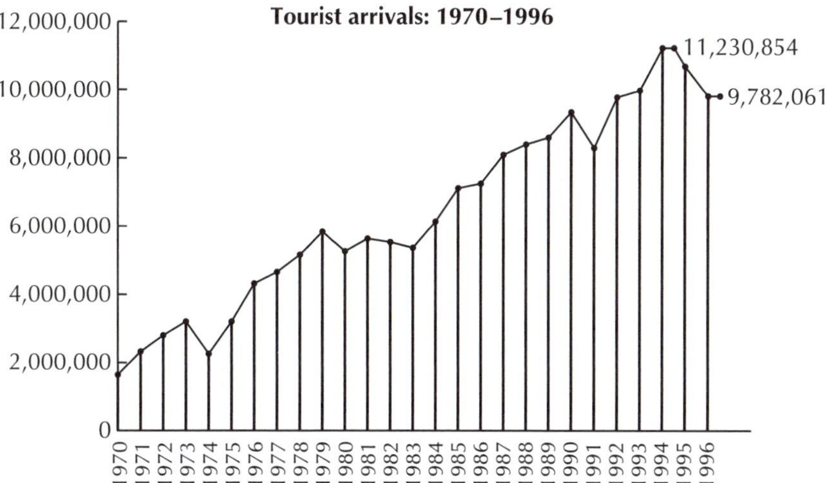

Fig. 5.1. Tourist arrivals: 1970–1996.
Source: Greek Statistical Service.

To the same category of projects belongs the major programme to unite archaeological sites in Athens.

Designing Cultural Routes

The above programmes are designed to create cultural routes that will be used both by tourists with specialist interests, and by those in search of new forms of tourist enjoyment that will increase their knowledge of the local cultural identity, help them to enjoy new cultural experiences, and reduce the potential for conflicts. More generally, these programmes are part of a broader endeavour aimed at attracting cultural tourists, for which proposals and suggestions have repeatedly been advanced, mainly at scientific and cultural meetings. It must be noted, of course, that tourism, as developed in Greece, invariably involved 'cultural routes' that included organized visits to major archaeological sites and museums. The forms of cultural tourism in Greece may be divided into two major categories. First, there are international programmes of cultural tourism. This category includes cultural tours which are designed as part of the activities of European and international organizations, are involved with the public sector, and take the form of cultural networks. Second, there are cultural routes studied and proposed in the context of European programmes supported by the European Union (Council of Europe, 1996a).

Figures 5.1 to 5.4 show the magnitude of the tourist movement, the number of visitors to archaeological sites and museums and the income derived from them.

Entrance to the sites is by ticket. Very few categories of citizens are exempt and permitted free entrance. Entrance is free only on Sundays, though

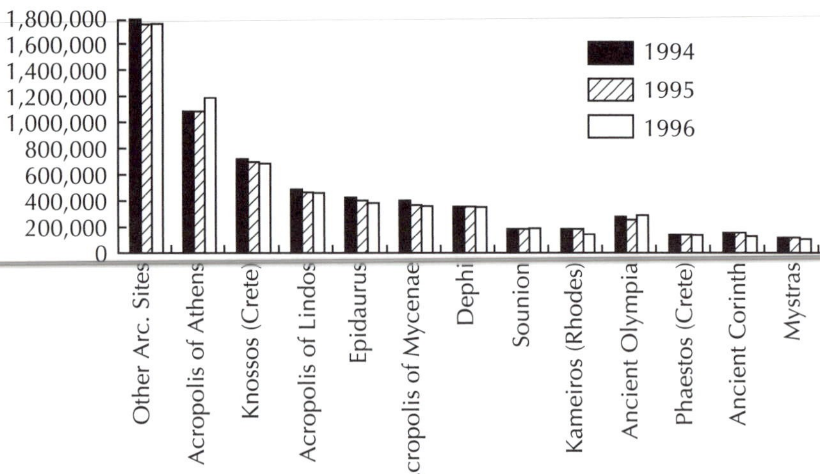

Fig. 5.2. Visitors to archaeological sites.
Source: Greek Statistical Service.

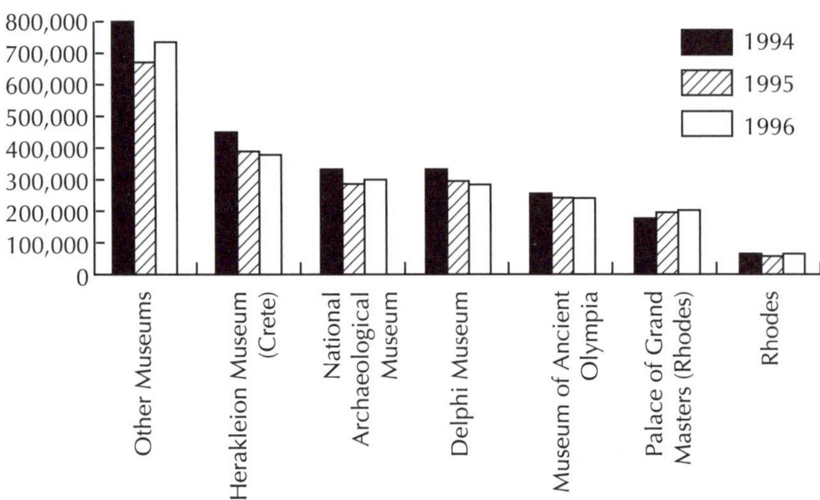

Fig. 5.3. Museum visitors.
Source: Greek Statistical Service.

some museums cancel this right when they are entertaining major exhibitions, for which they anticipate increased attendances.

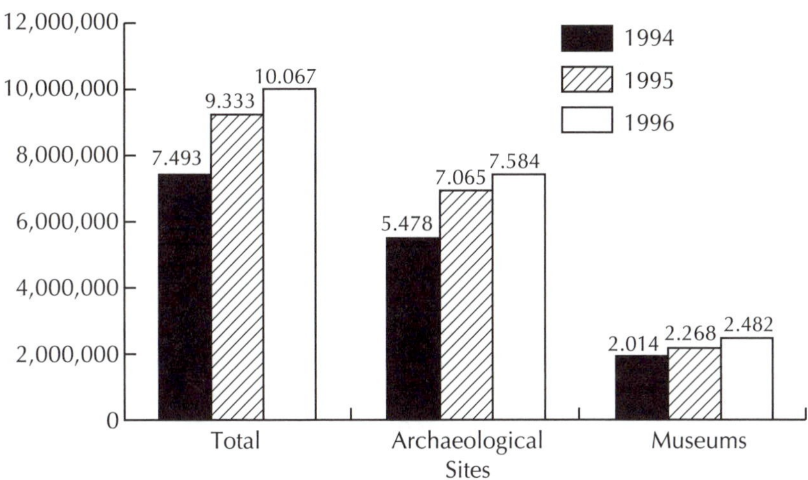

Fig. 5.4. Income (in GRD).
Source: Greek Statistical Service.

The Silk Roads: roads on dialogue

This is a well-known, ambitious programme inaugurated and advanced as part of the UNESCO decade of Cultural Development, which is designed to promote human understanding and communication in connection with the different cultures that evolved along commercial routes, and the influences they exercised. The programme involves the organization of international missions, meetings of scientists and tourists, seminars, exhibitions and research programmes, in an endeavour to allow people to understand not only the links between the past and the present, but also the influence that may be exercised on the formation of the future by a 'knowledge of our common heritage' (Droulia, 1991; Reid 1994).

Greece participated in this programme, especially in the section dealing with the sea route, which lasted four months, starting in Venice and ending in Osaka, in the *Ship of Peace*. Three Greek scientists took part in three of the four sections of this route. As part of the scientific meetings and conferences held at the various ports of the voyage, visits and guided tours of representative sites were organized while the ship was in Greece, and there was a one-day meeting at the Centre for Modern Greek Studies under the general title 'Cultural and commercial exchanges between the Greek world and the East'. The programme for this meeting covered three subjects: silk in the Greek world, communications, and cultural influences (CNR NHRF, 1990; Droulia, 1991).

Silk Roads was a proposal for an alternative form of tourism that took advantage of package tours. Within the excursions on offer travel agents included a number of tours that, in general terms, corresponded to the ancient route and covered the geographical area of Asia. As part of the organization for the Cultural Capital of Europe, Thessaloniki 1997, two motorcyclists representing the Cultural Capital revived the ancient route and carried a piece of unworked silk presented by the municipal authorities of Beijing to Thessaloniki.

Cultural Routes of the Council of Europe – Silk Roads

This was a sub-programme of the broader programme of Cultural Routes of the Council of Europe (Council of Europe, 1996b). The Programme of Cultural Routes was inaugurated in 1987 and applied in many parts of Europe with a broad theme, designed to encourage the mutual acquaintance of peoples through their historical and cultural traditions, their monuments, and their artistic expression. In 1990, in cooperation with the Centre for Modern Greek Studies of the National Research Foundation and the Ministry of Culture, Greece organized a European Meeting in Alexandroupolis and Souphli (an area with a silk-rearing tradition), attended by European experts and scientists who contributed to the development of this cultural route. The Cultural Routes were actual journeys in space and time; in most of the countries in which they were held, they contributed to the cultural environment, the improvement of life and the establishment of alternative forms of tourism.

Cultural Routes – roads of orthodox monasticism

Another 'cultural journey' elaborated as part of the broader programme of Cultural Routes of the Council of Europe, has, as its theme, monasticism in Europe. The programme first took place in 1991 in Poland and then Portugal with the aim of promoting educational and cultural exchanges. The aims of the Greek programme are on the one hand to disseminate a knowledge of monasticism in the Greek East, and on the other to present monasteries and churches in Greece that covered the entire area of the Greek world, selected according to specific criteria, such as their antiquity, cultural and historical importance, and contribution to the national consciousness. The programme enables tourists with cultural interests to become acquainted with the spirit of monasticism, its history and evolution, the principles that govern monastic life and its importance for the Orthodox East, and to experience the cultural and artistic activity developed in different monasteries.

As part of the programme, an International Symposium was organized in collaboration with the Greek Ministry of Culture, the Centre for Byzantine Research of the National Research Foundation and the Council of Europe. This was held in the Vlatadon Patriarchal Monastery and focused on 'Trends in Orthodox Monasticism 9th–20th century' (Council of Europe, 1994). At this symposium, in addition to the scientific papers, there were special sessions aimed at examining the possibility of applying the Greek programme more widely. The Greek representatives emphasized the great interest of the programme, and the social and economic benefits that could accrue from its implementation, and set out their thinking on how it should be approached in the light of the special character of the monasteries as living institutions.

The assessment of the programme took place at a special seminar on the Programme of Cultural Routes that was organized on 9–11 October 1996 in Bourglinster Castle (Grand Duchy of Luxembourg) under the aegis of the Council of Europe, in collaboration with the Luxembourg Ministry of Culture and Service for National Monuments and Sites (Council of Europe, 1996b). The Programme for Monasticism has developed into an independent network, in which France, Romania, Greece, Norway and Portugal are participants, and which aspires to develop both cultural and educational activities involving mainly young people, and to sensitize them to the religious heritage and the role of religion in the modern world. The cultural issue of religion was the starting point for the creation of 'the first university of European citizenship, a multidisciplinary, mobile university that meets on monastic heritage sites in the countries concerned' (Council of Europe, 1996b). Greek participation is represented by the Inter-Orthodox Academy of Crete, which promotes the creation of a 'Euromediterranean Youth Centre', whose aim is, through tourism, to help young people to find a solution to their problems and satisfy their spiritual and cultural needs.

Cultural Routes in the Context of European Union Programmes

Cultural tourism is promoted by the European Commission as an element in its strategy for cooperation, sensitization to cultural heritage issues, creation of infrastructure, and the economic development of member countries of the European Union (Commission of the European Communities, 1996). According to the report which was submitted to the European Parliament (5 February 1996), efforts were made to strengthen this form of tourism through both independent and broader programmes. Programmes such as 'Villes d'art en Europe' or 'Routes to the roots – retrouver ses racines', are singled out in this report as being of importance in the development of this kind of tourism. The Kaleidoscope and Raphael programmes contribute indirectly to the development of cultural tourism. So, too, does the Erasmus programme. The same end is also served by the institutions of the European Cultural Capital and the European Cultural Month. Cultural tourism works with, or is favoured by, other community programmes (Leader, Petra, Interreg). Many forms of alternative tourism (agrotourism, social, religious and educational tourism) also help to attract tourists whose motivation is of a cultural or artistic nature.

Of the programmes in which Greece participates, developed in the context of community funding, mention may be made here, indicatively, of the programme 'Via Mediterranea', in which other Mediterranean countries, including France, Spain and Portugal also participate. These countries originally evolved a cooperative network designed to promote agrotourism. Ten local organizations participate in the network. Since 1992, the network has turned its attention to proposals in the sector of cultural tourism, which are a combination of recreation, holidays and 'cultural adventure', and include visits and guided tours both to areas of natural beauty and to traditional settlements and places of historical memory. The areas of Greece participating in the network are the Zagorochoria in Epiros and Siteia on Crete.

Of the cultural tourism programmes resulting from cooperation in the context of European Funding, the programme 'Routes to the roots – Retrouver ses racines' is of particular importance. It has ten participating countries (Ireland, Denmark, the Netherlands, Great Britain, Norway, Finland, Iceland, Spain, Greece and USA) and is designed to encourage American tourists to rediscover the roots of their ancestors by exploiting and promoting cultural routes that already exist in some countries (Germany, Great Britain, Ireland, the Netherlands, Denmark). This is a comprehensive programme that strives to turn the attention of tourists not to the well-known and well-populated sites, but to those that are less well known but by no means insignificant. In this programme, efforts will be made to cooperate with the American tourist trade to make the results known to as wide a public as possible and spread knowledge of the routes proposed; it is also planned to publish a tourist guide and produce a video in cooperation with all the bodies involved.

Comprehensive proposals for the development of alternative cultural tourism that fall within the above category include the Euronautica programme, the theme of which is the naval tradition. It was drawn up by the Greek Society for Cultural Development and Self-Administration, in recognition of the fact that the naval tradition forms a connecting link between many European peoples, and may therefore serve as a proposal for alternative tourism. This is a well-prepared programme that envisages much work to implement it and disseminate the information, and also involves cultural choices, helping tourists to select the way in which they use their leisure time, and the routes or subject areas they wish to pursue. The approach is a broad one and covers a wide range of expressions of social and traditional life from antiquity to the present day, at the same time promoting cultural and natural resources.

Plans have also been drawn up for cultural tourism as part of the Kaleidoscope programme (for example, the programme 'Odyssey-Periplous 2000'), consistently taking account of the aim of improving the quality of the tourist product. Moreover, plans that have been or are being implemented as part of the Raphael programme, also indirectly foster the development of cultural tourism. A recent example is the MINOTEC programme, relating to the enhancement and effective development of ancient sites used for performances. The emphasis is upon the Greek and Roman theatres and arenas, which are now being turned to new uses as places of cultural and artistic recreation; participants in this programme include parts of Greece (Ancient

Messene), France (Lyon) and Italy (Verona). In the spirit of utilizing cultural heritage spaces for tourism, a number of further initiatives involving the private sector have taken place including the development of 'cultural cruises'.

Finally a special reference should be made to the programme 'Wine routes in Macedonia' focusing on local wine production and promoted by local wine producers. Regional events were organized in the summer of 1997 under the broad framework of the activities of Thessaloniki, Europe's Cultural Capital and included visits to the vineyards and wine factories, as well as exhibitions of folk material and representations of traditional grape-harvest with accompanying traditional dance and music.

Conclusion

Tourism in Greece continues to be approached in a developmental framework. In recognition of the potential conflicts which exist as part of the development process, the aims are to harmonize the natural, social and cultural environment through the creation of alternative, benign forms of tourism. Utilizing culture as the basis for tourism development in Greece entails that culture and heritage can be preserved, developed and promoted at both national and local level, and the very issues that can generate cultural conflicts can be controlled.

Culture, thus, emerges as an essential element in the new tourism policy of Greece, and is in harmony with the spirit prevailing at European level. As well as helping to generate consensus amongst the population, culture and its promotion to tourists remains important for economic reasons and provides a useful tool to stimulate economic development in the widest sense.

With its rich cultural heritage, traditions and natural resources, Greece is well placed to focus on cultural tourism. However, how tourism is organized and structured in order that it will be able to contribute to the economy at both local and regional level, unburdened by the over-exploitation of cultural goods and the over-use of well-known centres of interest, requires further study. What is required are further measures to protect and promote the cultural heritage, the harnessing of new technologies (which are at present limited), and the coordination of activities, mainly at the level of the organization of events (festivals, exhibitions, etc.). This will involve comprehensive programmes that will reinforce both the sensitivity of the host community and cultural tourists, so they will 'respect and protect the authenticity and diversity of the cultural values'.

In any event, the promotion of cultural tourism as an independent form of tourism in Greece is still somewhat limited. This is due in part to the fact that the philosophy of cultural tourism and its possible consequences remains little studied and although it is recognized as the most effective form of tourist development, it is viewed at a practical level as a specialized form aimed at a limited number of tourists. But as the various European Union initiatives are showing, cultural tourism can be a useful vehicle, not only for economic development, but also for the protection of heritage and the affirmation of Greek culture at all levels.

References

Auge, M. (1997) *L'impossible voyage – Le tourisme et ses images*, 'Rivages Poche' in the series 'Petite Bibliotheque'.

Burgel, G. (1981) La Grece rurale revisitee. In: *Greek Review of Social Research, Aspects du Changement Social dans la Campagne Grecque*, Athens.

CNR NHRF (1990) *Cultural Commercial Exchanges between the Orient and the Greek World, Integral Study of the Silk Roads: Roads on Dialogue*, Seminar papers, Maritime Route Expedition, 25–28 October, Athens.

Commission of the European Communities (1996) *Rapport sur les Actions communautaires affectant sur le Tourism*, Bruxelles 5 February, COM (96), Final Report.

Council of Europe (1994) Trends in Orthodox Monasticism 9th–20th century. *Proceedings of the International Symposium, Roads of Orthodox Monasticism: Come ye and learn*, Cultural Routes, Directorate of Cultural Affairs, Ministry of Culture, 28 September–2 October.

Council of Europe (1996a) Culture and Tourism Initiative, *Introduction to the Seminars, 'Culture and Tourism. Opportunities and Prospects'*. Milan Fair 28 February–1 March.

Council of Europe (1996b) *Introductive Report, Seminar on Cultural Routes, Challenges of Citizenship and Sustainable Development*, Bourglinster Castle, 9–11 October.

Derruau, M. (1987), *Geographie Humaine*, Athens, pp. 356–357 (in Greek).

Drakatos, K. (1997) Towards a new tourism policy – The Greek economy, *Epilogi*, special edition, pp. 186–192 (in Greek).

Droulia, L. (1991) Silk in the West and East, *Symposium Proceedings*, Museum of Greek Folk Art, 22–23 May, Athens.

Greek National Tourism Office, GNTO (1990) *Preservation and Development of Traditional Settlements in Greece*, the Programme (1975–1992), Special Edition in the European Year of Tourism 1990.

Holloway, C.J. (1989) *The Business of Tourism*, Pitman, London, pp. 177–181.

Karpodini-Dimitriadi, E. (1995) *Ethnography of European Traditional Cultures. Society, Cultural Tradition and Built Environment*, Athens.

Karpodini-Dimitriadi, E. (1996) Les guides touristiques et l'identite culturelle. In: *De l'Europe. Identites et identite. Memoires et memoire*, sous la direction de Charles-Olivier Carbonell, Presses de l'Université des Sciences Sociales de Toulouse.

MacCannell, D. (1976) *The Tourist: A New Theory of the Leisure Class*, Schocken Books, New York.

O'Barr, W.M. (1994) *Culture and the A: Exploring Otherness in the World of Advertising*, Westview Press, London.

Reid, S. (1994) *The Silk and Copper Routes, Peoples and Civilizations*, Belitha Press/UNESCO.

Technika Chronika (1995) Tourism and monuments – cultural tourism. Proceedings of two-day meeting, *Technika Chronika,* special edition (in Greek).

UNESCO (1996) *Culture, Tourism, Development: Crucial Issues for the XXIst century,* Proceedings of a Round Table, Paris 26–27 June, UNESCO, Paris.

6

Tourism Development in De-industrializing Centres of the UK: Change, Culture and Conflict

Mike Robinson

We live in an age when unnecessary things are our only necessities.

Oscar Wilde, *The Picture of Dorian Gray*

Introduction

Cities and large urban centres appear to work wonderfully well as repositories for tourist activity. Their multi functionality meets the needs of the multi motivational user (Ashworth and Tunbridge, 1990). The landscape of urban centres, their diverse ethnoscape (Appadurai, 1990), apparent capacity for absorbing 'outsiders', and their role as loci of cultural capital, all fits well with the desire of tourists to be satisfied both physically, emotionally and spiritually. Even if ascribing to the anti-urban tradition which sees cities as providing 'an unnatural setting for the anonymous interaction of an alienated population' (Short, 1991, p. 44), tourists will find themselves drawn to cities and towns in their capacity as nodes of service, information, social activity (Ashworth, 1992; Haywood, 1992; Law, 1993; Shaw and Williams, 1994; Page 1995), as well as providers of primary and secondary attractions (Jansen-Verbeke, 1986). The growth in urban tourism, and the more extant phenomenon of urban regeneration, would seem to illustrate a symbiotic state between host community and visitor, and host community and tourism development. At the most, the tourist is offered the opportunity to share in the celebration of the urban; the agglomeration of cultural capital, liveliness, creativity and a forum for individualism. At the very least, the tourist is granted anonymity. The urban community is offered money from tourists who seek either open expression for their desires, or refuge. The community can also share in the upgrading of the cityscape, its amenities and its image.

All would seem well. However, although there has been increasing attention focused on the urban tourism phenomenon, we can identify gaps in our understanding at two levels. First, while there exists a reasonably strong tradition in the study of urban culture, there are limited analyses of the cultural implications of tourism in urban settings *per se*. Second, and not surprisingly, studies which have focused upon cultural transformations in urban life have tended to utilize 'world cities' as cases (see for instance: Hannerz, 1996 on Amsterdam; Zukin, 1997 on New York). Little attention has generally been given to the cultural consequences of urban tourism in the smaller cities and large towns where tourism development is locked into the wider processes of de-industrialization and the shift from manufacturing to service sector economies. These are not the expansive 'megacities' of Bangkok, the large metropolitan centres such as New York, Tokyo or Paris, nor the historical centres of Venice or Rome, but, borrowing from Gault's (1989) typology, those second, third and even fourth league cities, which usually have populations of less than 500,000. According to the World Commission on Culture and Development's (1995) estimate, some 56% of the world's urban population lives in such cities and large towns; they may not be massive or glamorous but there are a lot of them (Byrne, 1997). These centres may lack cultural diversity, may not display the cultural mingling relative to megacities, and are often politically and economically peripheral. It is difficult to define these centres precisely by any one parameter, there being considerable variation in terms of population, history, economic and social profiles. In the UK, these are the provincial cities and large towns which experienced rapid development and population expansion as a consequence of industrialization and have subsequently undergone (and are still undergoing) a process of economic and social transformation. Such centres have neither the cushion of cosmopolitanism, nor the tenure of the historic, yet they are now challenging hard for recognition as tourist destinations and exhibit their own diversity and individualism (Sachs, 1994).

Unlike an increasing number of studies which consider the tourism/culture interface in the context of the developing world and indigenous peoples (see for instance: Smith, 1989; Butler and Hinch, 1996), the (still) limited literature which has developed in the field of urban tourism has tended to bypass detailed examination of its social and cultural impacts. Whilst to some extent this is explained by reference to methodological issues and the difficulties of disaggregating urban populations, types of urban tourists and the processes surrounding urban tourism generally, it also reflects a range of other issues.

First, the negative and positive impacts of tourism upon cultures are interestingly perceived in the context of the unique. Issues such as community resentment and antagonism (or acceptance), erosion of values (the evolving of new social norms), and the dilution of tradition (or preservation) are seen as chiefly emerging from encounters with the different, the specific and the exotic. Studies considering the outcomes of contact between tourists and indigenous cultures, for instance, often carry a subtext of First World romanticism, whereby the tourist is seen to threaten the unique; the very element which qualifies a culture's attractiveness (otherness?). Not surprisingly, studies have tended to focus on tourism's cultural impacts in rural settings, lesser developed countries and on indigenous peoples, partly because there is a real need to understand such impacts for management purposes, and partly because such impacts are usually highly visible and immediate.

Second, and arguably, attention is given more to the outcomes of tourist–host encounters (particularly if they are clearly identifiable as negative or positive), whereby the complexities of cultural relationships are portrayed as reducible to a series of impacts or end-points. In this sense there is the risk of neglecting the processes which are involved in the construction, and destruction, of tourism/culture relationships. The processes of cultural change are more apparent within a developing context, and where cultures are particularly differentiated; traditionally the destinations of the long-haul, independent traveller. What we are looking for within an urban context is a more obscure and elongated process of cultural change of which tourism is only one amongst a myriad of influences.

Third, we need to distinguish between the role of *tourists* as agents of cultural change, and *tourism* as a complex, but disjointed amalgam of economically driven structures and institutions supplying the desires of the tourist. Clearly the two are interdependent to a greater or lesser degree. In terms of examining cultural change, the literature is particularly strong on the impacts of *tourists*, and the interactions of visiting individuals and groups with host communities. Changes in the way societies are organized, and the values and meanings upon which they are based can be stimulated by different 'contact' situations between tourists and host cultures (de Kadt, 1979; Reisinger, 1994). Studies are thus concerned with the behaviour of tourists, the cultural influences on this behaviour, the social, economic and political context of contact with the visited culture, and the distribution and authority of power. However, the role that the *supply* and development of tourism plays in changing host community cultures, and how provision is developed, is under-researched, particularly with regard to provincial urban locations.

Fourthly, and fundamentally, there exists an implied agenda in urban tourism which is fashioned on economic success, or at least a belief in success. Although the economic benefits may be problematic to measure, their promise is the main driver for urban tourism policy. There has generally been an uncritical acceptance by policy makers and academics that tourism in urban areas bestows a range of benefits at relatively low cost, low risk and limited opportunity cost. Certainly set against the 'boosterist' agendas of the

1980s and early 1990s, tourism and leisure were recognized as important levers for capital investment, the generation of income and the creation of employment (Buckley and Witt, 1985, 1989; Owen, 1990; van den Berg *et al.*, 1994). Despite the fact that claims made for urban tourism are often dependent on assessment methods which are increasingly open to challenge (Loftman and Spirou, 1996), the economic impacts are generally taken to be wholly positive and 'upbeat'. So too are the cultural effects of tourism development. Again, we need to distinguish between tourism development at the level of supply and the impacts of tourists. With regard to the latter, tourists are cited as stimulating benefits such as the preservation of arts, crafts and rituals (de Kadt, 1979). Regarding the former, social and cultural betterment is also promised to the host community, although this is noticeably often couched in terms of the shared utilization of cultural capital with tourists, and greater choice. As Lengkeek (1993, p. 12) suggests: 'the assumption has tended to be that recreation facilities should be provided as a quasi-collective good'.

Leaving aside the advocacy which is arguably endemic in tourism development, it is difficult to deny that tourism can and does generate economic, environmental and social benefits. However, it does so with cultural consequences. The influential anthropologist Franz Boas (1928) argued that although we cannot explain all of cultural life by reference to economic conditions and developments, we nevertheless need to give our attention to the economic background within which cultural forms emerge. This chapter explores the extent and nature of cultural conflict as a result of tourism development, within de-industrializing, provincial urban centres of the United Kingdom. In doing so it works on the premise that any analysis of cultural change (of which conflict is only one mechanism) needs to be understood within the context of economic change and the political structures which shape it (Rubinstein, 1990; Roche 1992). This is not at odds with Urry's (1990) observation that the economics of tourism need to be culturally defined, it merely starts at a different point of the same circle.

The emphasis here is upon the supply of tourism as opposed to the demands of tourists. Roche observes:

> At the most general level it seems that the *cultural impact* of the modern tourism economy is enormous and that it is threatening to be an all-pervasive impact making tourists of us all in *every* aspect of our lives, not just when we are on holiday.
>
> (Roche, 1992, p. 593)

Urry's (1994, p. 237) view that 'tourist practices have become indelibly part of contemporary culture' may well be correct. Contemporary studies of tourist activities are increasingly framed by a deeper understanding of the consumerist, capitalist culture which they simultaneously emanate from and participate in. Further, one cannot expect to consider tourism in urban areas without some recourse to the social realities of tourist experience. However, the cultural consequences produced via the provision of amenity and services, position tourism as a conspicuous agent of change; a consciously constructed economic strategy with outputs, rather than some by-product of post-modern society. As Morris puts it:

> Wherever tourism is an economic strategy as well as a money-making activity, and wherever it is a policy of state, a process of social and *cultural* change is initiated which involves transforming not only the 'physical' (in other words, the *lived*) environment of 'toured' communities, and the intimate details of the practice of everyday life, but also the series of relations by which cultural identity (and therefore, difference) is constituted for both the tourist and the toured in any given context.
>
> (Morris, 1995, p. 180)

The relatively recent emergence (within the last 15 to 20 years) of tourism as having a substituting role within de-industrializing economies and the political legitimation accorded to this, defines our goal to consider the cultural outcomes. This chapter explores the productive aspects of tourism in transitional, developed urban economies in the UK, its cultural impacts, and goes on to discuss possible areas of cultural conflict.

De-industrializing Urban Economies in the UK

To some degree representing the triumph of the post-modern tourist, and a historical process of de-differentiation whereby the importance of designated tourist resort areas declined, the increasing relevance of tourism for many urban centres in the United Kingdom represents fundamental, often dramatic, changes in their structure and function. The development of infrastructure to serve the needs and desires of visitors (although the local community may share facilities) is a way of responding to the deep-seated economic decline and restructuring which has marked British capitalism since the 19th century. Harris (1997) examines a range of responses to economic restructuring in large cities and majors on the replacement role of the growing service sector (interestingly he does not identify tourism *per se*). The idea of tourism development as a *reaction* to a changing set of economic stimuli, rather than as a proactive process to meet market demand, provides a more fitting framework by which we can understand tourism developments in former industrial areas.

The term de-industrialization is used here to refer to the broad process of economic change which has both cultural inputs and outputs. It is a far from satisfactory term to use. It refers to structural changes in economy and society brought about by micro- and macro-economic and political factors difficult to isolate and locate in time. It carries the theme of economic decline, which although far from unusual in capitalist societies (Cippola, 1970), transforms it into an emotive and politicized term (Coates, 1994). At its heart, de-industrialization is normally taken to mean the dismantling of manufacturing industry, particularly the productive primary and secondary industrial sectors (Rowthorn, 1986). The demise of 'traditional' and highly labour intensive units of production which have included coal mining, steel production, shipbuilding, engineering, automotive production and textile working, has taken place at different rates, but was particularly rapid during the 1970s and 1980s. However, while de-industrialization goes some way to explain the realities of a reduced role of manufacturing industry in society, it says little about the emergence of new economies linked more to patterns of consumption than production. Thus, reference is inevitably made to the terms post-industrialism and post-Fordism (we could also add the related terms of post-nationalism and post-materialism). Though such terms are equally unsatisfactory, and often contradictory (Roche, 1992; Urry, 1995), they nevertheless help to locate tourism within the context of an economy increasingly dominated by the production and consumption of cultural products.

A transformation in capitalism has simultaneously transformed cities (Jewson and MacGregor, 1997), but it is in the provincial industrial cities and towns of the UK where transformations in economy, society and space have been the most striking (Law, 1996). In the UK as a whole, some 55% of the working population were employed in the combined sectors of agriculture/fisheries, mining/quarrying and construction in 1950, which by 1994 had declined to 27% (Johnes and Taylor, 1996). Of further significance has been the dramatic expansion of employment in the service industries including hotel/catering, education and health (23% employed in 1971 and 40% in 1994). There has also been a scaling-down of company size so that some 95% of businesses now fall within the small to medium enterprise (SME) sector employing less than 250 people, with a substantial majority employing less than 10 people. Martin (1995), for instance, relates these changes to Birmingham's economy, noting not only the rapidity of change, but changes in structure whereby the city's role has been transformed from a major manufacturing centre to that focusing upon conferences, exhibitions and servicing the needs of the business traveller.

In common with the East and West Midlands, South Wales, and Clydeside in Scotland, the North of England has been particularly hard hit by an often dramatic scaling-down of manufacturing industry, accentuated by over-dependence on a limited range of industrial sectors. Moreover, parts of the urban North have experienced an often slow recovery process built around overseas inward investment and service sector expansion (Smith, 1989; Smith and Stone, 1989). Provincial cities and large conurbations such as Bradford/Leeds (West Yorkshire), Sheffield/Doncaster (South Yorkshire), Manchester/Salford/Bolton (Greater Manchester), Liverpool (Merseyside), Newcastle upon Tyne/Sunderland (Tyneside and Wearside) have, to varying degrees and over various time scales, experienced sustained periods of de-industrialization. The reasons for this are complex and reflect specific locational characteristics. However, these centres, which combined represent approximately 20% of the UK's population, all share the consequences of economic and structural change (though not exclusively).

High levels of unemployment

The loss of work remains the most critical feature of these urban centres. Average unemployment levels of 11% in the North of England in 1995 (Office for National Statistics, 1997) masks the rate of change (4.6% in 1970) and considerable local variation, with some neighbourhoods registering much higher rates. In Newcastle upon Tyne, for instance, male unemployment across the city is some 21% and in the west end of the city over 40% (Newcastle upon Tyne City Council, 1997). It is the rate of change that is the critical feature. Manchester, to take one example, lost nearly 50,000 jobs in textiles, steel and engineering between 1971 and 1981 (Tye and Williams, 1994). To take another example, Sheffield, the 'steel city', lost some 33,469 jobs in metals and engineering between 1981 and 1991 (Dabinett, 1995). This involuntary 'loss of work' is far removed from the optimism implicit within modernist visions of the 'leisure society'. Further, the fact that it has occurred within the time-frame of one generation, although against a longer history of decline (Weiner, 1985), means that it has resulted in communities having little time for re-adjustment in both economic and socio-cultural terms. As Urry (1995) observes in his consideration of the transformation of industrial Lancashire, a unique history and culture shaped by two centuries of industry is rapidly being eroded.

Associated social problems

Whilst it remains debatable as to the extent of the influence, unemployment, loss of income, the growth in income support dependency and the loss of social status are certainly factors which have contributed to urban poverty, community fragmentation, rising crime rates, increased drug abuse and vandalism (Kotler *et al.*, 1993). These are certainly not specifically urban issues, but their manifestation has challenged the more romantic notions of the civilized city. In particular it has been the unemployment phenomenon which has defined de-industrializing centres, fundamentally creating two social groupings of those that work and those that do not. Subordinate are two increasingly polarized sets of values, strikingly evident in the riots which occurred in the suburbs of Newcastle and Cardiff in the early 1990s, but still on display in the estates and marginalized neighbourhoods of many former production centres across the UK (Campbell, 1993; Danziger, 1996).

For the image-conscious tourism industry, the culture of the displaced, disinterested and disenchanted populations of the young and the long-term unemployed, can pose thorny problems (Boyle and Hughes, 1991). Prospective tourists are invited to consume the culture of museums, galleries and the theatre, but not the equally creative cultural forms which include car theft, ram-raiding, bus shelter demolition and the paint spraying of graffiti on apparently inaccessible railway bridges. The two cultures share the same urban space, though not always at the same time. Some tourism agencies prefer to ignore the realities of urban life, while others at least note it. For example, the 1997 Liverpool and Merseyside Visitor Guide informs readers:

> As with any large city, Liverpool has its share of minor safety and security problems but we do welcome millions of visitors every year . . . remember when you leave your car to ensure it is locked. Keep to the main thoroughfares and avoid unlit streets after dark.

Changing spaces

Evaluating the extent of physical changes in urban centres is highly subjective and assessments will vary considerably with insider or outsider status. Some centres of provincial cities and towns have changed little over the past 100 years, in part as testimony to the great Victorian building programmes and their enduring public appeal. But there has also been substantial transformation. This manifests itself on a number of levels. On a physical level the closure of industrial plants has released substantial land and buildings for redevelopment. Local authorities, development corporations and the private sector have been reasonably successful in the physical reclamation of derelict land in the centres and urban fringe, remaking and re-creating the urban landscape and its social character. On another level, this process is the most highly symbolic of the transformation from a productive to a consumptive economy. The substitution of industrial spaces with leisure and recreational spaces can also represent the finality of change; we are not only speaking of scaling-down and reduced employment in some manufacturing sectors, but the wholesale removal of industries which provided communities with purpose and identity. By way of an example, Table 6.1 illustrates this through the consideration of changes which have taken place in the cities of Newcastle upon Tyne, Sunderland, and the Tyne and Wear conurbation over a relatively recent time-frame of 30 years. Sites of coal mines now provide for leisure, large industrial buildings are taking on new 'high' culture roles, and places which once displayed their productive histories are renamed. New spaces, new landmarks and new names have replaced what was the 'familiar'. Aside from the quick rates involved, this is nothing more than the normative process of change; but this does not alter the impacts.

The Response of Tourism Development

What has emerged from the de-industrializing process and the experience of decline is a political, economic and moral agenda to 'regenerate' the de-

Table 6.1. Indicative spatial and cultural transformations in the Tyne and Wear region 1968–1998.

Former space/landmark/name	'New' development/identity
North Sands Ship Yard, Sunderland	National Glass Centre
Wearmouth Colliery, Sunderland	Sunderland Football Ground 'Stadium of Light'
Silksworth Colliery, Sunderland	Dry Ski Slope and Tennis Centre
North Hylton Colliery, Sunderland	Retail Park, American Grill Bar/Hotel
Sunderland Royal Infirmary	Building earmarked for Leisure and Housing Development
South Tyneside	Promoted as Catherine Cookson Country
Boldon Colliery Railway Station	Re-named as Brockley Whins
Baltic Flour Mills, Gateshead	To be converted into an Arts Centre
City of Newcastle upon Tyne	Increasingly promoted as the 'Party City'
River Tyne Shipbuilding	Hosting of the Tall Ships Race 1993
Co-operative Wholesale Society Warehouse, Newcastle Quayside	Four Star Malmaison Hotel
Manors Goods Yard, Newcastle	Technopole Office Development

industrialized urban centres. Paradoxically, this has required a level of intervention which was at odds with the Thatcherite ideologies which had contributed to decline (Hutton, 1996). However, it has been an intervention of private capital, private ownership (Zukin, 1997) and a planning process which side-stepped traditional democratic politics (Bianchini and Schwengel, 1991).

The reasons for the expansion in urban tourism provision are multifarious and complex, but they summarily reflect the formalization of tourism and cultural development as part of economic regenerative strategies, which are themselves responses to the problems of economic restructuring and the management of decline (Chang *et al.*, 1996; Zukin, 1996). In the UK this has considerably extended the number of urban locations now involved with tourism to include the larger industrial cities and towns (Urry, 1990).

At this juncture, it is valuable to emphasize two points. First, tourism in former industrial centres is chiefly supply led. The decline of manufacturing industry and the growth in the service sector has affected the majority of urban locations, even those towns and cities which, superficially, have always existed for the benefit of tourist and pilgrim. The city of York, for example, as Meethan (1996) points out, is increasingly structured around consumption, although it carries a strong, and recent, past in manufacturing, particularly railway engineering. The historic role of York, together with its heritage core, has arguably guaranteed tourist demand independent of the de-industrializing process. Page (1997) has drawn together an eclectic list of the principal motivating factors for urban tourists ranging from business travel and conference attendance to shopping and visiting friends and relatives. Through substantial investment over recent years, the majority of urban centres, including former industrial cities and towns, are now in a position to proffer a highly sophisticated range of services and amenities to an increasingly diverse range of tourist types. Moreover, in recognizing that tourists are increasingly adaptive as they attempt to achieve satisfaction (Ryan, 1995), the urban environment is readily able to offer the visitor a number of substitute experiences in the fields of art, food and shopping. If we don't fancy the Greek restaurant we can try Italian. However, what is interesting is not that tourists have the opportunity to sample Mongolian, Lebanese and German cuisine in New York, or even York, but that they can now do the same in Newcastle upon Tyne.

Second, tourism development is linked with the wider context of service provision and the new forms of cultural production. There has been an increasing convergence of economic development policy with cultural policy, partly in recognition of the post-modern consumer and the post-modern tourist (if indeed, these are the same) and partly, and more fundamentally, because of the economics of cultural production (Harvey, 1989). Cultural capital, in a range of physical and symbolic forms including shopping centres, culturally orientated tourist attractions and events, and entertainment centres (Britton, 1991), and in the more ethereal sense as distinctive and historic communities, is considered as having 'real economic value' (Zukin, 1991). Thus, tourism, culture and associated leisure development remain at the heart of many regenerative strategies in the Western World (Bianchini and Parkinson, 1993).

Scott (1997) explores the ways that cities have harnessed cultural capital for productive purposes. He considers the cases of Los Angeles and Paris, and points to the employment and income generating benefits which can be identified. To some degree, one can understand this with reference to 'world' cities such as Paris which have been instrumental in the generation of cultural forms. However, to speak of the cultural economies of some UK provincial industrial cities and towns is more problematic. Whilst culture in the Arnoldian 'high' sense is present in the Wakefields and Wigans of the world, it is increasingly commodified and contrived and its pulling power in tourism terms is limited. Moreover, in focusing on the presentation of cultural achievements for tourists, there is a danger of masking the more important dimensions of culture – akin to Raymond William's notion of the 'ordinary' –

which define a destination and underpin its social identity (Williams, 1993).

Mirroring urban strategies developed in North America in the 1970s and 1980s (Hewison, 1995), with few exceptions and within a highly competitive climate, former industrial centres in the UK have followed similar patterns in developing tourism; the development of tourist accommodation (usually of a high standard), of associated leisure and retailing spaces, the creation of attractions with a strong heritage theme, large and costly 'flagship' projects (Smyth, 1994), and the establishment of cultural events and festivals. Even the reclamation of derelict land and the temporary make-overs of 'garden festivals' in provincial centres of Liverpool, Stoke, Glasgow, Gateshead and Ebbw Vale seemed to demonstrate that the very process of de-industrialization could attract tourists.

Manchester exhibits the dominant ideology of tourism as a response to its industrial decline. It has, since the early 1980s, invested considerable public and private sector funding and European Structural Funds in developing a wide range of tourism amenities including conference facilities, the major attraction of Granada Studios (TV and film-based theme park) and the Castlefield area, billed as 'Britain's first urban heritage park'. In addition, Manchester has invested heavily in the development of sports complexes to underpin its failed Olympic bid (Law, 1996; Loftman and Spirou, 1996). In a recent brochure, Greater Manchester boasts of the existence of 'over 100 industrial heritage themed attractions'. Taken together all these developments represent dramatic economic change. But, they also represent a similarly dramatic re-orientation of culture.

Recent developments in Liverpool and Merseyside also typify the ways in which provincial post-industrial cities are still physically re-creating themselves and looking to tourism and leisure to effect economic success. Table 6.2 identifies a range of recent initiatives on Liverpool and Merseyside and emphasizes a number of themes of this chapter – the move from productive to consumption orientated space, strong cultural themes, the availability of private and public capital for such ventures, and the hope of attracting visitors. But also conveyed by these changes is an implicit sense of failure of past economies.

Dawson and Parkinson (1991) in an evaluation of the Merseyside Development Corporation during the 1980s quote from *The Economist* which argued that Liverpool is:

> a museum to the depression, failing to hype itself back to prosperity in the fashion of Glasgow and Newcastle upon Tyne . . . stuck in the past, in a time-warp of Beatlemania and class solidarity.
>
> (*The Economist*, 1989, p. 25)

Nearly ten years on, it appears the museum is still under construction.

To urban centres and the authorities and agencies that manage them, such tourism developments promise a relatively swift and cost effective way

Table 6.2. Tourism and associated leisure developments in Liverpool/Merseyside.

Development	Description
Chinatown Re-development	£28 million plan is underway to make Chinatown more of a tourist attraction. Elements include a ceremonial arch, a Chinese garden and pavement mosaics.
Devonshire House Hotel Development	£3 million extension through the conversion of Holly House, a former student hostel, into a 60-bedroom three-star hotel.
Hope Quarter Development	£40 million bid to Millennium Fund to develop area between Liverpool's two cathedrals to attract tourism and investment. A 1960s history trail of clubs, cafes and historical features relating to the city is planned.
Chavasse Discovery Park	£25 million bid shortlisted by the Millennium Commission to help fund a 'Discovery' Park in Chavasse Park.
Princes Dock Re-development	Private sector development plans for £13.3 million luxury hotel near to the Liver Building. The 174-bed hotel, under the Holiday Inn Crown Plaza banner would include a conference centre for 700 people. The Merseyside Development Corporation has awarded the project £4.5 million.
Speke Hall Visitor and Conference Centre	National Trust has submitted a planning application for a £5.5 million development of redundant farm buildings at Speke Hall including glass-fronted exhibition and visitor centre. £3.8 million is sought from the National Lottery and £1 million from the Merseyside Objective One Fund.
Kings Dock Cinema and Leisure Complex	£80 million proposal for 30-screen Multiplex cinema and developments of leisure/health centre, virtual reality hall, bingo hall and cafe-bars.
St Georges Hall	£17 million application for National Lottery funds to improve the building and turn the north section of the building into a Visitor Centre.
Wolstenholme Square	Proposed scheme to transform the area into a centre for tourism and creative industries similar to the Temple Bar area of Dublin. English partnerships have pledged £30 million towards the scheme.
Hamilton Quarter	An £81 million scheme to redevelop the Square into a major arts and cultural quarter with continental style street bars and pavement cafes.
Cammell Laird Shipyard Project	£60 million project to regenerate the Cammell Laird shipyard area to include a hovercraft link to Liverpool Airport, a marina, leisure centre and marine technology park. The scheme has secured £20 million of government money through the Single Regeneration Budget.

Source: Extracts from Merseyside Tourism and Conference Bureau (1997), Digest of Merseyside Tourism Facts and Figures and 'What's New', October, City of Liverpool, Leisure Services Directorate.

to fill the physical and emotional gaps left by de-industrialization. Tourism is still recognized as an important element in the diversification of economies and is driven by the following.

Perceived market demand

The idea of the post-tourist (Rojek, 1993) seeking an increasingly diverse set of commodified cultural experiences goes some way to explaining the attraction of the de-industrialized town and city. Trends in the domestic market towards the taking of additional shorter, 'out-of-season' holidays and themed stays, together with an increase in business travel focusing upon accessible service centres, reflect the emergence of the post-tourist. However, the idea of identifying and quantifying the true nature of demand, prior to tourism developments, frequently amounts to no more than a good guess and a certain degree of hope.

Increased funding opportunities

This reflects the belief by successive UK administrations and the European Union, that the cultural sector has a major role to play in urban regeneration and the creation of employment. The tourism and leisure dimensions of culture are seen as a partial payback mechanism, and projects which feature a tourism dimension are now well established priority areas for a variety of funding agencies (European Union Structural Funds, National Lottery, City Challenge and Single Regeneration Budget). In 1993/94 some £1.7 billion was spent by central and local government, businesses, trusts, foundations and private donors in support of cultural activities (Casey *et al.*, 1997). Moreover, the blurring of the boundaries between tourism and cultural policies, and the ideology of 'partnership' between public and private sectors, has effectively increased funding opportunities. Casey *et al.* (1997) indicate, for instance, that in addition to the Department of the Environment spending £39 million on the cultural sector through its urban regeneration programmes in 1993/94, some 25% of central government funding came from government departments not directly responsible for culture. At the same time, however, the competitive nature of such funding programmes seems to encourage over-ambition at the expense of market and social need (Edwards, 1997).

Low barriers to entry

There are lower barriers to entry in tourism compared with manufacturing industry. Because UK labour costs are low in the tourism and leisure fields (and relatively higher in most other European Union nations) tourism development remains a viable strategy for economic development agencies. Buckley and Witt (1989, p. 138) reflected this philosophy: 'the labour intensive nature of tourism and its unskilled job generating capacity make it an ideal element in a strategy of regeneration'. According to a publication produced by the Association of District Councils (1986) extolling the benefits of tourism development, it cost approximately £35,000 to create a full-time job in manufacturing and only £5000 to create a full-time job in leisure and tourism.

Limited development choices

For many former industrial centres, there has been little choice but to encourage growth in the service sector. Indeed, the UK expansion of tourism and leisure in the 1980s was ideologically driven. Thatcherism made a significant contribution to destroying the ideal of full employment centred on manufacturing industry. Unemployment was the 'price worth paying' for zero inflation. Manufacturing was refused subsidies and allowed to decline together with its unionized labour, and the service sector was encouraged to expand. For some, strategies to encourage tourism, heralded the fulfilment of post-industrial prophecies. But, following Zukin's (1996, p. 229) wider point that cultural strategies often represent a 'worst-case scenario of economic development', for former industrialized and peripheral urban centres, frustrated at not being able to attract manufacturing industry, such strategies are indicative of the economics of desperation.

Re-imaging

In addition to the re-creation of industrial space, considerable resources have gone into the creation and competitive marketing of new images and 'makeovers' (see for instance: Ashworth and Voogd, 1990; Sadler, 1993; Barke and Harrop, 1994; Holcomb, 1994; Bramwell and Rawding, 1994, 1996). Conspicuous consumption of culture is now the platform upon which post-industrial cities are having to compete. Thus, in its 1997 'Visitors Guide', the City of Leeds promotes itself as 'a major European Cultural Centre', a city which has 'embraced the continental lifestyle' and with the arrival of the London store Harvey Nichols, portrays itself as the 'Knightsbridge of the North'.

The rationale of attempting to negate images of industrial decline and dereliction is hardly surprising, but the central issues relate to the extent to which the images projected are unique, and presumably therefore effective, and, paraphrasing Harvey (1989), whether they are more about aesthetics, rather than the ethics of dealing with social and economic realities.

In the de-industrialized city, tourism development and promotion are heavily dependent upon the rediscovery and reinvention of Victorian high cultural life. This is indeed ironic given that in the times of industrial achievement and robust economic performance, formal, recreational tourism was limited, save for the continental excursions of the élite. In terms of supply, urban centres were invariably functional; and in terms of demand, the two vital elements for movement (aside from transport), time and money, were restricted to the minority until relatively late into the 20th century. The utilization of tourism for regenerative purposes now is perversely ever reliant on the leftovers of industrialism. Attractive Victorian townscapes now devoid of their original use are packaged for the tourist gaze. Art galleries and museums, established under the patronage of industrial leaders, are often beacons of former municipal wealth in now run-down towns and cities. Other, once functional features such as canals, railways and industrial sites provide essential tourist resources for destinations which are not blessed with natural beauty.

What all this tells us is that urban policy generally, and tourism policy in particular, is both imbued and legitimized with a cultural text, but it is a text constructed around the consumption of culture; the visual and performing arts, sports, shopping and heritage. This, and the structures, artefacts and symbols of industrial ordinariness are now promoted as extraordinary, and, as Urry (1990) tells us, it is the extraordinary, and the distance from the norm that creates the tourist gaze.

Cultural Conflicts in Provincial Urban Tourism

In the smaller, less diverse, de-industrializing cities and towns of the UK, which have relatively low throughputs of international tourists, it remains tempting to bypass the idea of any sort of cultural conflict. But conflicts do occur though it is argued they are more directly related to the processes of tourism development and economic restructuring rather than at the level of tourist–host contact. In rural societies, remote and fragile communities, and amongst the world's indigenous peoples, cultural conflicts are chiefly viewed as a product of inappropriate tourist behaviour and it is usual to portray the visitor as the *agent provocateur*. Debate also focuses upon tourism as a series of disruptive interventions such as inappropriate development and the rate of development, and issues surrounding acculturation, the demonstration effect, and the inequities of the tourism trade.

However, such interventions are commonplace in de-industrialized provincial urban centres of the UK, though they are frequently obscured and little researched. Given the urban context, arguably the visitor is less visible, the host community less sensitive, the economy more diverse, distinct cultural groupings are often located away from tourist centres, and socio-cultural norms are apparently more eclectic and dynamic. As Conforti (1996) notes, in the context of large cities, it is the fact that urban cultures are so diverse which makes them attractive to tourists. The problem is (if it is a problem) that this diversity becomes structured through ghettos, which in turn can justify their preservation.

Cultural diversity and multiculturalism are a feature of most UK provincial towns and cities, to varying degrees. But whatever the age, ethnic and socio-economic composition of this diversity, there is an indigenous population which experiences contact with tourists and visitors and the positive and negative impacts of tourism development. Whilst recognizing that the term 'indigenous peoples' has developed its own, commonly accepted meaning, in part defined by 'historical continuity with pre-invasion and pre-colonial societies that developed on their territories' (United Nations 1986/87), and not wishing to undermine the importance of the issues facing them, it is nonetheless instructive to highlight some further aspects of the definition of indigenous peoples. In addition to the characteristic of pre-existence, the Independent Commission on International Humanitarian Issues (1996) points to three further defining traits of non-dominance, cultural difference and self-identification.

Clearly there are substantive differences between aboriginal peoples and the residents of a suburban housing estate in Manchester, but without wishing to overly stretch the semantics, there are also striking similarities. The urban underclass, the unemployed and the old represent the non-dominant sectors of society, observing and experiencing change without being able to shape it. Such groups are marginal politically, socially, economically and, often, spatially. Yet collectively they represent a significant dimension of the local culture which helps define the difference of a destination. The westernized concept of the 'other' and 'otherness' invariably label peoples and cultures as exotic, unique and foreign, rather than merely different. The displaced communities caught up in the rapidity of transition are also the 'other', and although authentic their lack of exoticism means that tourists seldom seek them out.

In the restricted cosmopolitanism of the UK's provincial towns and cities, where the desire of connecting with the global is reflected in the increasingly predictable retail profile of the high street, it is the 'indigenous' peoples that help create the identity and distinctiveness of place. Although they may not have historical continuity beyond the 500 years usually referred to as a qualifying characteristic of first peoples, they inhabit this world, identify with it, witness change and continuity, are both proud and ashamed of it, and believe they own it. It is their city.

It is perhaps rather fanciful and abstract to extend the idea of indigenousness to the populations of urban areas being considered here. However, an understanding of the cultural character of these centres as tourist destinations, and their vulnerability, helps in paving the way for the following discussion on three interrelated areas of cultural conflict.

Marginalization through Work and Non-work

As markedly as unemployment has driven the development of tourism and leisure, so too have new patterns of employment impacted upon urban cultures. Culture, in the sense of being a 'way of life', resonates strongly with the nature and performance of an economy (Rubinstein, 1990). Despite what post-industrial theorists have argued, a large proportion of the urban population would still seem to connect with a culture rooted in an economy focused on manufacturing through large production units. Nostalgia aside, the messages of recent films such as *Brassed Off* and *The Full Monty* point to a residual way of life which still carries public empathy. The success of these films is heavy with irony – symbols of the UK's increasingly successful cultural industries and at the same time providing insights into the hardships of industrial failure. De-industrialization has become a cultural commodity.

What we now have is an economy, two-thirds of which is constituted by the service sector, with 95% of all companies classed as small and medium sized enterprises (employing less than 250 people). It appears that we are out of synchronization; our culture is framed by a past which we may desire, but which we do not have. For the manufacturing economy not only provided us with high levels of employment (indeed, it remains the most prized goal for economic development organizations of whatever political hue), it also provided social and cultural cohesiveness, a sense of identity (independent of class) and a focus for communication and shared beliefs (Edwards and Llurdés i Coit, 1996). Of course one can over-romanticize about cultural consensus and social cohesion, just as one can forget that poverty, environmental degradation and social depravity were inherent by-products of an essentially exploitative industrial system. However, the prospect of progress through manufacturing and a measure of industrial spirit still appear to carry important values.

In some senses the Victorian values of entrepreneurship, self-reliance and philanthropy were re-invented by Mrs Thatcher and her belief in an enterprise culture (Morris, 1991). However, these qualities emerged from, and were suited to, a *growing* manufacturing economy, not an economy in decline. Similarly there appears little in the nature of the service sector from which we can expect any gestalt-like shift in cultural values. It has merely provided us with additional cultural capital. Arguably what we are left with, is a situation of cultural stagnation in which our values have remained fixed to ideas of industrial success which we no longer enjoy.

Supplying the needs of tourists in urban centres has brought the prospect of work, but work within a different cultural context. The issues of low pay, long working hours, seasonal uncertainty and the psychological leap needed to 'serve' in, rather than contribute to, an economy, are arguably likely to create greater social tensions and resentment in Bradford and Birmingham, than they would in Bangkok. Somewhat paradoxically, against the background of the UK's ageing demographic profile, work within tourism and leisure has tended to focus on the younger age groups. A ready supply of labour amongst 16 to 20 year olds, their flexibility, and as Purcell and Quinn (1996) note, their apparent willingness to tolerate low pay and long hours in order to work within a lively and perceived glamorous environment, is creating new social norms which will impact well into the future. In addition, the UK's Secretary of State for Culture, Media and Sport has announced the expectation that the tourism and leisure sectors are likely to absorb a large proportion of the young unemployed in the 'New Deal' Welfare to Work scheme (Department for Culture, Media and Sport, 1997). Ironically, the tourist is probably not concerned whether those serving him or her in a hotel restaurant are local, previously unemployed, and currently being paid £2.50 per hour, as long as the service they receive meets their expectations. In this, there is a real danger that the older sections of the community are marginalized, excluded from the world of work, not just in terms of their skills, but because of their increasing distance from the contemporary value sets which underpin tourism developments.

Krippendorf's (1987) common sense observation that while tourists are engaged in leisure, the host is at work, clearly points to potential conflict which exhibits itself in many situations of tourist–host contact. The idea of two cultures surrounding those serving and those being served takes on another dimension in the context of de-industrialization. Unlike resort tourism which is contained and focused on tourism as the dominant economic sector, urban tourism works within flexible and shifting boundaries, and is not the sole activity. Thus tourists are not only in contact with those who work for them; their presence and activities and the developments created for them are also observed by other workers and the unemployed. To some of the unemployed, tourists, tourism and leisure developments may represent opportunities. To others they are likely to be symbolic of what they are unable to experience, and also of more restrictive choice in employment futures.

The Creation of 'New' Cultural Territories

Parkinson (1996) provides a useful commentary on the UK policy responses to urban problems from the late 1960s. He notes the emergence of several key elements which continue to re-shape urban life and particularly those of public and private sector partnership, in which the latter has dominated by virtue of resources and political favour, and the mechanism of competition, which has, by definition, created winners and losers.

A further dominant theme of urban policy is the degree to which it has been dominated by the creation of landscapes. The recent rapidity of the physical transformations which have taken place in de-industrializing urban centres is awesome. Property-led regeneration has majored on the creation of urban spaces designed for the service sector, of which tourism, leisure and recreational usage have been central. Developments inspired by North American successes such as Baltimore and Boston, enticed by good access, lax planning restraints (particularly where Urban Development Corporations have been active), public subsidy and the promise of an often desperate and cheap supply of workers, are now a common feature of UK provincial towns and cities. Developments may vary in the relative emphasis given to their component elements, but the overall formula is unrelentingly consistent; a visitor attraction, visitor centre, hotel, health and leisure club, multiplex cinema, retail/business park, 'executive' housing, and if possible a marina complex or water-based feature. The elements are linked by their post-modernist building style, their ambitions to attract tourists, their overt appeal to the higher socio-economic groupings, their complete success in covering up any traces of previously industrial space and their substitutability. The lone concession to place is perhaps through a heritage attraction which emphasizes an uniqueness rooted in the past.

The creation of new urban spaces provides 'new' or more precisely different cultural territories for the local community as well as the visitor. Territory implies a sense of collective and individual ownership on the part of the local community. This is not ownership in the legal sense, but an emotional sense of connectedness with an area, a set of buildings or streets-cape, as spatial expression of cultures. It is much more about 'placeness' (Cohen, 1995) than place. The boundaries of cultural territories may not be recognizable from the outside, but are learned and recognized from within (Cohen, 1985). These boundaries continually shift in both aesthetic and functional terms. Old mills and warehouses have been restored and now provide for housing, offices and art centres; remade to fit with the new 'symbolic economies' (Zukin, 1997, p. 7). For the local population the familiar has become the exotic only to become the familiar again.

Urry (1995, p. 192) notes that in order to satisfy the tourist gaze, 'environments, places and people are being regularly made and re-made as tourist objects'. The reconstruction process is more than cosmetic, it involves substantive economic and social change. This process is perhaps more marked in those provincial urban cities and towns which have previously been immune from some of the more dramatic redevelopment and expansion programmes of the very large centres. Lengkeek (1993, p. 8) notes that 'the creation of tourist/recreation places to visit and things worth seeing has a guiding function in our community, telling us what is beautiful and worthwhile and what is nice'. But developing city space, particularly 'inner' city space, to make it more attractive to tourists, has not always been accompanied by attempts to maintain viable communities there. Emphasis has been upon space rather place, what Keith and Rogers (1991) term the 'spatial fetish'. Spiralling rents, loss of ownership, and the primacy of aesthetics over function (Edwards, 1997) have contributed to changing the social patterns of the indigenous community and migration out of town. On the latter issue, as

Zukin (1991) discusses, suburbanization itself can be viewed as a form of consumption. She makes the point that making centres more attractive to visitors and encouraging suburban growth merely relocates social and economic problems to the edge of cities.

An issue which is resonant of tourism in developing nations and indigenous peoples, is that of ownership; where cultural territories have been and remain appropriated from minority groups, and tourism and leisure developments are owned, and effectively controlled, from outside of the local community. But this pattern of power relations is not restricted to Third World economies, it is replicated within the provincial de-industrialized centres. Furthermore, the ownership issue and the fact that decisions can be taken from a distance relates also to manufacturing industry and other parts of the service sector. The economic consequences of this transnationality, in terms of revenue leaking out of the local economy, is often the other side of the employment creation aspect. In tourism, however, where arguably the economic and social value of employment is relatively low, generation and circulation of revenue in the local economy becomes more important and its absence a potential source of resentment.

Martinotti (1996, p. 6) differentiates between city 'inhabitants' and city 'users', the latter group acting to swell city populations and using (and abusing) public spaces and facilities. Leisure and business tourists clearly belong in this user group (along with shoppers, concert-goers, football fans and other transient groups). In cities such as Venice, the swollen number of users can induce conflict with the inhabitants as they compete for space and services (albeit in key commercial neighbourhoods), and although in provincial cities they are unlikely to be very large in number, they can nevertheless be significant in relative terms.

In cultural terms, seeing developments created for, and owned by, 'outsiders' can also generate conflict. Papson (1981) speaks of the problems of creating 'spurious realities' as events and attractions have been created or imposed by sources outside of the local community. Boyle and Hughes (1991) take to task the developments and re-imaging of Glasgow through the Garden Festival and the labelling of 'European City of Culture' in 1990 and identify the tensions created between the planners and promoters and the realities of working-class communities. Territories become redefined in accordance with the aspirations, tastes, preferences and budgets of developers, architects and government agencies, often without local consultation. Although communities would perhaps rather see their environment evolve in an organic manner, provincial cities in the UK are littered with recently created and radically different spaces symbolic of major, rapid, economic and cultural change. Moreover, the more fundamental choice regarding whether to invest in tourism and leisure, or in manufacturing say, is also frequently an 'outside' choice. McGuigan summarizes the consequences of external decision-making:

> Urban regeneration . . . articulates the interests and tastes of the post modern professional and managerial class without solving the problems of a diminishing production base, growing disparities of wealth and opportunity, and the multiple forms of social exclusion.
>
> (McGuigan, 1996, p. 99)

Although play may be made of community 'ownership' and access, this can often be selective with access prioritized for the high spending visitors (no doubt identified at the feasibility study stage). The promise of tourists can encourage price rises amongst local suppliers. This inflationary feature of tourism development is therefore also a source of resentment amongst the poorer sections of the host community, as they are confronted with the stark contrast between what has been created for others and what they are left with. Following Clarke and Critcher (1985), it is perhaps one of the successes of late capitalism that societies have been persuaded control and choice of leisure are unrelated. Control, for instance, has been exercised by Urban Development Corporations (Parkinson, 1996), whose portfolios of projects have included strong cultural and tourism themes, but choice has often been what *they* provide in terms of an attraction or leisure facility.

In the town of Hartlepool on the coast of the north-east of England, where the largest employer was once shipbuilding, the Teesside Development Corporation has spent some £200 million on a marina complex including the 'historic quay', an 'authentically reconstructed' seaport of the 1800s. Nearby, the Jacksons Landing factory outlet shopping mall offers the visitors and residents of Hartlepool discounted designer fashion from Calvin Klein and Christian Lacroix. Whatever the economics of this reaction to Hartlepool's 22% unemployment rate of the mid-1980s (still 13% in 1996), it is not hard to see how the new cultural spaces can seem daunting to a large part of the community whose values and behaviour were forged in a different time and space. It is the landscape of consumption that now provides the cultural context for the population of the town. Whilst some may welcome this as a new territorial gain, some react against it, and others are merely bewildered by it. As well as the 'tourist gaze' (Urry, 1990) there is also the community gaze engaged when communities encounter the new, often dramatic, physical and emotional spaces designed for tourists. But as tourists seek the unfamiliar, the different and the exotic (the features requested of the tourism development process), communities look for continuation, evolution, stability and familiarity.

From Identity to Image

The notion that the development of tourism can contribute to a sense of social cohesion and cultural identity is well established. As Friedman (1994, p. 110) notes, for instance, in his discussion of the Ainu peoples of northern Japan: 'tourism production and display have become a central process in the conscious reconstruction of Ainu identity'. Indeed, tourism development can be partly legitimized by its claims to maintain traditions and preserve cultures (Lanfant, 1995), particularly in societies where cultural identities reflect long, unbroken histories and powerful continuity. Where tourism does challenge and overcome such continuous cultural identities, the manifestations are often dramatic. Perhaps in the context of indigenous peoples and discrete cultures, Greenwood's (1989) vehemence about the capacity of tourism to commodify culture and tradition, erode authenticity and violate the rights of host communities, is easy to appreciate. In the context of de-industrialized urban centres, cultural identities are already hybridized, in part as a function of economic restructuring and its social effects. Consequently, given this implicit historical discontinuity, it is not straightforward to recognize the manifestations of cultural change, nor does it generate so much attention.

Wearing and Wearing (1992) describe identity as emerging from both the core of the individual and from within the core of communal culture. In the less cosmopolitan provincial towns and cities, cultural identities have closely reflected patterns of industrial production and have been communal in practice and in emotional terms. As noted earlier, and particularly affecting the older generations, there is still a residual power of the past (Taylor and Jameson, 1997) which allows communities to hang on to the real economy of production as an identity defining characteristic. This is amplified, not negated, by the commodification which has occurred in UK domestic tourism over the past 20 years. West Yorkshire wool weaving, South Yorkshire steel making, Lancashire cotton spinning, Staffordshire china production, South Wales coal mining, and North East England heavy engineering, all retain a local community currency but as museums and heritage attractions. Narratives of work and production are now framed in the past tense and are referenced with talk of 'tradition' and inherited pride. True, we can still distinguish destinations by their industrial pasts and in tourism marketing this is recognized as important. As Law (1993, p. 170) puts it: 'it is very unlikely that visitors will want to travel to clone cities'. What is remarkable is that we do, though we pretend we do not. Against the pressures of globalization and the threat of homogenization, provincial cities and towns are increasingly differentiated on the basis of their past economies and their manufacturing traditions. This may say nothing of real contemporary social identities but the fact is that service sector economies are of little use in tourism marketing terms; there is little about them to distinguish a sense of place and difference.

The impact of tourism and leisure developments on the identities of host communities in de-industrialized centres is poorly explored, partly reflecting the problems of disengaging tourism projects from the wider contexts of service sector expansion, media impacts and the process of globalization. Bourdieu's (1984) view that identity (self-identification) is increasingly shaped through consumptive behaviour and 'lifestyle' is helpful in explaining the role of the tourist, but the identity of the host community is surely something greater than a collection of individuals seeking to differentiate themselves through distinctive consumption.

Two issues emerge. The first is the extent to which urban societies are the 'consumed' (Urry, 1995). In contrast to tourist visits to rural societies, the expectation (however misplaced) of gazing on traditional work patterns and urban ways of life is either diminished, or wholly absent. However, inasmuch as the local community is associated with the provision of tourism, either directly through working in a shop or hotel, or indirectly by just being there, they are consumed. Indeed, in the urban context, some parts of the community are consumed more than others, which itself can contribute to cultural fragmentation and conflict, involving isolation, poverty and the break-up of cities into what Sachs-Jeantet (1996, p. 6) terms 'outlaw zones'.

The second point concerns the nature of the relationship between place and social identity. Arguably, this relationship was/is more intimate in the provincial centres than large cosmopolitan cities. The culture-generating capacity of economic activity (Scott, 1997) is at the root of the modernist identities of old industrial towns and cities which we still recognize. Identity was narrowly defined by what people did, and what they produced and provincial centres thus reflected this. Bauman (1996, p. 23) quotes Lasch (1985) who points out that identity 'refers both to persons and to things' and continues, 'both have lost their solidity in modern society, their definiteness and continuity'. In the wake of de-industrialization, identities have floundered, and attention has moved from endogenously constructed narratives of reality, to externally generated images of aspiration.

Whilst tourism is not causally responsible for the loss of social identities, it remains an influence in the creation of *new* urban images. Barke and Harrop's (1994) research points out that the promotion of such images is more common in industrial towns. They draw upon a number of examples of industrial centres which have sought to compete on an often uneasy combination of nostalgia and the desire to recapture new industries. Although it is likely that new and very different industries are at the centre of urban economies, these are relatively unattractive to the tourist gaze. Ironically, it is the re-invention/re-creation of the industrial past and its socio-cultural setting which are so important to the new images, enabling places to maintain, albeit superficially, distinct identities for place and people. A full discussion of the conflicts surrounding the use of heritage and nostalgia in relation to tourism and culture is outside of the scope of this chapter. Issues regarding commodification/preservation of the cultural past, its use and mis-use, selectivity, and Hewison's (1987, 1996) well articulated theme of heritage's contribution to cultural stagnation, clearly extend beyond the urban sphere, but are nevertheless a source of conflict in policy, if not in practice.

Conclusion: The Meaningfulness of Tourism

Few urban centres remain unexplored by tourists (Page, 1995). Fewer still would claim not to have aspirations to share in tourism's perceived benefits; none more so than those centres which are engaged in the process of de-industrialization. Specific tourism developments, developments with tourists in mind, and newly constructed images remain as an integral part of the reaction to the processes of de-industrialization. In some cases the missionary zeal with which local authorities, development agencies and the private sector welcome the regenerative promises of tourism can miss more mainstream industrial development opportunities which may generate more long-term economic benefits (Karski, 1990), and which may be more culturally appropriate. It was not that long ago that political and economic commentators were bemoaning the over-dependency of provincial towns and cities on monolithic industrial production. There are limits to tourism development too – limits imposed by the market and normal competition, limits of economic effectiveness and cultural limits (Craik, 1995). If present trends of provincial urban tourism development continue, these limits increasingly become exposed and we may well be looking at a new and radically different form of cultural dependency.

Crick (1989, p. 335) notes the dangers of using tourism as a 'conspicuous scapegoat' for problems which are invariably shaped by a far greater expanse of variables. In the context of the urban centres alluded to here, tourism development is clearly not the sole agent of cultural change. Indeed, in emphasizing the merging of tourism and culture (Rojek and Urry, 1997), it is problematic in both physical and intellectual terms to isolate tourism from closely related phenomena such as retailing, catering and sport. Nevertheless, while accepting Crick's warning, this post-modern merging only promotes the role of tourism as a driver of cultural change, and a cause for conflict. In attempting to replace industrial economies and new forms of employment, by the creation of new physical landmarks, in promoting style over substance, and by disenfranchising those sections of the community which are not attractive, tourism development in provincial de-industrializing urban centres of the UK, is perhaps not as different in its cultural effects as it is in, say, Bali or Belize.

Increasingly, key elements in any discussion of the tourism–culture relationship are those of consent and ownership; having the power and ability to make decisions regarding tourism development and being able to gain adequate economic reward for what, in consensus terms, is commensurate with one's own culture. Such an approach would allow for social justice of the kind described by Rawls (1971), simply paraphrased as not advancing the causes of the 'better-off' if it does not benefit those which are not so advantaged. Commercial exploitation of otherness, objectification of cultures, trivialization of traditions and rituals, exploitation of artefacts and the environment by 'outsiders', have been key themes in the literature over many years. The bulk of studies have focused upon First–Third World/first peoples, developed–developing country/region clashes, and despite sometimes being tinged with a degree of ethnocentrism and romantic élitism, they clearly reflect some very real and pressing problems. Root causes of conflict are where decisions regarding tourism development are taken without the consent of the host community by those who do not 'own', or live in, the area of development and where cultural sensitivities and nuances are neglected, and although tourism may be recognized as a legitimate, economic and culturally worthwhile goal, an imbalance in power relations and ownership entails there may not be any recompense.

In the urban context as discussed, apart from being problematic to identify and isolate, conflicts may remain submerged under a powerful ideology of economic and 'cultural' regeneration. It has become difficult to argue against the fact that a derelict riverside, for instance, should be transformed into a marina, visitor centre and shopping complex. Few would dispute the aesthetics, and although the economic arguments may be challenged, in the de-industrializing context they retain considerable currency. However, it is legitimate to enquire of the cultural impacts of such developments and the ideologies behind them.

Although extracted from a discussion of cultural citizenship and the resilience of national cultures in the globalization debate, Stevenson (1997, p. 53) notes that 'culture, if it is about anything, is intimately connected with meaningfulness'. As the novelty value of tourism begins to wear thin and as the boundaries between it and culture also dissolve, we need to turn our attention to what the supply and development end of tourism means in cultural terms, and in a variety of contexts.

Kearns and Philo (1993) focus on meaning and utilize the term of 'other peoples' in their critique of the processes by which places are being 'sold'. Though requiring development and further analysis in the tourism context, their observations are important:

> these 'other peoples' have relationships with the city – or, to be more precise, with the particular city places in which they live, work, rest and play and dream; often the places 'left over' after those with power have chosen theirs – that differ (often quite dramatically) from both the relationship lived by the bourgeoisie and the 'respectable' relationship intended for them by the bourgeoisie. And what we further want to claim is that these 'other peoples' hence possess other attachments to the city that differ from the arguably superficial attachments of the bourgeoisie – those to do with property-ownership and fancy possessions, the surface badges of cultural capital – and that alternative attachments of this sort are always shot through with meanings, though not necessarily in all that reflected upon a fashion, to the extent that these 'other peoples' will feel their lives to be seriously compromised if their particular city places are mistreated in any way.
>
> (Kearns and Philo, 1993, p. 16)

The 'other' is alive and well and living in Sunderland, and Doncaster, and

Glasgow, and Liverpool, and so on. The cultural renaissance of provincial Britain and its touristic consequences are inviting the 'other' to ask some probing questions such as; 'what the hell's this?', 'what use is that?', and 'why can't the money be better spent on *the other*?'

Without claims to exclusivity, this chapter has sought to highlight the context of UK de-industrializing provincial cities and towns. Tourism development as one of a number of elements in economic regeneration has been real, rapid and dramatic, and we need to know from those who are living through transition and within new cultural landscapes what this *means* to them in economic and cultural terms. There is clearly much that tourism can contribute to the visited urban communities, but without being able to identify the parameters of its meaningfulness we are in the dark when it comes to understanding its long-term cultural effects and the full extent of actual and potential conflicts. Hopefully the discussions contained in this chapter will spark interest in this matter, and further interdisciplinary research will extend the work that has been carried out in a developing world context to the urban centres of developed nations, allowing us to shed more light on these issues.

References

Appadurai, A. (1990) Disjuncture and difference in the global cultural economy. In: Featherstone, M. (ed.) *Global Culture – Nationalism, Globalization and Modernity*, Sage Publications Ltd, London, pp. 295–310.

Ashworth, G.J. (1992) Is there an urban tourism? *Tourism Recreation Research*, 17(2), pp. 3–8.

Ashworth, G.J. and Tunbridge, J.E. (1990) *The Tourist – Historic City*, Belhaven, London.

Ashworth, G.J. and Voogd, H. (1990) *Selling the City: Marketing Approaches in Public Sector Urban Planning*, Belhaven, London.

Association of District Councils (1986) *Tourism: It's the Districts Who Deliver*, Association of District Councils, London.

Barke, M. and Harrop, K. (1994) Selling the industrial town: identity, image and illusion. In: Gold, J.R. and Ward, S.V. (eds) *Place Promotion: The Use of Publicity and Marketing to Sell Towns and Regions*, John Wiley & Sons, Chichester, pp. 93–114.

Bauman, Z. (1996) From pilgrim to tourist – or a short history of identity. In: Hall, S. and DuGay, P. (eds) *Questions of Cultural Identity*, Sage Publications Ltd, London, pp. 18–36.

Bianchini, F. and Parkinson, M. (eds) (1993) *Cultural Policy and Urban Regeneration: The Western European Experience*, Manchester University Press, Manchester.

Bianchini, F. and Schwengel, H. (1991) Re-imagining the city. In: Corner, J. and Harvey, J. (eds) *Enterprise and Heritage – Crosscurrents of National Culture*, Routledge, London.

Boas, F. (1928) *Anthropology and Modern Life*, W.W. Norton & Co., New York.

Bourdieu, P. (1984) *Distinction: A Social Critique of the Judgement of Taste*, Routledge, London.

Boyle, M. and Hughes, G. (1991) The politics of 'the real': discourses from the Left on Glasgow's role as European City of Culture 1990, *Area*, 23, pp. 217–228.

Bramwell, B. and Rawding, L. (1994) Tourism marketing organizations in industrial cities: organizations, objectives and urban governance, *Tourism Management*, 15, pp. 425–435.

Bramwell, B. and Rawding, L. (1996) Tourism marketing images of industrial cities, *Annals of Tourism Research*, 23, pp. 201–221.

Britton, S. (1991) Tourism, capital and place: towards a critical geography of tourism, *Environment and Planning D: Society and Space*, 9, pp. 451–578.

Buckley, P.J. and Witt, S.F. (1985) Tourism in difficult areas: case studies of Bradford, Bristol, Glasgow and Hamm, *Tourism Management*, 6, pp. 205–213.

Buckley, P.J. and Witt, S.F. (1989) Tourism in difficult areas: case studies of Calderdale, Leeds, Manchester and Scunthorpe, *Tourism Management*, 10, pp. 138–152.

Butler, R. and Hinch, T. (eds) (1996) *Tourism and Indigenous Peoples*, Routledge, London.

Byrne, D. (1997) Chaotic places or complex places? Cities in a post-industrial era. In: Westwood, S. and Williams, J. (eds) *Imagined Cities: Scripts, Signs and Memories*, Routledge, London, pp. 50–73.

Campbell, B. (1993) *Goliath – Britain's Dangerous Places*, Methuen, London.

Casey, B., Selwood, S. and Dunlop, R. (1997) *Culture as Commodity? The Economics of the Arts and the Built Heritage in the UK*, Policy Studies Institute, London.

Chang, T.C., Milne, S., Fallon, D. and Pohlmann, C. (1996) Urban heritage tourism: the global–local nexus, *Annals of Tourism Research*, 23, pp. 284–305.

Cippola, C.M. (ed.) (1970) *The Economic Decline of Empires*, Penguin Books, London.

Clarke, J. and Critcher, C. (1985) *The Devil Makes Work: Leisure in Capitalist Britain*, Macmillan Press, London.

Coates, D. (1994) *The Question of UK Decline – The Economy, State and Society*, Harvester Wheatsheaf, London.

Cohen, A.P. (1985) *The Symbolic Construction of Community*, Ellis Horwood Ltd, Chichester.

Cohen, E. (1995) Contemporary tourism – trends and challenges: sustainable authenticity or contrived post-modernity? In: Butler, R. and Pearce, D. (eds) *Change in Tourism – People, Places, Processes*, Routledge, London, pp. 12–29.

Conforti, J.M. (1996) Ghettos as tourism attractions, *Annals of Tourism Research*, 23, pp. 830–842.

Craik, J. (1995) Are there cultural limits to tourism?, *Journal of Sustainable Tourism*, 3(2), pp. 87–98.

Crick, M. (1989) Representations of international tourism in the social sciences, *Annual Review of Anthropology*, 18, pp. 307–344.

Dabinett, G. (1995) Economic regeneration in Sheffield – urban modernization or the management of decline? In: Turner, R. (ed.) *The British Economy in Transition: From the Old to the New*, Routledge, London, pp. 218–239.

Danziger, N. (1996) *Danziger's Britain: A Journey to the Edge*, Harper Collins, London.

Dawson, J. and Parkinson, M. (1991) Merseyside Development Corporation

1981–1989 – Physical regeneration, accountability and economic challenge. In: Keith, M. and Rogers, A. (eds) *Hollow Promises? Rhetoric and Reality in the Inner City*, Mansell, London, pp. 43–61.

de Kadt, E. (ed.) (1979) *Tourism: Passport to Development?*, Oxford University Press, London.

Department for Culture, Media and Sport (1997) 'New deal offers a great deal says Chris Smith', *Press Release, DCMS 129/97*, 24 November, Department for Culture, Media and Sport.

Edwards, J. (1997) Urban policy: the victory of form over substance?, *Urban Studies*, 34(5), pp. 825–845.

Edwards, A. and Llurdés i Coit, J.C. (1996) Mines and quarries – industrial heritage tourism, *Annals of Tourism Research*, 1, pp. 341–363.

Friedman, J. (1994) *Cultural Identity and Global Process*, Sage Publications Ltd, London.

Gault, M. (1989) *Villes Intermediairies pour L'Europe*, Syros, Paris.

Greenwood, D. (1989) Culture by the pound: an anthropological perspective on tourism as cultural commoditization. In: Smith, V. (ed.) *Hosts and Guests: The Anthropology of Tourism*, 2nd edn., University of Pennsylvania Press, Philadelphia, pp. 171–185.

Hannerz, U. (1996) *Transnational Connections – Culture, People, Places*, Routledge, London.

Harris, N. (1997) Cities in a global economy: structural change and policy reactions, *Urban Studies*, 34(10), pp. 1693–1705.

Harvey, D. (1989) *The Urban Experience*, Blackwell, Oxford.

Haywood, K.M. (1992) Identifying and responding to challenges posed by urban tourism, *Tourism Recreation Research*, 17(2), pp. 9–23.

Hewison, R. (1987) *The Heritage Industry: Britain in a Climate of Decline*, Methuen, London.

Hewison, R. (1995) *Culture and Consensus – England, Art and Politics since 1940*, Methuen, London.

Hewison, R. (1996) Cultural policy and the heritage business, *The European Journal of Cultural Policy*, 3(1), pp. 1–13.

Holcomb, B. (1994) City make-overs: marketing the post-industrial city. In: Gold, J.R. and Ward, S.V. (eds) *Place Promotion: The Use of Publicity and Marketing to Sell Towns and Regions*, John Wiley & Sons, Chichester, pp. 115–131.

Hutton, W. (1996) *The State We're In*, Vintage, London.

Independent Commission on International Humanitarian Issues (1996) *Indigenous Peoples – A Global Quest for Justice*, Zed Books Ltd, London.

Jansen-Verbeke, M. (1986) Inner city tourism – resources, tourists and promoters, *Annals of Tourism Research*, 13, pp. 79–100.

Jewson, N. and MacGregor, S. (eds) (1997) *Transforming Cities: Contested Governance and New Spatial Divisions*, Routledge, London.

Johnes, G. and Taylor, J. (1996) The structure of the economy. In: Artis, M.J. (ed.) *The UK Economy – A Manual of Applied Statistics*, Oxford University Press, Oxford, pp. 29–51.

Karski, A. (1990) Urban tourism – a key to urban regeneration?, *The Planner*, 6 April, pp. 15–17.

Kearns, G. and Philo, C. (1993) Culture, history, capital: a critical introduction to the selling of places. In: Kearns, G. and Philo, C. (eds) *Selling Places – The City as*

Cultural Capital, Past and Present, Pergamon Press, Oxford, pp. 1–32.

Keith, M. and Rogers, A. (eds) (1991) *Hollow Promises? Rhetoric and Reality in the Inner City,* Mansell, London.

Kotler, P., Haider, D.H. and Rein, I. (1993) *Marketing Places: Attracting Investment, Industry and Tourism to Cities, States and Nations,* Free Press, New York.

Krippendorf, J. (1987) *The Holiday Makers – Understanding the Impact of Leisure and Travel,* Heinemann, Oxford.

Lanfant, M.F. (1995) International tourism, internationalization and the challenge to identity. In: Lanfant, M.F., Allcock, J.B., Bruner, E.M. (eds) *International Tourism – Identity and Change,* pp. 24–43.

Lasch, C. (1985) *The Minimal Self: Psychic Survival in Troubled Times.* Pan Books, London.

Law, C.M. (1993) *Urban Tourism – Attracting Visitors to Large Cities,* Mansell, London.

Law, C.M. (1996) Tourism in British provincial cities: a tale of four cities. In: Law, C.M. (ed.) *Tourism in Major Cities,* International Thomson Business Press, London, pp. 179–205.

Lengkeek, J. (1993) Collective and private interest in recreation and tourism – the Dutch case: concerning consequences of a shift from citizen role to consumer role, *Leisure Studies,* 12, pp. 7–32.

Loftman, P. and Spirou, C.S. (1996) Sports, stadiums and urban regeneration: the British and United States experience. Paper presented at the conference Tourism and Culture: Towards the 21st Century, University of Northumbria, Longhirst Hall, Morpeth.

McGuigan, J. (1996) *Culture and the Public Sphere,* Routledge, London.

Martin, S. (1995) From workshop to meeting place? – the Birmingham economy in transition. In: Turner, R. (ed.) *The British Economy in Transition: From the Old to the New,* Routledge, London, pp. 199–217.

Martinotti, G. (1996) The new social morphology of cities, *Management of Social Transformations Discussion Papers Series,* No.16, UNESCO, Paris.

Meethan, K. (1996) Consuming (in) the civilized city, *Annals of Tourism Research,* 23, pp. 322–340.

Merseyside Tourism and Conference Bureau (1997) *Liverpool and Merseyside Visitor Guide,* Merseyside Tourism and Conference Bureau.

Morris, M. (1995) Life as a tourist object in Australia. In: Lanfant, M.F., Allcock, J. and Bruner, E. (eds) *International Tourism: Identity and Change,* Sage Publications Ltd, London, pp. 177–191.

Morris, P. (1991) Freeing the spirit of enterprise: the genesis and development of the concept of enterprise. In: Keat, R. and Abercrombie, N. (eds) *Enterprise Culture,* Routledge, London, pp. 21–38.

Newcastle upon Tyne City Council (1997) *Newcastle City Profiles – Results from the 1996 Inter-Censusal Survey,* Newcastle upon Tyne City Council.

Office for National Statistics (1997) *Annual Abstract of Statistics,* The Stationery Office, London.

Owen, C. (1990) Tourism and urban regeneration, *Cities,* August, pp. 194–201.

Page, S. (1995) *Urban Tourism,* Routledge, London.

Page, S. (1997) Urban tourism: analysing and evaluating the tourist experience. In: Ryan, C. (ed.) *The Tourist Experience – A New Introduction,* Cassell, London, pp. 112–135.

Papson, S. (1981) Spuriousness and tourism: politics of two Canadian provincial governments, *Annals of Tourism Research*, 8, pp. 220–235.

Parkinson, M. (1996) Twenty-five years of urban policy in Britain – partnership, entrepreneurialism or competition?, *Public Money and Management*, July–September, CIPFA, pp. 7–14.

Purcell, K. and Quinn, J. (1996) Exploring the education–employment equation in hospitality management: a comparision of graduates and HNDs, *International Journal of Hospitality Management*, 15, pp. 51–68.

Rawls, J. (1971) *A Theory of Justice*, Harvard University Press, Cambridge.

Reisinger, Y. (1994) Social contact between tourists and hosts of different cultural backgrounds. In: Seaton, A.V. (ed.) *Tourism – The State of the Art*, John Wiley & Sons, Chichester, pp. 743–755.

Roche, M. (1992) Mega-events and micro-modernization: on the sociology of the new urban tourism, *British Journal of Sociology*, 43(4), pp. 563–600.

Rojek, C. (1993) *Ways of Escape: Modern Transformations in Leisure and Travel*, Macmillan, Basingstoke.

Rojek, C. and Urry, J. (1997) Transformations of travel and theory. In: Rojek, C. and Urry, J. (eds) *Touring Cultures – Transformations of Travel and Theory*, Routledge, London, pp. 1–19.

Rowthorn, B. (1986) Deindustrialization in Britain, In: Martin, R. and Rowthorn, B. (eds) *The Geography of Deindustrialization*, Macmillan, London, pp. 1–30.

Rubinstein, W.D. (1990) Cultural explanations for Britain's economic decline: how true? In: Collins, B. and Robbins, K. (eds) *British Culture and Economic Decline*, Weidenfeld and Nicolson, London, pp. 59–91.

Ryan, C. (1995) *Researching Tourism Satisfaction: Issues, Concepts, Problems*, Routledge, London.

Sachs, I. (1994) The environmental challenge. In: Salomon, J.J., Sagasti, F. and Sachs-Jeantet, C. (eds) *The Uncertain Quest*, United Nations University, Tokyo, pp. 302–339.

Sachs-Jeantet, C. (1996) Managing social transformations in cities, *Management of Social Transformations Discussion Papers Series*, No. 2, UNESCO, Paris.

Sadler, D. (1993) Place-marketing, competitive places and the construction of hegemony in Britain in the 1980s. In: Kearns, G. and Philo, C. (eds) *Selling Places – The City as Cultural Capital, Past and Present*, Pergamon Press, Oxford, pp. 175–192.

Scott, A.J. (1997) The cultural economy of cities, *International Journal of Urban and Regional Research*, 21(2), pp. 323–329.

Shaw, G. and Williams, A.M. (1994) *Critical Issues in Tourism: A Geographical Perspective*, Blackwell, Oxford.

Short, J.R. (1991) *Imagined Country – Society, Culture and Environment*, Routledge, London.

Smith, D.M. (1989) *North and South – Britain's Economic, Social and Political Divide*, Penguin Books, Harmondsworth.

Smith, V. ed. (1989) *Hosts and Guests*: The Anthropology of Tourism, 2nd edn., University of Pennsylvania Press, Philadelphia.

Smith, I. and Stone, I. (1989) Foreign investment in the North: distinguishing fact from hype, *Northern Economic Review*, 18, pp. 50–61.

Smyth, H. (1994) *Marketing the City: The Role of Flagship Developments in Urban Regeneration*, E & F.N. Spon, London.

Stevenson, N. (1997) Globalization, national cultures and cultural citizenship, *The Sociological Quarterly*, 38(1), pp. 41–66.

Taylor, I. and Jameson, R. (1997) Proper little mesters – nostalgia and protest, masculinity in deindustrialized Sheffield. In: Westwood, S. and Williams, J. (eds) *Imagined Cities: Scripts, Signs and Memories*, Routledge, London, pp. 152–178.

Tye, R. and Williams, G. (1994) Urban regeneration and Central–Local Government relations: the case of East Manchester, *Progress in Planning*, 42, pp. 1–97.

United Nations (1986/87) *Document No. E/CN.4/Sub.2/Add.4*, para 379.

Urry, J. (1990) *The Tourist Gaze: Leisure and Travel in Contemporary Society*, Sage Publications Ltd, London.

Urry, J. (1994) Cultural change and contemporary tourism, *Leisure Studies*, 13, pp. 233–238.

Urry, J. (1995) *Consuming Places*, Routledge, London.

van den Berg, L. van der Borg, J. and van der Meer, J. (1994) *Urban Tourism*, Erasmus University, Rotterdam.

Wearing, B. and Wearing, S. (1992) Identity and the commodification of leisure, *Leisure Studies*, 11, p. 8.

Weiner, M.J. (1985) *English Culture and the Decline of the Industrial Spirit 1850–1980*, Penguin Books, Harmondsworth.

Williams, R. (1993) Culture is ordinary. In: Gray, A. and McGuigan, J. (eds) *Studying Culture: An Introductory Reader*, Edward Arnold, London, pp. 5–14.

World Commission on Culture and Development (1995) *Our Creative Diversity – Report of the World Commission on Culture and Development*, UNESCO Publishing, Paris.

Zukin, S. (1991) *Landscapes of Power*, University of California Press, Berkley.

Zukin, S. (1996) Cultural strategies of economic development and the hegemony of vision. In: Merrifield, A. and Swyngedou, E. (eds) *The Urbanization of Injustice*, Lawrence & Wishart, London, pp. 223–243.

Zukin, S. (1997) *The Cultures of Cities*, 2nd edn., Blackwell, Oxford.

7

Trading Culture: Tourism and Tourist Art in Pisac, Peru

Jane Henrici

Introduction

The following chapter will argue that touristic discourse yields a 'misrecognition' of economic and social relations by circulating distorted representations; such misrecognition helps perpetuate conflicts and inequalities. Touristic discourse is seen here as including narratives such as those used in promoting tourism to the southern highland Peruvian village of Pisac as well as in re-creating the village through everyday acts of selling and manufacturing tourist art. While the term 'touristic discourse' indicates the circulation of tourism, its participants, and their exchanges, 'southern highland' references the geography and peoples of the Andes Mountains south of the Amazon Basin. Both categories currently encompass Pisac crafts and their sales.

The space of the village of Pisac contains within it diversity and disparity, yet touristic representations of Pisac and its art present a sense of uniform timelessness. Shifting relations and acts of discomforting disadvantage do not appear within touristic expressions of local identity. Touristic discourse instead emphasizes cultural stereotypes, stressing similarity or contrast in style and custom, and eclipses existing inequalities in power and wealth.

Pisac craftspersons paint reproductions of archaeological motifs on ceramics and participate in reproducing certain stereotypic and conventional images regarding themselves and their visitors in order to sell crafts. Stylized presentations of identity are common within types of social interactions everywhere. However, as will be argued below, standardized representations within international tourism turn attention away from disparities that

 Tourism and Cultural Conflicts
(eds M. Robinson and P. Boniface)

exist among residents of a tourist site as well as between them and the tourists who visit. Circumstances in Pisac are representative of this.

Pisac village is a district centre resting along a river bank underneath mountain peaks, a grid of dusty streets at about 3000 metres above sea level, built up around a colonial-era square with its elements of a church façade, government building and tourist hotel. The valley village straddles, with inns and dining halls, the paved road that connects the historical city of Cuzco to the archaeological site of Machu Picchu. Its location, somewhere between urban centre and ancient outpost, is the primary feature of tourism promotions: Pisac carries the label of a 'traditional market' with the implication that visitors there will experience a display of local rural ethnicity and old-style forms of commerce. This touristic image emphasizes the rustic context of the little town as it sits with agricultural fields spreading into the distance on either side, although it somewhat ignores the complex archaeological Inca ruins nestling on mountain ledges and terraces in the distance above the colonial-period plaza. Contemporary stucco buildings in Pisac contain fragments of pre-Conquest walls while the mould-made crafts there display notations of ancient designs; all such attributes are maintained carefully by tourism industrialists and locals in presenting the centrepiece of the village as its market square filled with vendors (see Fig. 7.1).

Meanwhile, the mountain peaks behind and above the village of Pisac support smaller communities and single homes that are part of the Pisac district. These mountain dwellings belong to the individuals who typically wear ethnic clothing, speak the indigenous idiom of Quechua as their primary language, and hike down to Pisac for certain transactions and events. These are the persons who primarily form the colourful subject matter for tourism advertising of the valley-based market despite the fact that many of them live outside the village.

On geopolitical maps, Pisac district forms a long rectangle that slices back and up from the Vilcanota River bank, surrounds the village's smaller square inside the section of the river valley and includes the ascending mountain tops with their households and communities. Within touristic discourse, the village is the centre of all craft production and exchange while the other communities of the district are absent or appear merely as suppliers of the costumed farmers who come in to the town each Sunday to trade or sell their land's produce.

Misrecognition and Touristic Discourse

Touristic imaging and tourism's participants assist in the perpetuation of conflict through manifesting a 'misrecognition' of relations of power. Pierre Bourdieu (1977) first presented the term misrecognition as part of his model describing the gift, in which gift-giving excludes even the possibility of disinterestedness through an accepted but non-vocalized implementation of

Fig. 7.1. Pisac market plaza and church façade.

time on the part of those making an exchange. It is tacit that the recipient of a present or other gesture should not respond immediately with a reciprocal gift in order to avoid making obvious either obligation or ritual element. Once time 'passes', then a shared illusion of altruism permits a misrecognition of social relations. Bourdieu later elaborated misrecognition as part of the operation of maintaining dominance within a society. Pressure, authority and demand become tempered and hidden. This occurs through a complicit but denied disguising of relationships as if all are equal but separated only by time, that is, by historical situation and position (Bourdieu and Wacquant, 1992). Within global tourism, assumed distinctions of time appear in terms of relative level of modernization, development, societal complexity or sophistication and thus achieve parity for participants while marking differences only of detail. That only one sector of those involved in an exchange actually sets the operation in motion and defines its terms and conditions remains without mention. Unfairness and differentiation seem absent as long as everyone goes along with the illusion of a relative equality merely seasoned by cultural diversity and historical circumstance.

The circulation of tourist art, and of touristic discourse in general, is an aspect of modernity and its power relations. Tourist art production is a particular form of 'modernization' insofar as it tends to be the domain of persons in so-called developing societies. As is generally the case with constructs of social change such as that of 'modernization', seemingly contradictory images appear and reappear in touristic discourse (Williams, 1973; and with specific reference to tourism see: Turner, 1976; Feifer, 1985; Urry, 1990; Buzard, 1993; Kinnaird *et al.*, 1994).

Such contradictions pattern images of tourism's participants and of tourist art within social scientific texts, industry advertising and market-place dialogues (Crang, 1997). Certain researchers have suggested alternatives (Richter, 1995; Butler and Hinch, 1996). Nevertheless, misrecognition of relationships within tourism occurs through the tendency of touristic discourse to conflate certain oppositions and conventionalize others and in this way elude criticism. Ethnographic reports and analyses also yield easily to such obscuring demarcations and various presentation styles now seek to resist this. In the following, this chapter uses a device established in contemporary anthropological literature of acknowledging the presence of the ethnographer as the 'I' who also participates in confusions and conflicts within the discourse. Presentation of text from field narratives in the first person is an attempt to avoid disguising the voice of the researcher as neutral and authoritative.

The issue of authority is important within the character of touristic discourse and relates to the issue of what is called 'authenticity' in tourism and travel. Authenticity as a problematic might be seen in some ways as the attempt to reconcile connotation and denotation within sales and other narratives among tourists, agents and vendors. In analysis of this, Dean MacCannell (1973, 1976) asserts that all tourism experiences are 'staged' while other authors argue against the existence of an authentic tourism experience and consider any communicative act as imitation (for a response see Bourdieu and Haacke, 1995). Regardless, discussion has thrived in touristic discourse measuring the validity of travellers' assessments of a scene, as well as measuring the validity of the scene itself, even though such commentary shows that all such classifications and evaluations cannot be quantifiable given their ethnocentric quality (Megaw, 1982; MacCannell, 1984; Ascher, 1985; Pearce and Moscardo, 1985, 1986; Cohen, 1988; Crick, 1989; Crew and Sims, 1991; Shiner, 1994; van den Berghe, 1994; Kirshenblatt-Gimblett, 1995; Castañeda, 1996; Crang, 1997).

Authenticity as a marker of awareness and, simultaneously, of ingenuousness or innocence in turn connects to the concern within modernizing tendencies to note difference among social groups as respective stages of societal evolution and economic development (Crang, 1997). Stamping people and their products and practices with labels of 'traditional' or 'commercialized', 'discriminating' or 'ignorant', can reinforce a Western model of balance between the masses visited and those who come to explore, and between those who supposedly recognize the authentic from those who supposedly represent it. With an emphasis on cultural exchange as neutral and equal, any disparities within the event or image may be construed as due to variance in levels of modernization or socialization among those involved in touristic transactions rather than to relational separation and an imbalance of control. Ethnicity as an aspect of identity becomes a label of authenticity that certain people, those with the 'authority' of expertise, may give to other people or an art form.

Classifications of tourism's participants in literature and market-place gossip elaborate on such labels of assumed similarity and difference. Descriptions abound regarding a relative awareness and appreciation among an élite, sometimes called 'travellers', in contrast to a credulity and/or corruptibility among those who are merely 'tourists' as well as among those who are toured (Feifer, 1985; Urry, 1990; Buzard, 1993; Rojek, 1993; Trinh, 1994). Meanwhile, ethnicity and identity are defined as imagined by one group, performed and produced by another, and then discussed in terms of whether the consumer-creator is able to discriminate the fake from the real (Boynton, 1997).

Cultural and personal attributes are linked within touristic discourse to certain stages in development, or lack of development, which contributes to misrecognition of power relations. Through highlighting cultural exchange as if it is a broad form of gift-giving between equals separated merely by relative position on a formative time-line, touristic discourse obscures any disadvantaged interchange among groups or populations.

Comings and Goings in Pisac

As a manifestation of Bourdieu's concept of misrecognition, touristic discourse evades rather than acknowledges disparity among tourism's participants while asserting claims to the contrary. Important in the Peruvian tourist site of Pisac is the observable and ongoing economic differentiation separating those living in the mercantile valley village from district residents living in surrounding mountainside farming communities, and between resident villagers and visiting tourists. Tourism does bring a supply, albeit an unreliable one, of cash into Pisac and is a major part of survival there. It is unsurprising that the portrayals generated locally and elsewhere of Pisac tourism and its art ignore relative disadvantages and celebrate cultural trades. Stylized images used by Pisac artisans and vendors respond to the elements of misrecognition found in touristic discourse such as demands for authenticity and emphases on cultural difference. Throughout touristic discourse the whims of some and the hardships of others determine exchanges and, through distortion of that situation, misrecognition serves to maintain it.

Fig. 7.2. Pisac vendor's display.

As elsewhere in the world, development tourism did not begin what is called modernization in Pisac. Economic differentiation, cultural diversity, wage labour, and mercantilism existed in the district long before the presence of the touristic as an entrepreneurial form. With the fomentation of tourist art production, such village phenomena became predominantly touristic over three decades. In particular, hand-painted clay beads have gone into mass production and marketing along with craftwork of a variety of media. Those artisans who set up many of the first workshops as part of a national tourism development project have continued to make or have made delicate ceramic objects with elaborate, pre-Hispanic style painted designs; now, almost everyone in the village makes or at least sells small mould-ware clay pieces, jewellery beads and other similarly portable touristic goods (Figs 7.2 and 7.3).

Both the village of Pisac and its surrounding district have been researched over decades, and reports show that cultural and economic diversities within the zone were present before and despite tourism development (Castillo Ardiles, 1970; Nuñez del Prado, 1973). Ceramic manufacture for tourist and export sale began in Pisac in the late 1960s through government-sponsored training as part of a national tourism development plan. Individual artisans later established workshops with piece labourers and expanded sales. Several non-governmental organizations (NGOs) and alternative trading organizations (ATOs) joined the government in taking an interest in Pisac artisanry. Ceramic production for tourist and export sale dominated the

Fig. 7.3. Mixed motifs on tourist ware.

activities of the Peruvian village of Pisac by the 1980s and influenced some involvement on the part of mountain-dwellers in the surrounding district as well. With this change in subsistence source, *piseños* interviewed during 1988–1990 stated that they were able to an extent to subsidize both traditional and more modernizing customs despite extreme national economic fluctuations.

Subsequent research conducted in 1996 with support from the PromPerú Summer Internship Programme indicates that the ceramic art of Pisac and nearby sites expanded in output during recent years among the primary craftspersons who continued production. In addition, artisans from Pisac who left during low tourism years and migrated to other Latin American nations have influenced production and design elsewhere, so that there is a small diffusion of Cuzco–Pisac designs and techniques at present. A cactus and llama motif, painted in diverse colours and surrounded by pre-Hispanic patterns, has become popularized on beads worn on jewellery internationally (Fig. 7.4). Foreign importers continue to arrive in Pisac in order to make personal contacts for long-term purchasing and shipping contracts; these contacts remain the secrets of importers in their home nations while local craftspersons pocket business cards printed in English and Japanese and hope that payment materializes. Smoky orange fires from eucalyptus-burning clay kilns appear at night in the village along with the smaller red lamps of occasional electric kilns and the buttery glow of workshop light bulbs. Throughout Pisac, individuals and entrepreneurs with full-time employees keep working at the business of craft production for tourist and export sale.

Fig. 7.4. Hand-painted Pisac bead necklaces.

According to the residents of Pisac, tourist art activities have increased distinctions among those participating in tourist sales from others in the village, whether the others are wage labourers in other occupations, small-scale farmers or local store owners. Reportedly, those in tourism have greater access to cash and credit and this justifies villagers continuing with, or switching to, tourist art manufacture and merchandising despite their difficulties. Different villagers said that plans or desires such as putting together a more adorned saint's day dance costume or sending a child to a reportedly better school in Cuzco would rest on the financial ability accorded by tourist and export art sales. Certain families seek to send a member to vend goods in another country while others try to feed themselves through purchased foodstuffs, since some consider farm land to be unavailable and most consider it cost-ineffective. Recently, tourist art sales continued to be financially supportive although most of those who had become ceramic workshop owners by the 1980s had become, by the 1990s, middle merchants of goods crafted elsewhere.

As an income source, tourism to Peru had a large decline in the late 1980s for a variety of reasons, including the infamy of insurgent and counter-insurgent violence as well as a cholera epidemic that began along Peru's coast. That decline reversed somewhat with the well-publicized Peruvian military actions to end anti-government militancy and the reduction of the cholera threat. Peruvian national tourism development programming resumed in importance in the 1990s. Another factor within Peruvian tourism in the 1990s is the intensification of travels by nationals throughout Peru, particularly in the form of so-called adventure holidays. This tendency towards national tourism has somewhat changed Peru's emphasis on international visitors but has not eliminated them as significant within the GNP. It has also modified the near certainty of visiting Pisac within standard tours; however, the people of Pisac observed by mid-decade a general return of tourism as a relatively steady income source (Powers, 1994).

During the years 1984–1990, the quantity of foreign tourists to Pisac decreased but economic inflation increased. Political dangers and sudden jumps in prices became routine at that time, particularly for those in the provinces, and this included to some extent those of the district of Pisac. Craft production and selling nevertheless continued within the southern highland area, and some village craft vendors have expanded their work into the hostelry and restaurant trades now that tourism has revived.

Determination and desperation have combined at different moments within Pisac tourist art production. In addition, there remain the ongoing and ancient frictions: among families, between the village and the city of Cuzco which dominates the region, between men as artisans and women as vendors, between villagers and foreign craft workers and sellers who try to set up competing stalls in Pisac, between villagers and the farmers dwelling in the mountainside communities, and among villager political parties and aspirants. These ongoing tensions were not minor in comparison, for example, to an assassination on Pisac's bridge in 1988, but are relational. The incursion of tourists and its requisite complexities are also an aspect of these interconnections and conflicts.

Artisans of the Touristic: Misrecognition and Authenticity

Locals to a tourist site might calculate and even give 'staged' performances but generally may not determine which so-called authenticity is authoritative. Many Pisac villagers take one approach or another to attempt to take from outsiders any domination over their situation but the disparities between *piseños* and others are evident in what may be categorized as issues of class, gender, ethnicity and nationalism.

In particular, Pisac residents, tourists and development workers have become complicit with the misrecognition found in a sense of authenticity and changelessness associated with the mountain-dwelling *indios* (those wearing traditional clothing and of whom tourists take photos). Villagers have long expected and even demanded on occasion that those of the mountain communities of the district – often Quechua speakers and generally poorer farmers – would descend from the hillsides as they have for centuries on Sunday market days and feast days. However, now this effort occurs not only for the long-established objectives of selling produce, attending mass and taking care of political business but also in order to lure tourists. This expectation on the part of village merchants may be seen as a re-engagement of customary pressures and obligations between valley and mountain residents and among the different valley dwellers (Castillo Ardiles, 1970). It is important to note, however, that any bond of unequal but mutual dependence is weaker in these circumstances than in farmer–trader exchanges: the physical presence of the *indios* as an invocation of the indigenous and the past is itself no longer essential to a maintenance of the touristic in Pisac. Indeed, when hillside *comuneros* are absent, sometimes in protest regarding local political conditions, the mixed-ancestry villagers simply assert their own genetic and cultural connections to a native heritage while selling to incoming tourists. Such merchandising stresses inherited rather than contemporary ties. This self-perpetuation of a touristic myth of Pisac reveals the distancing and misrecognition that characterizes the current and unacknowledged relationship between these two groups; perhaps the touristic influence separates these populations even further in that little agrarian productivity or labour now influences valley economic activity, and full-time mountain farmers, regardless of ethnic costume, have less power than ever before. Indeed, recent activities on the part of aid organizations formerly dedicated exclusively to farming and herding in Pisac now seek to assist hillside residents' supplemental involvement in tourist and export art production (Alex Chavez, Director, CEDEP-Allyu, Cuzco, July 1996, personal communication). Tensions and difficulties dividing those with the power connected to national politics and the routes to commerce from those in the isolated mountain peaks thus continue and take on new terms within the tourism trade. Meanwhile, the representation of Pisac within tourist discourse as a site of 'traditional' Andean marketing becomes both a mask villagers assume when useful and a now broken weapon once wielded by *comuneros* in their attempts to claim demands of the merchants.

Another important disparity in relations exacerbated as part of touristic discourse is that between genders. Men more than women may be artisans, the former judging the latter as generally not very good at ceramic crafts. Pisac villagers themselves no longer weave textiles as a rule, although women in the village often share a great deal of information about traditional designs, dyes and techniques, and might be the family specialists in purchasing older weavings from others to sell in the market. Women also tend to be the most respected vendors in the market-place to individual shoppers. However, men dominate the tourist business that dominates the village – of making, buying, and selling for export, quantities of tourist ceramic ware.

Most villagers, men and women, take for granted that every Sunday and holiday, quantities of poorer but more 'colourful' *indios*, particularly the photogenic young girls and old men in their respective costumes, will walk for the hours it takes to come down from the mountain peaks and enter the village by its back way through ancient Inca ruins. Meanwhile, *piseños* pause often in their handicraft work to look anxiously for tourist buses descending along the mountain highway at Pisac's front entrance. The merchants and artisans, and the *comuneros* posing for photographs, have learned to labour within the circulation of touristic discourse to persuade customers to enjoy buying representations of local identity. However, the consumer as participant receives greater power to authenticate than the local even, as each vendor of Pisac works hard to keep the tourist shopping.

Pisac merchants meanwhile have taught themselves to debate with any traveller the authenticity of any item. Cries in various languages appear among the plaza stalls of 'genuine baby alpaca [wool]' and 'hand-made'. Only within the tourist market, Pisac women argue, would buyers not know enough about the product to have to ask if the item is 'real' and expect in their ignorance an honest answer from the struggling vendor even if it lost a sale. Conversely, merchant women in Pisac made a show for tourists of challenging the authenticity of the US 100 dollar bills the buyers submitted for exchange, insisting that a visiting US ethnographer test her nation's product of paper money for forgeries before completing each transaction. Villagers thus contribute to a weaker position for themselves through a reproduction of touristic imagery, but occasionally subvert touristic discourse by challenging, within the rhetoric, the authority of visitors.

> Initially, villagers attempted to identify me by requesting assistance with tasks that appeared to involve somewhat gender-specific activities such as child care and my performance usually elicited criticism or laughter. Viewing me as an outsider, some *piseños* alleged that I was a trouble-maker while others said that I had links to authority and great quantities of money with the power to intervene in local issues. In part, the identification of an individual's role in village life seemed to be according to the use to which s/he might be put and I thus felt more accepted when townspeople gave me chores they decided I handled all right.
>
> I eventually began to feel comfortably taken for granted. With this, villagers could evaluate out loud my hair, skin, and weight and profession; I learned to wear clothing that could gain approval without appearing insultingly distinctive, and my lifestyle at least did not give grounds for scandal. I imagined that I was a familiar outsider and of no particular interest. By this time, those persons who pointed me out in Pisac as entirely separate, unique, and out-of-place – to the point of speaking to me as if no *piseños* were present – were those who were themselves also transitory or marginal to the town. I include in that category most of the gigolo-type men from the city seeking tourists with cash, some of the villagers' relatives who visited for holidays and family celebrations, and, most particularly, the tourists.
>
> Once, I was peeling corn in order to make a cake; cake baking having turned out to be my most valued ability in the village apart from translating dialogue and 'testing' US currency in market transactions. I peeled with my thumbnails the tooth-sized yellow kernels into a bowl while sitting in the stall of María Luisa, my landlady. She herself twisted with her steel needle-nose pliers a coil of silver alloy wire into necklace hooks. María Luisa and I chatted with neighboring vendors between attempted sales as we perched on the alpaca shawls and sweaters purchased for resale now layering her stall's wooden-slatted platform. Part of our concentration remained on the tourists who cruised the crowded and labyrinthine paths among the blue plastic-

sheltered stalls and occasionally stopped to finger and sometimes buy goods.

One tourist, a tall, pale man dressed in wrinkled and beige-toned clothes, approached with his *mestizo* translator-guide in tow. Both men moved with intensity and evaded my friends' hawking cries and gestures. Abruptly, in the midst of examining the items in an adjacent stall, the tourist grabbed my ponytail and held it up for the inspection of the translator and said with a pause-laden German accent, 'No. . . . es . . . local!'

The nearby male vendors responded as they had come to do in imitation of the most successful women merchants regarding any issue of authenticity and protested that the object of discussion was indeed of local provenance. Laughing, they took the joke they were making on the tourist, on me, and on village selling tactics even further and made it one on the orientation of the entire tourist town: they claimed with exclamations to the foreigner that I, too, was for sale.

In making these assertions, the men only occasionally employed their memorized phrases of German or English. Their carefulness seemed as clever as their attempted use of these languages in other contexts. That is, the presence of the translator and the tourist's own awkward speech indicated that the man could be safely ridiculed in Spanish. He could be mocked through a reinforcing of difference as someone merely beginning in his learning of that market language (as opposed to the Quechua spoken to many old people, certain laborers, and those of the communities) if indeed he were not comprehending their words. In addition, through this very lack of comprehension, he remained a still-potential customer to avoid offending.

María Luisa laughed briefly at all of this without raising her eyes from her fingers working the jewelry wire. She thus gave the performing men, with their family's intergenerationally tense relationship to her own, a listening but not viewing audience. She made no verbal response in this context to their loose invocation of 'authenticity' although at other times, when sales of artisanry were involved, she had expressed anger regarding that strategy.

Finally, María Luisa looked up just long enough to eye the tourist and his lack of interest in buying anything from her display of craftwork. She then returned to twisting her wire, Rosario and Nicolas let off teasing the tourist, and I returned to peeling the corn kernels. The Sunday-market visitor moved on to look elsewhere and dragged his guide with him.

(excerpted from Henrici, 1996a, 1996b)

Crafting a Future Past

Centuries of travel – by settlers, traders, colonizers and tourists – have been intrinsic to interactions among diverse groups in Peru. Nevertheless, points of contact seem, in certain dialogue, as demarcations of rupture rather than as episodes elemental to, and participating with, ongoing situations and relations. This perspective of 'loss' or 'discovery' in turn contributes to the concretizing of spatial and temporal characteristics found within the misrecognition of dominant touristic discourse (Diller and Scofidio, 1994).

Fig. 7.5. Hand-painted Pisac ash trays.

Ruptures of contact show up throughout tourism's histories as both educating to the modern (by means of a 'glimpse of the past') and modernizing, or at least also educating, to the non-modern. In this way, tourism appears as complementary to modernization as well as its tool. Texts show touristic and tourist art as functions of modernization and functioning to produce it. Conditions of disparity do not appear within the misrecognition of these representations so 'cultures' meeting each other seem like neutral forces making contact (see Pratt, 1992).

The 'past' remains significantly present within traditional Peruvian historiography and Peru's established, if altering, tourism business; it also conditions the daily exchanges among those of the village of Pisac and those shopping for souvenirs there. This sense of 'loss' connects to nostalgia for an 'authenticity', and both are features of the assumed historical and cultural gulf between tourist artisan and client. In order to successfully keep a demand for their goods, artisans and small-scale businesses must work with the not-for-sale connotations of tourist art – a sort of purity and innocence that employs terms such as authentic, 'made-by-hand', and 'all natural materials' – while selling such goods through entrepreneurship and exportation (Fig. 7.5).

Certain items which have come to be called 'tourist art' are designed, made, bought and displayed globally. Throughout the world, crafts are turned out for sale as gifts or souvenirs. The collecting of mementoes from what is past or passing has become a component of virtually all travel. Advice on selective shopping now forms part of any tour guide and newspaper, and classification of touring types by sociologists and anthropologists often incorporates Bourdieu-like descriptions of distinctive souvenir practices (Urry, 1990). In addition, exporting handicrafts remains an important business for countries seeking new forms of trade with economically stronger and industrialized nations. Large quantities of goods are in demand from small-scale producers like the villagers in Pisac in order to minimize training and infrastructure needs in poorer regions while yielding high profit-margin and tariff-free items for sale.

Three aspects of small-scale tourist art manufacture remain problematic worldwide: (i) the dependence on fashion tastes, generally of the non-producing culture; (ii) the use of resources that are expedient in the short term but which may have socially or environmentally negative repercussions in the long term; and (iii) the rapid expansion of production to the point of saturated supply and unprofitable prices (Henrici, 1997). These characteristics occur within Pisac. However, none are unique to tourist art as a product as opposed to any other insurgent industry, and it is impossible to isolate tourism or tourism development as the cause. Rhetoric surrounding tourism development, as with that surrounding modernization in general, nevertheless ascribes such changes as either somewhat progressive or immoral, depending on the stance. Assumptions about the power of tourism to alter forever the quality and character of a people or place, ironically the very features marketed as unchanged within tourism business, colour judgements regarding tourist art as an activity and a product, even though actual inequalities seem to be invisible. Sometimes, seeking tourist art as an income source might be a challenge to existing circumstances on the part of those persons who are the most disempowered.

> A group of mountain dwellers from the community of Cuyo Grande asked my assistance in approaching non-governmental organizations for export trade. These *comuneros* (as the Quechua-speakers called themselves in Spanish) hoped to evade what they told me was *explotación* [exploitation] on the part of those of the village of Pisac (15 July 1989). When asked, the men told me that their tiny ceramic figurines were the heritage of centuries.
>
> I noticed one design in particular, on a ceramic whistle of pre-Columbian form, a red and black Asiatic motif with colorful surrounding samurai figures. I had seen this imagery in a Polaroid photograph sent from Japan to Hipolito's workshop in the village. That design had been part of a February work order from Tokyo. Now, a few months later, it was claimed as the traditional work of Andean farmers who presented it to me, as an 'authority' on development funding. When asked later about these Japanese-style decorations, Hipolito responded that no such forms ever had come from his workshop. Then, when I described the design again, he told me that it was an order for matching hand-painted whistles for physical education classes in Japan, provided one-time only because it had cost more in production than yielded in profit.
>
> Regardless of my musings about authenticity, I gave names and phone numbers in Lima for a few non-profit, non-governmental organizations to the

> *comuneros* and they selected, after asking around with agricultural development workers, that of Minka. When these artisans requested, I also photographed them together and then their craftworks, using the camera they as a guild had bought for that purpose. They explained that they never got copies of the photos travelers take of them in the village marketplace and needed these for promotional purposes. The artisanal association of six members told me then that they would mail samples of their works and photos to the Minka director and request her help. I didn't check back with them but learned later in Lima that they'd done so and, indeed, that they continue to work with Minka eight years later although their president has now migrated down into the valley village.
>
> (excerpted from Henrici, 1996a, 1996b).

Comuneros generally remain observably poorer and politically weaker even with the current resurgence of tourism into the Pisac district, just as the artisan-vendors of Pisac constantly do battle to retain rights and profits with regard to those of Cuzco, Lima and international importers. Nevertheless, regardless of village hostilities and frictions, residents of Pisac district involved with tourism and tourist art unite in defining themselves as 'artisans' primarily and as merchants secondarily and as representatives of a local culture rather than as full participants in a worldwide exchange. This imaging, also part of common touristic discourse, seems partly provided to the *piseños* as their expected role by NGOs, ATOs, foreign import companies and the Peruvian government. The imaging also seems important to those of the district of Pisac even though it seems to be part of the misrecognition denying one set of differences and heralding others, manipulated by those of Pisac as entrepreneurs within a global system.

In addition, since men and boys more than women or girls may work on ceramics, the artisanal association with status is associated with the masculine in Pisac (Fig. 7.6). Boys apprentice while still in elementary school, receive small wages for their painting or ceramistry, and in recent decades tend to marry while young thanks to an income that encourages a sense of independence. Their image in turn is articulated with that of being a successful artisan, and competition results not only in designs and techniques but in sales. With changes in tourism fashions and promotion, an identity of the masculine in Pisac might alter.

Indeed, the two global market forces of tourism and export continue to affect artisan development practices and the role and status of the crafts producer. Government and non-profit agencies with widely diverse political views involve themselves in new and modifying handicraft projects. For the immediate future, among an increasingly influential element of such agencies in Peru and within certain recent efforts for the economic development of small-scale production, indigenous and local distinctions of artisanal production are becoming erased as elements. The Spanish words *artesanía* and *artesanal* obtained, within Peru in the 1960s, a legal status as small-commodity or simple service without necessary affiliation to the traditional

Fig. 7.6. Part-time worker painting while waiting for customers.

or ancient, but these connotations remained firmly in place within marketing and fund-raising. Registration as an 'artisan' entitled an individual to certain rights and exemptions and remains a category of some professional respect. Thirty years later, part of the Peruvian government and private sector affiliates have re-defined the handicrafts they are promoting for export as *industria manual* rather than as *artesanía*. This is an attempt to separate export goods from the economic whims of ethnic tourism and the restricting nostalgia of its discourse, particularly while current national tourism development campaigns are stressing instead the internationally-fashionable eco- and adventure tourisms. The move towards re-designing crafts as more global in production, style and marketability is also an effort by the Fujimori administration to eliminate a dependency on rural identity and its political associations of the past decade (ADEX-USAID, 1996).

In some respects, this trend is a furthering of development and modernization objectives and in others it is analogous to the tendency of Pisac villagers to distance themselves from a need for the physical presence of *indios* to make sales. However, at this point the Pisac villagers themselves and their own hybrid cultural distinctiveness are becoming irrelevant to selling Peruvian crafts. For decades tourist art producers in Pisac previously sold export and tourist market goods through expressions of ethnicity as well as through pride in their imaged identity as a village of craftspersons with a traditional-style market-place. Yet, these distinctions may be disappearing from the discourse. By simply changing the rhetoric describing an artisanal form, representation of relative powerlessness as nothing more than a cultural essence and backwardness enables certain agencies to claim victory over threats to a modernizing nation. Misrecognition in its current touristic manifestation supports certain interests in the governing of Peru.

Conclusion

Tourist art development is a global phenomenon and has been constitutive of contemporary life in Pisac. Examination of the touristic and the artisanal within Pisac reveals much that is exemplary of tourism's articulation with diverse groups and cultural identities. Conversely, exploration of the rhetoric surrounding and forming the touristic and the artisanal is critical to a depiction of Pisac. As argued, touristic portrayal tends to highlight cultural oppositions even as it eclipses other differences among the peoples involved, and stresses a timelessness while emphasizing transformation.

A culturally specific non-traveller who is representative of an imagined past and who is approachable at any moment convenient to a visitor representative of a uniformly modernized future has been a dominant theme in touristic discourse. While frustrations and disappointments arise from this limited portrayal, nevertheless both tourists and those who are toured generally reproduce, and sometimes agree with, the image. Those who are part of a discourse of misrecognition tend to perpetuate it, or alter it only within terms of existing paradoxes in the rhetoric, and existing differentiation and disparity continue without challenge.

Pisac recapitulates general touristic trends in that its plaza became within tourism development requisite for travellers wishing to obtain a view of, and to buy from, a 'typical' and 'indigenous' Andean market. Affiliations occur among all those participating in such imagery and exchange. In this mapping out of roles and representations, the 'modernized' can meet the 'modernizing'. Distinctions collapse into contradictions as those involved allege severe contrasts among themselves only in terms of 'culture', 'level of sophistication' (or ignorance), or 'level of development'; these concerns in turn arise from a presumed unilinear transformation and relative parity in power with variation determined only by 'history', or the passing of time.

Within all forms of misrecognition, the reproduction of misleading imagery is not deliberate but rather unquestioned. Social scientific and development aid concerns, the national interests of Peruvian policy, and stereotypes of cultural difference articulate within a discursive domination that affects tensions among travellers, tourism developers, *piseños* and *comuneros*. Pisac artisans, their ceramics, and their sales techniques participate within a touristic discourse filled with the misrecognition found in assumptions and expectations. Lack of acknowledgement of disparity in economic and power relations serves to perpetuate conflict. The situation in forthcoming decades needs observation as touristic discourse shifts away from a focus on international tourism and local ethnicity towards an emphasis on national tourism and the ecotouristic; changing touristic discourse might further distort problems in the relationships among peoples, or its intrinsic contradictions might allow for greater alternative expression of identity.

References

ADEX-USAID (1996) *Maqi Wasi, Boletín de Artesanías*, 1, 1.

Ascher, F. (1985) *Tourism: Transnational Corporations and Cultural Identities*, UNESCO, Paris.

Bourdieu, P. (1977) *Outline of a Theory of Practice*, Cambridge University Press, Cambridge.

Bourdieu, P. and Haacke, H. (1995) *Free Exchange*, Stanford University Press, Stanford, California.

Bourdieu, P. and Wacquant, L.J.D. (1992) *An Invitation to Reflexive Sociology*, University of Chicago Press, Chicago.

Boynton, G. (1997) The search for authenticity, or destroying the village in order to save it, *The Nation*, 265, pp. 18–19.

Butler, R. and Hinch, T. (1996) Indigenous tourism: a common ground for discussion. In: Butler, R. and Hinch, T (eds) *Tourism and Indigenous Peoples*, International Thomson Business Press, London, pp. 1–19.

Buzard, J. (1993) *The Beaten Track: European Tourism, Literature, and the Ways to Culture, 1800–1910*, Clarendon Press, Oxford.

Castañeda, Q. (1996) *In the Museum of Maya Culture: Touring Chichen Itzá*, University of Minnesota Press, Minneapolis, Minnesota.

Castillo Ardiles, H. (1970) *Pisac: Estructura y Mecanismos de Dominación en una Región de Refugio*, Instituto Indigenista Interamericano, Mexico City.

Cohen, E. (1988) Authenticity and commoditization in tourism. *Annals of Tourism Research*, 15, pp. 371–386.

Crang, P. (1997) Performing the tourist product. In: Rojek, C. and Urry, J. (eds) *Touring Cultures: Transformations of Travel and Theory*, Routledge, London, pp. 137–154.

Crew, S.R. and Sims, J.E. (1991) Locating authenticity: fragments of a dialogue. In: Karp, I. and Lavine, S.D. (eds) *Exhibiting Cultures: The Poetics and Politics of Museum Display*, Smithsonian Institution Press, Washington, DC, pp. 159–175.

Crick, M. (1989) Representations of international tourism in the social sciences: sun, sex, sights, savings, and servility, *Annual Review of Anthropology*, 18, pp. 307–344.

Diller, E. and Scofidio, R. (1994) Tourisms: suitcase studies. In: *Flesh: Architectural Probes*, Princeton Architectural Press, New York, pp. 198–220.

Feifer, M. (1985) *Tourism in History: From Imperial Rome to the Present*, Stein and Day Publishers, New York.

Henrici, J. (1996a) The artisanal and the touristic in Pisac, Peru. Unpublished Doctoral dissertation, University of Texas, Austin.

Henrici, J. (1996b) Clay beads and plastic paints: paradoxes of the touristic in Pisac,

Peru. In: Robinson, M., Evans, N. and Callaghan, P. (eds) *Culture as the Tourist Product*, Vol. I of *Proceedings of Tourism and Culture: Towards the 21st Century*. Centre for Travel and Tourism and Business Education Publishers Ltd, University of Northumbria at Newcastle, UK, pp. 165–184.

Henrici, J. (1997) Promoting Peruvian crafts and selling culture. In: *PromPerú Summer Internship Program 1996 Reports*, PromPerú, Lima, Peru, n.p.

Kendrigan, M.L. (ed.) (1991) *Gender Differences: Their Impact on Public Policy*, Contributions in Women's Studies No. 121. Greenwood Press, New York,

Kinnaird, V., Kothari, U. and Hall, D. (1994) Tourism: gender perspectives. In: Kinnaird, V. and Hall, D. (eds) *Tourism: A Gender Analysis*, John Wiley & Sons, New York, pp. 3–34.

Kirshenblatt-Gimblett, B. (1995) Confusing pleasures. In: Marcus, G.E. and Myers, F.R. (eds) *The Traffic in Culture: Refiguring Art and Anthropology*, University of California Press, Berkeley, California, pp. 224–255.

MacCannell, D. (1973) Staged authenticity: arrangements of social space in tourist settings, *American Journal of Sociology*, 79, pp. 589–603.

MacCannell, D. (1976) *The Tourist: A New Theory of the Leisure Class*, Schocken Books, New York.

MacCannell, D. (1984) Reconstructed ethnicity: tourism and cultural identity in Third World communities, *Annals of Tourism Research*, 11, pp. 75–392.

Megaw, V. (1982) Western desert acrylic painting – artifact or art?, *Art History*, 5, pp. 205–218.

Nuñez del Prado, O. (1973) *Kuyo Chico: Applied Anthropology in an Indian Community*, The University of Chicago Press, Chicago.

Pearce, P.L. and Moscardo, G.M. (1985) The relationship between travellers' career levels and the concept of authenticity, *Australian Journal of Psychology*, 14, pp. 311–313.

Pearce, P.L. and Moscardo, G.M. (1986) The concept of authenticity in tourist experiences, *Australian and New Zealand Journal of Sociology*, 22, pp. 121–132.

Powers, M. (1994) 'Battered tourism industry seeks comeback', LEXIS/NEXIS: Reuters North American Wire, 14 June.

Pratt, M.L. (1992) *Imperial Eyes: Travel Writing and Transculturation*, Routledge, New York.

Richter, L.K. (1995) Gender and race: neglected variables in tourism research. In: Butler, R. and Pearce, D. (eds) *Change In Tourism: People, Places, Processes*, Routledge, London, pp. 71–91.

Rojek, C. (1993) *Ways of Escape: Modern Transformations in Leisure and Travel*, Macmillan, Basingstoke.

Shiner, L. (1994) 'Primitive fakes', 'tourist art', and the ideology of authenticity, *The Journal of Aesthetics and Art Criticism*, 52, pp. 225–234.

Trinh, T.M. (1994) Other than myself/my other self. In: Robertson, G., Mash, M., Tickner, L., Bird, J., Curtis, B. and Putnam, T. (eds) *Travellers' Tales: Narratives of Home and Displacement*, Routledge, London, pp. 9–26.

Tsing, A.L. (1993) *In the Realm of the Diamond Queen*, Princeton University Press, Princeton, New Jersey.

Turner, L. (1976) The International Division of Leisure: Tourism and the Third World, *World Development*, 4, pp. 253–260.

Urry, J. (1990) *The Tourist Gaze*, Sage Publications Ltd, London.

van den Berghe, P. (1994) *The Quest for the Other: Ethnic Tourism in San Cristóbal, Mexico*, University of Washington Press, Seattle.
Williams, R. (1973) *The Country and the City*, Oxford University Press, New York.

Social and Cultural Impacts of Tourism Policy in Tunisia

8

Sue Bleasdale and Sue Tapsell

Introduction

Over the last three decades Tunisia has developed a substantial, largely coastal, resort-based tourist industry. The sustainability of this industry is crucial to the continued economic stability of the country. Achieving this sustainability will require changes in the industry, and in this context the Tunisian Tourism Ministry is seeking to change and diversify the tourist product. One attempt at diversification has led to the development of tourism in the south, bordering on the Sahara desert.

This chapter examines some of the issues surrounding the socio-cultural impact of this development on the small town of Tozeur and its hinterland by drawing on surveys and fieldwork undertaken over a period of some five years. Observation has been supplemented by interviews and conversations with local residents, tourists, tourism employees and representatives of the Office Nationale du Tourisme Tunisien (ONTT). The nature of resident attitudes and adaptations to the growth of tourism is explored, problems arising from tourism impact are identified, and the needs of a more culturally focused form of tourism are considered with a view to providing some suggestions for future policy modification.

National Tourism Policy in Tunisia

Tourism policy aims remain targeted on economic growth, employment potential and foreign exchange earnings, with regional economic develop-

(eds M. Robinson and P. Boniface)

Box 8.1. Main areas of official concern in Tunisia.

Regional inequality and underdevelopment of the south of the country

Unemployment – compounded by a very youthful population

Balance of payments problems and a rising national debt (structural adjustment policies have led to a more active pursuit of economic growth; specifically to the search for sources of international finance and to diminishing the role of the state in economic development)

The need to maintain (and enhance) political stability

The need to improve rural infrastructure and social development

Source: National Plans 1987–1996; various government statements.

ment as a strong secondary aim. The main areas of official concern in Tunisia shown in current National Plans and government statements are shown in Box 8.1 and current tourism policy addresses these issues. Tunisia currently receives over three million tourists a year and aims to increase this (*Tunisia News*, November 1995). A very high percentage of these visitors (62.7% in 1994, ONTT) come from Europe, and 80% of these come in groups (Poirier and Wright, 1993, p. 156).

Box 8.2 outlines the planned objectives for tourism identified in recent National Plans (1987–1991 and 1992–1996). Along with these objectives are the continued expansion and improvement of facilities and infrastructure in all existing centres of tourist activity and the specific targeting of new markets, for example in Eastern Europe, with ONTT offices opening in Moscow, Budapest and Warsaw. Policies therefore focus on consolidating Tunisia's place in the market, building upon the successes of the 1970s and 1980s by seeking to maintain and upgrade the quality of the tourist experience, whilst diversifying to new markets, new forms of tourism and new regions.

One area targeted for the expansion of tourism is the south (Fig. 8.1). Currently this area (here defined as the Gafsa–Tozeur tourist region as specified by the Ministry of Tourism) has only 5% of Tunisia's national tourism capacity (ONTT, 1994), although this has risen from 3% in 1988 (Poirier and Wright, 1993, p. 157). The ONTT have devised a specific term for tourism in the south – 'le tourisme saharien'. This label taps into romantic images and ideas which are relatively well defined among Tunisia's dominant tourist groups. These are variously derived from Second World War experiences, literature and film (*Star Wars* and *The English Patient* were both largely shot in Tunisia). Tunisia has always been marketed as a destination combining good climate and beaches with an exotic culture within easy

Box 8.2. Planned objectives for tourism in National Plans (1987–1991 and 1992–1996).

The development of tourism in the south – 'le tourisme saharien'

The development of tourism in the northern region

Increasing incentives to overseas investors

Continued investment both by the state and by private investors in tourism education

More attention to quality and enhancement of existing quality

Mitigation of the negative features of tourism development (waste and sewage disposal, etc.)

Expansion of specialist tourism (heritage tours, nature tours, thermalisme, water sports, golf, etc.)

Source: *Tunisia News* 158 (November 1995); *Tunisia News* 159 (December 1995); Tunisian Ministry of Tourism (1987); Anon (1996).

reach of most West European countries. Adding Saharan tourism to Tunisia's existing image is a mechanism for consolidating Tunisia's place in the market whilst also tapping into the expanding market for holidays that are a bit more adventurous. Whilst this may be a sound and logical marketing ploy the development of tourism in Tunisia's south will have profound implications for all aspects of the desert fringe: culture, society, economy, as well as the physical environment.

Southern Tunisia

The southern landscape has many elements that are attractive to tourists. Large areas of semi-desert plain merge into sandy and stony desert and there are several salt lakes (chotts). The plains are broken by hill and mountain ranges and where water is available at the surface there are oasis settlements. The area is renowned for its sunsets and mirages. The contrast provided by the dense greenery of the oases with their palm groves, intensive agriculture, warm springs and flowing water adds to the region's attractiveness (Stannard, 1991).

Tozeur has a long, complex history (e.g. as a Roman border post, a stopping point for the Saharan caravan trade) and unique architectural features in the form of geometrically-laid brickwork designs. Today the town is the main centre for exploring the south, and is best known as a centre for the export of dates. Views over the palmerie in the evening and early

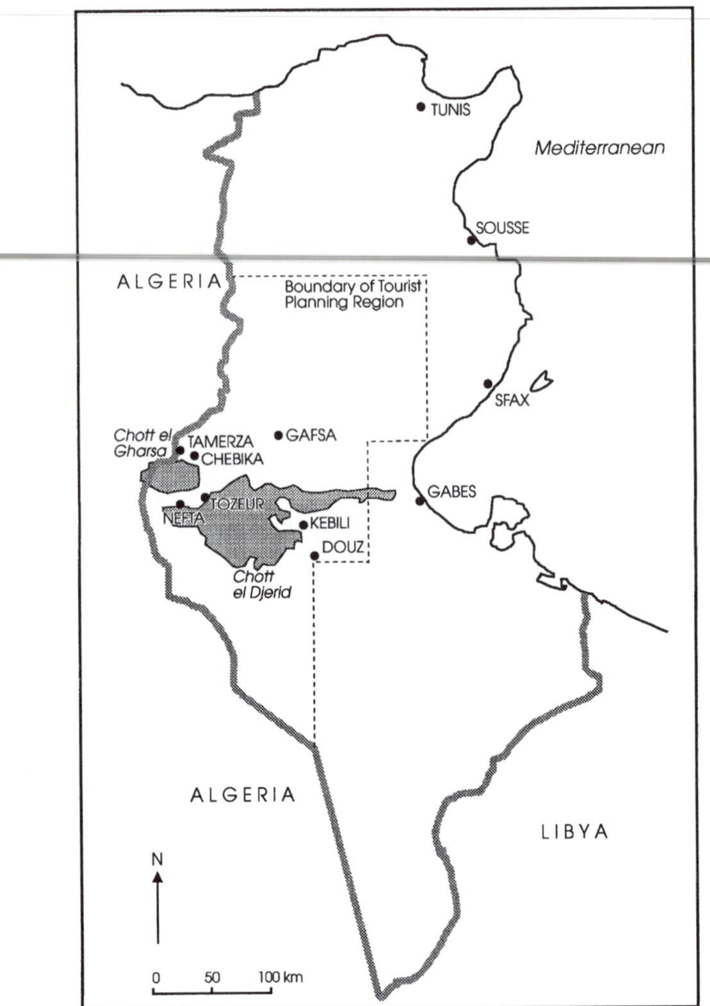

Fig. 8.1. Tunisia showing Gafsa–Tozeur tourist region.

morning, when steam rises from the springs and drifts up through the palm trees, are an important part of Tozeur's attraction. Date production is still the mainstay of the economy in terms of year-round employment. Income from date exports has suffered in recent years but this has been compensated to a degree by the increase in income from tourism. Nearby, Nefta is visually and culturally quite distinct from Tozeur, being an important religious centre for Sufi pilgrims. Douz, a traditional market centre well known for the Festival of the Sahara, is seen as the gateway to the 'true' Sahara. To the north of Tozeur is a line of small oases (including Chebika and Tamerza) at the foot of a rocky mountain range.

The Development of Tourism in Southern Tunisia

Tourist development in the region falls into two main categories: desert journeys by camel or Landrover, which can be long and arduous expeditions, and (more frequently) short circular tours of 2–5 days starting and ending on the coast and taken as add-ons to beach package holidays; literally day trips to the desert. Centres visited include Matmata, Douz, Tozeur and mountain oases. Most tours include a journey across the chott, a camel ride and maybe a 'Bedouin feast or wedding'. There are some 'hallmark events' which are an integral part of the tourism strategy for the area. These include: rallying, a biathlon, the Festival of the Sahara, the National Day of Saharan Tourism, the Festival of the Oases, hot-air ballooning and sand yachting conventions. More recently, packages using direct flights to Tozeur or combining a week on the coast with a week in the south have been added but are still relatively unimportant.

Tourism Infrastructure and Official Policy Towards Saharan Tourism

The Tunisian government has actively encouraged the development of tourism in the south since 1987 through various initiatives and incentives, the provision of infrastructure and fiscal structures. Entrepreneurs in the Gafsa–Tozeur region have responded vigorously to these incentives. A number of new hotels have been built in the last ten years and there has been a progressive movement up-market with the addition of some 5-star hotels. As Table 8.1 shows, Tozeur now boasts over 60 hotels, and the number of beds in the Gafsa–Tozeur region has more than doubled from 3309 in 1987 to 8366 in 1996 (C. Houcine, ONTT Tozeur, 1996, personal communication). In Nefta, development has been slower, with only four hotels established. (Anon, 1995). In all towns, hotels are gathered into a 'zone touristique' away from the original town centre (Fig. 8.2). The zones are on raised ground with good views over the chott, sand dunes and oasis. There are no accommodation facilities in Chebika but in Tamerza there are two hotels. One is older with very basic palm frond cabanas but the second is the 5-star Tamerza Palace, which is situated on the cliff-top edge of the main wadi.

Communication links to the south have also improved. The airport in Tozeur has facilitated the transportation of visitors to the region (Table 8.2). There are now four direct flights each week from Paris, Lyons, Bern and Brussels, with plans to develop flights from Italy and Spain. Main roads have also been improved as part of general upgrading of tourist and rural infrastructure, supported by government investment.

There is a degree of external dependency in terms of consumer goods for tourists such as food and vehicles. However, in terms of industrial capacity,

Table 8.1. Tourism trends in the Gafsa–Tozeur region, Tunisia 1988–1994.

	1988	1990	1992	1994	1996
Beds	3309 (1987)	5084	6821	7658	8366
Hotels	39 (1989)	51	60	62	–
Arrivals	377,685 (1987)	488,337	–	722,017	–
Tourist nights	432,902	566,995	827,228 (1993)	872,066	–
Occupancy (%)	–	40.7	37.0	35.2	–
Length of stay (days)	–	1.1	1.2	1.2	–

Note: Use of 1991 figures has been avoided as far as possible as 1991 was exceptional because of the Gulf War.
Source: ONTT 1991, 1994; ONTT Tozeur 1995, 1996, personal communication.

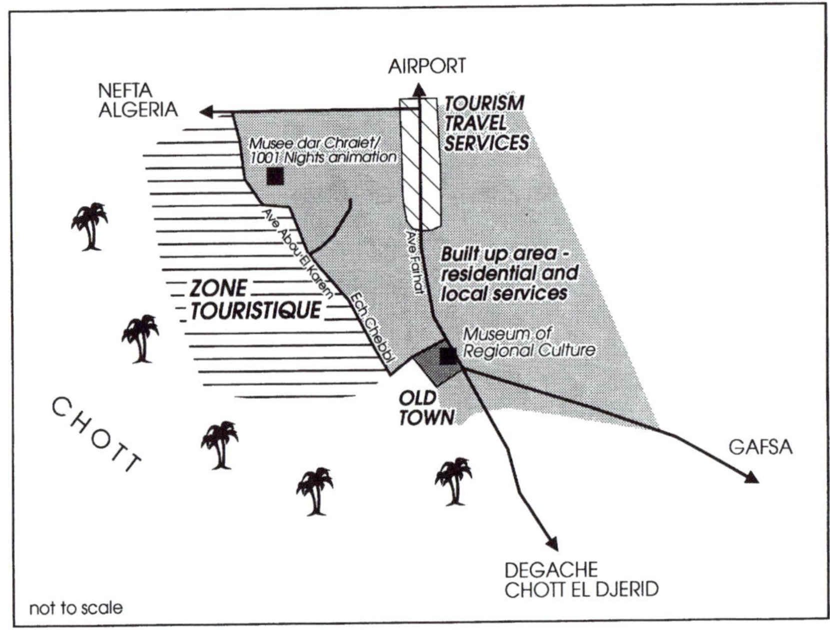

Fig. 8.2. Tozeur – key features of tourist industry.

Table 8.2. International traffic through Tozeur airport.

	1990	1991	1993	1994
Regular flights	11	21	101	166
Irregular flights	143	25	111	115
Passengers	11,099	3517	17,603	23,204

Note: Figures for 1991 show the impact of the Gulf War.
Source: ONTT 1991 and 1994.

there is a considerable degree of non-dependence. Almost all the hotels are locally or Tunisian owned. This seems to be where the government's policy of Tunisian ownership established in the 1960s is paying off. Tunisia has an established tradition of indigenous investment in tourism, but it is not clear whether this feature will survive in the economic climate of the 1990s. There is already evidence of joint ventures with Middle Eastern finance in some of the larger new hotels in Tozeur. Current government policy is further encouraging this by increasing the proportion of ownership by foreign investors in these ventures.

Service industries have expanded to cater for tourists wishing to explore the south. Numerous car and four-wheel drive (4WD) hire firms and travel agencies are ready examples of spontaneous enterprise (21 are listed in the directory in *Profession Tourisme* (Anon, 1995)). Many of these are offshoots of firms already established on the coast (e.g. Tunisie Voyages) which emphasizes the fact that much of the tourism in the Tozeur area is an add-on to the basic beach holiday. Other facilities include a firm which offers hot-air balloon trips over the chott.

The tourist zone is well connected to the town centre by wide, clean streets with broad European-style pavements. There is a very active trade in horse drawn taxis (*caleches*) making a 'picturesque' link with the old town centre. A recent addition is the museum Dar Chraiet, with extensive displays of Tunisian history, jewellery and costume. Adjacent to this is Tozeur's major 'animation', a theme park depicting the tales of the 1001 Arabian Nights. The museum and the 'theme park' are located in the 'zone touristique' and it is noticeable that some souvenir shops have been opened in the immediate vicinity. If this trend continues, there is a danger of trade in the original town centre being undermined.

Information about the town and its facilities remains limited. There are no town guidebooks or leaflets readily available for visitors. The ONTT office does have some information, but the office is not obvious visually, and the Syndicat d'Initiative in the main square is often closed (at least in November and December). This probably reflects the fact that most visitors come to Tozeur by coach and therefore rely on the courier/coach driver for information about Tozeur and its environs; few need to find their own way around the town. This encourages 'bubble' or enclave tourism and discourages interaction between local residents and tourists. Although many visitors to Tunisia today certainly appear to be better informed, and more interested in being informed than in the past, more accessible literature is still needed. Guidebooks are available in the UK but not in Tunisia. Recent glossy booklets published by the Ministry of Culture (on Berbers, Islam, Romans, etc.) are a good start and are produced in several languages. However, these could be more widely available. Many of the maps on sale are also of limited value. Some improvement has been noted, however, in the last few years, consistent with government diversification policy.

The town centre of Tozeur itself is dominated by tourist activity even in the off-season of November–December. The old town has a map at one entrance, a museum of regional culture, and there are informal guides available. The main street in Tozeur is largely taken over by shops selling carpets, basketware, desert roses (crystals formed in the desert) and dates – mainly orientated to the tourist trade. So far these shops have not penetrated the old town, which remains dominantly residential in character.

Tozeur is clearly the main service centre for tourism in the area, other locations are short-stop centres. In contrast, the town centre of Nefta remains almost untouched by tourism. Chebika and Tamerza have become centres of attraction for tourists on 4WD excursions from Tozeur and here the main development has been the setting up of roadside stalls selling souvenirs and drinks.

Social–Cultural Impacts of Tourism Development on Tozeur

With any discussion of the socio-cultural impacts of tourism there is the difficulty of separating the social from the cultural, and divisions can be largely arbitrary. On looking at the impacts on society and culture in the region of Tozeur, it is immediately apparent that these are both positive and negative. This view also appears to be that held by local residents interviewed, although in general, regardless of location, there were more positive comments made than negative. However, one factor largely missing from the analysis is the perspective of Tunisian women.

Employment and economic impacts

One of the positive impacts of tourism in the region has been the creation of employment opportunities in the blossoming number of hotels and service industries. Since the late 1980s, both direct and indirect employment has more than doubled (Table 8.3). The ONTT in Tozeur estimate that each new hotel creates between 50 and 100 new jobs (C. Houcine, ONTT Tozeur,

Table 8.3. Tourism receipts and employment 1988–1994

	1988	1990	1992	1994
Receipts (millions of dinars)	14 (1987)	24	–	45.9
Direct employment	1416	2034	2728	3074
Indirect employment	3516 (1987)	5112	–	7752

Note: Use of 1991 figures has been avoided as far as possible as 1991 was exceptional because of the Gulf War.
Source: ONTT 1991, 1994; ONTT Tozeur 1995.

1995, personal communication). In the hotels, the direct employment opportunities created are filled by mostly local applicants, and a new training school recently opened in Tozeur is likely to contribute to this, being part of the move to upgrade tourism quality. In the south, most of the higher paid contact positions (e.g. receptionists and waiters) are filled by men. Women work mostly as chambermaids and cleaners. This is in contrast to the coastal resorts where many women are employed as receptionists.

Indirect employment is also very important with numerous new opportunities being provided in the growing service industries. These include: increased demand for rugs and carpets, guides in the old town and the oasis, horse and cart rides through the oasis and onto the chotts, driving for travel and tour operators, positions in banking (Tozeur now has five banks) and other commercial services, cafe and restaurant work. Many of these jobs represent self-employed locally-generated opportunities. These opportunities appear to fall almost exclusively to males, and predominantly to young males. The self-employed seem to be more vulnerable to the seasonal and other vicissitudes of the tourist industry. However, to some extent these new jobs can be combined with farm work which has its labour demand peaks in the spring (date palm pollination) and late autumn, i.e. outside the peak demand periods of tourism.

According to the ONTT (C. Houcine, ONTT Tozeur, 1995, personal communication), tourism is not likely to undermine local farming, but is absorbing the surplus labour created by demographic changes in the population, which is currently very youthful. However, there have been reports of labour shortages in the oasis making it difficult to maintain date production. Other reports indicate that jobs in tourism *are* taking labour away from agriculture and that tourism is providing physically easier work and richer rewards. Education also appears to be reinforcing this process. Boys who previously learnt the intricacies of date palm pollination (undertaken by hand) and the date harvest are now in school and unavailable to carry out these tasks.

From the perspective of the 90 local residents interviewed in Tozeur and the coastal resorts (over half of whom were employed in tourism, either directly or indirectly), there is a widespread appreciation of the employment benefits from tourism, even among those not employed in the industry. Moreover, this appreciation went beyond the provision of jobs and individual household benefit, with residents speaking of wider economic benefits and of the importance of tourism to the national economy. There was also an appreciation of the wider benefits in terms of improved facilities such as health care and a generally higher standard of living. Some residents also spoke of tourism bringing liberalization and positive cultural change, as well as more shops, business and entertainment in the towns, from which they could also benefit.

On the negative side, some residents showed an awareness of the dangers of over-dependence on tourism by referring to such negative impacts as migration from the interior regions to the coast, rising prices, the decline of agriculture, and over-development of resorts such as Sousse. In general, residents displayed a very pragmatic attitude towards tourism and showed a realistic and balanced view of the impacts, the 'no tourists, no jobs' philosophy. This balance was also seen to extend beyond the economic sphere to include the social and cultural.

Host behaviour and attitudes

It is largely through the diversification of employment that opportunities for interaction between the host community and tourists arise. Most of this interaction is confined to commercial transactions and requests for information and services. In Tozeur and the surrounding region various changes in local behaviour and attitudes are becoming apparent.

The demonstration effect

In terms of the demonstration effect, the impact of tourism is obvious, but so far appears only to have penetrated that sector of the population which has direct contact with the tourist, mainly younger men. There are few opportunities for interaction with local women or with older members of the community. The impact on the young male members of the population is demonstrated in several ways. Dress mode is frequently Western with jeans and the black leather jacket being a preferred style of clothing. In contrast the women in the local community still retain predominantly traditional modes of dress (full-length black robes or berber dress). Older male members of the community also tend to retain more traditional styles – the grey overall or brown burnous with red felt cap and leather mules can still be seen among the older men in the town's cafes. Local workers in the oasis also retain traditional forms of dress (cloth head-dress, white shift, bare feet).

Many of the tourists visiting Tozeur and its environs are highly insensitive to local socio-cultural traditions. Bare limbs and the wearing of shorts are not acceptable in Islam and are likely to have a more negative impact in the south than in the coastal resorts, where local residents have been exposed to these Western customs for a much longer period. Many locals, particularly women, may find the tourists' dress offensive. Comments from local residents, particularly in Sousse, referred to other more negative aspects of tourist behaviour such as rudeness, drunkenness and a general disrespect for Tunisians and their culture.

Where tourists were friendly and respectful and demonstrated an interest in Tunisia beyond the beaches, local residents were positive about their impacts. Some even mentioned that they perceived tourists as guests, with tourism giving them an opportunity to demonstrate pride in their Tunisian culture. Other comments indicated an internationalist perspective by some of the local residents who commented on the opportunities for interpersonal contact, the learning and use of other languages, and pleasure in meeting people which came out of tourism development. Contact and knowledge of other countries was seen as important, as was the opening up of Tunisia to the outside world.

Attitudes of traders

The multilingual capabilities of the local traders, acquired from interaction with the tourists, are well demonstrated during commercial transactions. Conversation with young traders is easily initiated and attitudes to tourists quickly become apparent. Traders differentiate in their behaviour between tourists of different nationalities, showing an astute awareness of cultural and economic variations. Local residents interviewed recognized that not all tourists who visit Tunisia are alike. Attitudes and expectations, and levels of friendliness, were said to vary with tourists' nationality and level of affluence.

Some traders indicated a wish to move away from traditional forms of exchange, i.e. haggling over prices, having found tourist enthusiasm for this process wearing. In other parts of Tunisia where tourism is more established (as in Hammamet) a trend towards 'fixed price' selling has emerged, which could be seen to undermine cultural authenticity. Perhaps Tozeur traders will follow suit. This will, of course, remove one aspect of the 'otherness' which is one of the attractions of Tunisia for tourists. Among the more highly motivated traders there is a tendency to see the tourist only as a source of business and those without money are quickly recognized and conversations cut short. This is a clear indication of the depth of penetration of commercialization into trading, since traditionally even small transactions would involve a great deal of discussion.

Restaurants and cafes outside the hotels are relatively few in number, but again they show a willingness to adapt to the demands of tourists. In the main street cafes, tourists often outnumber locals and older local clients will often move aside (or be moved) to make way for the more lucrative tourist trade, thus disturbing a long-time local practice for male elders. Some of this cultural adaptation undoubtedly dates from the colonial period (e.g. serving French-style bread as an accompaniment with meals). Several outlets seem to have originated to serve Tunisian customers but they are extensively used by tourists and offer a good opportunity to try something approaching local cuisine. It is noticeable that few have adapted to the point of serving alcohol, which is still largely restricted to the tourist hotels. Whether this indicates the strength of the local culture, which is firmly embedded in Islam, or difficulties with local legislation is not clear. However, it seems clear that the presence of tourism certainly encourages alcohol consumption among Tunisian males. This is demonstrated by the fact that during the evenings, the bars in many of the tourist hotels are largely full of Tunisian men, often making it difficult for the tourists themselves to get served.

Deviant behaviour

One social impact which is frequently associated with the growth of tourism is prostitution, both male and female. In Tozeur, and in the coastal resorts, there are definite signs of male prostitution, and very occasional signs of female prostitution, although this seems largely to serve the local population or visiting Tunisians. It seems likely that the traditional position of women is sufficiently entrenched to make the development of female prostitution unlikely (and this is supported by the local strength of Islam). However, a much more negative development in recent years, particularly evident in Tozeur, has been the increase in child prostitution and paedophile activity. Many local residents interviewed spoke openly about this and showed concern at the increase.

Sexual relations between Tunisian males and Western female tourists is also widespread, especially in the more developed coastal resorts such as Sousse. There appears to be increasing evidence that the young men take Western female attitudes towards dress, for example, as a sign of loose morals. For many of these relationships, however, sexual motives are not the most important, and many Tunisians demonstrate a self-seeking relationship with the objective of receiving gifts from the tourists, marriage, or gaining help in obtaining employment in the tourists' country of origin. Several young males interviewed admitted to overseas fiancées, girlfriends or wives. This may be perceived as a positive outcome of sexual contacts by the young men involved, but may be perceived differently by the older Tunisian population who suggest that Western women are contaminating the young men with their lax morals. There were indications that some of the older men are trying to put a stop to the fraternization between their young men and female tourists.

A second social feature which is often associated with tourism in the developing world is begging – particularly by children. This feature is rarely seen in Tozeur, but is more common in Chebika and some parts of Nefta. The low incidence of begging may reflect the fact that there is almost universal schooling.

Finally, there is evidence of some increase in crime rates in Tunisia which may be largely attributed to tourism, and to the frustration felt by some young Tunisian males when faced with the affluence of the tourists. Juvenile delinquency has risen along with theft, pickpocketing and aggressive behaviour against tourists. The availability and use of drugs also appears to be on the increase in Tunisia.

The built environment and physical infrastructure

There have been both positive and negative impacts on the built environment (and infrastructure) from the development of tourism. In Tozeur the main mosque has been extensively rebuilt – a sign of the increased affluence of the town. There is also much upgrading and rebuilding work in progress. To some extent this is necessitated by damage caused by the flooding of the town centre in 1988/89, but much is undoubtedly made possible by the revenue which tourists bring into the town in increasing numbers. The conservation and rehabilitation of the buildings in the old town, and the addition of town guides and maps at the entrance, show an awareness of the potential of the town for tourists with an interest in more than just sunsets and sunshine. Local residents indicate that since there is more money, town houses are being restored and are once again becoming sought after as residences. There is little sign in the residential old town in Tozeur of a breakdown in traditional building practices and the area appears to be undergoing a revival as a residential quarter. As yet there is no sign of it being fossilized as a sort of living museum, although increasingly the locals seem to be willing to show tourists around their homes. Local residents have been told to paint their outer doors green (previously many were blue or simply varnished). This could be a revival of an old tradition, although the motives are not clear.

Comments from some local residents in other Tunisian towns point to the demolition of some areas in the medinas with the view that tourism is leading to a loss of traditional urban form through such modification for tourism purposes. In Tozeur, the old (traditional) covered market for food and produce, which functioned as an outlet for local produce, was demolished in 1996 to make way for a new shopping centre for tourists. A new market for local residents is being built to the rear of the old town. However, the traditional market was a focal point for the town centre, both for residents and tourists.

One area of further conflict is over the issue of water supply. Some local residents have complained at the amount of water used by the large tourist hotels in such an arid region, and there are fears that there may be serious implications for local farmers in reduced water supplies to the palmerie, as well as that available for local residents' consumption. When questioned on this, a local employee of the ONTT denied the possibility of any water shortages for local residents, stating that there was sufficient water available for everyone's needs until 2025 (C. Houcine, ONTT Tozeur, 1996, personal communication), with five new wells being provided in 1996 (*Tunisia News*, 1996). Other local residents spoke of contaminated water from the hotels affecting their crops, and in certain cases leading to crop failure.

'Animations'

Tozeur is fortunate in that it has two museums which offer quite different exhibits. The Museum of Regional Culture in the old town centre has a local focus and a display which explains the local water distribution system. However, a major positive contribution to the cultural landscape is the recent opening of the Dar Chraiet museum. This provides an opportunity for tourists and Tunisians alike to develop an awareness and appreciation of Tunisian history and culture. The displays offer a wealth of interesting exhibits, such as costume and jewellery, in a most attractive environment (a large purpose-built house in distinctive 'Arab' style). It is located in the tourist zone and is now an integral feature of coach tours to the area. However, there is little readily available information, hence it appears to be a somewhat wasted asset, although it does have real potential for enhancing tourist awareness of the richness and diversity of Tunisian culture, as well as for Tunisians themselves. The museum is visited by parties of local school children, as are other heritage sites such as El D'jem.

One feature of Tozeur's tourist landscape which remains somewhat of a puzzle is the so-called 'Museum' of 1001 Arabian Nights. This is in reality an amusement park built around the Arabian Nights theme and incorporating such characters as Aladdin, Ali Baba and Sinbad. The park is located immediately adjacent to the Dar Chraiet museum and provides a striking contrast. It is obviously targeted at tourists (with automated commentary in several languages) and clearly represents a major investment. Whilst it is hi-tech in the local context, it cannot compare technically with the Jorvik ride of York or the Pageant of London ride. It is also much less informative than these British examples, assuming a level of knowledge of the Arabian Nights that many Europeans will not have, and with no copies of the tales themselves on sale. It seems oddly out of place in Tozeur, especially since the tales are of Middle Eastern origin. It does, however, represent a diversification of tourist facilities, providing jobs and opportunities for commercial exploitation. This is a definite attempt to develop a new aspect of cultural tourism in the area but it can be questioned whether it is Tunisian culture that is being promoted.

Handicrafts and souvenirs

Local production of traditional craft goods, particularly carpets, rugs, blankets, ceramics and basketware has been stimulated by the growth of the tourist trade, and economically this has to be seen as a positive benefit. It can also be argued that tourists are helping to keep traditional skills alive. In 1994 the Tunisian government responded by creating a Ministry of Tourism and Handicrafts (*Tunisia News*, November 1995). Most of the goods on sale in Tozeur are still locally made by women working in the home. However, the products show signs of adaptation to the tourist market and some traditions have been modified. The range of colours used in weaving has been extended beyond the traditional, and many of the dyes being used are synthetic and imported rather than locally produced vegetable dyes. Basketware has been extended to a much wider range of products and these are now decorated with symbolic coloured pictures of camels and palm trees to satisfy tourist demand. Carpet design has also been adapted. Traditionally the area is renowned for its geometric designs in muted colours and whilst these are still widely available, camel and palm tree images have been incorporated into many of the rugs and carpets. Other forms of trade that are flourishing include the sale of dates and desert roses, and the dubious (from the viewpoint of wildlife impact) sale of snakes and scorpions in bottles. Date sales may, however, contribute to the continued well-being of oasis agriculture and may be more lucrative than export production which is becoming more difficult.

Authenticity

'Staged authenticity' is a commonly reported feature of tourism in the developing world and Tunisia is no exception. Most hotels offer 'entertainment' in the form of belly dancers, snake charmers and troupes of dancers and musicians. To these have been added, and specifically in southern Tunisia, 'Bedouin feasts' and 'wedding feasts'. The food and drink served may have only a passing resemblance to Tunisian cuisine and indeed the whole concept of these feasts seems to have been created for the tourist industry. Similarly the displays of belly dancing and snake charming are often so far removed from the authentic as to be unrecognizable. On the other hand, some of the music and dancing entertainments do retain a large measure of local authenticity. A useful measure of this can be gleaned from the reaction of the local population to such displays.

Tozeur entertainments seem to have reached the point of losing touch with 'real' local culture. This is ironic considering that one of the most splendid new buildings in Tozeur is the local cultural centre (not currently promoted to tourists). Perhaps the tourist office needs to give this more proactive consideration – especially since one of their biggest concerns is the lack of 'animations' in the area. The International Festival of Maghrebian Music and Dance held in Tozeur in December 1994 could provide some useful lessons for the future. The Festival of the Oasis (held annually in November) is a major local event currently little publicized outside Tunisia. This could be a useful platform for broadening the base of tourism.

Most tourists also visit the oasis as part of a tour, and staged displays of some of the more spectacular aspects of cultivation (such as harvesting and pollination) are becoming quite common. It can be argued that such visits and displays represent not only an additional economic opportunity but provide a rationale for the upkeep of the oasis and its agriculture. However, there is a danger of the oasis becoming, or being seen to become, a tourist attraction rather than an area of sustainable agriculture underpinning a thriving local economy. Perhaps the demand for food from the tourists could be used to stimulate positive change in the oasis – integrating it into tourism development rather than having it be seen as an alternative economy.

Overall then, there are clear signs of increasing commercialization impinging on traditional social relations and behaviour. Interaction with tourists is mainly limited to commerce, service and curiosity. Perhaps the most significant social impact lies in the enhanced status and freedom which accrues to the many young males who are working in tourism. This represents a significant shift in intergenerational relations. On the other hand, some local patterns are very resilient – notably relating to the position of women in society. As to whether these changes represent a positive or a negative force in the community, it is often difficult to judge. Moreover, the impact of increasingly large numbers of tourists in the peak season on the relatively small local population is a likely source of future conflict.

It is true here, as it is in many other tourism destinations, that the local culture is an important part of the region's attraction. It follows therefore that if tourism has negative socio-cultural effects, and/or produces major changes in the visible aspects of the society and culture, there is a danger that the area's attractiveness to tourists will diminish. Increasingly it will be in the economic interests of the region to monitor and positively manage the impacts of tourism, if it is to be sustainable.

The town of Tozeur itself has obviously benefited from the revenue from tourism. However, many tourists do not venture out of the 'zone touristique'. This may be a good thing, helping to prevent the spread of commercialization, depending upon your point of view. It does appear, however, that more could be done by the ONTT to promote the cultural features of the area to attract a larger number of culturally-aware tourists.

So far only the Tunisian perspective on the issues raised has been discussed; however, tourism's impacts are also a reflection of tourist attitudes and expectations which also need to be considered.

Tourist Attitudes, Expectations and Experiences

Tourists today are showing an increasing degree of sophistication when it comes to travel. Many tourists are now more experienced travellers, have larger disposable incomes and increased leisure time, and often therefore seek more than a typical beach–sun holiday. The homogenization of destinations and packages, largely due to the increased vertical integration within major travel corporations, has led some visitors to search for destinations with something different to offer, either a touch of adventure or the provision of specialist activities within their holiday experience.

Although some attitudes and expectations of tourists visiting Tunisia have remained largely consistent over the last two decades, there have been some discernible changes which will have implications for future tourism policy. Comparisons of data from surveys in 1975 (Groupe Huit, 1979) and 1996 (by Middlesex University) highlight some of these consistencies and changes. The main consistencies relate to the reasons for choosing Tunisia as a holiday destination; the good weather, the beaches and the low price of the holidays being the main motives. Moreover, package visitors have remained the main type of tourists in Tunisia over the last 30 years.

Despite the efforts of the Tunisian government to attract more higher-spending cultural tourists, the numbers visiting the country on cultural and special-interest tours are still small. One factor which had attracted a small percentage of the 1996 tourists was that Tunisia was considered different, exotic and African. However, when asked what they had enjoyed most about their visit, the most common feature cited was again the weather, followed by the hotels and the relaxation. None of these are related to Tunisia specifically, and although the medinas, Roman sites and camel rides in the desert were mentioned by some visitors, the history, culture and society of Tunisia is still the main point of interest for only a minority.

Visitors do, however, appear to be more adventurous now, with many venturing out of their hotel complex to visit other towns and regions of Tunisia. Increasing awareness of, and interest in, other cultures may also have played a part in encouraging tourists to venture beyond the immediate confines of their hotels. The 1975 survey showed that on average most tourists spent 22 hours a day in their hotel complex, most not even bothering to visit the nearby town (Groupe Huit, 1979, p. 299). In 1996, however, the majority of the 110 tourists interviewed had visited, or intended to visit, other towns or regions within the country and over a third of them had been on excursions to the south. Comments from visitors were mixed but generally positive, and over half said that they had enjoyed the experience. Although some made negative comments, e.g. about poverty, the high cost of the excursions, as well as the length of time involved in reaching the destinations, others spoke of the south as exciting, being more 'cultural', 'native', and more Muslim than expected – the 'best part of Tunisia'. Half of the 1996 visitors had also visited heritage sites in Tunisia with others planning to visit: El D'jem was the most popular site mentioned, followed by museums and the Great Mosque at Kairouan. This indicates that the marketing of these attractions is now paying off, although other attractions such as the beaches still remain more popular.

The increased confidence of the tourists was also evident when asked about the local services they had used during their stay. In 1996, 95% of tourists interviewed said that they had used local services and facilities while in Tunisia. Taxis were the most popular local service, followed by restaurants and trains. Other services mentioned were buses, the Noddy train, shops, cafes, boats and banks. Moreover, almost three-quarters of visitors said that they had purchased souvenirs from their trip, and others said that they probably would. The most popular souvenirs mentioned were ceramics, carpets, toys (mostly fluffy camels), jewellery, leather goods and clothing. All of this reinforces the diverse number of employment opportunities available for local residents in tourism-related enterprises. It also increases the penetration of tourism into the economy and society of Tunisia, and therefore the intensity and scale of the impact.

Contact between tourists and residents is largely restricted to those employed in the tourism industry. Few, if any, of the 1996 visitors appeared to have had any intensive contact with the local population. However, when questioned on the response they had received from the Tunisian people, 83% said that they had found them to be friendly or very friendly, and several said they had enjoyed visiting local people's homes. More negative aspects of host–guest interaction were mentioned by visitors, with one commenting that the local people were over-friendly. This positive attitude towards tourists could be related to government policy in the increased level of tourism education in recent years, particularly with the opening of new hotel training schools. However, those indirectly employed in tourism such as shopkeepers and traders were criticized by tourists who often reported being hassled, and found local traders aggressive and too persistent when trying to sell their goods, while several female tourists mentioned sexual harassment from local men. Experiences such as these could discourage future host–guest interaction.

Tourists felt that there were both positive and negative effects on the local populations from tourism development, however, the positive effects were thought to be more numerous. The fact that tourism brings in income and is good for the economy was frequently mentioned. Several visitors felt that tourism increases cultural exchange, which they saw to be a positive effect, while other comments included that it enables local people to learn new languages, and that it revives traditions. The most negative effect of tourism mentioned by visitors was the impact on local cultures. Tourism was said to 'spoil' the host's culture and lead to Western values and behaviour being adopted. 'They should keep their culture and not copy the West.' However, several visitors obviously felt this to be a positive impact: 'introducing the locals to more sophisticated Western culture'.

Overall, although tourists expressed some criticism about various aspects of their experiences in Tunisia, the general impression from them was positive. Tourist facilities and the local people were generally praised and there appears to be a desire to experience aspects of local culture beyond the confines of the hotel and nearest beach. The Tunisian government therefore needs to continue its focus on the marketing of the culture and heritage of Tunisia and on improving this aspect of their tourism product. Consideration should be given to the problems mentioned by tourists, such as the length of the journey for excursions to the south for a two-day trip. A few tour operators have now introduced two-centre holidays which would be one way around the problem. The government could also try to reduce the amount of hassle and pressure from local traders that many tourists experience by raising the awareness among traders of the detrimental effects they might be having. In addition, the tourists themselves need to be made more aware of Islamic culture in order that they respect local customs and values. This is where tour operators and travel agents could also play a more pro-active role.

Discussion – The Implications for Policy

Suggestions for modification to government tourism policy must be realistic and should seek to satisfy a number of aims. The first of these is continued expansion of the tourist industry through diversification and consolidation (for the sake of the national economy, employment, debt reduction, foreign exchange earnings, etc.). Within this expansion there must be increased attention to 'new' forms of tourism, i.e. Saharan tourism, golf tourism, hunting, heritage, etc. Some of these will use 'culture' as a major and necessary resource and will therefore lead to increased potential for (and intensity of) socio-cultural impacts of tourism and for increased resident–tourist conflict. They will involve using cultural features specifically for tourist consumption and marketing these features internationally. Recent tourist brochures (e.g. *Panorama 1997/98* when compared with earlier editions) clearly demonstrate that this increased focus on cultural features is already feeding through into the marketing literature, and official ONTT campaigns in the UK in early 1997 also feature cultural and heritage resources quite explicitly, i.e. government diversification policy is becoming reality.

Policies must seek to mitigate and avoid the negative aspects of tourism's socio-cultural impact – not only is this necessary if Tunisians are not to be alienated but it will help to ensure a good 'quality' experience for the tourist.

Tourism which focuses more on the cultural features of a country is more likely to involve a greater degree of tourist–resident interaction. Resident satisfaction with tourism development policy is critical to the success of new developments. Sustainability can only be achieved if tourist experiences are positive.

To satisfy these aims the ONTT will need to be more pro-active and seek actively to incorporate culture into the tourist experience without excessive commercialization, loss of authenticity and without alienating the local population. A participative process in planning and developing new tourism ventures may hold out a better chance of success. To date such processes seem to be lacking in Tunisia which has a rather structured top-down planning system.

Other possible examples of 'pro-action' which might benefit tourism development, tourists and residents are suggested below:

- Using the national education system to develop a stronger, more overt sense of pride in Tunisian culture and heritage. A training scheme for National Guides would absorb some youth unemployment and enhance the tourist experience. There is currently much scope for guides at key heritage sites. Although interviews indicate that Tunisians do have pride in their culture and that they would like tourists to be more interested, the government does need to ensure that Tunisians do not see culture and heritage as 'belonging' only to the international tourist sector. The question of 'ownership' of culture is critical. A comparison can be made here with Malta. Like the Maltese, Tunisian residents are adapting, developing coping strategies and would support positive development of more 'cultural' tourism (Black, 1996).
- A recent report by the World Bank (1996) recommends that Tunisia should seek to reduce the number of tourist arrivals (largely due to the adverse environmental impacts of tourism which are not discussed here) and aim for higher-quality, higher-spending visitors. This proposed shift in tourist make-up is supported by local resident interviews.
- The quality of the tourist experience needs to be improved. This should include upgrading the presentation of cultural features and providing better information both in towns and at heritage sites.
- Tourist awareness of Tunisia's cultural diversity and richness needs to be raised. Most information currently available to tourists is found in the hotels, is commercially biased (excursion information only) and general rather than specialized. Little is done to entice the tourist to venture out of the tourist 'bubble'. Hotels could do more in this area and the Syndicats d'Initiatives need a major upgrade.
- Tourists need educating about appropriate behaviour in a predominantly Islamic country. Tour operators and/or airlines need to be encouraged to do this.
- More independent travellers/tourists need to be encouraged. The govern-

ment still seems nervous of independent travel (e.g. its insistence on groups travelling with a guide) and this is incompatible with forms of tourism that encourage smaller groups, independent travel, more local–tourist interaction. Evidence is that they are more likely to be culturally aware (and they spend more), and to go out into the rural and more remote areas which would help the policy of geographical diversification. This can only work if there is supporting infrastructure and information.

- Tourist–resident interaction needs to be diversified. Relationships are currently too focused on servant–master, buyer–seller interaction. There is a definite appreciation of the internationalization aspect of tourism among Tunisians, with a positive welcome to opportunities for mixing with other nationalities and learning about other cultures. Emphasis on smaller groups rather than large coach parties would help. This brings into focus the difficulty of matching the expansion aim with the cultural integrity aim.
- Improvements in international marketing. Although there have been some changes in current marketing of Tunisia in the UK (see above), overall the campaigns still focus on sunshine and beach holidays, winter warmth and cheapness, plus proximity to Europe. Most brochures make passing reference to Tunisia's culture and some now include information on excursions into the south. Recent brochures mention Chenini, Tatouine, Cap Bon and the north so there is some broadening of the geographical range. The ONTT will need to work more closely with tour operators if this trend is to be developed.
- If the south is to develop tourism successfully it needs to find a way to make it the focus of a trip rather than an 'add-on' to a beach holiday. More direct flights would help, although a great deal could be achieved by re-opening the railway line (after upgrading) to Tozeur to passengers – the nostalgic aspects of train travel are very attractive to Westerners.
- The issue of gender needs to be raised. Comparisons emerge between the coast and the interior in terms of employment opportunities for women. Fewer opportunities exist for females resident in the interior and this must have potential for creating tensions, isolating Tunisian women and creating a population of men with different, i.e. Western values, behaviour, dress and distorting tourist–resident relations.

Conclusions

Attempts to assess tourism's impact on society and culture empirically are fraught with methodological difficulties. These include the following:

- The boundary between societal and cultural impacts is indistinct and there is overlap with economic and environmental aspects.
- Local, regional and national influences are difficult to separate.

- Tourism is not the only agent of change – other forces such as education and television are at work.
- Tourists and residents are not homogeneous groups – distinct interest groups will all have differing perspectives on tourism.
- Research undertaken by Western academics is necessarily culturally constrained.

This chapter offers no solutions to these problems but it is important to note our recognition of these constraints.

Tunisian government policy appears to be going all out for growth in tourist numbers and there is little evidence of sensitivity to potential problems. Unless there is a firm move to involve local people more in forward planning, a future problem may not be external dependency but internal colonialism, i.e. dependence on Tunis and the dominant coastal areas. It is not yet too late to avoid the worst excesses.

To conclude, in the Tozeur region, some of the more negative features associated with tourism development reported elsewhere (external dependency, expatriate employment, large-scale prostitution, gross commodification of culture) are not apparent. This may be because development is as yet too small (in terms of tourist numbers) and too recent; these features, however, could become more of a problem. Several areas of potential future conflict can, however, be identified as likely to develop: conflicting behaviour between hedonistic secular tourists and the local Muslim society, water resources, and neglect of the oasis.

According to *Profession Tourisme* (Anon, 1995), the 1001 qualities that represent the grand tourist destinations can be found in southern Tunisia. It remains to be seen whether many of the negative impacts of tourism can be avoided in and around Tozeur. Will 'le tourisme saharien' prosper and bloom in the 21st century, like the desert roses so readily sold to tourists, or will the 1001 qualities for tourists become 1001 nightmares for local culture and society?

Acknowledgements

The authors would like to acknowledge the assistance given by employees at the ONTT in Tozeur over the last two years, in particular M. Chouchen Houcine. Thanks are also due to the students from Middlesex University who carried out the 1996 tourist interviews and many of the local residents' interviews, and to Steve Chilton of the Technical Unit, School of Social Science, Middlesex University, for producing the maps of Tunisia and Tozeur.

References

Anon (1995) Tourisme Saharien, le Nouveau Souffle, *Profession Tourisme*, 23, November, pp. 9–24.

Anon (1996) *1992–1996: A New Stage in Tunisia's Development*, Tunisian Information Service.

Black, A. (1996) Negotiating the tourist gaze: the example of Malta. In: Boissevain, J. (ed.) *Coping with Tourists: European Reactions to Mass Tourism*. Berghahn Books, Oxford, pp. 112–142.

Groupe Huit (1979) The sociocultural effects of tourism in Tunisia: a case study of Sousse. In: de Kadt, E. (ed.) *Tourism – Passport to Development?* Oxford University Press, Oxford, pp. 285–304.

Office National du Tourisme Tunisien (1991 and 1994) *Le Tourisme Tunisien en chiffres*. ONTT, Tunis.

Poirier, R. and Wright, S. (1993) The political economy of tourism in Tunisia, *Journal of Modern African Studies*, 31(1), pp. 149–162.

Stannard, D. (ed.) (1991) *Insight Guides – Tunisia*, APA Publications, London.

Tunisia News various editions: no. 158, November 1995; no. 159, December 1995; nos. 208 and 209 November 1996.

Tunisian Ministry of Tourism (1987) Le tourisme en 1991. *Information Touristique*, February 1987, Tunisian Ministry of Tourism, Tunis.

World Bank (1996) *Tunisia's Global Integration and Sustainable Development: Strategic Choices for the 21st Century*, World Bank, Washington DC.

Cornishness, Conflict and Tourism Development

9

Michael Ireland

Introduction

Conflict centred on Cornish identity and economic interest is not a new phenomenon in Cornwall. Cornwall is both a Celtic country within Europe and a county of England. Cornwall forms the 'toe of Britain' stretching from Land's End in the south-west to the River Tamar, a distance of approximately 80 miles. It is claimed that Cornwall is a poorer area than South Yorkshire and Mersyside and 'on a par with regions in Greece and Spain' (Atherton cited in Jobson, 1998). Cornwall has a history of conflict covering a period of 600 years. The issue of Cornishness has always been at the core of its people's fight for separate identity and economic development.

The most recent vehicle for development has been tourism. Discussions about the impact of tourism on Cornwall are a mixture of economic forecasts and concern about cultural change. Tourism has been seen by some as unwelcome colonization which has had two principal effects: economic leakage and a breakdown of Cornish culture (Hodge, 1990). Conflict resulting from debates about tourism in Cornwall is never out of the headlines of local papers. Such reports reflect the multidimensional nature of conflict. For example, 'Cornwall must stand united' (*Western Morning News*, 23 March 1998) refers to the loss of the mining industry, with the closure of the last tin mine in Europe. The assertion that 'the theme park has replaced the engine house' (Calder, 1992) is now a fact.

It is against this background of conflict at European, national and local level that this chapter shows why the issue of Cornishness for tourism development is not parochial. The first section of the chapter asks the question, 'Why is this issue important?' The chapter then goes on to consider why Cornishness is contested in its meaning, drawing on attempts to explain Cornishness using history. The chapter provides an overview of significant work done by local historians and those academics who have explored the meaning and significance of Cornishness.

The interpretation taken by historians is compared with the sociological and social anthropological analysis of the concept by asking the question, 'What is Cornishness today?' This question is explored using a paradigm which draws on the disciplines of psychology, linguistics and social anthropology. The question is examined by looking at difference and commonality of meaning attached to Cornishness by a heterogeneous resident population. Using survey material gathered in 1996 from north and west Cornwall, and a case study of the conflict surrounding the first sale of Land's End in 1981–82, the chapter examines what constitutes sources of conflict between politicians, planners, tourism officers and entrepreneurs on the one hand, and members of the local community on the other. The penultimate section of the chapter attempts to place the argument in the wider context. This is achieved by looking at the duality of Cornishness for the tourism industry. It is at once a cultural identity for a people, and the source of a product identity for the tourism industry.

Conflict and Cultural Identity

Conflict between a wish to retain cultural identity and the commercial need to develop tourism is not just confined to Cornwall (Cooper and Wanhill, 1997). Anthropologists have been concerned about the hegemony of tourism development since the 1970s; for example, Nash's early work on tourism as a form of imperialism and more recently Fees' (1996) work in England's Cotswolds charting the cultural impact of the incomers on the tours of Chipping Camden.

The issue of Cornishness and tourism development is also important with regard to what anthropologists can say about cultural difference and conflict. Anthropologists have been traditionally more sensitive in understanding cultural diversity (Stolcke, 1995, p. 1). Yet as Stolcke (1995, p. 2) laments, few anthropologists have looked at how cultural distinctiveness is being used as a divisive force.

In Cornwall, Cornishness has been, and continues to be, a catalyst for conflict with regard to tourism development in the county. However, such conflict is based on a constructed cultural identity rather than genetic traits. As Harvey *et al.* (1986, p. 199) conclude, the Cornish do not share strongly the genetic characteristics of the other Celtic peoples in Western Europe. Notwithstanding Harvey *et al.*'s conclusions, the struggle for Cornwall and its people to gain recognition as a nation state has a history which spans 600 years. Conflict between the Cornish and the English state reached a crisis in

1497 when an estimated 15,000 'rebels' marched from St Keverne in west Cornwall to Blackheath near London. The Cornish challenged the right of the Parliament of Henry VII to raise taxes in Cornwall to fight another Celtic nation, Scotland (Jackson, 1997, p. 17). Jackson reports that a rally and march to commemorate this event held in May 1997 received the support of Prince Charles, Prince of Wales and Duke of Cornwall. Opposition to this rally came not from England, but within Cornwall. A representative of the local area, the leader of the Conservatives on Cornwall County Council, is reported to have said, 'I am scared Cornish nationalists could use the march for their own ends and discredit the county' (Jackson, 1997, p. 17). This example from history shows that the struggle for Cornish identity and the recognition of Cornwall is not just a conflict between a unified England and a peripheral Celtic nation. Today the conflict between what is regarded as Cornish and what is defined as non-Cornish is not just fought out across the physical and administrative boundary of the River Tamar, which separates Devon from Cornwall. Conflict arises across relational boundaries (Cohen, 1985) which exist between Cornish people, non-Cornish residents in Cornwall and the ever present but transient tourist population.

Attempts to answer the question, 'What is Cornishness?' have been debated long before it became a signifier of a relational boundary (Cohen, 1985). There are at least two schools of thought when considering this question: those who represent the local historians who produce monographs in the style of '*Notes and Queries*' of an anecdotal nature, and academic historians. What is usually absent from the discourse of local historians and academics is the contribution of the social scientist. The absence of the social science, namely the sociological and social anthropological discourse, is indicative of a wider problem and thus gives this apparently local question a much greater significance. The problem is succinctly put by Burke (1980, p. 18) who says, 'many historians rejected sociology because it was too scientific, in the sense that it was abstract and reductionist, that it did not allow for the uniqueness of individuals or events'.

This problem illustrates the school of thought which exists within Cornish studies today. However, this is not to say that the findings published in *Cornish Studies* cannot be useful in formulating sociological research. Rowse (1969, p. 83) in his book *Tudor Cornwall* makes reference to characteristics associated with Cornishness in Tudor times which it is still possible to acknowledge today. In his chapter on 'Social structure and Government' Rowse make a link between geographical remoteness, the social characteristics of the people, e.g. clannishness and kinship patterns, and Cornishness. The most controversial point he makes in this chapter is describing Cornwall as a 'primitive society'. The question remains to be answered with regard to Rowse's work: how much of what he says is based on historical fact and how much is his interpretative view based on his own life experience?

The work of Jenkin (1933) *Cornwall and the Cornish* follows a similar line of reasoning to Rowse. The book is a mixture of historical fact (however defined) and myth. Notwithstanding this criticism, the work rather surprisingly points to many of the elements which have been identified for use in a semantic differential scale and used in the research presented here to signify Cornishness. Jenkin (1933) refers to the cosmology, ideology, social structure, social characteristics and personality of the Cornish people. He makes reference to the work of Evans-Pritchard, and Collingwood (Jenkin, 1933, pp. 255–256)in discussing the transmission of culture. Jenkin's work is more a blend of ethnology and history than a conventional history of Tudor Cornwall. The value of the book is that it acts as a pointer to characteristics of Cornishness which have survived into the late 20th century.

A note of caution is needed if we think Jenkin and Rowse have provided us with a basis to answer the question, 'What is Cornishness?' By comparing the work of Probert (1971) with Jenkin (1933) it is possible to demonstrate that definitions of Cornishness which have validity across time and space are untenable. Probert looked at the circumstances which fostered the growth of Methodism (often attributed as an element of Cornishness) in Cornwall. He argues that there were localized political and economic circumstances which gave rise to Methodism in the farming communities of 18th century Cornwall. Whilst particular circumstance cannot be replicated, Probert argues that this period developed the growth of a 'conscience collective' which has persisted into the 20th century. This point has been identified by Jenner (1920, p. 2) in his essay on Cornish nationality. Jenner describes what he sees as the Cornish 'conscience collective', defining the Cornish as a nation 'who usually by reason of their history have a sense of consensus, a sentiment if one may call it so, of a separate nationality and possess individual national characteristics'.

Among recent attempts by historians to solve the riddle of why a sense of national character exists in Cornwall is the work of Payton (1992), *The Making of Modern Cornwall.* In the preface to this work Payton (1992, p. ix) asks the question, 'How is it that, even at the end of the 20th century there remains an abiding and all pervading sense of "Cornishness" and separate identity?' Payton asserts that he is going to tell the 'real' story of Cornwall and in doing so hopes to combine objectivity with 'a deeply personal interpretation' (Payton, 1992, p. x). This assertion appears to contradict his earlier claim, with which I agree, that explanations of Cornishness are highly subjective, metaphysical and romantic (Payton, 1992, p. ix).

There are a number of problems with Payton's approach that need to be addressed. Firstly, in the preface to his book, Payton places inverted commas around the word Cornishness. This raises the question what does Payton believe Cornishness really is? Is Cornishness for Payton synonymous with difference? It would seem that Payton (1992, p. 2) is actually referring to Cornwall's difference from England in terms of the historical experience of its people. Secondly, Payton in common with this author, asks the question, 'How does one make sense of Cornishness today?' This question is never really answered. Payton is more concerned with models of the periphery and the analysis of Cornwall's political history. As Stolcke (1995, p. 2) says, 'History may explain the origins of these different political traditions, but it is not the cause of their continuity, each period interprets history according to contemporary needs'. Instead the answer to the question 'What is Cornishness today?' is more likely to be found in the key semantic terrain (Stolcke, 1995, p. 4) to emerge in contemporary Cornish culture.

What is Cornishness Today?

Cornishness is a deeply emotional and personal statement about being part of a living culture. The question 'What is Cornishness?' raises a number of important issues. For example, what aspects of Cornish culture are being commoditized by the tourist industry? To what extent is Cornishness a finite economic resource? Why is there a perceived threat to Cornishness as claimed by people living in Cornwall? These questions are also of great importance to policy makers in Cornwall. At a recent conference hosted by Cornwall County Council it was argued that Cornishness had implications for housing, health and education as well as tourism policy in the county. However, in this chapter the focus will be on the implications for tourism development.

Interest in the question, 'What is Cornishness?' and in what way does the answer have implications for tourism in the county began when fieldwork was being conducted in west Cornwall in the early 1980s (Ireland, 1987, 1993, 1997). It was then clear that tourist expectations of what Cornwall had to offer them as a holiday destination and collective notions of Cornishness, for both visitors and indigenous people, could not be divorced. The preceding section has shown that attempts to answer this question have been drawn primarily from historical sources. These enquiries were not entirely irrelevant. It is the existence of objective cultural differences in the remote past which provide continuity with the present (Nute, 1995). There are also positive economic rewards to be gained from enhancing cultural difference, real or invented. Recent research leads to the conclusion that a shared consciousness of what Cornishness is exists, at least among people who live in Cornwall. However, it should be remembered this is a population, not all of whom can claim to be Cornish.

The question 'What is Cornishness?' remains still largely unanswered. One reason for this has been put forward by the Research Unit of Cornwall County Council, who explained why it is important that we understand what Cornishness means. They point out that there are very few facts about Cornishness. From the point of view of County Council policy, it is necessary to understand the links between Cornishness, housing, health and education. This has become important because in the last 30 years 'the county has experienced a rate of population growth which has been much faster than the national trend, increasing by over 39% from 339,000 in 1961 to 473,000 in

1991' (Griffin, 1993, p. 5). Notwithstanding this growth there is 'very little information on the interaction between groups within Cornwall'. Recent research in the county points to one reason for this dearth of information: a preoccupation with the past, an attempt to explain Cornish identity through tenuous links with traditions, medieval legislation and folklore. In this context Payton (1995) has argued that Cornish Studies as a discipline needs to be reinvented. In this chapter I take issue with that view. It is not the discipline of Cornish Studies that needs to be reinvented, but new paradigms and methodologies need to be employed to look at the meaning of Cornishness in contemporary Cornwall.

The problematic to be addressed here is, 'What is Cornishness today?' From this general question, three questions were formulated which have a direct bearing on tourism development in the county and have relevance in other parts of the UK:

1. What aspects of Cornish culture are being commoditized by the tourist industry?
2. What are the implications of Cornishness as a form of cultural identity for tourism?
3. What are the perceived threats to Cornishness as it is understood by the indigenous people?

Issues in Measuring Cornishness?

These questions cannot be answered until we understand what Cornishness is. One problem has been to use concepts such as Cornishness 'simultaneously to define culture and to investigate it' (Bohannan, 1973, p. 357). This problem cannot be overcome completely, because in order to make dialogue possible we have to accept that there is something which is recognized as Cornish culture. What this chapter seeks to demonstrate is the level of agreement which exists between people living in Cornwall as to what it (Cornishness) actually is. In doing so it draws upon research undertaken in north and west Cornwall in 1996.

By adopting a multi-paradigm approach to the question posed, research has enabled a model to be constructed as to what is in the minds of respondents when answering the question 'What is Cornishness today?' This further presents a subset of questions to be answered, including for example; 'Does Cornishness have the same meaning to Cornish and non-Cornish respondents?' and how does time, expressed through length of residence, affect the response to this question? Respondents use and understanding of the word 'Cornishness' must relate to a particular experience. Following Hunt and Agnoli's (1991, p. 387) point that 'language is too human to be confined to a single discipline', the methodologies and research designs which were used to investigate this question reflected a blend of social scientific inquiry. In practice, semantic differential scaling was combined with more conventional survey research.

The semantic differential scale was used to ascertain what respondents understood by their use of the word 'Cornishness' as a concept in their everyday language. The semantic differential scale identified three dimensions of meaning in the respondent's scoring on the scale: (i) evaluation relating to the overall positive or negative meaning attached to Cornishness; (ii) potency describing the overall strength or importance of notions of Cornishness; and (iii) activity regarding the extent to which Cornishness is associated with social action.

Osgood *et al.* summarized the relationship between these dimensions in the following way:

> It is because language signs have certain meanings in the psychological sense that they are used consistently in certain situations and consistently produce certain behaviours (sociological meaning) and this is also the reason in part at least, they occur in predictable association with other signs in messages (linguistic meaning).
>
> (Osgood *et al.*, 1957, p. 10)

In the context of the research carried out the 'other signs in messages' were those the respondent made about tourism as a social process affecting their lives. Notwithstanding the persuasiveness of this argument, Osgood *et al.* (1957, p. 30) admits 'that the theoretical conception of the nature of meaning and the procedure for measuring it have no relations to each other'. Likewise, the anthropologist might claim to understand people through the intuitive process of fieldwork, but do they (Cicourel, 1964, p. 176)? This poses an epistemological problem: 'the actors experience of events and objects in their environment and the thought patterns and the meaning to which they are linked cannot be dismissed' (Cicourel, 1964, p. 178).

A Survey of North and West Cornwall

Taking these methodological issues into account, research was carried out in Padstow in north Cornwall and St Just in west Cornwall (see Fig 9.1) using a self-complete questionnaire mailed to a 10% sample of all residents in the areas selected. St Just in Penwith (west Cornwall) and Padstow in north Cornwall were chosen because they reflect the demographic changes which have taken place in Cornwall in the last 30 years. These areas were also chosen because they are considered to be typically Cornish. Data from the 1991 census showed that migrants in households as a proportion of the population index for Cornwall were almost three times as high for Padstow (271 : 67) as for the county as a whole (100). For St Just the figure was marginally higher than for Cornwall as a whole at 107:45. Those settlements with index figures over 100 are more attractive to migrants.

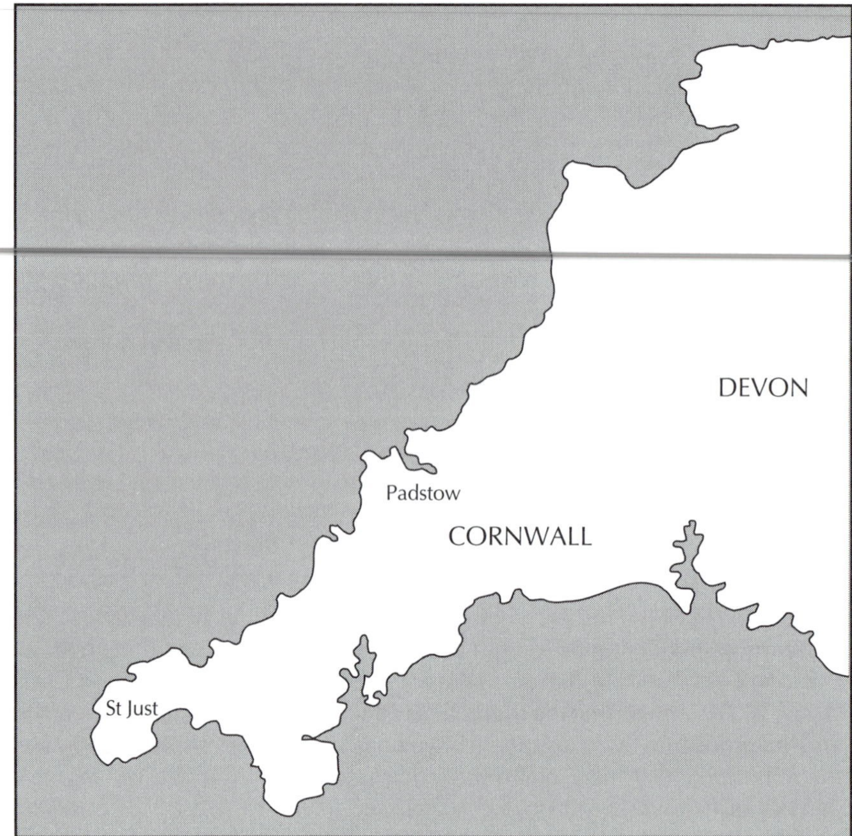

Fig. 9.1. Cornish towns included in Cornishness survey.

A simple random sample was used with every tenth name on the electoral registers for the wards selected. A questionnaire and covering letter were sent with a stamped addressed envelope to 400 households in St Just and Padstow.

A total of 82 valid responses were received giving a 20% response rate. The mean age of the respondents was 55, with the majority being female (57%). Just over half (53%) were born outside Cornwall. Most migrants came from South East England, a fifth (21%) of the respondents born there and a similar percentage (19.5%) with one parent from that area. Of those respondents born in Cornwall (47%) just under half had a parent not born in the county (39%). The questionnaires contained three sets of questions. Firstly, respondents were asked to provide information about the people they live with. This included questions on place of birth and length of residence in Cornwall. Secondly, they were asked to say what they thought Cornishness *is*. There were three types of question in this sub set: a semantic differential

Box 9.1. Sets of adjectives used to indicate dimensions of Cornishness.

Proud	Ashamed
Reserved	Outgoing
Religious	Secular
Celtic	Saxon
Impulsive	Cautious
Independent	Dependent
Superstitious	Agnostic
Clannish	Open

Table 9.1. Median scores for pairs of adjectives.

Adjectives		Score	Rank
Proud	Ashamed	6.5	1 =
Reserved	Outgoing	4.5	
Religious	Secular	4.5	
Celtic	Saxon	6.5	1 =
Impulsive	Cautious	2.5	
Independent	Dependent	6.5	1 =
Superstitious	Agnostic	5.5	2 =
Clannish	Open	5.5	2 =

scale, word association and an open question which asked the respondent, 'How would you describe Cornishness?' The final set of questions examined the links between Cornishness and the tourism industry.

It is important to note the way in which the adjectives used to make up the semantic differential scale were chosen. Eight sets of adjectives were used to indicate dimensions of Cornishness as shown in Table 9.1. These adjectives were chosen in two ways: from a review of literature written about Cornwall and its people, and from words used by informants in transcripts of interviews conducted in the field. The questionnaire asked respondents to place a tick at whatever point along a blank separating two opposing adjectives, to reflect the extent to which they thought the words in Table 9.1 described Cornishness. There is no absolute zero point on the scale, so the results are summarized as median scores, for each pair of adjectives (Osgood *et al.*, 1957). Table 9.2 sets out the pairs of adjectives, the median score and the rank order.

The adjectives highlighted are the main components which respondents

Table 9.2. Median scores indicating the strength of association between social and cultural characteristics and Cornishness.

Characteristic	Score	Rank
Handicrafts	5.5	3 =
Language	5.0	4
Traditions	6.5	2
Food	5.5	3 =
Art and music	4.75	6
Working life	5.5	3 =
Religion	4.5	5 =
Architecture	4.5	5 =
Style of dress	3.5	8
Leisure activities	4.5	7
History	6.5	1

believe described what Cornishness is. An independent and proud person with a Celtic ancestry remains important. Unlike popular descriptions of the Cornish and their links with Methodism (Probert, 1971) the responses indicate an ambivalence towards religion.

Respondents were then asked to select from a list of eleven social and cultural characteristics those they would associate with Cornishness. The scale from 1 (not associated) to 7 (strongly associated) was scored using the median to summarize responses (Table 9.3).

History, traditions, handicrafts, working life and food are the most tangible characteristics associated with Cornishness. When compared with elements identified in the semantic differential scale it is possible to postulate a link between psychological meaning and observable social and cultural characteristics. For example, Celtic people could be described as proud with a history and lifestyle which can still be recognized in the physical and cultural landscape of Cornwall today. One of the aims of the research was to ascertain the extent to which the tourism industry in Cornwall has commoditized the meaning which these symbols have for people living in the county today.

The questionnaire attempted to bring together respondents' understanding of what Cornishness meant to them through the open question: 'How would you describe Cornishness?' The following quotations from the responses received should be seen as apt illustrations:

> Cornishness is a way of life – to people who don't live in Cornwall it always seems to them that we are very relaxed and things are done at a slow pace, but this is not necessarily true. We just don't make so much fuss! Cornish people are very proud people who generally rally when needed.
>
> Single male, aged 20, not born in Cornwall. Born in Australia.

> People who are very proud of being Cornish, they don't welcome outsiders immediately and when they do eventually accept you, you still remain non-Cornish. Very clannish.
>
> Single female, aged 30, not born in Cornwall.

> The sense of belonging and having roots for generations in this unique county. The strong bonding between proud Celtic tribes. People who have time to care for each other like one large family. Only really happy when in Cornwall.
>
> Married female, aged 50, born in Cornwall.

> Pride of being born in a beautiful part of the country. A caring concern for their family and friends and to keep the county from being spoiled by too much development.
>
> Married male, aged 63, not born in Cornwall.

> A strong Celtic influence as with their Welsh cousins, independent and clannish even within themselves; this has to some extent restricted growth and development.
>
> Married male, aged 84, not born in Cornwall.

These descriptions of what respondents actually describe as Cornishness encapsulate the salient elements expressed in response to the previous questions (Tables 9.2 and 9.3). What is interesting is the recognition by non-Cornish as well as Cornish residents that Cornishness has a meaning in their everyday lives, not just as a vestige of the past but as part of a living culture. This point is well illustrated in the following case study of the sale of Land's End and the emotions it provoked.

Cornishness, Conflict and Tourism: The Sale of Land's End

This case study demonstrates how the conflict arising from the proposal to sell a small piece of Cornwall's coastline, the Land's End, can spread far beyond the boundaries of the county, to take on national and international significance. The case study draws heavily on accounts in the *Cornishman*, a weekly newspaper which covers the Penwith district of Cornwall, and *The Times*. The intention is to present a view of the conflict surrounding the sale as it might have been seen by the local person.

Land's End is situated in the far south-west of Cornwall in the parish of Sennen, which forms part of the administrative district of Penwith. It is approximately 300 miles from London; the journey to Penzance taking about 5 hours by train. Figure 9.2 shows the area of coastal headland which was the focus of so much debate.

Over the period of the sale, August 1981 to January 1982, various themes which appeared in the press, began to take on the status of myths and were capitalized on by the various interested parties. The myths were of three kinds: (i) uncertainty over the vendor's, (Charles Neave-Hills) intention to

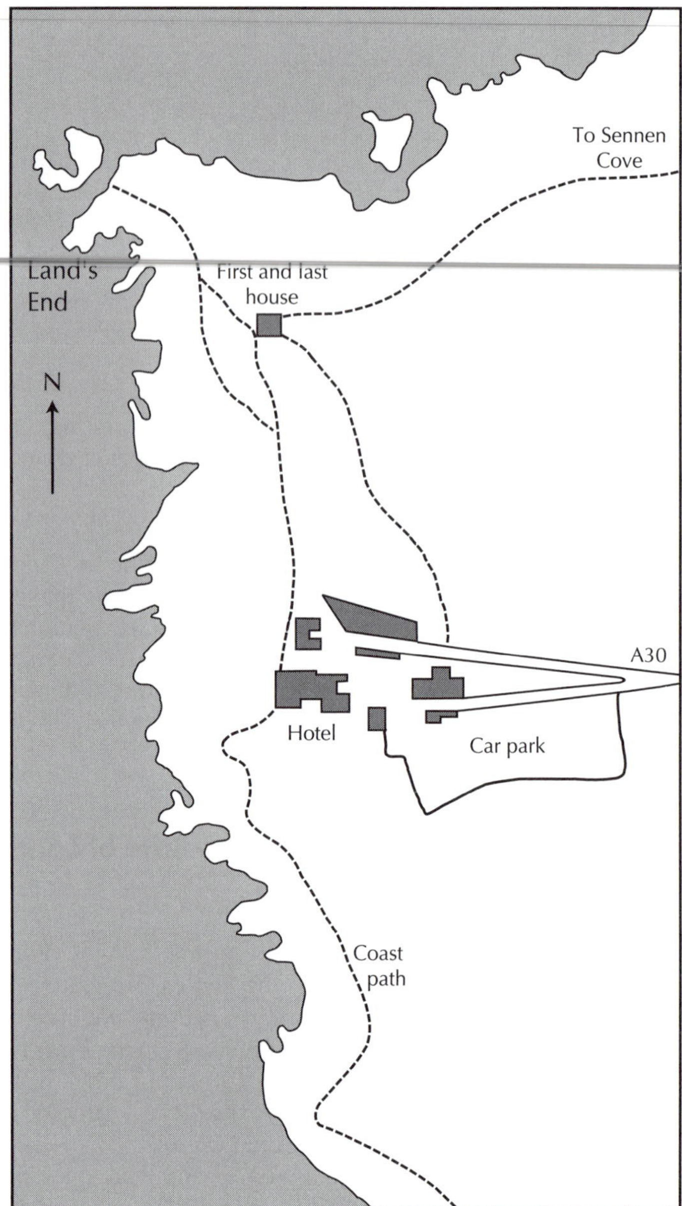

Fig. 9.2. Land's End, Cornwall.

sell, which was linked to management failure; (ii) conflicting opinions as to the intention of national heritage and conservation bodies, principally the National Trust, regarding the sale; and (iii) conflict fuelled by xenophobia, the fear of Land's End being bought by Americans. The realization of these myths had two immediate effects. Firstly, their cultivation had the effect of selling or marketing the property for the vendors. Secondly, the myths created among prospective visitors' prior expectations of a promised experience when visiting Land's End. The idea of expectation and promised experience strengthens the contention that culture, social and material, can be produced and sold as a commodity. What this case study is testimony to is the re-creation and eventual repackaging of a well used touristic commodity, the Land's End.

The origins of the sale stem from a conflict by the owner and Penwith District Council on how Land's End as a major tourist attraction should be redeveloped. Immediately prior to the decision to sell, the owner had submitted a scheme which gave the impression of wanting to conserve rather than further commercialize Land's End. Details of the scheme appeared in the *Cornishman* (9 April 1981) under the headline: 'Strong support for new proposals at Land's End'. This is a reference to the fact that the plans had the backing of the main environmental pressure groups, the National Trust and the Council for the Preservation of Rural England, and government bodies which included the Countryside Commission, English Tourist Board and the West Country Tourist Board. The plan received little local publicity until June 1981 when the *Cornishman* (18 June 1981) carried a headline: 'Land's End: Penwith and County disagree'. The disagreement arose over a proposed visitor centre at Land's End.

The County Council had made their position clear with regard to Land's End. Its Planning and Employment Committee had passed a resolution to advise Penwith District Council of the County's support for the proposal to restore eroded areas, carry out environmental improvements and improve facilities. The importance of this resolution can be interpreted in two ways. Firstly, it allowed the blame for any subsequent mismanagement of Land's End to be laid at the door of Penwith District Council. Secondly, the people of Cornwall (who are not necessarily Cornish people) were by no means united on the fate of Land's End.

The Origins of Land's End Myth

News of the sale of Land's End originated as a rumour in the *Cornishman* (27 August 1981, p. 3). The official comment from Land's End was that this was only a rumour! Within the space of about three weeks this rumour became a little more credible. *The Times* (19 September 1981, p. 3) carried a headline: 'Land's End may be sold'. The article was very brief, yet important. The importance lies in the identification of three themes which ran through both national and local press in the months leading up to the eventual sale of Land's End. Firstly, that two to three million tourists visit Land's End each year; a statement which would have the effect of provoking speculation on the revenue to be gained from a seemingly thriving tourist industry. Secondly,

The Times reported that the National Trust was interested in adding the property to the coastline it already owned in Cornwall. From this point on, the National Trust featured in almost every serious article on the sale, regardless of its actual involvement. Finally, an element of mystery entered the saga, through reports of the whereabouts of the elusive owner, who was rarely at Land's End, often believed to be in America. This seemingly trivial point is important because it introduced mystery into the sale, which helped create a state of national and international fear as to the eventual fate of Land's End.

Rumour of the sale was confirmed in late September 1981 (*The Times*, 22 September 1981, p. 4) and confirmed the National Trust's interest in buying Land's End. The report also hinted at 'possible American buyers'. It is this hint, which while remaining no more than a hint, became the most contentious aspect of the sale. As with so many of the conflicts which surround tourism development in Cornwall, there existed dissension within the county as to whether or not the National Trust should be supported in their campaign to buy Land's End. Whilst the *West Briton*, a weekly paper for mid Cornwall was running a headline: 'Drive starts to buy Land's End for the Nation' (*West Briton*, 24 September 1981), in contrast the *Cornishman* (24 September 1981) dwelt on a fear which was never substantiated: 'Land's End to be American owned?'

Prominence is given to the remarks of a 'leading' local and County Councillor who expressed two main fears concerning the possibility of American ownership of Land's End. The Councillor was concerned that Land's End would be ruined if it fell into American hands. It was not entirely clear whether the Councillor was referring to the further degradation of the physical environment by tourists aiding the forces of nature, or ruination for the local entrepreneurs who had traded at Land's End for so long. On one issue he was very clear; that American ownership would result in a monopoly at the site.

Events have shown that the most prophetic statement made by the Councillor was the reference to the new owner's relationship with the planning authority. He warned of a running battle between the planning authorities and the people down there (whoever bought Land's End).

Xenophobia in the National Parliament

Conflict over the sale of Land's End took on a national and, by implication, international dimension in the autumn of 1981. Cornish and British national feeling appears to have been united against a common enemy, the mythical American buyer, such was the strength of a report in the *Cornishman* (22 October 1981) on a debate on the future of Land's End which took place in the House of Lords. Lord Molloy (Labour) introduced the debate and the root of the conflict, with the following question:

> To ask Her Majesty's Government whether they will take all necessary steps to prevent the sale of Land's End to non-British individuals or organisations; and whether they will consider providing financial aid to the National Trust to purchase Land's End on behalf of the British people.
>
> (*Parliamentary Debates,* V series, 1981a p. 559).

The debate had three clearly identifiable themes. Firstly, to prevent the sale of Land's End to a non-British individual, through the use of Government aid. Secondly, to make the Government aware of public concern over the sale. Finally, to highlight the symbolic importance of the sale to a foreigner, as a mark of national decline and a threat to nationhood. This last sentiment was expressed most succinctly by Lord Somers. He said: 'My Lords, would not the sale of Land's End be the beginning of Britain's end?' (*Parliamentary Debates,* V series, 1981a p. 560).

These comments made by the Noble Lords highlight the growth of a fear voiced through emotive statements which became increasingly nationalistic and less concerned with conservation and environmental issues as the sale approached. The power of such remarks to fuel conflict over the sale of Land's End is evident from comments to the editor of the *Cornishman.* The paper has an international as well as national circulation among Cornish expatriates. Letters to the editor dated in the November editions of the paper illustrate the strength of feeling. A housewife from Australia wrote that she was sure that 'all Cornish people all over the World' will be filled 'with absolute horror and grief at the thought of an American buying Land's End' (*Cornishman,* 5 November 1981, p. 9). Another reader writing from California described herself as being very upset at the thought of maybe an American buying Land's End. In her opinion, 'Cornwall belongs to the Cornish'.

These remarks demonstrate that any attempt to treat the sale of Land's End as merely a sale of 105 acres of coastal headland with commercial potential, was futile. National identity and the conflict over ownership were inextricably linked. The 'keep foreigners out' theme (Horsnell, 9 November 1981, p. 10) and appeals to patriotism continued in the hope of raising money for the National Trust to purchase Land's End. Support for the Trust came from an unusual quarter, the Cornish Nationalist Party who were reported as saying that 'every support should be given to the efforts of the National Trust to purchase the headland' (*Cornishman,* 19 November 1981, p. 3).

Just what Land's End represented to the different parties was not at all clear. This is evident from the comments of Earl Avon speaking about the sale in the House of Lords. He said: 'one of the difficulties about Land's End is that it is difficult to know what actually we are trying to preserve . . . a hotel, the land itself, the car park, the litter bin, or what? (*Parliamentary Debates* V series, 1981b p. 1433). The answer to this question would, of course, have been different according to whom one talked to at the time, and illustrates the very nature of the conflict over the sale. At a national level the replies centred on the symbolic aspects of the sale and the perceived threats to national identity. At a local level, replies would have been more complex, with people torn between employment and conservation and the erosion of Cornwall both actually and metaphorically when seen in terms of Cornish national identity.

The Sale and the Aftermath

Shortly before the sale was completed, support for the National Trust disappeared. Cornwall County Council were of the view that there was no need to spend public money on helping to purchase Land's End, because planning laws would control development. As subsequent events have shown, the local authority did not have control over developments at Land's End. It is difficult to comment further on the reasons for the withdrawal of support for the National Trust both at a local and national level, except to say that it was a political decision. The decision can be seen more as a battle between the conflicting ideologies with the Trust and conservationist bodies on one hand, and national and local government on the other.

January 1982 saw the death of the National Trust's attempts to buy Land's End. The *Cornishman* (14 January 1982) reported that the Trust's first bid of £800,000 was not accepted and that another bid of 'over £1 million' had been tendered. The announcement on the completed sale came on 22 January 1982 with the *Guardian* carrying a report headed 'National Trust loses Land's End to £1.75 million bid'. *The Times* headline was less sympathetic with the Trust proclaiming 'Land's End bought by British Businessman' (Phillips, 1982). Both the *Guardian* and *The Times* described the new owner as a 'self made socialist millionaire'. In an effort to reconcile himself with the defeated environmentalist lobby the new owner was quoted in *The Times* as saying:

> We fully appreciate that we have achieved the acquisition of not only a remarkable investment opportunity but also a unique part of the national heritage and folklore and our approach to the realization in the investment opportunity will always have due regard to this latter fact.
>
> (Phillips, 22 January 1982, p. 22)

The initial statement by the new owner can be seen as an attempt at conflict resolution between private capital and the large pro-National Trust lobby in the country at that time.

Almost as a postscript to the sale, the *Cornishman* (18 March 1982, p. 3) carried three reports on the new owner of Land's End. One report is of interest because it could be described as an obituary to the National Trust. The report deals with the Council for the Protection of Rural England's (Cornwall Branch) reaction to the sale. The concluding paragraph illustrates a contradiction inherent in the development of tourism in Cornwall. The reports states that:

> Everyone who lives in Cornwall recognises the vital importance of the tourist industry to the county's economy, but . . . many did not recognise the immense danger which could be caused to that industry if the traditional Cornwall and its way of life that every tourist came to see and enjoy, continued to be destroyed.
>
> (*Cornishman*, 18 March 1982, p. 3).

This comment focuses attention on just what exactly it is the tourist industry is trying to provide for the visitor. The new owner gives some indication in the *Cornishman* (28 March 1982): 'No Fun Fairs at Land's End'. Referring to the way the tourists spend their time at Land's End he is reported to have said, 'The only thing they [tourists] can say is they have seen Land's End. There is no more to the experience than that' (*Cornishman*, 28 March 1982, p. 1).

Just what the new owner intended that experience to be and how much it conflicted with local culture forms the postscript to this case study. One year after the sale the new owner, Davstone Holdings, made headlines in the *Daily Telegraph* (Shields, 8 March 1983) with: 'Trippers must pay £1.50 to visit Land's End'. The headline referred to 'the charge being imposed from March 28th [1983] by Davstone Holdings'. The report explained that the money would be used for repairs to erosion damage caused by walkers and the weather. The Planning and Development Officer for Penwith District Council said, 'There has been quite a lot of reaction against the price. It used to cost 40 pence to park your car and walk down the coastal path' (Shields, 1983, p. 17). There was, however, some concession to Cornish residents who were able to buy a season ticket costing £3.00! This concession was not enough to satisfy the Cornish Nationalists.

Conflict between the Cornish Nationalist Party and Davstone Holdings came to a head in August 1983, with a demonstration against the new charges taking place at Land's End. The photograph (Fig. 9.3) shows a tourist being stopped and asked to pay the admission charge of £1.50 per person. For the four adults in the car shown, this would have meant a total admission of £6.00. The second photograph (Fig. 9.4) illustrates the point of conflict between the Cornish Nationalist and the management of Land's End. The final photograph (Fig. 9.5) symbolizes, through the flag of St Piran (a white cross on a black background), the Nationalists' defiant stand against the imposition of admission charges for access to a headland which Cornish people would claim as a right.

Cornishness in the Wider Context

Payton (1992, p. 170) has argued that Cornwall's economic development was in effect based on 'an act of faith in the panacea of tourism'. If this panacea is to continue to bear fruit then it has to be acknowledged that

Fig. 9.3. 'Tourists are charged admission to the Land's End for the first time' (M. Ireland).

Fig. 9.4. 'Cornish nationalist in conflict with Land's End management' (M. Ireland).

Fig. 9.5. 'St Piran's Flag symbolizes a defiant stand by Cornish nationalists against the imposition of admission charges to Land's End' (M. Ireland).

Cornishness, which gives the county its separate cultural and product identity, is a finite resource.

The tourist industry and those firms who supply its needs have already come to realize that cultural difference and uniqueness must be maintained in the minds of the tourists as consumers. The globalization of Cornwall's traditional food and the text promoting it, is one source of evidence for this view. In Cornwall a publication promoting the county's industries states: 'Traditional golden crusted Cornish clotted cream – once a home made delicacy found only in domestic kitchens – is today exported as far as Hong-Kong' (Cornwall County Council, 1995).

The argument advanced here, using food as one example, is that culture as an economic resource embodied in commodities to enhance the exchange value, is finite. Each culture possesses symbols which have come to represent it, whether it is Cornish pasties or Devon cream teas. The living culture of the respective peoples with which these and other symbols are associated are not reliant on them to give meaning to their everyday life. The important point for the development of tourism, if conflict is to be avoided, is 'the need for care and accuracy in the transmittal of the images of host cultures and communities, and the correct identification of the needs and desires of those indigenous people who wish to become involved in the tourist industry' (Butler and Hinch, 1996, p. 278).

The influx of tourists to Cornwall has sought to heighten awareness of cultural boundaries and create new ones. When asked to describe Cornishness the response frequently referred to the perceived effects of tourism. The main themes to emerge from this research were that: (i) many people living in Cornwall have become intolerant of the visitor; (ii) visitors are referred to openly by derogatory names; and (iii) there is hostility among some local people to the management of tourism businesses by non-Cornish. Non-Cornish residents have become perceived as a threat to the maintenance of Cornishness, and leading to a growth of South East England values.

The debate within Britain about the cultural impact of migrants to Cornwall from other regions of the country has its parallels in Europe. Stolcke (1995) has coined the term 'extra-communitarian immigrants' to describe population movements within Europe. Stolcke (1995) argues that the concepts of cultural identity and distinctiveness once used by the anthropologist have become the language of anti-immigration sentiments and policies. The consequences for peripheral countries within the European Union is that socio-economic ills resulting from the recession and capitalist readjustment, for example unemployment, housing shortages, inadequate social services and crime, will be blamed on those who comprise the cultural 'other'.

Tensions based on such assumptions can be seen to manifest themselves throughout the recent history of Europe, in places as geographically and culturally diverse as Karalia (Finnish/Russian border), Northern Ireland and the former Yugoslavia.

Conclusion

This chapter has raised a number of questions for future research in peripheral areas in Europe which, like Cornwall, are dependent on tourism for economic development. It has been shown that cultural difference expressed through language, and used as a divisive force is an under-researched area with regard to tourism development.

A review of the existing literature which addressed the question, 'What is Cornishness?' raised questions about the need for greater cooperation between social science disciplines in the study of cultural difference. This failure to cooperate calls into question the status of some historical research on Cornishness. In particular, the suitability of the methodologies used and the impressionistic conclusions drawn.

Fieldwork in Padstow, St Just and Land's End has shown that the question: 'What is Cornishness today?' generates deeply emotional and personal statements which contain generalizable elements. Research has shown that the concept of Cornishness is of importance to local people, tourists, planners, politicians and those of Cornish descent living overseas. This research has demonstrated that a new paradigmatic perspective is required to understand the meaning of Cornishness in the context of tourism development.

Cornishness is only able to exist in relationship to the cultural 'other', e.g., tourists, developers or 'foreigners'. Cornishness and tourism development do not, as this chapter has shown, sit comfortably together. They are in binary opposition. Put simply, the reaction to tourism development can only be understood through the language which gives locals and tourists a shared cultural understanding of what unites, and at the same time, divides them – Cornishness.

References

Atherton C. (1998) cited in Jobson 'Special Euro status is number one objective' *Western Morning News*, 23rd March.

Bohannan (1973) Rethinking culture: a project for current anthropologists, *Current Anthropology*, 14(4), pp. 357–372.

Burke (1980) *Sociology and History*, George Allen and Unwin, London.

Butler, R. and Hinch T. (eds) (1996) *Tourism and Indigenous Peoples*, International Thomson Business Press, London.

Calder, S. (1992) 'Pasties on the camomile lawn', *Independent*, 21st March.

Cicourel, A.V. (1964) *Method and Measurement in Sociology*, Free Press, New York.

Cohen, A.P. (1985) *The Symbolic Construction of Community*, Ellis Horwood Ltd, Chichester.

Cooper C. and Wanhill S. (1997) *Tourism Development: Environmental and Community Issues*, John Wiley, Chichester.

Cornishman (1981) 'Strong support for new proposals at Land's End'. *Cornishman*, 9th April.

Cornishman (1981) 'Land's End: Penwith and County disagree'. *Cornishman*, 18th June.

Cornishman (1981) 'Land's End "rumour" '. *Cornishman*, 27th August.

Cornishman (1981) 'Land's End to be American owned'. *Cornishman*, 24th September.

Cornishman (1981) 'Lords discuss Land's End'. *Cornishman*, 22nd October.

Cornishman (1981) Letters to the Editor, 5th November.

Cornishman (1981) 'CNP supports Trust purchase of Land's End'. *Cornishman*, 19th November.

Cornishman (1982) 'Prince Charles considered buying Land's End'. *Cornishman*, 14th January.

Cornishman (1982) 'Regrets that National Trust failed in bid for Land's End'. *Cornishman*, 18th March.
Cornishman (1982) 'No funfairs at Land's End'. *Cornishman*, 28th March.
Cornwall County Council (1995) *In Pursuit of Excellence*, Cornwall County Council, Truro.
Fees, C. (1996) Tourism and politics of authenticity in a North Cotswold town. In: Selwyn, T. (ed.) *The Tourist Image: Myth and Myth Making in Tourism*, John Wiley, Chichester, pp. 121–146.
Griffin C.G. (1993) *Cornwall Structure Plan – Explanatory Memorandum*, Cornwall County Council, Truro.
Guardian (1982) 'National Trust loses Land's End to £1.75 m bid.' *Guardian*, 22nd January.
Harvey R.G., Smith, M.T., Sherron, S., Bailey, L. and Hyndinan S.J. (1986) How Celtic are the Cornish? A study of biological affinities, *MAN*, 21, pp. 177–201.
Hodge, P. (1990) Tourism or whorism?, *Kernow*, September–October, No.10.
Horsnell, M. (1981) 'Mystery trip', *The Times*, 9th November.
Hunt and Agnoli (1991) The Whorfian hypothesis: a cognitive psychology perspective, *Psychological Review*, 98(3), pp. 377–389.
Ireland, M. (1987) Planning policy and holiday homes in Cornwall. In: Bouquet, M. and Winter, M. (eds) *Who From Their Labours Rest?: Conflict and Practice in Rural Tourism*, Avebury, Aldershot.
Ireland, M. (1993) Gender and class relations in domestic employment in tourism: a case study of West Cornwall, *Annals of Tourism Research*, 20(4), pp. 666–684.
Ireland, M. (1997) Tourism and social responsibility. In: Stabler M.J. (ed.) *Tourism and Sustainability*, CAB International, Wallingford, Oxford.
Jackson, L. (1997) 'Prince backs Cornish march', *Sunday Telegraph*, 16th February.
Jenkin, A.K.H. (1933) *Cornwall and the Cornish*, J.M. Dent and Sons, London.
Jenner, H. (1920) *Cornish Nationality – An Essay*, Courtney Library, Truro.
Nute, E.R. (1995) *Protect your Cornish Inheritance*, Cornish Stannary Parliament, Truro.
Osgood C.E., Suci, G.J. and Tannenbaum, P.H. (1957) *The Measurement of Meaning*, University of Illinois Press, Illinois.
Parliamentary Debates (Hansard) (1981a) *'Land's End*', V Series, 424, pp. 559–560, HMSO, London.
Parliamentary Debates (Hansard) (1981b) *'Land's End*', V Series, 425, pp. 1432–1433, HMSO, London.
Payton, P. (1992) *The Making of Modern Cornwall*, Dyllansow Truran, Redruth.
Payton, P. (ed.) (1995) *Cornish Studies* (Second Series) 3, Exeter University Press.
Phillips, B. (1982) 'Land's End bought by British businessman', *The Times*, 22nd January.
Probert, J.C.C. (1971) *The Sociology of Cornish Methodism*, Redruth.
Rowse, A.L. (1969) *Tudor Cornwall*, Macmillan, London.
Shields, J. (1983) 'Trippers must pay £1.50 to visit Land's End', *Daily Telegraph*, 8th March.
Stolcke, V. (1995) Talking culture: new boundaries, new rhetorics of exclusion in Europe, Sidney, W., Mintz Lecture 1993, *Current Anthropology*, 36(1), February, pp. 1–24.
The Times (1981) 'Land's End may be sold', *The Times*, 19th September.
The Times (1981) 'Trust wants to buy Land's End', *The Times*, 22nd September.

West Briton (1981) 'Drive starts to buy Land's End for the Nation', *West Briton,* 24th September.

Western Morning News (1998) 'Cornwall must stand united', *Western Morning News,* 23rd March.

Some Dimensions of Maori Involvement in Tourism

10

Chris Ryan

Introduction

This chapter has three foci. The first is a description of how the Te Arawa people have been involved with tourism for well over a century. The second analyses this history to explain why this involvement has been successful and why today other Maori groups wish to emulate this success. Drawing on this analysis and description of contemporary developments, in the third section a means is proposed of locating current Maori tourism products on a perceptual map formed by three axes consisting of: (i) the size and ownership of the product; (ii) the duration or intensity of the visitor experience; and (iii) the degree to which Maori culture forms the core of the tourism product on offer.

The History of Maori Involvement in Tourism

Maori involvement in New Zealand's tourism has a history of over 140 years. However, for much of the period that relationship has centred upon Rotorua in New Zealand's North Island. The consequences of this are described below. As noted, this chapter first traces some aspects of that history, and then describes contemporary developments. However, any such development occurs within a socio-political context which is the bi-cultural relationship between Maori and the predominantly European (or *Pakeha*) society that forms New Zealand. Moreover, Maoridom is beginning to further its aspirations at a time when New Zealand is changing from being a nation with a colonial past to one having close economic ties with the Asian powers of the Asia–Pacific region. This change impacts upon New Zealand in many ways, including immigration from Asia and the resultant emergence of a multicultural nation. Yet within these broad sweeps of history, New Zealand, like any nation with a history of immigration from the 19th century, also has its by-waters and quieter pools. Thus it includes a European tradition that is not British, and any history of New Zealand must note the contribution of Balkan and other European groups in addition to the past role of Chinese settlers. Maori are thus not the only group with an ethnic or national identity that seeks to gain from tourism. Although alternative initiatives are at different levels of maturity and of less importance, other ethnic groups seek similar gains from tourism, whether it is a Scandinavian tradition at Norsewood, an appeal to a French history at Akoroa or a Scottish identity in Dunedin. Hence this account of Maoridom and its use of tourism within New Zealand is but a partial picture of ethnicity and culture in tourism development within that country, although it is without doubt the main one. Indeed, it is one of the consequences of tourism that there is a perceived homogeneity of Maori culture, and while there is a truth in this perception in that there is one Maori language, the differences among tribal groups (*iwi*) are of significance.

Given that the early 19th century colonists found Maori inhabiting much of North Island, the first question to ask is why was it that the Te Arawa people of Rotorua were the first to develop tourism. Certainly that development has had significant economic implications. Today, while Maori form approximately 12.9% of the total population, they are over-represented in many of the indices of social dysfunctioning, whether it be statistics of unemployment, low income, receipt of benefits, juvenile suicides or prison population. The history of Maori in New Zealand from the early 1850s (when, as Belich (1986) and Butterworth (1988) point out, Maori were the equal of the colonists in wealth and business organizations, and the majority population) to the late 1890s is one of not only war, disease and rogue land deals, but of denigration of their culture (e.g., see McGeorge, 1993; Oppenshaw *et al.*, 1993). Indeed, by the turn of the 20th century commentators spoke of the possible extinction of Maori as a race. The recovery of identity, pride and economic well-being has been a difficult task, but one which is being accomplished. Yet in this scenario of deprivation the statistics of educational attainment, income, employment and entrepreneurship among the Te Arawa people differ little from those of mainstream New Zealand society, and in part this is a consequence of tourism (Ryan and Crotts, 1997).

Stafford (1977) traces the arrival of early tourists like the naturalist Bidwell in 1841, and the subsequent development of hotel accommodation in Rotorua. In 1898, Rotorua had 452 commercial rooms for tourist use. However, this was an early example of the theory of the marginalization of local enterprise in tourism (Kermath and Thomas, 1992). As Barnett notes:

> Initially, tourists' accommodation needs and guiding requirements were adequately met by Maori businesses – the first hotels and guiding operations in

> the district were either wholly or partly owned and operated by Maori. Gradually they were displaced by the *Pakeha*, and Maori land alienation in the area began to accelerate.
>
> (Barnett, 1997)

Two main reasons existed for tourism in Rotorua. The first was the presence of a volcanic scenery which attracted Victorian visitors by its strangeness, size, and health-giving qualities of hot springs. It appealed to those seeking medical cures and scenic attractions hard to find in Europe. It also had not only a smell of sulphur, but a whiff of danger, as the famous Pink and White Terraces were destroyed by volcanic action in 1886. The eruption of Mount Tarawera led to the loss of over 100 lives, most of whom were Maori, but if anything this was an impetus for renewed tourism interest in the area.

However, the second reason for the attraction of Rotorua was that much of the interpretation of the site was being provided by Maori guides. Stafford cites the comments of a Rotorua magistrate in an annual report of 1881 where it was noted:

> I regret to remark the extent to which the Natives of this district now neglect cultivation, depending in a great measure on what they get from tourists and other precarious sources for a living.
>
> (cited in Stafford, 1977, p. 26)

This touch of 'the native' was made all the more exotic by the fact that the most famous guides were females. Maggie Papakura, Guide Rangi, Guide Sophie and Bubbles were among the famous guides. The importance of these guides is not only due to their guiding, but to their role in popularizing Maori culture as displayed through song and dance, and through their organizing performances not only in Rotorua but also overseas. The extent of this past entrepreneurial activity is perhaps not fully realized by contemporary *Pakeha* society, but even a cursory examination of the papers of Maggie Papakura, which are lodged in the Pitt Rivers Museum Archives, Oxford, England, reveals the extent of this activity. Maggie Papakura, known as an outstandingly beautiful woman as well as being a talented organizer, died in Oxford in 1930, and had accompanied members of the British Royal Family when they visited Rotorua in 1901. The attraction of Rotorua was hence an attraction of an exotic 'other' as described by writers like Albers and James (1988), Cohen (1993), Edwards and Llurdes i Coit (1996). The late Victorian view of the South Pacific as an exotic 'other' was reinforced by a cultural community which included Robert Louis Stevenson, Conrad and Gauguin among others (Douglas, 1994); an exoticism reinforced by its distance from Britain and the time it took to travel there. Differences of culture and the various and disparate cultural norms attributed to Maori led to a process whereby Maori were perceived:

> for touristic purposes, anachronistically or 'allochronically', ahistorically or atemporally, as idealized and exotic, isolated and authentically living others,

> torn out of their wider contemporary socio-economic and socio-historical context.
>
> (Cohen, 1993, p. 37)

The exoticism of the Maori was further 'enhanced' by a Victorian view that it was a dying culture. Irvine and Alpers wrote:

> The maori is going to his doom – dying of a broken heart . . . The outlook for the race is undoubtedly gloomy. The census returns are the reverse of encouraging.
>
> (Irvine and Alpers, 1902, p. 399)

It can thus be contended that the Victorian generation was intrigued by a 'native people' who had proven their equal in recent wars (the Land Wars of the 1860s), who lived in a 'different' volcanic setting and whose hospitality included dances and performances with attractive females. Te Awekotuku (1991) advances another reason for the Victorian fascination with the 'other' – that Maori re-affirmed the notion of European supremacy as a civilized people. She writes:

> In the 1870's with the formalization of tourism in Aotearoa, Maori were romanticized as historical noble savages, replete in their barbaric and primitive culture, and as wild and 'tameable' as the new land. Early film, photography, travelogues and ethnographies concentrate attention on images of erotic/exotic game-playing Maori, while at the same time validating images of paternal, pioneering, civilizing Pakeha.
>
> (Te Awekotuku, 1991, p. 154)

Additionally the Te Arawa had one other asset. They had fought on the side of the Colonial forces during the 1860s. The success of the Te Arawa in establishing tourism can thus far be accounted for by their culture, their entrepreneurial flair, their being on the 'winning' side in the Land Wars, and the scenic and health-giving values of the land they settled.

A further factor was the willingness of European settlers to act as patrons and promoters of Rotorua tourism. By the late 1890s, hotel owners and Maori-philes like Hamilton and Nelson had aided Maori in the promotion of overseas trips by performance companies, and the sale and distribution of Maori carving. However, Neich comments that:

> Between them, these two men set up an orthodox doctrine of what 'unchanging traditional Maori culture' should be like. Furthermore, they had the economic power and influence to enforce this orthodoxy on the Ngati Tarawhai carvers.
>
> (Neich, 1983, pp. 255–257)

As already noted, the late Victorian view was that Maori culture and people were in decline. Certainly the Maori population, as far as can be judged, had declined from a population about 150,000 in the late 18th century to 42,113 as recorded by the census of 1896 (Butterworth, 1988, p. 23). Neich (1983) attributes the view to Hamilton that Maori culture had been an unchanging, timeless one which had only entered a degenerative stage with the coming of the Europeans. Thus, as Director of the Colonial Museum in Wellington, Hamilton had constructed a view of a Maori classical style of carving which too had been unchanging. Ryan and Crotts (1997) note, however, that the reality was far more complex, and that specific differences existed between Maori carvers in different parts of the country. The establishment of a Maori style, which was subjected to touristic needs of small scale and portability, at the turn of the 20th century has had surprisingly long lasting results. Not only has it diminished the importance of alternative Maori styles of work, but it created in the minds of European benefactors a stylistic understanding of what is Maori, which has perhaps made more difficult the acceptance of work by a modern generation of Maori artists like John Bevan Ford, Shane Cotton, Robert Jahake, Selwyn Muru Paenga, Ralph Hotere and Denise Tohiariki who adopt contemporary idioms of work informed by, challenged by and challenging to 'conventional' Maori styles. The tensions in Maori art between the old and new are described by a number of commentators (e.g. Ford, 1987), yet, when looking at the definition of what constitutes Maori art as established by the Aotearoa Maori Tourism Federation (namely, that it is conceived from the mind of a Maori, executed by a Maori, and is the work of someone with Maori *tapuna* (ancestry) (Aotearoa Maori Tourism Federation, 1994)), this modern generation of artists can only be deemed to be 'Maori'. Thus it can be argued that contemporary Maori art is just as important a part of the Maori tradition as the *poupou* panels to be found in *Marae*, and that the early touristic efforts of Hamilton and Nelson have had a long, if diffuse, shadow. It is also of interest to note that John Bevan Ford, in conversation with the author, noted that purchasers of his work included tourists who would purchase from commercial galleries because, he concluded, it stated something to them.

Canter (1977) stated that the psychology of place is derived from three elements: the physical attributes, the activities performed within the setting and the conceptions people carried to the place. The success of Maori tourism in Rotorua can therefore be explained by the successful creation of strong images/assets in each of these three dimensions. Smith (1996) has argued that the characteristics of indigenous people's tourism are explicable by reference to 4 'H's: namely, habitat, handicrafts, history and heritage. The first two have been touched upon, while for Maori, heritage and history are closely interlinked and, additionally, have a symbiotic relationship with land or place. Thus, when introducing themselves in any formal or semi-formal setting, a Maori person will commence with a brief statement of their genealogy (*whakapapa*) which is statement of identity with reference to place, ancestors and tribal affiliation, which are all linked. Thus, the loss of lands and denigration of culture that occurred in the last century must be understood as having grave psychological implications which in part account for the dysfunctioning of Maori society to which earlier reference was made. The 'history' and 'heritage' 'H's that contribute to tourism thus, it can be argued, contribute to a stronger sense of self-identity within the Maori psyche, and it is this that will now be considered within contemporary developments.

Since the mid-1980s there have been several reports and initiatives relating to Maori involvement in tourism, and general support from Maori communities themselves, albeit with an expression of concern about how tourism might negatively impact upon their culture. There is a high level of awareness of the dangers of stereotypical portrayals of Maori as, for example, portrayed in postcards. Ryan and Knox (1998) argue that compared with the late 19th century, today's postcards illustrate a much more limited display of Maori culture based upon the 'concert party' image of men sticking out their tongues (part of the *pukana* – a fearsome expression and a confirmation of the tongue as the conduit of words of meaning) and women whirling *poi* or wearing *piupiu*. It is interesting to compare this with posters printed by ATSIC (the Aboriginal and Torres Straits Islanders Council) in Northern Australia, where a poster dedicated to female Aboriginal women shows daily realities of being a barrister, weaving outside poor ramshackled housing, playing hockey, and in short presenting a series of images reflecting complex realities. Maori tourism representatives link this depiction with a loss of control over an ability to portray Maori culture. The Aotearoa Maori Tourism Federation has made this a central point in past reports. For example, in 1995, Bennett wrote:

> The authenticity of a particular tourism product is directly related to the quality of input by the *tangata whenua* into the development and operation of the venture. *Taonga* is the key determinant of ownership over an aspect of the culture. To retain the dignity of *Iwi* and the integrity of the New Zealand tourism industry a concerted effort must be made by all key stakeholders – *Iwi*, industry and Government – to acknowledge the role of the *tangata whenua* within each region; and to develop and enforce standards of authenticity of Maori tourism products.
>
> (Bennett, 1995, p. 20)

Tangata whenua (the original people) have a right of guardianship over Maori treasures, a phrase of constitutional importance dating from the Treaty of Waitangi in 1840. This treaty, which is the cornerstone of the New Zealand constitution, recognized the Crown as sovereign over New Zealand, but in return guaranteed traditional chieftain rights. Ryan (1998a) argues that in the Maori view there is an important relationship between constitutional rights and the rites of tourism and culture, and hence for some the development of tourism is not solely an economically motivated act but also one charged with political and cultural significance.

However, such wider concerns are of no avail if Maori tourism businesses do not prosper. What then is the current state of Maori involvement in tourism? While it is difficult to define specific periods it might be argued that the 'modern' period of Maori tourism commenced with the establishment of the Maori Arts and Crafts Institute at Whakarewarerwa, Rotorua, in 1963 under an Act of Parliament. While the prime purpose of the Institute was, and continues to be, a training and teaching role in the conservation and maintenance of Maori arts, it also had a promotional role which led to exhibitions and daily performances of Maori song and dance which are popular with tourists. The next significant development was the Manaakitanga *Hui* held in Rotorua on 25–27 September 1985 – a *Hui* (meeting) that discussed Maori involvement in tourism and which led to the Maori Tourism Task Force report and the establishment of the Maori Tourism Association in 1988, which was renamed the Aotearoa Maori Tourism Federation in 1991.

The Aotearoa Maori Tourism Federation has struggled to represent and maintain a Maori presence on various national tourism bodies on a small budget, but in 1996 received some additional funding and support from the Department of Maori Development (Te Puni Kokiri). The Department also appointed Dr Takiora Ingram to specifically aid Maori tourism initiatives. Since 1996 a number of new initiatives have commenced, which, for example, involve the setting up of training courses in the Gisborn region, and the establishment of a database of operations. This database is being linked into a geographical information system (GIS) of domestic tourism being established by a team of researchers led by Professors Pip Forer and David Simmons at Lincoln University under a major tourism research project funded by the Foundation for Research, Science and Technology in 1996.

One of the major developments of the last two years has been the organization of a Maori Tourism Trade Fair (Te Putanga Mai) by Aotearoa Maori Tourism Federation, which is held in Auckland. The first was held in 1996, and attracted approximately a dozen tourism operators. In 1997, however, Te Putanga Mai was a much larger affair, and was more indicative of the growing health of Maori tourism outside of Rotorua. It attracted 185 delegates even though, at present, best estimates indicate that Maori tourism attracts less than 1% of all tourism spending in New Zealand (Zeppel, 1997).

Outside of Rotorua it might be said that two other significant Maori tourism operations exist. The first is at Christchurch and is the Haga Hau Wha National Marae. This was opened in 1990 and its name means 'Marae of the Four Winds' – a name chosen to represent its function as a place of national importance. It actually consists of two meeting houses: Aoraki, which is in the traditional style, and the small Te Aritaua Pitama which is a more contemporary style. Tourists are offered guided tours of the *Marae* and, additionally, three nights a week, a 'Maori Magic Tour' is offered, which includes a *hangi* (meal cooked in an earth oven) and a performance of song and dance. There is also a nightly concert performance.

The second is Kaikoura Whalewatch. This operation has won two major awards: the British Airways Global Tourism for Tomorrow Award in 1994 and the New Zealand Tourism Board's best operator award in 1993. While obviously the watching of sperm whales is the major attraction, the business is wholly Maori owned and was originally initiated by members of Ngati

Kuru, a *hapu* of Nagai Tahu, as an attempt to address the unemployment of Maori that followed the closure of railworks and other state services in the 1980s (Warren and Taylor, 1994). The success of this operation is recorded by the fact that this small Canterbury settlement of 3700 inhabitants has over 350,000 visitors a year; while the serviced accommodation sector has risen sharply to the present number of 16 motels with over 150 unit rooms (Jasons, 1997). Indeed, such has been the impact of tourism the population of Kaikoura rose from 2004 to almost 4000 within 5 years. By comparison, Timaru, with a population of 43,000 has about the same number of motels (18).

Barnett (1996) estimates that today there are 153 Maori tourism businesses, but is careful to point out that there is an additional category which is not based on the sale of 'Maori culture'. She cites, for example, Maori who are motel operators. Their involvement in the tourism industry is that of supplying motel accommodation; yet the very fact that they are Maori may involve them in types of discussions with their guests that *Pakeha* moteliers would not have, as guests ask them their opinions about a range of topics. A comparison may be made with farmstay operators, where, as Pearce (1990) noted, the attraction was, for many guests, not the farm, but the people and their lifestyles and opinions. One example cited in some detail by Barnett is the fishing charter business, Te Moana Charters. The Maori owner will provide details of Maori traditional fishing practices and other information for tourists if they are interested, but otherwise his is a conventional fishing and scenic tour business.

The role and quality of Maori tourism was further indicated by the 1996 New Zealand Tourism Board awards. That year the main prize was won by Tamaki Tours which is based in Rotorua. This company began in 1990 with just one 16-seat bus, but in 1996 had an annual turnover of over NZ$2 million and entertained over 40,000 overseas visitors at Te Taw Ngahere, a re-created pre-European Maori *Pa* (fort) set in native forest on a lakefront. Further investment of NZ$3.2 million is planned.

Another major initiative starting in 1997 is another research project funded by the Foundation for Research, Science and Technology, which is a feasibility study of Maori involvement in tourism in Northland, and the types of social, cultural and economic implications that will follow. In 1994 Warren and Taylor noted that 'a lack of vision about the tourism potential of the Far North was identified as a barrier' (Warren and Taylor, 1994, p. 29). It is certainly an area of beauty, and social problems. Northland (Tai Tokerau) is located north of Auckland and Maori account for 28% of its population of 135,000. However, 50% of Maori households have incomes of less than NZ$10,000 and the unemployment rate is 31%.

In order to tackle this problem of a lack of vision, in June 1996 the New Zealand Tourism Board published its draft strategy for tourism development in the region. Amongst its recommendations was a strengthening of the Tai Tokerau Maori Association, and that it should work with the Northland

Regional Tourism Organization. The report also identified three main cultural and historic themes for touristic development, which were: (i) the area as 'The Cradle of the Nation' concentrating on early Maori–European contact leading to the Treaty of Waitangi; (ii) Maori culture prior to European settlement; and (iii) the early industries of the European period. The development of tourism among Maori in Northland is thus apparently motivated by economic reasons to generate employment and income, using Maori culture as a product.

This review of Maori involvement in tourism thus reveals many different strands which replicate concerns in the literature about the way tourism and indigenous peoples interact. First, and notably, tourism has been, in New Zealand, an important source of revenue for the Te Arawa in Rotorua and Nagai Tahu in Kaikoura. It has the potential to yield income for the Ngati Kamu, Te Nga Puhi, Ngati Hine and Ngati Wai to name but four Maori groups in Northland. The economic benefits are tangible and unquestioned. As Te Awekotuko, in 1981, noted: 'I am determined to expose tourism as a corrupter of pure culture, spawning cultural malaise', but instead, after two years work, concluded; 'There was indeed substance to my people's loud and frequent claims that tourism has not hurt *Te Arawa*; in many instances it has helped us' (cited by Barnett, 1996).

The help that tourism has provided is not solely economic, in that the revenues so derived are used for communal action. *Marae* are refurbished, and with the funds generated from tourism are better able to fulfil their roles as centres for Maori social life and education. The vitality of this life can be seen at various Maori festivals of Art and Performance – where *Marae*-based teams compete in the performance arts and are judged not solely by the polished nature of the performance, but by the creativity displayed. New *haka*, song and *poi* dances are still being created within Maoridom – the dances are not simply re-enactments of past choreography, but a dynamic and changing art form within the disciplines imposed by that art. Put simply, Maori have their equivalents of the choreographers of Western ballet and contemporary dance, unrecognized by *Pakeha* society, but having recognition and esteem among their own people.

The psychological benefits of this cannot be underestimated. As noted above, for a people where self-identity is related to a communal identity, recognition of achievement by one's own people is an important element in psychological maturation. In Maslow's (1954) terms, a sense of social belonging is created, and from this basis further maturation is possible. Part of this maturation is the risk-taking involved in playing a larger role in the wider affairs of New Zealand.

The stage that Maori tourism has reached today can be assessed with the use of two concepts. The first is the 'Spectrum of Cultural Opportunities for Tourism' devised by Sofield and Birtles (1996), which is illustrated in Fig. 10.1. The above text provides some illustrations of Maori involvement which can be allocated to the various stages devised by Sofield and Birtles (1996).

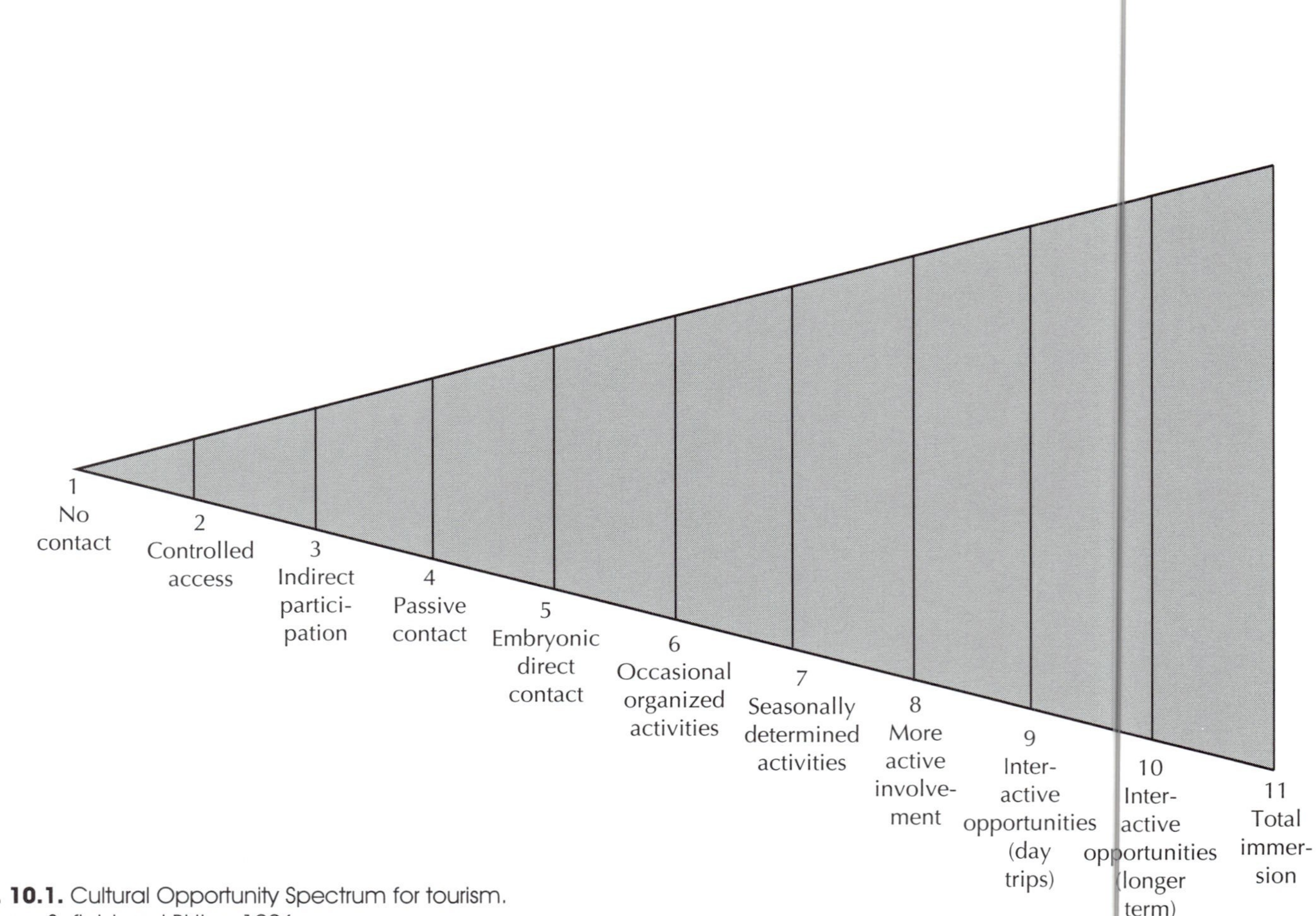

Fig. 10.1. Cultural Opportunity Spectrum for tourism. Source: Sofield and Birtles, 1996.

Although it is necessarily brief and incomplete, it is contended that the examples provided show that Maori involvement in tourism is not easily categorized, as practices vary between locations, industry sectors and stage of business. Some businesses are small, but reasonably well established (like Te Moana Charters), others receive state patronage (like the Institute of Arts and Crafts) while others like Tamaki Tours are emerging, at least on a local level, as important tourism enterprises. Indeed, Tamaki Tours has an interesting business history as the Tamaki family attempted the development of another tourism product in Rotorua based on Polynesian culture, but this form of business diversification did not achieve the hoped-for success. Hence, while Maori have their sacred sites in which no tourism development would be permitted (indeed, in some instances, Regional Planning Councils will only be informed of the approximate location of such a site (Ryan, 1998a), at the other end of the continuum Maori culture becomes but a theme within a New Zealand cultural presentation. It should not be thought that all Maori enterprise is small scale. Maori have significant property interests which range from hotels to executive suites in sports stadiums, and hence at one level operate in a manner similar to European or Asian tourism business interests, and tourists may be unaware that they are using Maori-owned assets.

Dimensions of Maori Tourism

Much of the literature on indigenous people's role in tourism emphasizes the role of their culture as a tourism product. The packaging of performances into two-hour stage shows is deemed to be part of a post-modernistic phenomenon of commoditization, where even the sacred is turned into a consumer experience. The debate that commenced in the 1960s with the work of Boorstin (1961), MacCannell (1976) and Fussell (1982) about whether authenticity exists within the tourist product has been overtaken by the marketing and promotion of products as offering 'an authentic experience'. The terminology used in the debate is itself of interest. In what way does the emotion attached to an 'experience' lack authenticity? Disappointment may be an authentic emotion. Hence it is not the experience *per se* which is suspect, but, as Ryan (1991, p. 45) noted the perception of the reality of the event, rather than the reality itself, which is the determinant of satisfaction from being present at an event which has meaning. If an event has meaning for tourists, does it lack authenticity? One of the implications of Foucault's (1978) 'gaze' is that an event has many who survey it, and hence many interpretations. However, the emergence of stronger Maori business enterprises and organizations means that the 'gaze' of the Maori is being more explicitly enunciated. Maori tourism operators straddle a number of 'gazes' or 'worlds'. They may operate in a world where Maori culture is commoditized for tourist consumption, and hence in a post-modernistic world of selective individual truths for those who participate in the act of consumption as suppliers or clients. Yet they also are members of an *iwi* or *hapu* whose culture identifies above all a sense of identity based not on individualism but on networks of belonging to other people, ancestors and land. Additionally, they deal in a world of business dominated by Western practices of contracts, due performance at set times and a need to cover costs and ensure profits. Furthermore, given the socio-political condition of Maoridom, many Maori operators have an additional responsibility not shared by European operators within New Zealand. Currently, at the start of the 21st century, Maori operators are linked to their culture and social history by ties which mean, like it or not, they are activists and role models for both Maori and *Pakeha* alike, and are judged as being representatives of their people.

Much of the literature on tourism and the culture of the developing world has implied that the only advantages that tourism offers are economic, with perhaps a revitalization of handicraft skills. For example, Lea (1988, pp. 70–72) notes this process, but adds that assimilation by a dominant Western culture does not always occur when 'active steps are taken to resist the forces of assimilation' (1988, p. 71). While this model might be imposed upon the experience of the Te Arawa, arguably such a view is incomplete. There is a need to consider additional features. First, the rate of development is important. In this respect, perhaps, Maori in general, and the Te Arawa in particular, have been fortunate due to having established a relationship with tourism over a century ago. They have not had to grapple, unprepared, with an onslaught of modern mass tourism. Second, tour operators in general have recognized that it is for Maori to interpret their culture. Examples to the contrary may be found, but the author believes that such examples are the exception rather than the rule. One exception though, is the question of the production of Maori artefacts as souvenirs, although how serious this issue is requires further research. As noted, Maori have claimed ownership of their culture under the Treaty of Waitangi, and New Zealand operators generally respect this. Additionally, Maori, based in part upon their notions of hospitality (Ryan, 1998a), have generally maintained a view that tourism represents a potential asset for income, employment and enhancement of a political recognition of the role and importance of Maori culture in New Zealand. (It should be noted that historically the notion of hospitality or *manaakitanga* within Maori culture could also have overtones of negotiation.) Indeed, one of the paradoxes of the success of Maori enterprise in New Zealand is that tourism development is increasingly viewed as an enterprise for individuals or families rather than for Maori Trust Boards due to the limited return to be had from tourism. Maori enterprise in New Zealand thus arguably gains more profit from its forestry, retail and other interests than from tourism.

The modelling of this process is hence more complex than that envisaged by Sofield and Birtles (1996). Their model was based primarily on Melanesian and Polynesian experience, and more specifically on that of the Solomons, and arguably there exist differences between situations where native peoples form a majority of the population and one where they do not, as in New Zealand, Australia or Canada. The above discussion indicates at least three dimensions to the situation of Maori tourism, and these are:

1. The level of Maori ownership and the size of the tourism operation. Arguably this dimension is really two – ownership and size – but in the late 1990s most Maori operations in tourism are wholly owned by Maori. However, for those tourism products which are large scale, ownership usually exists through Maori Trust Boards, and as a large business entity they may enter into agreements with, for example, hotel management groups. Hence size is related to ownership, in that the greater the scale of the operation, the higher is the possibility that some dilution of Maori ownership or management might exist.
2. The level of Maori culture involved in a product. As noted, Maori own motels and other attractions like helicopter sightseeing and fishing charter businesses. A Maori perspective may be provided when it is thought that clients would be responsive to the additional information, but it is not the main component of the product being offered. On the other hand, for Tamaki Tours as an example, the whole product rests upon a representation of Maori culture.
3. The intensity or duration of the experience. Again, two elements may exist within this dimension, as obviously intensity and duration are not synonymous terms. However, there is a significant difference between a 'concert party' performance in a Rotorua hotel and the type of experience offered by, say, Trek Wiranaki when clients have been known to break down in tears because of the emotion engendered by the *powhiri* after sharing time with Maori guides (Ryan, 1998b).

Thus, the three dimensions are themselves a simplification, but have the advantage of being easily used to plot current Maori tourism products on a diagram having three axes as shown in Fig. 10.2. The situation of a 200-bedroom hotel owned by Maori, but in which Maori culture is primarily represented by little more than aesthetics, may score high in size and Maori ownership, but low in level of cultural involvement or intensity of experience. On the other hand, a week's stay on a *Marae* in Northland represents a much lower level of Maori involvement in tourism in terms of capital value of assets, but represents a greater emotional involvement for the client, and perhaps the host. It is also a daily reality which is being experienced, and the guest will share in *powhiri* and other protocol whenever family or others visit the *Marae*. The performance of dance and song at a Rotorua hotel will, on the other hand, be a short representation of Maori culture, and while the dance group will be Maori 'owned', the performance takes place within a structure owned by others. The diagram thus enables a distinction to be drawn between Maori tourism products based on these elements of ownership/size of operation, cultural component and duration/intensity of experience.

There is a temptation to allocate the term 'authentic' to a given point on

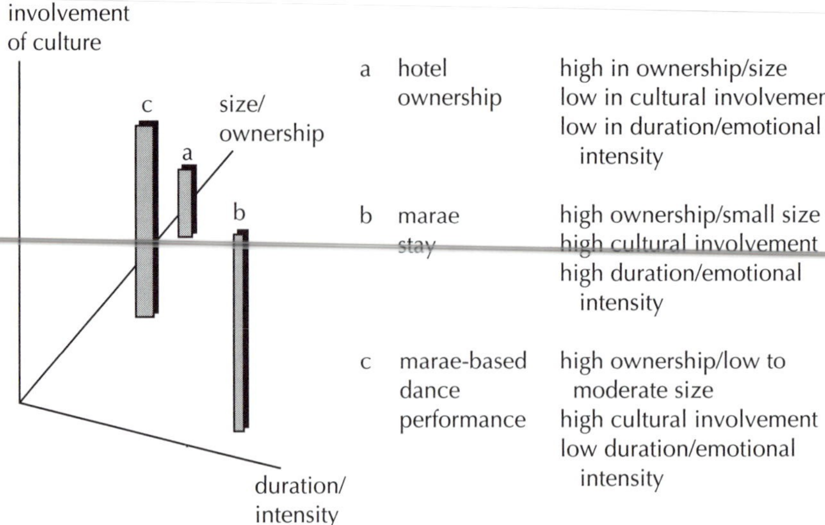

Fig. 10.2. Dimensions of Maori tourism product.

the diagram, but this would be a mistake. The epitome of the authentic cultural tourist product might be conceived as a long stay on a *Marae* with a small group of people, most of whom are Maori. Indeed, in some countries, such as Senegal, this has been upheld as good tourist practice (Saglio, 1979). However, this implies that authenticity is inversely related to size, and yet this cannot be true. For example, in New Zealand major Maori and Pacific Islander tourist events are associated with festivals and dance/song competitions, which attract several hundred competitors and which will last a week. These are important events for participants and audiences, can be emotionally charged for winners and losers, are a source of pride and self-identity, and are large scale. They are an expression of Maori and Pacific Islander creativity and indicate that the arts of these peoples are living, not static, and responsive to current situations. Lyrics of songs will, for example, range from comic comment on politicians and Maori celebrities to cries for justice under a Lands Tribunal Claim, while the *haka*, like ballet, permits endless permutations within a given dance form.

Maori tourism thus covers a wide gambit, from the small scale such as a group of weavers selling their traditional baskets, to ownership of large modern hotels, to the staging of major festivals where most of the tourists are themselves Maori, to yet other tourist products where Maori involvement is almost incidental. Yet, within this wide range of activity runs the common thread of 'being Maori': a sense of identity which links the individual to a wider set of relationships with people and place. It is one of the conundrums of modern tourism that it has been likened to a pilgrimage because it represents a search for identity through knowing places and forming relationships with others who live there (Smith, 1992). Such a perception of self-identity is found among many indigenous people (e.g. see Lockwood, 1961), and thus perhaps it is not unexpected that tourism has 'discovered' indigenous people in this modern context. In the past the 19th century English tourist 'discovered' Maori as a means of stating the Victorian self-assurance of being civilized and God fearing – today's tourist seeks another meaning from the encounter with Maori. Is it, as some Maori writers (e.g. O'Reagan, 1987) have suggested, simply another form of colonization? Does it take the form of an acquisition of culture to solve the angst of urban life? Such questions are beyond the scope of this chapter, but nonetheless serve to illustrate further the complex relationships contained within contemporary indigenous tourism, where the range of products being used, the way in which culture and heritage are used, and the 'etic' and 'emic' attributed to these processes are seemingly more varied and complex than was the case in even the recent past.

References

Albers, P. and James, W. (1988) Travel photography: a methodological approach, *Annals of Tourism Research,* 15(1), pp. 134–158.

Aotearoa Maori Tourism Federation (1994) *Position Paper: The Protection of Cultural and Intellectual Property Rights of Maori Within the Tourism Industry,* Rotorua, Aotearoa Maori Tourism Federation.

Barnett, S.J. (1996) Authenticity and commoditization of culture: a tourism perspective. Unpublished research report for MBS degree. Department of Management Systems: Massey University, Palmerston North, New Zealand.

Barnett, S.J. (1997) Maori Tourism, *Tourism Management* 18(7), in press.

Belich, J. (1986) *The New Zealand Wars and the Victorian Interpretation of Racial Conflict,* Auckland University Press, Auckland.

Bennett, R. (1995) *Report on the Current Market Position of Maori Tourism Product,* Rotorua: Aotearoa Maori Tourism Federation.

Boorstin, D.J. (1961) *The Image – A Guide to Pseudo-events in America,* Harper and Row, New York.

Butterworth, G.V. (1988) *Aotearoa 1769–1988 – Towards a Tribal Perspective,* Department of Maori Arts, Wellington.

Canter, D. (1977) *The Psychology of Place,* Architectural Press, London.

Cohen, E. (1993) The study of touristic images of native people – mitigating the stereotype of a stereotype. In: D.G. Pearce and R.W. Butler (eds) *Tourism Research – Critiques and Challenges,* Routledge, London.

Douglas, N. (1994) They came for savages: a comparative history of tourism development in Papua New Guinea, Solomon Islands and Vanautu 1884–1984. Unpublished PhD thesis, University of Queensland.

Edwards, J.A. and Llurdes i Coit, J.C. (1996) Mines and quarries – industrial heritage tourism, *Annals of Tourism Research,* 23(2), pp. 341–363.

Ford, J.B. (1987) *History of Maori Art,* Te Waka Tpi, Council for Maori and South Pacific Arts, Wellington.

Foucault, M. (1978) *Naissance de la clinique: une archéologie de regard médical Paris,* Presses Universitaires de France.

Fusell, P. (1982) *Abroad: British Literary Travelling Between the Wars,* Oxford University Press, New York.

Irvine, R.F. and Alpers, O.T.J. (1902) *The Progress of New Zealand in the Century,* London.

Jasons (1997) *Motels and Motor Lodges,* Jasons, Auckland, New Zealand.

Kermath, B.M. and Thomas, R.N. (1992) Spatial dynamics of resorts: Sousa, Dominican Republic, *Annals of Tourism Research,* 19(2), pp. 173–190.

Lea, J. (1988) *Tourism and Development in the Third World,* Routledge, London.

Lockwood, D. (1961) *I – the Aboriginal,* Seal Books, Sydney.

MacCannell, D. (1976) *The Tourist – A New Theory of the Leisure Class,* Schocken Books, New York.

McGeorge, C. (1993) Race, empire and the Maori in New Zealand primary school curriculum, 1880–1940, In: Mangan, J.A. (ed.) *The Imperial Curriculum – Racial Images and Education in the British Colonial Experience,* Routledge, London, pp. 64–78.

Maslow, A. (1954) *Motivation and Personality,* Harper and Row, New York.

Neich, R. (1983) The veil of orthodoxy: Rotorua Ngati Tarawhai woodcarving in a changing context. In: Mead, S.M. and Kernot, B. (eds) *Art and Artists of Oceania,* Dunmore Press and Mill Valley, Ethnographic Arts Publications, Palmerston North, California, pp. 245–265.

Oppenshaw, R., Lee, G. and Lee, H. (1993) Challenging the myths – rethinking New Zealand's educational history, chapter 3, *The Politics of Maori Education,* Dunmore Press, Palmerston North, pp. 38–59.

O'Regan, T. (1987) Who owns the past? Change in Maori perspectives of the past. In: Wilson, J. (ed.) *From the Beginning – The Archaeology of the Maori,* Penguin Books, Auckland, pp. 141–145.

Pearce, P.L. (1990) Farm tourism in New Zealand: a social situation analysis, *Annals of Tourism Research,* 17, pp. 337–352.

Ryan, C. (1991) *Recreational Tourism – A Social Science Perspective,* Routledge, London.

Ryan, C. (1998a) Maori and tourism: a relationship of history, constitutions and rites, *Journal of Sustainable Tourism* 5(4), 257–278.

Ryan, C. (1998b), Dolphins, Marae and canoes – eco-tourism in New Zealand. In: Laws, E., Faulkner, W. and Moscardo, G. (eds) *Embracing and Managing Change in Tourism – International Case Studies,* Routledge, London, pp. 285–306.

Ryan, C. and Crotts, J. (1997) Carving and tourism: a Maori perspective, *Annals of Tourism Research,* 24(4), pp. 898–918.

Ryan, C. and Knox, P. (1998) Postcard images of Maori – ambiguities of representation. Submitted to *Annals of Tourism Research.*

Saglio, C. (1979) Tourism for discovery: a project in Lower Casamance, Senegal. In: de Kadt, E. (ed.) *Tourism – Passport to Development?,* Oxford University Press, New York, pp. 321–335.

Smith, V. (1992) Introduction: the quest in guest, *Annals of Tourism Research,* 19(1), pp. 1–17.

Smith, V. (1996) Indigenous tourism – the four Hs. In: Butler, R. and Hinch, T. (eds) *Tourism and Indigenous Peoples,* Thomson International Press, London, pp. 283–307.

Sofield, T. and Birtles, R.A. (1996) Indigenous peoples' cultural opportunity spectrum of tourism (IPCOST). In: Butler, R. and Hinch, T. (eds) *Tourism and Indigenous Peoples,* Thomson International Press, London, pp. 396–434.

Stafford, D. (1977) *The Romantic Past of Rotorua,* A.H. and A.W. Reed, Wellington.

Te Awekotuku, N. (1981) The socio-cultural impact of tourism on the Te Arawa people of Rotorua, New Zealand, PhD thesis, University of Waikato.

Te Awekotuku, N. (1991) *Mana wahine Maori,* New Women's Press, Auckland.

Warren, J.A. and Taylor, C.N. (1994) *Developing Eco-tourism in New Zealand,* Institute for Social Research and Development, Christchurch, New Zealand.

Zeppel, H. (1997) Maori tourism in New Zealand, *Tourism Management,* 18(7), 475–478.

11

Tourism and Culture in Spain: A Case of Minimal Conflict?

Michael Barke

Introduction

This chapter will argue that, despite the massive numbers of tourists involved, the sheer rapidity of their growth, the variety of types of tourism and tourist destinations and the subsequent potential for conflict between tourists and their hosts, the relationship between hosts and tourists in Spain has been characterized by a remarkable lack of explicit conflict. To argue this case is not to deny that significant problems exist in the host/guest relationship or, more generally, with the impacts of tourism in Spain, but the limited conflict that has occurred can be demonstrated as an empirical reality. On balance, Spaniards have been extraordinarily accommodating of the tourist phenomenon and of tourists themselves. A number of factors are responsible for this situation and these will be discussed below. The economic significance of tourism, Spain's recent political history and the centralist/regionalist dichotomy all play some part in explaining the minimal conflict that has occurred. However, a deeper understanding of the paradox between massive tourist numbers and limited conflict may be gained through exploring some of the mechanisms adopted by Spanish hosts to cope with their guests and various aspects of their behaviour. It is further argued that, at a still deeper level, some aspects of Spanish social anthropology provide a more penetrative comprehension of the paradox, especially the concept of *sociocentrismo* (Caro Baroja, 1976), which provides many Spaniards with a strong sense of their self-worth (Mitchell, 1988) and a rational basis for their sense of 'difference'.

(eds M. Robinson and P. Boniface)

Bases for Conflict

The social and cultural impact of tourists and tourist activity upon their 'hosts' has received a great deal of attention in the academic literature (see Pearce, 1989 for a summary). Initially viewed in almost universally negative terms, the more recent literature demonstrates a more balanced perspective and an awareness of the subtleties and complexities upon which the relationship between 'hosts' and 'guests' may depend. Despite this broad tendency towards a more balanced viewpoint, much of the literature relating to this topic in Spain and, indeed, the broad consensus of popular perception, remains mainly negative. This is not altogether surprising as a number of factors relating to the very specific way that tourism developed in Spain from the middle of the 20th century would, at first sight, appear to provide the basis for substantial conflict between tourists and local peoples. The nature of the tourism activity and the characteristics of tourists as people, when juxtaposed against indigenous socio-economic characteristics and cultural norms, would appear to provide the circumstances ripe for friction from the 1950s onwards. First, there is the sheer rapidity of growth in tourism. Second, the actual numbers themselves may represent a major source of conflict especially in relation to their spatial concentration. Third, as implied above, there is the question of socio-economic and cultural conflicts between hosts and guests when the level of development, dominant political ideology and pattern of beliefs about social and cultural norms and mores are in stark contrast.

Although mass tourism is a relatively recent development in Spain, tourism itself is far from being a modern phenomenon and certainly travellers in Spain have been enthusiastic recorders of their experiences from the time of Richard Ford (the 1840s) up to the present (see Mitchell, 1990). However, it was not until the late 18th century and the advent of changes in taste – in favour of romantic scenery and more exotic cultures – that Spain became one of several new European tourist destinations (Towner, 1985). It is arguable that it was during this period that many of the persistent external images and perceptions of Spain and its cultural attributes were formed and that such images have continued to provide the basis – real or imagined – for potential conflict between Spanish hosts and their tourist guests.

However, it was the transport improvements of the 20th century which were to increase Spain's role in international tourism to a new order of significance, initially through road transport and eventually, of course, to an even higher order of magnitude, through air transport. Even in the 1920s and 1930s, however, Spain was either an innovator or a site of innovation in tourism in a number of respects, being one of the first countries to create a national tourism agency in 1905, developing a network of state-run hotels and inns (Barke and Towner, 1996a) and experiencing one of the first motor-based package tours, run by Motorways Ltd of London in 1929 and offering a 32-day package tour of Spain (Muirhead, 1929). Largely due to such developments, foreign visitors to Spain averaged over 260,000 by the early 1930s (Naylon, 1967) although this figure would certainly be exceeded by the number of (mainly middle-class) domestic tourists in the country. But it was the post-war growth, recommencing in the early 1950s, which is usually conceived of as providing a new type of tourism – mass tourism – with considerably greater potential for conflict between tourists and the residents of their destinations. It is certainly the case in Spain that numbers and their sheer rapidity of growth have been perceived as a basis for conflict (Villegas Molina, 1975). The number of tourists surpassed one million between 1950 and 1951, and in 1958 stood at over three million. The 1959 Stabilization Plan provided a major stimulus through the abolition of the requirement for foreign visas, a devaluation of the peseta and the introduction of favourable credit arrangements for the construction of accommodation (Tamames, 1986). The numbers then showed annual increases of never less than 6% until the oil crisis of 1973–74 but some 30 million tourists were still visiting Spain each year in this difficult period of the early 1970s. Recovery took place in 1976 and, whilst there have been some negative growth rates, for example, in the late 1970s and late 1980s, the annual number of tourists surpassed the total population of Spain in 1977 and has continued to do so ever since, increasing to over 40 million in 1980 and over 50 million in 1986. More recently, in the early 1990s, growth rates of 3% per annum have been the norm although the special year of 1992 saw an increase of over 7% with an additional four million tourists visiting the country. Within less than 50 years, therefore, the number of tourists in Spain has increased from a modest 80,000 in 1946 to well over 50 million per year. Although some of the specific implications will be dealt with below, it is clear that the simple reality of coping with the precipitous nature of this growth may be expected to be a source of many tensions. It seems unlikely that any other country in the world has gone so rapidly from so few tourists to so many in such a short expanse of time or been faced with the potential for the challenge to, and possible overwhelming of, indigenous cultural norms that is implied by such numbers and their rapid increase.

Whilst the speed of growth, the numbers involved and therefore the actual logistical implications of accommodating this growth are immense, it is clear that the spatial concentration of this phenomenon seems likely to exacerbate conflict. The pressure has not been evenly spread over the country or even over its coastal area but it has been markedly concentrated (García Manrique, 1989). In the early 1950s, hotels barely existed outside the largest cities but by the 1980s ten provinces accounted for three-quarters of the tourist bedspaces and seven (Alicante, Baleares, Barcelona, Gerona, Madrid, Malaga and Tarragona) for over 60% (Pearce and Grimmeau, 1985; Barke and France, 1986). At the more local scale, concentration is even more marked and Table 11.1 shows the ratio of hotel rooms to local population for a group of well known resorts.

In most cases, Table 11.1 underestimates the significance of the tourist

Table 11.1. Hotel rooms per 1000 resident population: selected resorts, 1991.

Resort	Hotel rooms per 1000 population
Benidorm	396
Mojacar	195
Roquetas de Mar	131
Calella	679
Sitges	193
Lloret de Mar	1122
Blanes	114
Tossa de Mar	1021
Salou	1404
Benalmadena	162
Fuengirola	104
Marbella	63
Torremolinos	368

Source: Ministerio de Comercio y Turismo, 1992

presence as it does not include accommodation in apartments, holiday homes or second homes. Nevertheless it is clear that, in a number of Spanish resorts, the local population is likely to be completely overwhelmed by tourist visitors at certain times of the year. This is especially the case in the Catalonian resorts of Salou, Tossa and Lloret. At the broader regional scale, Catalonia, with a resident population of six million, accounts for 29% of the total Spanish tourist market and attracts 15 million visitors. The Balearic Islands, with a resident population of 703,000, attracts between four and five million tourist visitors each year.

However, there are other potential bases for conflict in addition to sheer numbers, rapidity of growth and spatial concentration. Whilst numbers of tourists may be expected – theoretically at least – to provide a source of discord if not outright conflict, it is conceivable that conflict could also exist in areas where numbers are fewer. This is likely in situations where 'visitor' and 'host' cultures are substantially different and may in fact themselves be in conflict, in the sense that completely different norms and standards of behaviour are found within the two groups (Black, 1996). This raises two possibilities, first that conflict in some areas may have been greater in the past when, in fact, cultural contrasts were more marked and, second, that new forms of tourist activity, especially those which involve new locations, may potentially be more conflict prone. Thus, for different reasons, both 'mass' tourism and 'alternative' tourism may be hypothesized to give rise to conflict of various kinds. In addition to these categorizations, Spain has experienced a rapid development of 'residential' tourism over the last four decades, largely manifest in the growth of second homes and retirement homes for both foreigners and nationals. The superimposition of this form of tourist development, whilst very different from the classical resort-based mass tourism, seems likely to introduce a new set of potential conflicts.

Although the factors mentioned above are reasonably obvious in their probability of providing the basis for conflict, the precise nature of such conflict has so far not been made explicit, therefore it is necessary to consider in more detail the kinds of friction which are likely to result. Whilst some of these may appear, at first sight, to be only loosely related to the specific issue of cultural conflict, it is argued here that cultural norms and beliefs underlie attitudes to most phenomena, including the environment, land and resources as well as the nature of society itself. First there are a whole range of conflicts that relate to the two groups' – hosts and guests – demands for available resources. At the most basic level these could include access to the resource of space itself – especially social space – and, given the intensity of spatial concentration in a number of locations noted above, there is clear potential for the 'hosts' to feel that their own territory has been expropriated. Conflict over more tangible resources would include water and land, with the former being in high demand for irrigated agriculture and domestic use in areas of tourist development where there is an even greater, and potentially more wasteful, demand for water in hotels, other forms of tourist accommodation, the gardens of residential tourists and, of course, golf courses (Garcia Manrique, 1985; Kirkby, 1996). It has been asserted that tourists and the tourism industry use seven times more water per capita than do local residents (Jurdao Arrones, 1970). Land and land use conflict relates to the loss of agricultural land to touristic use, the potential for introducing discordant land uses, the possible fragmentation of farm holdings and severance of areas, loss of grazing and traditional rights of way (Jurdao Arrones, 1970; Greenwood, 1976; Gomez Moreno, 1983; Tyrakowski, 1986). Such conflicts may be expected to have been exacerbated in the past because of the weaknesses of the Spanish planning system and its particular weaknesses in relation to tourism development (Morris, 1985; Morris and Dickenson, 1987; Keyes *et al.*, 1993). A further potential source of considerable resentment in certain regions of Spain, especially during the phase of initial and rapid growth of mass tourism in the late 1950s and 1960s, was the way in which regional interests were subordinated to those of the centre. It was the peripheral regions of Spain which, in their coastal areas, provided the locations for the development of mass tourism and which had to bear the brunt of the conflicts or potential conflicts discussed in this section. However, the income generated through tourism was rarely re-invested in the peripheral areas but, instead, provided a major source of investment in the industrial areas of the north and Madrid (Torres Bernier, 1979).

Turning to the potential for conflict which arises more specifically from social and cultural contrasts between hosts and guests, a detailed typology has been constructed within the Spanish context by Figuerola (1976). Five main bases for friction are recognized – issues which relate to changing population structure, occupational change, the transformation of values through demonstration effects, the impact on traditional ways of life and changes in patterns of consumption. Figuerola also observes that tourists themselves are not solely active agents of change but are also recipients of impulses and impacts. Tourism development affects the size and structure of the resident population through the creation of new jobs and the likelihood of increased in-migration (Dumas, 1975). However, such trends may be expected to bring new tensions as they are age and sex selective, stimulate new demands on local infrastructure and introduce greater occupational and geographical mobility into societies which experienced little change for generations (Greenwood, 1972; Lever, 1987). Occupational change associated with tourism, although often perceived in a positive light in terms of job creation, may actually have disruptive effects upon local labour markets, leaving a shortage of workers in some sectors (Garcia Manrique, 1985). Occupational change may also link into changes in value systems. For example, tasks which hitherto were perceived as part of the expected routine and unpaid roles for women – cooking and cleaning – can become a source of paid employment, setting up a possible range of domestic and intergenerational tensions (Lever, 1987). Long-standing religious and moral values may also be increasingly questioned by the young when they come into contact with the apparently less restricted patterns of behaviour exhibited by youthful tourists. The impact of tourism upon traditional customs, folklore, music, etc., has been extensively studied with a broad consensus that the effects are negative, leading to an erosion and perhaps even eventual termination of traditional practices or to modifications which totally alter the meaning of the original event (Greenwood, 1978). Finally, the demonstration effect of visitors may eventually lead to change in local patterns of daily consumption in terms of food, clothing and other material goods, and the desire for such changes and possession of material goods may give rise to envy, frustration and a heightened awareness of relative differences in wealth (Pearce, 1989).

It is clear from the above that the development of tourism in the recent past in Spain is likely to have provided the opportunity for conflict of many sorts, and cultural conflict in particular. Against this background of the *potential* for antagonism, this essay will now turn to a consideration of the empirical evidence for such conflict.

Evidence for Conflict

A number of writers on Spanish tourism have either claimed or implicitly assumed that conflict does exist between Spanish hosts and their tourist visitors. Perhaps the most in-depth studies have been carried out in the municipality of Mijas, near Fuengirola in Andalusia by Francisco Jurdao Arrones (Jurdao Arrones, 1970; Jurdao Arrones and Sánchez, 1990) and, elsewhere, this work has been described as illustrating 'the dramatic socio-cultural changes associated with tourism development . . . [and] . . . the way in which outsiders have taken over' (Nash, 1996, p. 35). There is no doubt whatsoever that Mijas has changed beyond recognition through the development of residential tourism, but what is missing from the accounts of such change is an explicit consideration of conflict; its existence is hinted at or, more often, assumed. Furthermore, there is only limited explicit consideration of the reaction of indigenous residents apart from by the author himself. Of course, many problems do result from the presence of a majority foreign population within the municipality but most of these seem to be problems of communication rather than outright conflict *per se*. It could be argued that the indigenous residents of Mijas have actually coped with the foreign influx remarkably well. Some of the reasons for this will be dealt with later in this chapter but here it may be noted that Jurdao Arrones who, wearing his academic hat of critical social anthropologist, has been censorious of the process of social changes introduced by tourism and residential tourism in particular, but has worn a different hat as managing editor of *Mediterranean Magazine*, an expensive glossy English language magazine carrying many real estate advertisements and articles on the chic lifestyles led by wealthy foreign residents of the Costa del Sol.

Other examples may be cited which, again, tend to assume conflict rather than demonstrate it. For example: 'In recent years foreigners have moved in *frightening* [my emphasis] numbers into the pretty villages such as Competa and Frigiliana' (Jacobs, 1990, p. 37). It is not quite clear why this process should be frightening or who is actually frightened by it and, for this location, there is no evidence produced that indigenous Spaniards react in this way. Jacobs does, however, cite some indigenous concerns over the same process in other locations; for example in the village of Gaucin where there is a street with only one Spanish family still living there, all other houses being inhabited by foreigners and, in nearby Jimena de la Frontera, a local resident observed 'Pronto los Jimenatos serán los extranjeros (soon the people of Jimena will be the foreigners)' (Jacobs, 1990, p. 36). Yet, the question needs asking again – does this presence represent any real conflict? The evidence provided is limited in the extreme and the existence of conflict between hosts and guests is assumed. Furthermore, another writer on Andalusia has observed for this specific pueblo, 'in places like Jimena . . . there was no tension or even incongruity in two cultures existing side by side' (Luard, 1984, pp. 175–176).

In the same vein, numerous authors have testified to the friendliness and relative ease with which Spanish hosts have treated their tourist guests: 'tourists have never caused Spaniards any serious problems. Their aims . . . are easily understood, if not always shared; in any case they are birds of passage. Or, with the development of mass tourism, they might . . . be likened to a . . . perpetual crop, which can be reaped like lucerne throughout the year' (Boyd, 1992, p. 15). A detailed and light-hearted account of the development of tourism in Catalonia has noted: 'The art of welcoming and attending to strangers comes easily to the people of the province of Gerona, so easily that even newcomers to the hotel trade . . . are not long before rising to a worthy position in the profession' (Fàbregas i Barri, 1970, pp. 36–37). Official surveys of the reasons for visiting Spain and for returning have fairly consistently reported the importance of the friendliness of the hosts and the general social and cultural atmosphere or *ambiente* (Esteve Secall, 1982). This factor tends to come second only to the importance of the sun and good weather.

Nevertheless, there are some features of tourism development which appear to have led to serious consequences for individuals and which may be attributed to the clash between different cultures. Hooper (1986) notes the acceleration of various forms of physical and mental health problems experienced by young Spanish males in the early years of tourism development on the coast and, 'According to a study carried out in 1971, 90 per cent of all non-chronic mental illness in the rural parts of the province of Málaga was among teenage males who had gone to work on the coast' (Hooper, 1986, p. 29). It will be argued later that Spaniards have been adept at evolving various mechanisms to cope with the tourist influx but it is clear that, for some, at least in the early stages of tourism development, there were severe problems in coping with people from a different culture.

Perhaps more fundamentally, the role of tourism in reversing some traditional social and economic structures may be cited as a possible cause of cultural conflict. For example, older methods of cooperation between families may cease as some – especially those who have benefited from tourism – have the economic resources to no longer require such mutual aid. However, other families may not be in this position and be left in an even poorer situation (Greenwood, 1972). Traditional family structures and hierarchies may also be challenged through tourism development and the opportunities it represents. A frequently repeated experience in the Mediterranean region relates to the fact that, typically, poorer quality coastal land was owned by the youngest and least wealthy siblings but, with the development of tourism such land acquired massively increased value, thus reversing the economic position of its owners (Hermans, 1981; Selwyn, 1996). Although it is clear that most of these examples relate to conflict or potential conflict within the Spanish community rather than between hosts and guests they are, nevertheless, largely attributable to tourism and its impacts.

However, it would be misleading to pretend that the traditional way of life in Mediterranean Spain as practised by most small landowners and certainly by landless labourers, was one which was valued and within which there was no desire for change. Nothing could be further from the case. There is ample evidence that many Spaniards detested their way of life, for example 'there is a hatred of farming for what it has done to the previous generation' (Greenwood, 1976, p. 41), and substantial research in Andalusia has demonstrated the ambivalence or downright antipathy to the land and the way of life it represents (Pitt-Rivers, 1954; Gilmore, 1980). In such circumstances, rather than being a source of cultural conflict, it is quite likely that the opportunities brought by tourism may be a source of release.

Numerous authors, when discussing the impact of tourism, also draw attention to the way that some of the physical manifestations of a local culture, especially those of a folkloric nature, are colonized by external influences and lose much of their original meaning (Boissevain, 1992). Obvious examples from Spain include flamenco and bullfighting. In the case of the former it has been claimed that 'tourism has cheapened and trivialised flamenco into banal but accessible melodies accompanied by snapping castanets' (Luard, 1984, p. 152). This assertion is certainly true and many flamenco shows arranged for the entertainment of tourists are pale imitations of those which take place in front of a Spanish audience or which, more properly, occur spontaneously. But the point is that the latter still *do* occur. In other words, tourism has not destroyed flamenco but helped to create another, albeit less 'pure', form. The 'real thing' still exists. The existence of plural forms of the same 'entertainment' is evidenced by Boyd in a visit to the Bay of Cadiz where 'torn bullfight posters . . . spoke of the renowned bullrings of the Bay: San Fernando, El Puerto, Sanlúcar, all bywords for fastidious fans who despised the fraudulent showbiz fights of Puerto Banus and Marbella' (Boyd, 1992, p. 336).

The way that religious festivals and other fiestas have become commodified, changed and trivialized as a result of tourist influence is another example frequently cited of the cultural conflict produced by the tourist phenomenon. However, there are many features of such events which still remain closed to tourists (Mitchell, 1990) and for many Spaniards such fiestas fit into an annual cycle which is important for them, even if they are not religious or even if they live elsewhere. Very often, that is why the fiesta is important – it is a re-affirmation of belonging to that particular place. Black (1996) has shown how some of the mundane aspects of life for indigenous peoples remain linked to the religious calendar even when many such people cease to be 'religious' themselves. For many, therefore, it doesn't actually matter that tourists are present at the event, and most aspects of it remain within the control of the local population. There are some examples of local celebrations which appear to have been destroyed by tourist commodification (Greenwood, 1978), but they are few and far between and there is growing evidence that festivals and rituals can revive and others adapt in order to resist their packaging for external consumption (Crain, 1992; Cruces and Díaz de Rada, 1992; Driessen, 1992).

In fact, the changes that have been witnessed in various folk traditions such as fiestas and carnivals may owe more to attempts to control and, in some cases, ban such events for political reasons during the Franco regime. Either modifications were enforced or, upon resumption of the event, the changed socio-economic circumstances provided a different context (Nogués Pedregal, 1996). Although the advent of tourism may have been a part of that changing context, the point is that tourism seems unlikely to have been the principal cause of change and that the simple interruption of continuity of the folk tradition itself would make it more likely that many new influences would be incorporated.

One of the most frequently cited sources of cultural conflict in the early years of tourism related to the question of morality and the apparent major contrast between a mainly Catholic, conservative country and population, and tourists from the north who appeared to possess much looser moral standards. The Franco regime initially sought to control such conflict through insistence on particular standards of dress and behaviour on the part of tourist visitors (Grugel and Rees, 1997). However, it may well be that the moral 'shock' and potential for cultural conflict lay more in the minds of the dictator and some of his supporters than in the minds of the majority of the Spanish population. Ironically, some immediate members of Franco's family and a number of key figures in the regime appear to have exhibited rather different public and private moral positions (Preston, 1993). More importantly, the attitude of ordinary Spaniards to morality was certainly different from that of their rulers and it is significant, for example, that the Minister for Information and Tourism up to 1962 was Gabriel Arias Salgado, a well-known religious bigot (Hooper, 1995). It seems plausible that Spaniards may have been better able to cope with the cultural shock of bikini-clad females and similar manifestations of different cultures than was recognized at the time.

Whilst it would be foolish and misguided to pretend that the rapid development of tourism, especially mass tourism, in Spain has proceeded totally without conflict, the most remarkable fact to emerge from any study of this history is the absence of major friction. It is primarily the (foreign) travel writer who asserts the existence of major conflict but who then, in the time-honoured tradition of travel writers on Spain (Barke and Towner, 1996a), proceed to relate their discovery of some 'authentic' experience, place or event. Thus, Jacobs (1990) laments the presence of foreigners in villages such as Competa and Frigiliana but goes on to observe 'beyond this . . . you are again in unspoilt countryside where foreigners are few and far between' (p. 37). We should also remember that 'Travel writers hate, above any other category of humankind, tourists' (Ritchie, 1994, p. 3). There is, therefore, a significant paradox to be explained, namely the undoubted existence of, on the one hand, massive numbers of tourists with equally massive potential for causing social and cultural conflict with and between their hosts and, on the other, what appears to be the actual situation of limited antagonism.

Explaining the Paradox

One of the most basic reasons why the rapid development of tourism in Spain has taken place against a background of limited conflict relates to the economic significance of the industry within the overall Spanish economy and, more specifically, the historical association in the minds of many Spaniards between the growth of tourism, the overall growth of the national economy and the massive increase in material prosperity for many groups. It is estimated that, in the early 1990s, tourism contributed about 8% of GDP and 41% of the export of goods and services (Sinclair and Bote Gómez, 1996). Between 10% and 12% of the total labour force are calculated to be employed in tourism, about 1.4 million people (Salmon, 1995). It is widely recognized that income from tourism acted as a catalyst for the restructuring of the Spanish economy (Tamames, 1986; Sinclair and Bote Gómez, 1996) but crucial to Spain's ability to undertake such restructuring was its capacity to provide a large proportion of the necessary inputs into the tourism sector. Although weak in many ways, the Spanish economy was large enough and flexible enough to be able to adapt to the new demands and, consequently, much internal growth was directly stimulated by tourism. In the specific sector of agriculture there is more debate about the precise impact of tourism and whilst some commentators claim a destructive impact (Greenwood, 1976), others have demonstrated more beneficial and catalytic effects (Hermans, 1981). The direct and indirect contributions of tourism at the regional and local scales is, of course, much more marked than at the national aggregate scale. Despite the existence in the 1950s and 1960s of a core–periphery relationship due to the spatial mismatch between income generation from tourism and investment of that income, tourism has enabled some areas to significantly improve their relative position in Spain. For example, between 1960 and 1991 Málaga province leapt from 43rd (out of 50) place in terms of income per capita to 33rd, the Balearics from 15th to fifth and Gerona from 12th to second (El País, 1993). In circumstances where, within two generations, the realities of life have passed from a possible threat of starvation to the possibility of shopping in a hypermarket packed with commodities from all over the world, and where the development of tourism is widely perceived as the source of such a change, it is scarcely surprising that the levels of tolerance of tourists and what they represent are quite high.

Thus, whilst foreign travel writers could express the following opinion: 'On the Costa del Sol in a single generation mass tourism and foreign settlement have destroyed a social framework, an economy and an entire way of life. Whole villages and their communities have simply disappeared, swallowed up by one vast and constantly expanding concrete ghetto threaded by neon-lit highways.' (Luard, 1984, p. 110), the views of local residents were actually quite different: 'Try to find an Andalusian nostalgic for the good old days before the tourists came. Try to find an Andalusian resentful of the foreigners. I did try. I couldn't find one' (Ritchie, 1994, p. 186). Whilst, as we have seen, some studies of the local impact of tourist development have illustrated the negative consequences (Jurdao Arrones, 1970), more balanced ethnographic studies of the response of 'locals' to the tourist phenomenon have reached different conclusions and noted the 'gratitude' of local residents for tourism development which is perceived as easing most of the hardships of the past – 'An old goatherd remarks how happy he is to see the tourists in the streets: "Every time I can help one I do it gladly. Isn't it thanks to them that this village is prosperous now?"' (Fraser, 1973, pp. 183–184). Similar sentiments were voiced by the former communist mayor of Mijas who, although shocked at seeing Fuengirola after 33 years in hiding, felt that there 'was at least the consolation that a new era of prosperity had begun' (Jacobs, 1990, p. 229). The role of tourism in creating employment and improving much of the material basis of life is, therefore, widely recognized in the main areas affected (Fàbregas i Barri, 1970; Esteve Secall, 1982). This is not to argue that the many antagonisms and other problems stemming from the presence of tourists are ignored or fail to be recognized – they certainly are recognized by most Spaniards, but the simple fact that tourism is perceived to be the source of prosperity lessens the potential for outright and overt conflict. Nevertheless, it must be recognized that it is likely to be certain categories of hosts who are more likely to express or feel such mitigation and a number of authors have noted that the relationships between, for example, migrant workers in tourism and tourists themselves tend to be stronger and less conflict-prone than relationships with Spaniards not directly involved in the industry (Gaviria, 1974; Lever, 1987).

Independently of any economic considerations of the benefits or costs of tourism, a number of factors relating to Spain's recent political history have also been important in serving to dampen down the potential for conflict between hosts and guests. Most fundamentally, these relate to the initial influence and then subsequent legacy of the Franco dictatorship. Although the regime sought to promote tourism it was, initially at least, in a way that sought to superimpose the 'moral values' of the regime upon visitors especially, for example, in relation to dress and behaviour. This was despite the fact that one of the main reasons for tourist promotion was the increasing desire to be accepted and recognized internationally (Pi-Sunyer, 1996). However, the authoritarian nature of the regime also meant that any overt opposition to tourism in its areas of development could easily be suppressed. Some specific incidents indicate the importance attached to tourism and the presentation of an appropriate external 'image' at this time. Perhaps the clearest case was the 'Palomares incident' of 1966 when nuclear bombs were accidentally jettisoned in shallow water by a US bomber stationed at the Rota air base. The then Minister for Tourism, Manuel Fraga Irribarne, rushed to the scene and insisted on being photographed by the world's media, bathing in the apparently uncontaminated water (Jacobs, 1990).

It seems plausible that the long historical tradition of authoritarianism, stemming from the glaring inequalities in, for example, land ownership and from *caciquismo* (control of local bosses) also served to create a culture of acceptance amongst many. In a situation where the Franco regime was controlling access to information and many aspects of cultural life it was inevitable that, if the regime asserted that tourism was a good thing and should be welcomed, opposition would be muted (Grugel and Rees, 1997). However, it is arguable that the legacy of Francoism was influential in a much more fundamental way, apart from initially enforcing an acceptance of tourism and tourists. More significantly, the long isolation of Spain in international political and social terms which, despite opening up the country to tourism, continued into the late 1960s, had the effect of exacerbating the desire for international acceptance once the main obstacle had been removed. One way in which this could be achieved was through a continuation and, indeed, renewal of the enthusiastic acceptance of tourists from the mid-1970s onwards. Ironically, of course, this was one of the main motives for opening up the country for tourism in the 1950s but, in post-Franco Spain, the desire to take a place alongside other European nations became an important factor in tourism policy as in many other spheres of activity. In many ways, the culmination of this occurred in 1992 with the celebrations associated with the voyages of discovery and exploration, the Barcelona Olympics, the Seville Expo' and Madrid's year as Cultural Capital of Europe (Barke and Towner, 1996b). The desire for international acceptance and approval, against the historical background of rejection throughout the Franco years, appears likely to play some part in the attitude of Spanish hosts to tourist guests and partially helps to explain the generally positive relationship.

This factor links into a further consideration which is the desire to be perceived as a modern nation. The gradual 'opening up' of Spain with the erosion of the dictatorship's domination and control led to the internal realization of how 'different' Spain was and, in many senses, how backward (Grugel and Rees, 1997) and this, in turn, led to a desire for change. Growing economic prosperity led to the same set of desires, especially as Spaniards became more mobile and susceptible to external influences, for example, those communicated by television. Foreign influences penetrated much more easily and brought with them the growth of consumerism and mass culture (Vasquez Montalbán, 1980). This modernization of Spain (Esteve Secall, 1982) led to an apparent convergence of some aspects of Spanish culture and behaviour with those prevalent in many other Western countries. In other words, Spain – in a number of respects – ceased to be 'different'. If one of the potential sources of conflict related to 'differences' between hosts and guests in terms of cultural norms, attitudes and behaviour, then the convergence of such values may be expected to have lessened any such tensions. In the words of Jan Morris (1979), 'It was in the tourists that the Spaniards first recognized their future selves' (p. 140). Whilst not entirely agreeing with the full implications of this sentiment on the grounds that a total convergence has not taken place, it must be acknowledged that some elements of this particular demonstration effect have manifested themselves in Spanish society and, at least potentially, reduced some of the bases for cultural conflict.

As ever in Spain, most of the factors discussed above at the aggregated national level have their regional dimension. If Spain as a country was seeking international approval and acceptance then the various regions of Spain sought the same recognition for themselves and, to a certain extent, were vying within the country for acceptance outside its boundaries. This process was given additional momentum with the major decentralization of powers to the regions in the 1980s and the inevitable competition between them for shares of the tourism market. A clear illustration of this is provided by Galicia which, annoyed at being largely left out of the 1992 celebrations which focused on Seville, Barcelona and Madrid, announced in 1993 its own special year, the *Año Jacobeo*, to celebrate the pilgrimage to Santiago de Compostella but, more precisely, to cash in on its tourism potential (Hooper, 1995). The main point, however, is that in circumstances of intense regional competition the attitude of hosts to guests is a key component and any regional strategy which had not resolved problematic issues of conflict between the two would be unlikely to succeed. More importantly, such a strategy would have to be based on the reality of absence of conflict or the presence of only minimal and resolvable conflict.

All of the factors discussed so far go some way to explaining the paradox of a sudden and massive increase in tourist visitors and the apparent absence of any major tension between this phenomenon and their hosts. However, they do not explain the totality of this paradox in that they relate to the general 'atmosphere' within which the growth of tourism has taken place in Spain which, it is argued, favoured circumstances leading to minimal conflict. They do not explain in any specific way the ostensible lack of major conflict and the final part of this chapter will be concerned with these more specific and, in several senses, fundamental factors. These fall into two groups, first the role of coping mechanisms in allowing hosts to come to terms with their guests (Boissevain, 1996a) and, second and perhaps most fundamental of all, some of the pervasive and enduring aspects of Spanish society (Caro Baroja, 1957).

In the context of this final section it is important to record the author's view that the apparent lack of conflict does not necessarily signify a total and uncritical acceptance by Spanish hosts of the tourism phenomenon. More accurately, the lack of conflict may be explained by the ability of the hosts to find different and subtle ways of coping with tourists and the potential conflict situations their presence may initiate. Such coping strategies may take a variety of forms. As indicated earlier in this chapter, travel writers in particular are inclined to 'read off' a set of predictable social and cultural changes from the tangible physical and visual evidence of tourism development. The more massive such development the greater the social and cultural change implied (Turner and Ash, 1975). However, despite the apparent 'swamping' effects of mass tourism, local responses to such changes are varied and reflect the fact that host cultures possess their own internal dynamics and are not merely passive recipients (Black, 1996). Local people can and do select which aspects of tourist culture are appropriate for absorbing into their daily lives and very often have a clear perspective on the boundary between their own cultural identity and that of their visitors. A simple example concerns the restricted adaptation of the Spanish-owned sectors of the tourist infrastructure to the time-frame of their visitors. Whilst foreign-owned hotels, restaurants and bars adapt to the temporal requirements of tourists, most Spanish-owned establishments stick to their own time-frame in relation to meals and siesta periods.

Contrary to the view that the development of tourism has totally 'swamped' the social space of indigenous residents, there is ample evidence of the latter's ability to 'provide some cultural space for tourists while simultaneously preserving other, more private, spaces for themselves' (Selwyn, 1996, p. 249). This phenomenon is clearly similar to the notion of 'front regions' and 'back regions' (MacCannell, 1976) in apparently tourist-dominated areas but, in the case of many tourist areas in Spain, the 'back regions' are almost impossible for the tourist to penetrate, both physically and psychologically. In describing the impact of tourism on a Catalan village community, Pi-Sunyer has noted that 'Cape Lloc [a pseudonym] villagers remain in place and respond to tourists by erecting virtually insurmountable barriers to genuine human relations' (1978, p. 155). The marked physical segregation of space on the Costa del Sol has been discussed elsewhere (Barke and France, 1996) and, despite the absolute transformation of the environment and way of life in that area, it is clear that Spanish 'hosts' have either retained, re-created or initiated their own spaces in order to make a clear statement about their individuality and 'separateness'. There is no doubt that this represents a most important way of coping with tourists (Black, 1996; Boissevain, 1996b) and its importance on the Costa del Sol was recognized some time ago – 'The glory of Torremolinos is to have inwardly survived its ruin' (Honor Tracey, quoted in Mitchell, 1990, p. 170) – the emphasis should, of course, be placed on the word *inwardly*.

MacCannell (1976) argues that the penetration of the 'back regions' by tourists in search of authenticity leads to the development of 'fake' or 'staged' authenticity. This theme has been developed in the context of Spain with a number of authors arguing that traditional cultural practices have either been modified beyond recognition or have been usurped by the tourist phenomenon (see, for example, Moreno Navarro, 1984). Attention has been drawn to the changing nature of local religious festivals, fiestas and other folk celebrations and especially to the way that these have become 'commodified' for and by tourists. Many such events have indeed been 'highjacked' and may appear to have lost much of their original meaning (Greenwood, 1978). However, there is growing evidence that many local societies have been able to make a distinction between the 'performance' for tourists and part of the same event or an alternative event which is essentially for local consumption and an affirmation of local identity (Zarkia, 1996). This phenomenon has been noted in the case of one of Spain's most widely publicized and increasingly tourist-oriented *romerías* (pilgrimages), that of El Rocio where a number of alternatives (including the second *romería* of *el traslado*) have developed as a way of coping with the tourist pressure and of maintaining control over some of the basic religious symbolism of the site (Crain, 1996). Elsewhere, for example in the village of Zahara de los Atunes in Cadiz, the onset of tourism and some of the challenges it presented in terms of development has been noted as leading to an increased interest by local people in their own history (Nogués Pedregal, 1996).

Another defensive mechanism which has received some recognition by anthropologists working in Spain relates to the use of humour as a coping strategy. Although this was initially discussed in the context of the poor coping with the harsh realities of life in regions such as Andalusia (Brandes, 1980), the same phenomenon has applicability to the psychological demands made upon hosts in coping with their tourist guests. Nogués Pedregal (1996) has shown how the revival of the February Carnival in Zahara de los Atunes in Cadiz Province (a time of year when virtually no tourists are present) incorporated new themes and costumes, and humorous representations of foreign tourists were a significant part of the carnival display. Pi-Sunyer (1996) has discussed the role of humour in coping with the explosion of tourism in Catalonia and noted how it was used to subvert the censorship of outright criticism of tourism development in the Franco period. Similarly, the cartoons and stories of tourists and their exploits contained in an account of the development of the Costa Brava (Fàbregas i Barri, 1970) serve to give expression to local frustrations and feelings and provide for a continuation of a sense of self-worth whilst at the same time defusing any outright conflict. The use of humour to cope with tourists becomes an even more appropriate weapon and a potent guardian of self-value when the source of much of that humour is related to incomprehension about many of the things that tourists actually do. In the historical past, Spaniards could not understand why anyone should want to visit the crumbling Alhambra Palace in Granada and wondered why 'anyone should have come such a long way to look at stones' (Jacobs, 1990, p. 186). Although the appeal of sun and sea for modern mass tourists is more readily understood, there remains a degree of incomprehension amongst many Spaniards about the real appeal of their country for the foreigner (Jacobs, 1994). The lack of any real conflict may be readily understood in the face of such incomprehension. What seems to be valued by the tourists is not necessarily valued by indigenous residents. It is only very recently that Spanish tourism authorities have analysed this appeal in any detail and started to promote alternative forms of tourism related to environmental, cultural and heritage factors; factors which many Spaniards have traditionally largely ignored or taken for granted.

This ability to maintain a considerable degree of insulation from external pressures and to view oneself and one's beliefs and values as equal, or superior, to those of other people has been recognized as an enduring characteristic of Spanish society. The eminent Spanish historian, Salvador de Madariaga (1942), has written of the innate sense of moral equality which characterizes most Spaniards, independently of material wealth. Influential writers such as Ganivet and Unamuno gave powerful expression to this characteristic with their assertions that 'mere material improvements are largely irrelevant, since they do not affect the essence of a man's lot' (Shaw, 1975, p. 20). Such views have been echoed by authorities on most of Spain's regions. For example, Catalan traditional culture 'places substantial emphasis on the concept that each individual is a person, to be evaluated in terms of his or her merits' (Pi-Sunyer, 1978, p. 150). Caro Baroja has gone beyond this and argued that many Spaniards regard themselves as residing 'at the moral centre of the universe' (Caro Baroja, 1976, p. 119) and that the group one belongs to is the best of all possible groups (Mitchell, 1988). This concept can be linked to the identification of 'stoicism' as the essential 'psychological constitution of the Spanish soul' (Ganivet, 1946): 'amid all the chances of life, remember that you have within you a central indestructible force; a diamond hard axis, round which revolve the petty happenings which make up our daily existence' (p. 25). Thus, regardless of objective reality, Spaniards are inclined to feel themselves and their village or town of origin as superior to any other in terms of honour, morality or many other features. Such views are corroborated by more localized studies of Spanish culture (Brenan,1957). This sublime self-confidence then provides a substantial reservoir upon which to draw in the face of apparent challenges from other cultures, and included amongst these is the challenge posed by tourism. In one of the more perceptive foreign accounts of the Spanish national character, V.S. Pritchett has written: 'they regard the foreigner as fantastic, abnormal, absurd . . . the attitude is that it is we who live in a spiritual slum which the Spaniards could rescue us from, if they felt the effort worthwhile – but they do not' (Pritchett, 1954). In other words, what is being argued here is that Spanish culture has, to some degree, been able to resist or at least cope with the onslaught of tourism largely because of this phenomenon of *sociocentrismo* (Caro Baroja, 1957). This provides the mechanism for favourable comparisons between the 'in-group' (Spaniards of a particular locality) and the 'out-group' (tourists). The former possess a clear definition of their identity and it is one which has proved, for the most part, strong enough to provide a mechanism for absorbing the immense potential for cultural conflict represented by the tourism phenomenon. This does not mean to say that change has not taken place, the main point is that such change can be accepted or accommodated through the mechanism of sociocentrism without fundamentally disturbing the sense of cultural values of the hosts. Thus, sociocentrism is much more than a shield, in that it provides for more than merely deflecting pressures for change; it allows for the absorption of change within a framework of continuing moral superiority. This sense of a collective and superior culture enables the potential for hostility between hosts and guests to be deflected into other forms, for example, humour. Furthermore, the existence of such mocking does not carry with it any denial that the in-group needs the out-group of tourists. The conviction of superiority is sufficient for the hosts to put up with the tourist impact: they are, after all, a morally inferior 'other'.

Conclusion

This chapter has argued that Spain and Spaniards have been remarkably accommodating of the tourism phenomenon and that there has been surprisingly limited cultural conflict resulting from the rapid and massive development of tourism. This is not to deny that Spanish culture itself has changed. The development of state education and improved literacy, the widespread ownership of radio and television, the popularity of the cinema, experience of military service, the provision of easier communications and the major political change from dictatorship to democracy have all played some part in social and cultural change over the last four decades. But, just as Spanish society has largely absorbed such changes without major conflict, so too has it absorbed the development of tourism. To some extent, the absence of cultural conflict may be explained by the convergence of several factors which created an atmosphere within which the tourism phenomenon could be accepted by Spaniards. These included the experience of the Civil War and international isolation, the previous material poverty of many Spaniards and the obvious material benefits resulting from tourism's role in economic development, the general modernization of Spanish society and the inter-regional rivalries for the attention of external agencies. These factors helped to create the circumstances for large-scale acceptance but, even against the background they provide, one may still have expected substantial antagonism between hosts and guests. The fact that Spaniards most directly affected by the tourism phenomenon have been able to adopt a series of strategies to cope with tourists is one major explanation for this lack of conflict but for a rather more fundamental explanation, it is necessary to recognize the role of some distinctive features of Spanish social anthropology. Put simply, conflict is most likely when one feels inferior. The sense of moral and cultural superiority, which many Spaniards feel and which has been termed sociocentrism, does appear likely to provide an obvious mechanism for reducing potential conflict between hosts and guests in those areas affected by tourism development.

References

Barke, M. and France, L.A. (1986) Tourist accommodation in Spain, 1971–1981, *Tourism Management,* 7(3), pp. 181–197.

Barke, M. and France, L.A. (1996) The Costa del Sol. In: Barke, M., Towner, J. and Newton, M.T. (eds) *Tourism in Spain: Critical Issues,* CAB International, Wallingford, pp. 265–308.

Barke, M. and Towner, J. (1996a) Exploring the history of leisure and tourism in Spain.

In: Barke, M., Towner, J. and Newton, M.T. (eds) *Tourism in Spain: Critical Issues,* CAB International, Wallingford, pp. 3–34.

Barke, M. and Towner, J. (1996b) Urban tourism in Spain. In: Barke, M., Towner, J. and Newton, M.T. (eds) *Tourism in Spain: Critical Issues,* CAB International, Wallingford, pp. 343–374.

Black, A. (1996) Negotiating the tourist gaze: the example of Malta. In: Boissevain, J. (ed.) *Coping with Tourists: European Reactions to Mass Tourism,* Berghahn Books, Providence and Oxford, pp. 112–142.

Boissevain, J. (ed.) (1992) *Revitalizing European Rituals,* Routledge, London.

Boissevain, J. (ed.) (1996a) *Coping with Tourists: European Reactions to Mass Tourism,* Berghahn Books, Providence and Oxford.

Boissevain, J. (1996b) Ritual, tourism and cultural commoditization in Malta: culture by the pound? In: Selwyn, T. (ed.) *The Tourist Image: Myths and Myth Making in Tourism,* John Wiley, Chichester.

Boyd, A. (1992) *The Sierras of the South,* Harper Collins, London.

Brandes, S. (1980) *Metaphors of Masculinity: Sex and Status in Andalusian Folklore,* University of Pennsylvania Press, Philadelphia.

Brenan, G. (1957) *South from Granada,* Hamish Hamilton, London.

Caro Baroja, J. (1957) *Razas, Pueblos y Linajes.* Revista de Occidente, Madrid.

Caro Baroja, J. (1976) Algunos formas elementales de exposición y explicación de la historia, *Revista de Dialectologia y Tradiciones Populares* (32) pp. 103–122.

Crain, M.M. (1992) Pilgrims, 'yuppies', and media men: the transformation of an Andalusian pilgrimage. In: Boissevain, J. (ed.) *Revitalizing European Rituals,* Routledge, London, pp. 95–112.

Crain, M.M. (1996) Contested territories: the politics of touristic development at the shrine of El Rocio in Southwestern Andalusia. In: Boissevain, J. (ed.) *Coping with Tourists: European Reactions to Mass Tourism,* Berghahn Books, Providence and Oxford, pp. 27–55.

Cruces, F. and Díaz de Rada, A. (1992) Public celebrations in a Spanish valley. In: Boissevain, J. (ed.) *Revitalizing European Rituals,* Routledge, London, pp. 62–79.

de Madariaga, S. (1942) *Spain: A Modern History,* Jonathan Cape, London.

Driessen, H. (1992) Celebrations at daybreak in southern Spain. In: Boissevain, J. (ed.) *Revitalizing European Rituals,* Routledge, London, pp. 80–94.

Dumas, D. (1975) Evolution demographique récente et développement du tourisme dans la province d'Alicante, Espagne, *Méditerranée,* 21, pp. 3–22.

El País, (1993) *Anuario El País 1993,* Madrid.

Esteve Secall, R. (1982) *Ocio, Turismo y Hoteles en la Costa del Sol,* Universidad de Málaga, Málaga.

Fàbregas i Barri, E. (1970) *The Costa Brava: Before and After the Tourists,* Comercial Atheneum, Barcelona.

Figuerola, M. (1976) Turismo de masa y sociologia: el caso español, *Travel Research Journal,* 25–38.

Fraser, R. (1973) *The Pueblo,* Allen Lane, London.

Ganivet, A. (1946) *Spain: An Interpretation,* Eyre & Spottiswoode, London.

García Manrique, E. (1985) Turismo y agricultura en la Costa del Sol Malagueña, *Revista de Estudios Regionales, Extraordinario,* VI, pp. 81–96.

García Manrique, E. (1989) El turismo. In: Bielza de Ory, V. (ed.) *Territorio y Sociedad en España: Geografía Humana,* Taurus, Madrid.

Gaviria, M. (1974) *España A Go-Go*, Ediciones Turner, Madrid.
Gilmore, D.D. (1980) *The People of the Plain*, Columbia University Press, New York.
Gomez Moreno, M.L. (1983) Competencia entre agricultura y turismo por el dominio del espacio. El caso de Benalmádena, *Baetica*, 6, pp. 130–142.
Greenwood, D.J. (1972) Tourism as an agent of change: a Spanish Basque case, *Ethnology*, 11, pp. 80–91.
Greenwood, D.J. (1976) The demise of agriculture in Fuenterrabia. In: Aceves, J.B. and Douglass, W.A. (eds) *The Changing Faces of Rural Spain*, Schenkman Publishing Company, New York, pp. 29–44.
Greenwood, D.J. (1978) Culture by the pound: an anthropological perspective on tourism as cultural commoditization. In: Smith, V.L. (ed.) *Hosts and Guests*: The Anthropology of Tourism, Blackwell, Oxford, pp. 129–138.
Grugel, J. and Rees, T. (1997) *Franco's Spain*, Arnold, London.
Hermans, D. (1981) The encounter of agriculture and tourism: a Catalan case study, *Annals of Tourism Research*, 8(3), pp. 462–479.
Hooper, J. (1986) *The Spaniards*, Penguin Books, Harmondsworth.
Hooper, J. (1995) *The New Spaniards*, Penguin Books, Harmondsworth.
Jacobs, M. (1990) *A Guide to Andalusia*, Viking, London.
Jacobs, M. (1994) *Between Hopes and Memories: A Spanish Journey*, Picador, London.
Jurdao Arrones, F. (1970) *España en Venta*, Ediciones Endymion, Madrid.
Jurdao Arrones, F. and Sánchez, M. (1990) *Espana, Asilo de Europa*, Editorial Planeta, Barcelona.
Keyes, J., Munt, I. and Riera, P. (1993) The control of development in Spain, *Town Planning Review*, 64(1), pp. 47–63.
Kirkby, S.J. (1996) Recreation and the quality of Spanish coastal waters. In: Barke, M., Towner, J. and Newton, M.T. (eds) *Tourism in Spain: Critical Issues*, CAB International, Wallingford, pp. 189–212.
Lever, A. (1987) Spanish tourism migrants: the case of Lloret de Mar, *Annals of Tourism Research*, 14(4), pp. 449–470.
Luard, N. (1984) *Andalucía*, Century Publishing, London.
MacCannell, D. (1976) *The Tourist: A New Theory of the Leisure Class*, Macmillan, London.
Ministerio de Comercio y Turismo (1992) *Guia de Hoteles*, Ministerio de Comercio y Turismo, Madrid.
Mitchell, D. (1990) *Travellers in Spain*, Cassell, London.
Mitchell, T. (1988) *Violence and Piety in Spanish Folklore*, University of Pennsylvania Press, Philadelphia.
Mitchell, T. (1990) *Passional Culture: Emotion, Religion, and Society in Southern Spain*, University of Pennsylvania Press, Philadelphia.
Moreno Navarro, I. (1984) La antropología cultural in Andalucía: Estado actual y perspectiva de futuro. In: Rodriguez Becerra, S. (ed.) *Antropología Cultural de Andalucía*, Consejería de Cultura de la Junta de Andalucía, Seville, pp. 93–107.
Morris, A.S. (1985) Tourism and town planning in Catalonia, *Planning Outlook*, 28(2), pp. 77–82.
Morris, A.S. and Dickenson, G. (1987) Tourist development in Spain: growth versus conservation on the Costa Brava, *Geography*, 72(1), pp. 16–26.

Morris, J. (1979) *Spain*, Faber & Faber, London.
Muirhead, F. (1929) *Southern Spain and Portugal (The Blue Guide)*, Benn, London.
Nash, D. (1996) *Anthropology of Tourism*, Pergamon, Oxford.
Naylon, J. (1967) Tourism – Spain's most important industry, *Geography*, 52, pp. 23–40.
Nogués Pedregal, A.M. (1996) Tourism and self-consciousness in a south Spanish coastal community. In: Boissevain, J. (ed.) *Coping with Tourists: European Reactions to Mass Tourism*, Berghahn Books, Providence and Oxford, pp. 56–83.
Pearce, D.G. (1989) *Tourist Development*, 2nd edn. Longman, Harlow.
Pearce, D.G. and Grimmeau, J.P. (1985) The spatial structure of tourist accommodation and hotel demand in Spain, *Geoforum*, 16(1), pp. 37–50.
Pi-Sunyer, O. (1978) Through native eyes: tourists and tourism in a Catalan maritime community. In: Smith, V.L. (ed.) *Hosts and Guests: The Anthropology of Tourism*, Blackwell, Oxford, pp. 149–155.
Pi-Sunyer, O. (1996) Tourism in Catalonia. In: Barke, M., Towner, J. and Newton, M.T. (eds) *Tourism in Spain: Critical Issues*, CAB International, Wallingford, pp. 231–264.
Pitt-Rivers, J.A. (1954) *The People of the Sierra*, Weidenfeld and Nicolson, London.
Preston, P. (1993) *Franco: A Biography*, Fontana, London.
Pritchett, V.S. (1954) *The Spanish Temper*, Chatto & Windus, London.
Ritchie, H. (1994) *Here We Go*, Penguin Books, London.
Salmon, K. (1995) *The Modern Spanish Economy: Transformation and Integration into Europe*, 2nd edn., Pinter, London and New York.
Selwyn, T. (1996) Tourism, culture and cultural conflicts: a case study from Mallorca. In: Fsadani, C. and Selwyn, T. (eds) *Tourism, Culture and Regional Development in the Mediterranean*, University of Malata, Malta.
Shaw, D.L. (1975) *The Generation of 1898 in Spain*, Ernest Benn, London and Tonbridge.
Sinclair, M.T. and Bote Gómez, B. (1996) Tourism, the Spanish economy and the balance of payments. In: Barke, M., Towner, J. and Newton, M.T. (eds) *Tourism in Spain: Critical Issues*, CAB International, Wallingford, pp. 89–117.
Tamames, R. (1986) *The Spanish Economy*, C. Hurst & Co., London.
Torres Bernier, E. (1979) El sector turístico en Andalucía: instrumentalización y efectos impulsores, *Revista de Estudios Regionales*, 1, pp. 377–442.
Towner, J. (1985) The Grand Tour: a key phase in the history of Tourism, *Annals of Tourism Research* 12(3), pp. 297–333.
Turner, L. and Ash, J. (1975) *The Golden Hordes: International Tourism and the Pleasure Periphery*, Constable, London.
Tyrakowski, K. (1986) The role of tourism in land utilization conflicts on the Spanish Mediterranean coast, *GeoJournal*, 13(1), pp. 19–26.
Vasquez Montalbán, M. (1980) *Crónica Sentimental de España*, Barcelona.
Villegas Molina, F. (1975) El turismo en Andalucia: areas y consecuencias, *Informacion Commercial Española*, November, pp. 113–122.
Zarkia, C. (1996) *Philoxenia* receiving tourists – but not guests – on a Greek island. In: Boissevain, J. (ed.) *Coping with Tourists: European Reactions to Mass Tourism*, Berghahn Books, Providence and Oxford, pp. 143–173.

12

Partnerships Involving Indigenous Peoples in the Management of Heritage Sites

Geoffrey Wall

Introduction

With the growth of tourism and its fragmentation into increasingly specialized forms, such as ecotourism and cultural tourism, there has been increased pressure placed by tourists and the tourism industry on resources which have traditionally been used by indigenous peoples. This is particularly the case in parks and protected areas as well as some historic sites which have become increasingly important as tourist attractions because of both the relatively natural landscapes which they contain and the lifestyles of the inhabitants which they support. For the Masai in Kenya, Aboriginal peoples in Australia, the Maori in New Zealand, Indians and Inuit in Canada and the United States, and ethnic minorities in other parts of the world, tourism is bringing peoples with very different value systems into the territories which indigenous peoples have inhabited for centuries. This has brought to the fore a plethora of questions concerning control over such resources, the rights of indigenous peoples to determine appropriate uses for such resources, their interests in becoming involved in or discouraging the development of tourism, and the creation of acceptable mechanisms for arriving at such decisions. This chapter addresses the latter concern. It describes and evaluates the institutional arrangements which have evolved between governments and aboriginal peoples to address issues of shared management of national parks and historic sites. Alternative approaches to shared and cooperative management are identified and particular attention is given to the following issues:

1. The precise meaning of partnerships and shared and cooperative management;
2. The role indigenous people play in management;
3. The ownership of land;
4. Implementation mechanisms;
5. Relevant legal, constitutional and socio-economic contexts.

In essence, this chapter provides an overview of international experiences pertaining to the above topics. However, some American examples will be discussed to give a flavour of the types of issues and responses to be found.

While there is a rapidly-growing literature relevant to this chapter and some comparative studies of different protected areas both within and between countries exist, the author is not aware of any truly comprehensive assessment of the topic. In fact, Zube and Busch (1990, p. 119) indicated that, with respect to park–people relationships, 'There has not been to date . . . any attempt to survey current activities and practices from an international perspective.' However, in 1988, Rueggeberg prepared a document under terms of reference extremely similar to those which guided this investigation and Matowanyika *et al.* (1992) have prepared a review of the relationships between protected areas and people in Africa. Also, an annotated bibliography on principles of joint management agreements has been produced by Planning and Conservation Services, Northern British Columbia Region (1990).

Although land ownership and co-management constitute primary themes of the paper, it is apparent that these are not only goals in themselves for indigenous peoples; they are also means of addressing other concerns such as economic opportunity, cultural survival and self-determination. They also have substantial implications for the future of tourism in parks and protected areas. Thus, other issues, such as those relating to sacred sites, employment opportunities, human remains and cultural survival are very much intertwined with indigenous attitudes towards and involvement in tourism.

Indigenous people, members of the host society and tourists often have very different relationships to the land and the resources which it supports. Thus, they have divergent attitudes concerning what can be shared and what should be preserved at all costs, what activities are appropriate and inappropriate in protected areas, whose heritage is being protected and should receive priority, what stories should be told about that heritage and who should tell them, and the roles of indigenous and scientific knowledge in understanding and interpreting the heritage. Such issues can easily lead to conflict between individuals and groups who value a site or area for different reasons and would like to interact with it in different ways and use it for different purposes. Co-management schemes may be a means of reducing the likelihood of conflict by legitimizing and formalizing the input of different groups and different ways of knowing and understanding, in setting the goals, objectives and management strategies for protected areas. In this way, segments of society, including indigenous people, whose interests have often been ignored or, even worse, suppressed, may be empowered.

United States: An Overview and Some Examples

Legal, constitutional and socio-economic

Native land rights developed in the United States through a variety of treaties, legislation, and court rulings. Treaties signed by the federal government and Indian groups in the late 1800s resulted in the establishment of reservations which the natives held in title and the government managed in trust. Early government policies pursued the goal of assimilating natives into Western society. The Indian Reorganization Act (1934) ended the policy of cultural assimilation, terminated the government's land allotment strategy and gave some measure of self-determination for native groups. Native groups were encouraged to form formal governmental bodies and to develop formal laws but under the approval of the Department of the Interior. The Act also set up a legal process by which traditional lands could be re-acquired by native groups (Rueggeberg, 1988).

During the 1950s, the federal government withdrew from providing exclusive services for native Indian communities and removed federal trust protection from large tracts of land. The policy shift resulted in many Indian groups falling back upon a dependence on welfare. Native protests over adverse living conditions and a desire for self-determination in the 1970s forced a re-evaluation of the federal termination policy. In 1978, the American Indian Religious Freedom Act was passed and served to reaffirm the constitutional rights of native Americans to have access to lands and resources central to the conduct of their traditional religions. Federal government agencies, such as the National Parks Service (NPS), soon began to review and re-examine the impacts of their policies and procedures upon these rights (Halmo, 1994).

The NPS was created in 1916 by the US Congress as an administrative agency for national parklands. The NPS's early management philosophy towards national parks focused on the maintenance of 'pristine' wilderness to the exclusion of human habitation and placed strict limitations on human uses. Recognition of native culture within national parks was virtually absent even though many Indian tribes continued to hold close cultural ties to these lands (Cook, 1991; Ruppert, 1994). Past NPS–native relationships were characterized by one-way communication, the dominance of the NPS over native groups, and the use of Western models of negotiation and consensus building (Ruppert, 1994). In recent years, based in part on legislative developments such as the American Indian Religious Freedom Act (1978), the federal attitude towards native Indian involvement in protected area planning and management has changed and new efforts have been made to involve natives in this process. As an example, cultural anthropologists have been added to NPS's Anthropology Division in order to give it more expertise in traditional indigenous concerns (Rueggeberg, 1988).

Several new pieces of federal legislation are serving to redefine further the federal–native relationship with respect to NPS protected areas and areas of Native American significance:

- National Environmental Policy Act (NEPA) – addresses actions of the NPS affecting Indian tribal interests.
- American Indian Religious Freedom Act (AIRFA) – addresses actions of the NPS affecting Indian religious interests.
- Alaskan National Interest Lands Conservation Act (ANILCA) – addresses actions of NPS affecting subsistence activities and related ways of life.
- National Historic Preservation Act (NHPA) – addresses actions of NPS affecting ethnographic resources with National Register eligibility.
- Archaeological Resources Protection Act (ARPA) – addresses situations where the activities of archaeologists affect resources of concern to American Indians.
- Native American Graves Protection and Repatriation Act (NAGPRA) – addresses NPS collection of Native American artefacts, archaeological digs affecting Native American interests and accidental discoveries of grave articles and/or human remains.

Policies such as the Native American Graves Protection and Repatriation Act are forcing NPS staff to adopt new operational and negotiative approaches when addressing concerns such as the treatment of Indian burials and burial sites and the storage and collection of native items. They are also requiring NPS staff to accommodate sites, areas and cultural processes considered important by tribal communities within existing natural resources planning and management practices (Ruppert, 1994).

Partnerships and shared cooperative management

The legal obligation for federal government agencies to engage in consultation with native tribal groups over public land use and management and cultural preservation has resulted in a variety of innovative consensus-building and partnership-forming approaches; some of which are outlined below. The type of consultation and partnership-building process which is chosen for a particular situation must be sensitive to the fact that many Indian tribal governments and groups are limited in the amount of expertise, time and resources they can contribute towards such processes (Halmo, 1994).

Mesa Verde National Park

In 1992, a pipeline construction project unearthed Anazasi burial remains at Mesa Verde National Park. Acting under the Native American Graves Protection and Repatriation Act (NAGPRA), the park superintendent ordered the find to be back-filled and notified a number of native groups whose reservations bordered the discovery. No attempt was made to examine the site in detail using outside archaeologists prior to native consultation. After a series of meetings with native representatives, an agreement was reached on how best to store the remains already excavated, how to prepare the site for exhumation, where to locate a re-burial site, proper positioning for re-burial and respectful handling of the remains. The agreement also specified what actions should be taken if the pipeline construction unearthed any other remains (Ruppert, 1994).

The Native American Graves Protection and Repatriation Act (NAGPRA) requires consultations to take place with native groups when human remains or burial-associated artefacts are unearthed on federal lands. Within National Parks, park rangers are given the responsibility to repatriate native possessions upon request. Requests can be made on the remains of lineal ancestors or on funerary objects. Requests can also be made on cultural items to which a native group is culturally affiliated. These items can include human remains, funerary objects, sacred objects and items containing present-day cultural significance (McManamon, 1992; NAGPRA, 1992).

NAGPRA serves to address the issues that can arise from deliberate excavations and inadvertent discoveries of native heritage articles, and specifies what consultations should occur following such findings and how ownership is to be determined. Intentional or deliberate excavations must be done within the law and with the consent of the affected native group. Items excavated belong to the associated tribe or the proven descendant of the cultural items or human remains. If cultural items or human remains are found inadvertently, all excavations are required to stop and the proper authorities must be notified. Activities may resume after certification by these authorities. Federal officials are required to consult with associated tribes or lineal descendants or with tribes on whose land the activity is occurring. Notification is sent to the necessary tribes and information is provided to aid in the identification of the cultural items and/or human remains (NAGPRA, 1992).

The NPS is also required by the Act to summarize or catalogue in written form its holdings of sacred objects, unassociated funerary objects and objects of cultural patrimony and to send this summary to affected or interested tribal leaders and native organizations. An inventory of human remains and associated funerary objects on NPS lands was required to be completed by November 1995 (NAGPRA, 1992).

Badlands National Park

In 1968, Badlands National Park was extended to include lands within a nearby Indian reservation. A land use agreement between NPS and the reservation allowed members of the tribe to retain their right to hunt game within this area of the park. In 1993, the tribe decided to exercise this right and began to issue hunting permits to its members. Concerns over the possible impacts on park wildlife and the general issue of hunting within national parks, spurred the NPS to work with the tribe in preparing a joint game management plan. In late 1994, funds were provided to hire a cultural anthropologist/ecologist to work with the native-run Oglala Sioux Park and Recreation Authority in the identification of traditional Oglala methods of game and habitat management that could be incorporated into the plan and be combined with Western game management techniques towards the goal of maintaining a sustainable game population (Ruppert, 1994).

Devil's Tower National Monument

The original declaration of Devil's Tower National Monument in 1906 did not recognize the tower's significance as a sacred site for surrounding native tribal communities. In recent years, conflicts have emerged between the natives using the tower for vision quests and prayer sessions, and recreational rock climbers. In 1992, the park staff consulted several Indian groups, national climbing organizations, national environmental groups and county governments in its development of a Climbing Management Plan which assessed the impacts of this activity on the monument. This process served to highlight the extreme contrast in values held by natives and climbers towards use of this public area and was valuable in that it served to educate the two parties on the reasons underlying their uses of the tower and allowed them to examine alternative management solutions to the problem. After an 18-month consultative period, the management plan was released. It placed some restrictions on climbing but did not entirely ban it. The plan also required the NPS to communicate to the general public the range of traditional religious values that natives associated with the monument (Ruppert, 1994).

Grand Canyon National Park and the Havasupai Reservation

The Havasupai have inhabited the Grand Canyon since the 12th century. Originally, they occupied the central part of Grand Canyon National Park but were later moved to a small reservation along a nearby creek. Confinement to the reserve interfered with Havasupai traditional seasonal migration between the Canyon and the plateau and caused them economic, social and cultural hardships (Hough, 1991; White, 1993). The Grand Canyon National Park Enlargement Act 1975 was intended to improve the situation between the Havasupai and the NPS. Under the Act, the Havasupai were returned 74,866 ha of land and an additional 38,566 ha were set aside as Havasupai Use Lands to be utilized by the Havasupai under the NPS's jurisdiction (Hough, 1991). Once the Havasupai gained control over certain areas of land, they were able to charge camping and entrance fees which became a major source of income. Annual tourist visitations numbered 20,000 despite difficult access into the area. Although most tourists stay at facilities provided by the Havasupai, the tribe still suffers economically and incomes are generally below the state average (White, 1993).

Relations between the National Park Service and the Havasupai have been steadily improving even though each group maintains different philosophies about how the park should be managed. Cooperation has extended to a number of areas including tourism. The NPS wishes to provide visitors with a quality experience while protecting the environment. The Havasupai depend on the tourists for economic gain but also see them as an intrusion. Neither party has advertised the existence of any of the tourist lodgings; the Havasupai do not wish to advertise and the NPS wishes to disperse the tourists as much as possible (Hough, 1991).

In their cooperative undertakings, the NPS has trained Havasupai in park management techniques while the tribe has provided visitors with a unique tourism experience. Further, it is being recognized that the role of interpretation could also be beneficial to both parties in that the Havasupai would benefit by having the public understand more about their culture and the Park would benefit by improving the visitor experience (Hough, 1991).

Southwest Region

Many advancements have been made in the Southwest Region with regards to the involvement of American Indians in the management of National Parks. Programmes have been developed to train native Indians in park management skills while the NPS managers gain valuable traditional knowledge from them. NPS Southwest regional office employs American Indians in key positions such as regional curator and chief of Division of Indian Affairs. As well, maintenance workers are given training programmes in their native tongue. These activities have aided in building positive relationships between the NPS and the natives and their culture (Cook, 1991).

Native involvement in park operations has been extensive in the region. At Canyon de Chelly National Monument in Arizona, 80% of the park staff including the superintendent is Navajo. The park operates under a joint management plan between NPS and the Navajo. At Navajo National Monument, Arizona, the park superintendent, chief of maintenance and the administrative technician are all Navajo while the chief of the interpretation and resource management division is Pueblo. At the Petroglyph National Monument and El Mapais National Monument in New Mexico, consultations with appropriate Indian tribes has been ongoing.

Recently, a Council for American Indian Interpretation has been established in the region to increase the knowledge base of the region's park interpreters with regards to indigenous native culture and lore. This was in response to a concern that the majority of interpreters in the region's parks were still non-natives whose knowledge of native culture came from outside sources such as textbooks and non-native teachers (Cook, 1991).

Alaska

In 1971, the US Congress enacted the Alaska Native Claims Settlement Act mainly as a response to industry concerns over potential conflicts with native land claimants concerning a right-of-way for the construction of the Trans-Alaska Pipeline (Swan and Cahn, 1983). The Act extinguished all existing native land claims and entitled native peoples to select from 40 million acres (16.2 million ha) of unreserved federal land in the state. Twelve native regional corporations and about 200 native village corporations were established as 'privately owned companies' to select, own and manage these lands for native peoples. As well, the Joint Federal–State Land Use Planning Commission was established to set aside land for several federal agencies, including the NPS, Fish and Wildlife Service, Forest Service, and Bureau of Land Management, which were also recognized under the Act as land claimants. The Commission was also required to work with the native corporations and with the state government to resolve any overlapping or conflicting claims arising from this process (Gallagher and Epps, 1988).

The Commission's identification of suitable land areas for federal ownership resulted in the enactment of the Alaska National Interest Lands Conservation Act (1980) which set aside 104 million acres (42.1 million ha) of land primarily for the establishment of parks and wildlife refuges. Several existing conservation areas were enlarged and many new ones were created including five new national parks. Management plans for most of these areas were completed by the late 1980s. By this time, native corporations had also completed their land selections and had received interim ownership of these properties. Most land selections were centred upon existing villages and encompassed about 12% of the state. As well, most villages selected lands in a checkerboard pattern thus hoping to influence as large an area as possible. In the face of conflicting pressures to develop these lands for economic uses and to protect traditional hunting and fishing opportunities, most native corporations became involved in some form of land planning although the development of this process has been slow (Gallagher and Epps, 1988).

Given the complex ownership patterns that have now developed in Alaska, Gallagher and Epps (1988) stress the need for coordinating land use and land management activities between federal and native land managers and individual landowners. Alaska's wilderness landscape has been broken into an enormous number of potentially competing land parcels that are not designed for conservation of natural processes that extend over wide areas and cross jurisdictional boundaries. Gallagher and Epps advocate shared agency goals and some form of ongoing agreements with individual native landowners to have them understand and abide with broad, regional conservation objectives. Opportunities clearly exist to avoid similar land use conflicts that have developed in other parts of the US through the development of joint-management relationships and through the education and involvement of local landowners in decision-making for regional-scale conservation of Alaska's natural values.

The development of a coordination mechanism has not taken place. During the development of federal agency land use plans in the early 1980s, federal agencies, native corporations and landowners were brought together to review proposed land use plans and to engage in scoping sessions. Once the plans were completed, the consultations ended. Coordination is also made difficult by the large size of many land units, by uncertainties over exact unit sizes and boundaries, and by the difficulties in accessing remote native villages to engage in face-to-face consultations. Gallagher and Epps (1988) suggest the adoption of a regional approach, perhaps based on watershed boundaries, in order to make coordination schemes more logistically possible while maintaining general ecological integrity and local, social sensitivity.

Summary

As a large country with a substantial but diverse native population as well as a long history of national park and other protected area involvement, there is a long history of diverse and evolving relationships between native peoples and the managers of parks and protected areas. However, this history appears not to have been well-documented as a single phenomenon. One might expect that substantial differences may exist between areas as diverse as Alaska, Hawaii and the South-east United States.

The International Context

Considerable international interest has been generated in recent years in the status and well-being of indigenous peoples. For example, The International Work Group for Indigenous Affairs and Indigenous Peoples (IWGIA) produced a strategy paper in 1994 identifying relevant issues and principles for their resolution.

One specific issue identified was parks. Other issues, such as disposition of traditional lands and territories and the role of anti-hunting organizations, also impinge upon parks and protected areas and have implications for tourism. Somewhat similarly, the IUCN Inter-Commission Task Force on Indigenous Peoples and the Secretariat of IUCN, in collaboration with the International Institute for Sustainable Development (1993), has prepared a guide for action with respect to indigenous people and sustainability. Chapter 26 of Agenda 21, 'Recognizing and Strengthening the Role of Indigenous People and their Communities', stated that:

> In view of the interrelationship between the natural environment and its sustainable development and the cultural, social, economic and physical well-being of Indigenous people, national and international efforts to implement

> environmentally sound and sustainable development should recognize, accommodate, promote, and strengthen the role of Indigenous people and their communities.
>
> UNCED (1992)

Furthermore, both the UNCED Convention on Biological Diversity and the Draft Universal Declaration on the Rights of Indigenous Peoples emphasize the inextricable link between biological and cultural diversity by 'encouraging customary use of biological resources in accordance with traditional cultural practices that are compatible with conservation or sustainable use requirements'.

Thus, interest in the evolving roles of indigenous peoples in parks, historic sites and tourism can be seen as part of an international movement. Activities and decisions made to address issues related to and of concern to indigenous peoples, whether inside or outside of parks and protected areas, may have far-reaching implications for the management of such areas, including their potential for tourism and the forms which it might take. At the same time, because of the importance of the resources under their care, the managers of protected areas may have an opportunity to demonstrate a leadership role in addressing such issues. Certainly it is in their best long-term interests to do so.

In a paper which is often cited in the context of planning and public participation, Arnstein (1969) described a ladder of citizenship participation with successive rungs extending from manipulation, through therapy, informing, consultation, placation, partnership, delegated power and citizen control. The bottom rungs on the ladder were regarded as non-participation, those further up were viewed as types of tokenism, whereas those at the top were considered to represent varying degrees of citizen power. Recognition of the necessity for the involvement of aboriginal peoples in decisions which affect their lives can be seen as a specific aspect of the broader issues of public participation, self-determination, and the desire to enable individuals and groups to participate in the taking of decisions which influence their well-being. While the appropriateness of involvement is widely acknowledged, the form which that involvement should take, although tending to move up successive rungs of Arnstein's ladder over time, is far from clear or unanimous and varies from situation to situation both within and between countries.

The issue, particularly when viewed from an international perspective, is further complicated by variations in the meanings ascribed to: (i) indigenous peoples; (ii) parks and protected areas; and (iii) co-management. Each of these topics will be considered in turn.

Indigenous peoples

The international literature is not consistent in use of terminology concerning the peoples under consideration in relation to parks and protected areas. Thus, according to Brechin *et al.* (1991), the recent literature emphasizes 'traditional societies', 'native peoples' and 'indigenous peoples'. However, the terms are often not defined and are often used interchangeably although, for example, the International Labour Organization, in its 1989 Indigenous and Tribal Peoples Convention, has provided a lengthy definition. Furthermore, it is not always clear whether the concern is with people who live in and/or adjacent to protected areas, who once lived in or adjacent to protected areas, or who ascribe special values to such areas. Clearly, protected areas may be lived in or near and valued by people that do not claim aboriginal status.

In an attempt to clarify matters, Brechin *et al.* (1991) suggest a typology of residents as follows: tribal peoples, acculturated tribal peoples, peasant peoples, farmers and rural citizenry, and local entrepreneurs.

When members of the conservation community use terms such as 'aboriginal' or 'indigenous' peoples, they appear to wish to distinguish between those who live harmoniously with their immediate environment and those that do not. It is often presumed that traditional societies, native peoples and indigenous peoples lived in harmony with the environment in contrast to modern societies, colonists and other non-indigenous peoples. However, such presumptions can be questioned. For example, many aboriginal peoples had low standards of living, short expectancy of life at birth and high infant death rates. Furthermore, population size and distribution and available technology have changed markedly over time.

In summary, not only are there great variations in aboriginal cultures and the environments which they inhabit, and in their history of occupance and displacement, there are also substantial differences from place to place in the interpretation of relevant peoples, encompassing both very narrow and extremely broad definitions of those with claims of special status and interests.

Parks and protected areas

Somewhat similarly, there are great variations in definitions of parks and protected areas and the activities which are deemed to be appropriate in them. For the purposes of this chapter, no attempt is made to make a distinction between national parks and national historic sites for, although they may vary in size and have somewhat different purposes, there are considerable similarities in the issues involved with respect to aboriginal concerns.

In international comparisons of the roles of aboriginal peoples in protected areas, the specific name given to a site or area (such as a national, state or provincial park, biosphere reserve, wilderness area, nature reserve or game park) varies substantially. However, the critical factor is probably not the name itself but, rather, the extent to which the management regime permits human uses and alteration of the environment.

Nevertheless, most literature is concerned with so-called national parks with many developing countries adopting a modified form of the American model which has tended to exclude people from protected areas. However, there are other models, such as the British model, which has always included people. For indigenous people, the connection to the land and the relationships and obligations that arise from that connection are the core of their identity since it represents the basis of their economy and lifestyle. In recent years, the international trend has been increasingly away from the American model in the direction of the British model; away from the displacement of people who were viewed as being 'incompatible' with the park ideal, to finding ways of accommodating them within or adjacent to protected area boundaries. While displacement of people from protected areas is an important issue, it is only one among many which aboriginal peoples wish to address.

To a considerable extent, this changing perspective reflects increasing recognition that protected areas, even though a major objective may be the maintenance and enhancement of ecological processes, are cultural artefacts whose boundaries and management regimes are determined by human decisions and whose landscapes and ecological processes have long been influenced by human activities, the continuation of which may even be required for their perpetuation. Thus, perceptions of the dualism of humans and nature, which is a perspective which is foreign to many aboriginal peoples, are increasingly being replaced by a convergence between protected area establishment and management and cultural preservation so that, in many parts of the world, cultural heritage preservation, in the form of protecting the rights of aboriginal peoples, is taking place alongside the preservation of natural areas and historic sites as a legitimate policy. Nevertheless, the different world views of indigenous and mainstream societies make it difficult to translate ideas and concepts from one culture to another. Culture and language may inhibit communication and inhibit the ability of people and organizations of both societies to enter social encounters with relative ease. A major challenge facing both indigenous people and the wider society is to strengthen intercultural dialogue in the participation process.

As Brechin *et al.* (1991) point out, cultural preservation will be a more important concern for some resident peoples than others. For those for whom this is particularly important, the critical issue is the right of self-determination and the freedom to choose rather than a desire to live in an unchanging way in a form of 'enforced primitivism'. Key factors of concern are often: (i) recognition of territorial rights; (ii) protection from introduced diseases and social pathologies; (iii) adequate time to adapt to change; and, as has already been stated, (iv) the right of self-determination.

Co-management

There are a large number of ways of protecting the interest of aboriginal peoples. They include environmental and social impact assessments and conflict management (which attempts to integrate local cultural values into conservation decisions but may be very difficult to achieve whenever trade-offs between competing interests for the use of an area cannot be avoided). It is important to note that Western approaches to conflict resolution, such as litigation and other adversarial methods, may be inappropriate in many situations and new approaches for resolving disputes may be necessary if local people are to create shared solutions to meet their needs, protect traditional rights and maintain communication for mutual cooperation. However, as pointed out by Hough (1988), those with power will be required to take the initial steps to initiate action in a consensus–agreement approach.

Indigenous institutions are often poorly understood by outsiders but the effective functioning of indigenous resource management systems depends on the existence of appropriate institutions, and local people cannot be divorced from the social structures of which they are a part. If outsiders always make the assumption that there are always community-based institutions at work, then institutional arrangements would be based on a different footing than is usually the case. However, indigenous institutional arrangements may need reinforcing or rehabilitating so that they can meet the challenges of a changing world.

Co-management refers to a substantial sharing of protected site and area management responsibilities and authority among government agencies and interested peoples. Such an arrangement can take many forms and contains inherent tensions. Compromise and consensus are essential to the success of such processes. Although difficult to implement, the advantages of co-management can be significant. However, true co-management may be difficult to find and various forms of co-optation may be more common.

Co-management, and the similar term joint management, have been criticized as being terms with imprecise meanings. Piper (personal communication, 1995) on the basis of extensive Australian experience, stressed the importance of clear definitions and indicated that there is currently a debate about the use of the term 'joint management' in Queensland, particularly as it relates to national parks. Generally, the term has been used with regard to national parks, such as Kakadu and Uluru where, under legislation, there is equity in decision-making through Boards of Management (in fact there are aboriginal majorities on these boards). However, there has been a tendency recently for agencies to use the term 'joint management' in the context of lesser arrangements where aboriginal people have little power in decision-making. Not only does this cause confusion, it creates expectations of 'joint' decision-making which agencies may be unable to achieve under their legislation or policies.

Much like Arnstein, Piper sees a hierarchy in management arrangements although the division between the levels is fuzzy. This hierarchy is as follows:

1. Aboriginal people being in total control of the protected site or area.
2. Joint management (e.g. aboriginal land leased to a government agency with an aboriginal majority on the board of management).
3. Cooperative management (where aboriginal people do not have a great deal of power in the decision-making process but there is a close working relationship, possibly through a formal agreement).
4. Consultative arrangements (where aboriginal people are consulted about management matters but have no decision-making powers).

Piper advises that before agencies use a term such as 'joint management', they should clearly define what they mean by it. There has been a tendency for agencies to say to aboriginal peoples that they are prepared to discuss joint management without having a clear idea of what they mean by the term whereas aboriginal groups often have a clear idea of what the term means for them. As a result, agencies find themselves retreating from the use of such terms because they are unable to achieve what aboriginal groups see as joint management due to legislative, political or policy restrictions. Ownership of land and the role which aboriginal peoples play in management are but two of many concerns of aboriginal peoples. They include: the designation and delimitation of protected areas, compensation, indigenous uses, direct and indirect economic opportunities, interpretation (what and how landscapes, sites and artefacts are to be interpreted to visitors and who is to do this), the right to exclude visitors from specific sites and areas, protection and repatriation of human remains and cultural artefacts, copyright for traditional designs, etc. Slocombe and Nelson (1992), in an international comparative study of national parks, addressed eight management issues as follows: access, tourism, resource extraction, aboriginal role, administration, scientific research, interpretation and regional integration but, of course, the role of aboriginal people cannot be totally separated from all of the other topics. To a considerable extent, land ownership (which is a concept which, in its Western form, was alien to many aboriginal peoples) and the acquisition of management authority provide means of addressing many of the other related questions.

Zube and Busch (1990), in an international comparative survey, organized approaches into four major categories: local participation and residence in the protected area, services provided in and for the local community by the park, maintenance of traditional land and religious uses, and local participation in tourism activities. They suggested that four general models of relationships are being fostered, although the categories are not exclusive and most protected areas employ more than one of the models or strategies. These strategies are described briefly as follows:

1. Local Participation. Local participation is encouraged through ownership, in-park residence and traditional uses of park resources, serving as park administrators or some other form of participation in park advisory or policy committees, and employment on the park staff.
2. Park Services to Local Community. In this model, local people no longer have access to the protected area for traditional uses but park staff provide social services of various kinds to compensate for the lack of access.
3. Traditional Land Uses. Traditional land uses are permitted within protected area boundaries. Interactions occur between the local population and protected area staff, although the latter may be primarily in regard to regulations controlling access.
4. Tourism. Economic benefits are gained by local populations through involvement in tourism. Interactions are strongest between local persons and tourists, and relationships with protected area staff are often less direct and of a more regulatory nature.

Zube and Busch (1990) also note that all strategies are not equally adaptable and, hence, adoptable by all cultures and natural environments, and that some strategies may be employed as token efforts rather than as sincere desires to facilitate aboriginal involvement in decision-making. For example, local participation can result in co-optation and employment in only the lowest level service positions, the provision for access to park resources that are needed for subsistence can be a form of tokenism and so limited that local people are not compensated for their loss, and the promotion of local arts and crafts for sale to tourists can lead to commercialization and loss of quality and local pride in the articles produced for sale. On the other hand, the incorporation of local knowledge into management decisions and activities has many potential benefits and research will be required to determine the nature of such knowledge as well as to identify new models and structures to incorporate the knowledge into decision-making (Stankey 1989).

According to the IUCN agenda for action, key ingredients in achieving co-management include:

> joint research and information-sharing system combining Indigenous knowledge and modern science in order to establish sustainable levels of resource use and harvest, joint action plans and management objectives, a system of rights and obligations for those interested in the resource(s), procedures for making collective decisions affecting the interests of government agencies, user organizations, and individual users in all stages of strategy planning and implementation, including regular review and monitoring. It is suggested that indigenous institutions strongly involved in such a process, particularly in controls created and implemented locally, will achieve a greater degree of compliance, therefore requiring a minimum of

> enforcement while ensuring better results and solving/avoiding allocation and management conflicts.
>
> (IUCN, 1993, pp. 25–26)

In a general discussion of vision and objectives, the IUCN agenda for action suggests short, medium and long-term objectives for decision-makers. Under the former heading it is suggested that confidence-building consultations must be held with indigenous and traditional authorities by user agencies on use of national and rural resources within the context of their mutual concerns and interests, and with cognizance of indigenous people's strong attachment to their land for their very survival as a people. Priority should be given to indigenous and local people in employment opportunities and due respect must be given to their intellectual property rights.

In the medium term, in order for the 'subsistence culture' of indigenous people to keep pace with the growing demand for socio-economic development, there should be concerted efforts made to blend acceptable resource use strategies with tested modern methods that assure sustainability. Indigenous people must be provided with training opportunities to prepare them for incorporation into evolving management systems. In the longer term, consideration must be given to decentralization of political power, revenue retention in the indigenous communities for their socio-economic development and the people's right to self-determination.

Conclusions

It is suggested that government agencies must have a clear mandate for what they can achieve and base negotiations from a solid foundation, working up from there, rather than using imprecise terms which create unachievable expectations. However, indigenous practices are often very site-specific and this frustrates the implementation of general approaches. While legislation and formal administrative arrangements are required to empower aboriginal and other local peoples and to give them greater authority in decisions related to protected area management, in the absence of trust, relatively little may be achieved in real terms. Thus, such initiatives are a necessary but not sufficient requirement for successful co-management of protected areas. Personal relationships are a vital ingredient and it takes time, effort, understanding and patience, and even mediation (Ruppert, 1994) for these to develop to a level where co-management can be implemented successfully.

Thus, at the risk of oversimplification, three basic points can be made:

- Facilitating legislation is important because the legal situation circumscribes what various governmental authorities are able to do and it can also empower local people.
- True co-management requires trust, sharing and mutual respect and this takes time and effort on the part of all stakeholders.

- Indigenous peoples have varied cultures and a diversity of concerns reflecting different histories and opportunities. Different mechanisms are likely to evolve to meet the needs of differing situations. There is no quick fix for problems which have festered for centuries.

Acknowledgements

The research on which this paper is based was undertaken under contract to the Department of Canadian Heritage. Valuable research assistance was provided by Sara Hallman and Andrew Skibicki.

References

Arnstein, S.R. (1969) A ladder of citizen participation, *American Institute of Planners Journal*, 35, pp. 216–224.

Brechin, S.R., West, P.C., Harmon, D. and Kutay, K. (1991) Resident peoples and protected areas: a framework for inquiry. In: West, P.C. and Brechin, S.R. (eds) *Resident Peoples and National Parks: Social Dilemmas and Strategies in International Conservation*, The University of Arizona Press, Tucson, pp. 5–28.

Cook, J.E. (1991) The cultural legacy of America's national parklands, *National Forum*, 71(2), pp. 24–28.

Gallagher, J. and Epps, A.C. (1988) The great Alaskan land subdivision revisited, *Journal of Soil and Water Conservation*, 43, pp. 368–375.

IUCN Inter-Commission Task Force on Indigenous Peoples (1993) *Indigenous Peoples and Sustainability: A Guide for Action*, IUCN Inter-Commission Task Force on Indigenous Peoples and the Secretariat of IUCN in collaboration with the International Institute for Sustainable Development, Gland, Switzerland.

International Work Group for Indigenous Affairs and Indigenous Peoples (1994) *Strategy Paper*, IWGIA, Copenhagen.

Halmo, D.B. (1994) With one voice: collective action in cultural impact assessment, *Practicing Anthropology*, 16, pp. 14–16.

Hough, J. (1988). Obstacles to effective management of conflicts between National Parks and surrounding human communities in developing countries, *Environmental Conservation*, 15, pp. 129–136.

Hough, J. (1991). The Grand Canyon National Park and the Havasupai people. In: West, P.C. and Brechin, S.R. (eds) *Resident Peoples and National Parks*, University of Arizona Press, Tucson, pp. 215–230.

Matowanyika, J.Z.Z., Serafin, R. and Nelson, J.G. (1992) *Conservation and Development in Africa*, Heritage Resources Centre, University of Waterloo, Waterloo.

McManamon, F.P. (1992) Managing repatriation: implementing the Native American Graves Protection and Repatriation Act, *Cultural Resource Management*, 5, pp. 9–12.

North American Graves Protection and Repatriation Act (NAGPRA) (1992) National Park Service, United States Department of the Interior, Washington, DC.

Planning and Conservation Services, Northern British Columbia Region (1990) *Principles of Joint Management Agreements: A Literature Review*, Prince George, British Columbia, Canada.

Rueggeberg, H. (1988) Involvement of Aboriginal people in National Park management in other countries. Prepared for the Department of Environment – Parks, Nanaimo, British Columbia, Canada (mimeo).

Ruppert, D. (1994) Redefining relationships: American Indians and National Parks, *Practicing Anthropology*, 16(3), pp. 10–13.

Slocombe, D.S. and Nelson, J.G. (1992) Management issues in hinterland National Parks: a human ecological approach, *Natural Areas Journal*, 12, pp. 206–213.

Stankey, G.H. (1989) Linking parks to people: the key to effective management, *Society and Natural Resources*, 2, pp. 245–250.

Swan, T. and Cahn, R. (1983). The politics of parks in Alaska, *Ambio*, 12, pp. 14–19.

UNCED (United Nations Conference on Environment and Development) (1992) *Agenda 21*, UNCED, Rio de Janeiro, chapter 26, paragraph 1.

White, D. (1993) Tourism as economic development for native people in the shadow of a protected area: a North American case study, *Society and Natural Resources*, 6, pp. 339–345.

Zube, E.H. and Busch, M.L. (1990) Park–people relationships: an international review, *Landscape and Urban Planning*, 19, pp. 117–131.

13

Tourism and Cultures: Consensus in the Making?

Priscilla Boniface

Introduction

Tourism's expansion continues apace. Culture is now recognized as a significant feature in tourism, both as an object of the tourist gaze and as a factor likely to condition tourism's participants. So, that there is more tourism is likely to be strongly significant in relation to the development of cultural conflict. The burgeoning of tourism is exemplified in three main ways. First, is that overall there is a growth and complexity of structure, policy and planning to cope with the increase. Second, people are simply travelling more, though, and this seems an important element in terms of stages being set for cultural conflict, tourists still only derive from a limited selection of the world's countries. Third, the number of destinations is increasing following the tourism industry's need to offer 'new' experiences to maintain appeal and serve larger markets. Greater than these individual aspects, culture, as a feature of permeation in various guises, is present in tourism in an additional and major way. Culture is present in tourism generally, but cultures play a crucial role because in their differences they offer variety and the possibility of product differentiation (Craik, 1997).

Although culture plays a fundamental role in tourism, it is as the material of different attraction that it serves the vital position of keeping the attention of a wide and novelty-seeking audience. This is more than enough reason for culture to be seen in the tourism industry as requiring to be maintained by hosts and put on show at destinations. The increase in tourism has resulted in many more outsiders arriving among resident communities. So, a scenario is offered by this growth, as two groups encounter one another as strangers and

 Tourism and Cultural Conflicts (eds M. Robinson and P. Boniface)

participants shaped by varying cultural conditionings, of more occasions being presented for the revelation and appearance of cultural difference. The framework of activity and operation in relation to tourism and culture as it is presented among tourists and hosts has been depicted by Shaw and Williams (1994, p. 15). The interface in the Shaw and Williams framework is cultural, with demonstration effects and tourist demands occurring intrusively within the host cultural boundary.

Surrounding and influencing the actual tourist–host contact is a range of inputs, influences and infrastructure extending beyond the immediate bounds of tourism. Fundamentally, this wide participation and involvement is present because tourism is regarded as likely to deliver economic benefits. Therefore, the stage and players to be viewed are necessarily extensive in considering how cultural conflicts in tourism might be resolved.

Due to the size of tourism, providers need to set in place a more complex and extensive infrastructure which in itself effects major impacts in cultural terms. Tourism's players, whether of the public or private sector, are often outsiders to the cultures and communities they impinge upon, so causing a potential source of friction. The central aspect is that culture is not only at the root of tourism as part of the tourism product but also a key source of motivation in becoming a tourist.

While cultural conflict may emerge at any level, its inevitable obvious presence is likely to be at the actual scene of the tourist–host encounter. Degrees of conflict can vary with the attitudes of the host; culture may itself influence whether the host demeanour is hostile, welcoming or merely apathetic. It should not be forgotten that culture is not the ultimate starting point of the process. Culture does not emerge out of a vacuum but is generally perceived as being forged from a combination of such influences as landscape, climate, history, circumstance, or as Hannerz presents it, by the influence of ecology (1996). Krippendorf (1987) remarks on the power of defence against tourism's influence by the host's firm adherence to his or her own culture and possession of in-built confidence. Of relevance to the discussion is Hannerz's observation that some people may opt not to espouse their own culture, with its implication that those 'of' a culture could decide not to relate to it or operate to its dictates.

Regarding the visitors, the situation of being on holiday, on tour, and away from home can heighten their mood and state and accentuate their conduct. It is probable that the state of minds of host and visitor will be, at best, at variance. Turner and Ash describe how the tourist does not want sightseeing spoilt by the intrusion of unpleasant features, saying:

> even when his tourism is directly concerned with culture and history the tourist is not encouraged to develop any real sense of history. Nor is he encouraged to view a foreign culture as a totality (of people and environment, art and religion, past and present). The touristic view of culture is necessarily schizoid and fragmented.
>
> (Turner and Ash, 1975, p. 139)

So, immediately, with a host grounded in an entire home context of the everyday and a tourist only choosing to recognize and interact with selected portions of it, contrasting perspectives and interests are present in their encounter.

Among cultural dissimilarities for consideration are those where host and visitor attach differences of meaning or status. Where a deep significance is attached, for example, regarding a spiritual or religious matter, which is not recognized by the visitor, aggravation can be a consequence. Notable within the careful tourism development in the Maldives, prescribed by its government, is that it is managed, so that 'Islamic codes and customs are carefully maintained' and tourism and tourists have to make the necessary accommodation (WTO, 1997, p. 166). In this instance, potential for conflict has not only been recognized but arrangements provided towards its avoidance. Cathedrals, churches and their artefacts, as well as being used for worship by the resident community, are often also attractions for visitors among whom may be many who do not attach the same, or any, religious significance to what to them is merely a site of spectacle. These buildings have thus taken on dual functions; their original purpose and the purpose of tourist attraction, and as such are often in a delicate and difficult position.

The political, economic and cultural dimensions of the First World culture may so strongly differentiate from those of the Third World that common meeting points of comprehension and shared views may be hard to discover, and the peculiarities and priorities of needs between developed and developing nations are likely to be dissimilar. However, respect of difference, particularly in cultural terms, is fundamental. The demand for cultural respect is a main plank of the position of the World Commission on Cultural Development in the report *Our Creative Diversity*. The Commission's call is for 'cultural freedom' which, it says, 'refers to the right of a group of people to follow a way of life of its choice' (de Cuéllar *et al.*, 1996, p. 15). In opining 'Cultural freedom leaves us free to meet one of the most basic needs, the need to define our own basic needs', the Commission says of this need that it is 'now threatened by global pressures and global neglect'. In this aspect is again provided a potential and fundamental source of conflict.

Culture's Critical Role

Culture is now recognized to be a supreme factor, guiding and influencing many aspects of life. A direct concentration upon the search about how to conserve the environment, in relation to the tourism impact, has shifted to include more focus upon culture. De Cuéllar as Secretary of the United Nations, in his Presidential role of the World Commission on Cultural Development (WCCD), says 'culture shapes all our thinking, imagining and behaviour'. He provides the key item: 'The challenge to humanity is to adopt new ways of thinking, new ways of acting, new ways of organizing itself in society, in short, new ways of living.' He continues: 'The challenge is also to promote different paths of development, informed by a recognition of how cultural factors shape the way in which societies conceive their own futures and choose the means to attain these futures.' Among the WCCD President's deliberation, culture and peace are linked in the depiction of concern with 'the "culture of peace"' (de Cuéllar, 1996, p. 11). The cultivation of peace and a culture of peace, as instruments towards conflict resolution and as opposites to conflict, will be considered below.

Cultural Conflict: Inevitable or Alterable?

Tourism brings into contact people who are not in usual, everyday or routine encounters. They are not, therefore, accustomed to each other's characters and circumstances which are programmed and produced by culture. Due to this, some degree of conflict may be anticipated. The front-line participants experiencing aggravation and discomfort of the situation are the tourist and host. That pivotal arena of disharmony and the conflict itself may be, however, the creation and outcome of decisions, objectives and activities selected by initiators away from the scene of encounter. It is the major players and participants in world tourism – governments, major public sector agencies, tourism industry operators – who are, through their policies and actions, helping to stage cultural conflict.

Governments, for instance will be pursuing dual and potentially contradictory objectives; those of economic development and cultural conservation. It can be said that the tourist and host meet in the holiday and travel experience somewhat as pawns and victims to giants' and bystanders' actions and objectives. In this respect, ground initiatives towards cultural harmony cannot fully achieve their aims unless instigators, such as those elucidated above, have provided the appropriate context for dialogue and reconciliation. For example, for the project 'Come visit our country' of the Associated Schools Project (a UNESCO network in Senegal, Morocco, Sweden and India), booklets of information are prepared for and by the young (United Nations/UNESCO, 1994, p. 27). The booklets address aspects of potential conflict relating to issues of the cultural past and religion. Such specific and 'on the ground' projects as this can be seen as isolated initiatives of worthiness. The recommendation could be made that they need to be established within a context of adequate attention being given to major issues, and of enough dialogue being created by and among those bearing the capacity to alter radically situations which dispose towards conflict.

Rhetoric and Reality: A Difference Between Them?

In the experience of being a tourist, a person travels from his or her home into another and different one, that of the host, and two distinct mores will confront one another. But as has been suggested, there is a difference of position among tourists and hosts who serve as the front-line agents in comparison to those behind them such as major agencies – both public and private sector, governments, planners, decision-makers and commercial operators – who possess the ability to make decisions about tourism and to shape its direction. The work of national tourism administrations is presented by Gee *et al.* (1997) who emphasize that government's role in tourism is essentially to deliver public benefits from tourism.

If the background of the tourism encounter shows some causes of responsibility and sources of instigation towards conflict, then it ought to consider what key organizations say and do. The general perspective is of tourism as an agent of economic development for both its direct and multiplier effects (Smith, 1989; WTO, 1997). Tourism is also frequently regarded by nations and agencies, despite many problems, as a tool towards bringing social benefit and cohesion and community well-being (WTO, 1997). And while it is recognized as having a capacity as potential destroyer and changer of cultures, tourism is hoped and regarded to be a mechanism for cultures' preservation (WTO, 1997), re-emergence and strengthening. Of the governments, organizations and private sector operations with various vested interests in using culture for tourism and receiving benefits in some way, all among them could be expected to be saying, believing or acting as though either no cultural harm is being done by tourism, or as if cultural denigration and alteration are under limitation or reasonable control. On the other hand, it would be reasonable to expect that some global or disinterested organizations who can afford to stand back are providing a truer picture and recommendation on the matter. In actuality, it can be questioned whether there is, maybe, a gap between the rhetoric and the reality of such bodies and inquired whether these organizations are, in seeking to advise and help progress the front, perhaps looking to inappropriate areas for attention and supporting the wrong mechanisms?

It must be clear that cultural conflict in tourism is produced, partially at least, at the macro level of endeavour and by power imbalances at that stratum. Yet, much of the direction of initiative and support – from either misbelief or due to difficulty of major influences and imponderables being addressed – is focused upon the small level in a piecemeal way. It can be wondered, therefore, how much pressure, valuable warning and advice is being delivered to the places which require it. The World Commission on Culture and Development (WCCD) is not very sanguine in its view saying: 'cultural expressions are being commercialized worldwide with scant respect for the communities in which they originate' (de Cuéllar *et al.*, 1996, p. 195).

Investigation into whether tourism's major players fully recognize the situation they are producing and if they understand, as far as possible, the nature of its provenance, is an idea towards improving the situation of cultural conflict. From this it can be asked whether they are doing all they can to bring about a situation of maximum reduction of aggravation in the tourist–host encounter. It can then be inquired: (i) whether the key players' and influencers' current initiatives in the area are the most suitable; (ii) whether their attention is directed at the correct level; and (iii) whether the suitable dialogues are being engaged in, with all the necessary and suitable people, and in the suitable way.

Peace, Equality and Understanding?

There is a train of thought among organizations and individuals to endow tourism with the capacity of generating peace, or to wish for tourism to develop the capacity. The sentiment was articulated in 1982 in the WTO's Charter of Acapulco; Vukonic (1996, p. 104) reports in the process of describing how Travis encapsulates the ensuing dialogue as demanding 'peaceful encounter' (1996, p. 105). It can be argued that in some parts of the world such as Europe, with its obvious device of the European Union, peace has long been the norm from which conflict is the aberration. It is all too understandable that with the desire for peace so strong and natural, situations can emerge in which, for good feeling and reputation, conflict is concealed and not admitted to. Either the conflict may not be noticed by those who should observe it, or it is avoided because by resolving the conflict other worse difficulties could be created or revealed, or conflict is seen but efforts of improvement are misplaced.

Peace features for consideration among the discussion about culture and tourism and conflict, not just as the opposite of aggression but, equally significantly, as a conditioner of a culture of aspiration, action and activity. Indicative of the sector of belief which holds tourism as an agent to reduce conflict was the establishment of the International Institute of Peace through Tourism (IIPT) and its activities of global conferences. Queen Noor of Jordan in her programme introduction for the IIPT 2nd Conference, asserts her opinion of 'the important contribution that tourism can make to . . . shared goals of peace, understanding and sustainable economic interaction among all people'. She continues with the optimistic prediction: 'travel and tourism now faces major new opportunities to match its economic scope with parallel contributions to social and even political interaction among the peoples and cultures of the world' (Queen Noor of Jordan, 1994, inside facing page). The message contained seems to be that of searching for equality and balance of existence with travel and tourism as mechanisms of help.

UNESCO is required in its constitution to build 'peace in the minds of men' (United Nations/UNESCO, 1994, p. 26); its World Decade of Cultural Development has 'the symbols *roads* and *encounters*'. The cynic might argue that fine words cost those involved in tourism nothing and that peaceful protestations encourage a warm glow about tourism which regards any conflict, such as has been the extreme in Egypt with tourists the target of religious cultural extremists (Hall, 1994), as a departure from the norm. This is not to dismiss the ideal but to say that for its achievement, peace demands the initiative of true identification of the catalysts and agents towards it, and above all the effort of thorough understanding. Clear guidelines or rules of encounter which are known by both sides of the cultural representation are likely to be of help in the process. Ignorance is its own instigator of disagreement. Against any endeavour towards harmony between cultures is the tourism industry's need for cultural difference to be present as novel encouragement to the tourist's curiosity and interest for travel. If the tourism experience provided by operators, of bringing people of different cultures together, is such as to offer a type of situation to allow participants the opportunity and context for developing understanding, then the claims for tourism as an agent of peace could have substance. The critical thing, as is the case with other aspects concerning cultural encounters, is that those immediately engaged in the meeting often do not have very much control over its arrangement and displacement.

The long-standing 'town-twinning' initiative stands as an example of travel and exchange as a process being used as a mechanism to generate peace and understanding. Though this is an effort lodged in officialdom, its characteristic is that it is particular and long term, so allowing relationship and understanding to be developed and built upon slowly and in some depth. There is careful movement from stranger to friend on the host–guest continuum (Ryan, 1991). The logical result of such activity might be the tourist 'going native' or a cultural merge and exchange being attained along the lines of acculturation theory as Nuñez reports (1989, p. 266). Overall, however, with the consumer requirement upon novelty and new stimulation, a slow developing and long-standing relationship is unlikely to be a standard product of tourism.

Though tourism can be the medium for generating cultural knowledge and awareness, it cannot be regarded that a peaceful impulse towards the owners of that culture is the automatic accompaniment to the experience. One objective of amelioration for host and holidaymaker doing things in different ways could be for both 'sides' to a find an acceptable level of compromise and methodology, and this would represent, effectively, a new cultural formulation. But such a *modus operandi* would require knowledge and information for a formula of action to be reached which both groups would regard as fair and acceptable.

At 'grass roots' level, if only on grounds of pragmatism and to provide a protective mechanism, peace or at least tolerance can be the usual or 'natural' situation. However, with an encounter so frequently orchestrated from beyond them, tourists and hosts are often not free to do as they regard best for their joint situation and interest but may be under subjugation to the structures, systems and demands, and clashes and divergences of outside ordinators. So, if differences of aims and viewpoints of orchestrators are the fault, if there is lack of dialogue, agreed compromise, and choice of a suitable system among them, then it can be as much external to the touristic encounter where peace fails to be found and where conflict has presence and influence. This is to reflect the wider situation in relation to cultural conflict. This is to say that it may be at structural level, among developers and multi/transnational operators, where the crucial absence of cultural harmony and understanding exists.

Common Points of Interest

A way forward out of cultural conflict is to use common points of interest as the basis for building understanding (Krippendorf, 1987). There are certain things we all do as human beings and, importantly, which tourists and hosts both do in the territory of potential conflict. The traditional hotel package and 'ghetto' resorts, with everything provided within their perimeters, mitigate against such opportunities of shared contact and necessary endeavour. An argument is (Krippendorf, 1987) that exclusive developments which contain tourists and keep them largely separate serve to help maintain host cultures and assist to remove points of ignition between hosts and tourists due to imbalances of wealth and differences of attitude. One such example is Hawaii's Waikiki Beach which effectively represents a tourism zone apart and different from the more routine and mixed activity of the remainder of the island of Oahu. The perspective also takes the view that containment is the best solution and way of avoiding conflict, by tourists not being 'let out' into an increased portion of host territory. The counter-argument is that if contact points are carefully chosen and directed to be of a type of basic activity of general human endeavour (for example, grocery shopping), the two 'sides' can be brought to a point of departure towards cultural harmony. Relevant to the discussion of whether keeping hosts and tourists separate is a reasonable contemporary idea for avoiding conflict between them and a best option, is de Kadt's opinion (1979, p. 136) that 'tourists have considerably less desire for intense inter-cultural encounters than is alleged'.

Balance and Equality

An imbalance between hosts and tourists may only be felt, and envy generated as a result, though, if judgements are made by them by the same criteria. For example, differences in spending power may deliver conflict. However, if one apparently disadvantaged group is not actually worried about lack of spending power, because of not being part of a consumerist culture and therefore not culturally inclined to place value upon high spending or perceive status as being its accompaniment, then they will not experience resentment at high spenders. The example can be applied to other items of potential conflict: if one side does not attach importance to the matter then they will not be disposed to be exercised about it. Difference, such as could be between an isolated indigenous tribe and a group of stereotypical 'rich' tourists, could be so great that the groups' perspectives and attitudes simply pass each other by, causing no friction.

Conflict is, nonetheless, a product frequently resulting from imbalance among the number of hosts and guests in some areas of the world and at certain seasons (WTO, 1997). The simple mechanism for avoidance of conflict therefore might be to regulate ratios suitably (Hall, 1996), but this is to suppose that no counter pressures would be in place to bring inappropriately large numbers of tourists to a destination, and the reality is that this last situation is often the case. Contradictions and sways are as much among host communities – between conservationists, the rich and poor, those benefiting from tourism, residents in tourists' direct path and those not, and so on – as among tourists and hosts. Of course the differences of outlook in the tourism arena are reflected – albeit often with different concerns to the foremost and often with more financially at stake – among tourism's deciders and initiators.

Hosts' Strengths

Of deep importance and relevance is how host inequality of strength and assets may pertain to encourage or bring about situations and feelings of conflict. The World Commission on Culture and Development makes the particular plea 'that cultural heritage does not become an exclusive commodity to serve tourism (and is degraded and despoiled in the process), but is brought into a mutually supportive relationship with it' (de Cuéllar *et al.*, 1996, p. 184). Highlighting the control aspect, the Commission describes a way in which the indigenous community of Lake Titicaca in Peru, in response to a monopolistic situation 'organized themselves to respond to the upsurge and external control of local tourism so as to improve the local economy yet preserve the culture' (de Cuéllar *et al.*, 1996). Here it might be said, the local community produced action such as would be expected to produce conflict, but in so doing served its own interests and culture. The example reveals an important point which is that a community in an apparent situation of weakness nevertheless possesses the strengths inherent in being on home territory and therefore knowing about its resources and potential. With a unique resource at its disposal, in the development of a conflict situation, a community has quite considerable influence because it possesses the object of tourist desire and outside interest. The further strength hosts may possess is the strength of confidence to serve as a barrier to conflict, and an impulse to behave and expect to be treated as equal, or even superior, to the tourist.

The Power of Information and Knowledge

The location of power is the essence of the tourism–culture relationship. Lukes (1974, p. 56) identified that 'locating power is to fix responsibility for consequences held to flow from the action, or inaction, of certain specifiable agents'. Projects which are 'bottom up' only hold control if for some reason or another a local group has an item to give them power of authority in their life and endeavour. An unique resource, an unreplicable cultural artefact of some kind, for example, is such a feature. An interesting and relevant aspect to power is provided by Mowforth and Munt (1998, p. 277) in their suggested development of Doxey's Irridex for allowing the capacity 'to speculate on the association between Doxey's levels of irritation and the degree of local control'. Information and knowledge, and with whom and where necessary parts of these are located, distinguish outcomes and whether they are felicitous or antagonistic (Reisinger, 1994). As a fundamental matter, tourists and hosts need the equipment of knowledge about each other, about each other's tastes, tendencies and pre-occupations (WTO, 1997). Often this information is not present. To find out when cultural conflict has occurred that with the presence of pre-information could have been avoided, is to make a discovery far too late to be useful. The argument needs to be where the responsibility for providing and obtaining information rests. Again it can be suggested that the formulating agencies and participants in tourism are not providing what is needed to make the touristic encounter a success and without conflict. Currently, participants are not equipped, to an extent. If, as is the case with agencies such as UNESCO and the European Union, support is to local projects, then valuable and useful information needs to be given to local communities, for example about their tourist guests and their attendant cultures.

The Secretary-General of the World Tourism Organization states that:

> Well managed and properly planned ... [tourism] permits the survival of traditions and cultural practices that would otherwise have an uncertain future. It offers exceptional opportunities for encounters between peoples who would otherwise know little of each other.
>
> (Frangialli, 1997, p. 2)

While being undoubtedly well-meaning and optimistic, such sentiments scarcely portray the full picture of involvement needing to be addressed. Such organizations as the WTO need to inquire deeper into the relevance and involvement of agencies at the macro stratum and whether they are appropriate to influence the context for the management and avoidance of conflicts.

The Effect of Ownership

Inextricably linked to the aspects of power, control, and information and knowledge, is the matter of ownership. Having knowledge of the touristic situation involving a unique tourism resource or having rights to it and/or holding control of an item needed for tourism, all endow power and therefore provide a capacity for influence. By such information and/or exclusivity, many apparently disadvantaged groups, such as First Nations peoples, being visited by affluent tourists from the Western world, are, or could be in control. They have an influence which they can bring to the touristic engagement to render them equal to their guests and the masters of the tourism they both share.

One example of how hosts can be in control is shown by the First Nations peoples in Canada. These realize that their 'healing culture are [*sic*] hot ticket items for international tour operators' (Parker, 1997). They have the knowledge and understanding of the value of their product. Aboriginals across Canada are proactively seeking to inform tourists by, acting in concert, placing a tourist information site on the World Wide Web.

Types and Levels of Partnerships to Bring Influence

The Canadian item mentioned draws attention to the necessity of partnership. If properly chosen and constituted, partnership brings strength, range and diversity, and also probably economies of scale. If the problem of cultural conflict is to be addressed effectively a multidisciplinary effort and approach will be a prerequisite. As the Commission of the European Communities (CEC) *Cohesion Policy and Culture: A Contribution to Employment* articulates (1996, p. 8): 'cultural measures are most effective where they form part of a strategic concept'. The document continues, though somewhat cautiously: 'economic development, social cohesion, environmental protection and cultural action are interrelated and not necessarily opposed to each other'. This depicts the jumping-off point while recognizing that conflict is often an outcome of attempts at cooperative action. The challenge is to avoid such potential conflict at the crucial level of decision and influence. As a cooperative and large international cultural tourism initiative to watch, the 'Partners for Livable Places' (McNulty, 1993) may deliver some useful lessons for application. To support and encourage local endeavours and be focused on task-specific individual initiatives is perhaps to partly avoid the issue and follow an easier option of addressing symptoms rather seeing to and removing their cause. As the CEC distinguishes, the strategic level of planning and decision is the important area necessary for focus. The dialogue and interaction of public and private sector parties are necessary, and to be of appropriate calibre, intensity and commitment. In itself, attention on the ground is insufficient.

As was recognized by the introduction to the United Nations World Decade for Cultural Development 1988–1997 round table meeting in 1996 (which itself showed an encouragingly wide sector of representation), the need is for:

> Encouraging the development of partnerships with a view to undertaking actions . . . and . . . associating, both at the conceptual and implementation levels: United Nations system organizations, major international organizations, States, business firms, experts, and public and private representatives from the world of culture and tourism.
>
> (UNESCO, 1997 p. 9)

Echoing this, it was reported in *WTO News* No 4 (November 1996, p. 2) that WTO's Bali Declaration of 1996 stressed: 'Tourism development should be carried out on the basis of careful planning with the broad involvement and active participation of local communities, including women, young people and the private sector.' For success, dialogue and initiative need both firm horizontal and vertical axes and dimensions.

Policy Locations and Derivations

Change and intention need to be represented at the level of policy. Nash (1996, p. 96) describes how, in the north-east of the USA, policy for tourism development at the Foxwoods resort is being determined by the local Mashsantucket Pequot Indians through their tribal council. It was opined in the introduction to the UNESCO World Decade meeting referred to above – perhaps optimistically at this stage but it is to be hoped prophetically – that:

> the growth of ill-planned tourism, imposed from outside, and leading to the wrong kind of development and to socio-cultural disruption is not inevitable. Political decision-makers at the national and local levels, in co-operation with the various actors involved in tourism, have the possibility of choosing what type of tourism they want for their country or their community. Questions of orientation will not be resolved by technology and investment, which can only support the implementation of tourism policy choices.
>
> (UNESCO, 1997, p. 8)

Multiculturalism's Role

Among the matters concerning partnership, producing new and democratic balance and equality and linked to matters of policy, is the whole aspect of multiculturalism. The UNESCO MOST (Management of Social Transformations) programme is concerned with such issues and conflicts as are revealed when tourism and culture meet. A UNESCO MOST Policy Paper No 4 (1996, pp. 10–11) speaks of 'an increasing awareness among decision makers of the need to develop policies which contribute to the development of harmonious relations between diverse ethnic groups' and points to 'the potential of multiculturalism to constitute such a policy response'. It portrays multiculturalism as offering 'some way forward in addressing the challenges posed by the growth of conflict and violence associated with ethnic differences' but suggests that it can be perceived as depicting 'the dangerous divisiveness associated with ethnic and cultural diversity'. The MOST paper focuses on policy initiatives in Sweden, Canada and Australia. With regards to conflict it can be said that it is perhaps easier to resolve where there is literally plenty of room for maneouvre as is the case with all these countries. Ryan (1991, p. 164) draws attention to the relationship between impacts and the size and population of a tourism area. How those endeavours, as MOST describes, pass among the area of tourism should be watched carefully. Ethnic conflict, often featuring in the tourism experience, is of course a feature of the world's wider stage. Among attempts, not specifically related to tourism but with relevance for it, to address and find solutions to ethnic conflict was the 1993 gathering in Hawaii at which Eastern Europe and Russia were to the fore in representation and looking to avoid the impediment of ethnic conflict in a post-Communist era. A resulting Kona Statement (Council for Ethnic Accord of the Project on Ethnic Relations, 1993, p. 3) identified four stages to ethnic conflict which were 'latency, manifestation, actualization and aftermath'. Clearly it is to the latency period that planners and managers need to give remedial attention as a last resort if they are still to avoid conflict they have not anticipated and which is already showing early signs of emergence.

Social Evaluation

Essentially it is social issues and features which are to the fore and which imbue the circumstance of the combination of tourism, culture and conflict. As the UNESCO MOST Policy Paper No 2 (1995, p. 18) on social matters declares quite unequivocally, 'the world crisis is social'. A sign that there is now a degree of recognition at high level about the socio-cultural impacts of tourism was the 1997 WTO and Philippine Department of Tourism 'World Tourism Leaders' meeting on the 'Social Impacts of Tourism' (WTO press release, 23 May 1997). The MOST Policy Paper No 2, a 1995 symposium report, emphasizes the point of a wholesale approach, saying 'social demands cannot be satisfied by narrow, sector-based policies' and recommends 'the elaboration of more holistic strategies for development are urgently needed'. Later in the document, the call is for 'social accounting' (UNESCO, 1995, p. 25).

The Tibet tourism plan incorporates the evaluation of social impacts, and interestingly concludes that they are insubstantial in the case considered due to 'the relatively modest level of tourism proposed and the strong Buddhist-based cultural values of Tibetans' (WTO, 1997, p. 172). Regarding how equability can come to be among strategies for sustainability in relation to indigenous peoples, the IUCN Inter-Commission Task Force on Indigenous Peoples depicts (IUCN, 1997, pp. 151–152) the expected aspects of a Social Impact Assessment for the context and in showing political orientation. Though mechanisms for addressing the relevant impacts due to tourism do not feature as such, much of the action listed by the Commission as necessary – research, citizen participation, etc. – would apply to the tourism situation.

It seems that social impact auditing and the pre-knowledge it can generate could provide a positive contribution towards the resolution of conflict in the tourism and culture domain. Retrospective information can help the next situation but will be too late to save the situation being analysed of costs and benefits already experienced. Ways need to be found of analysing and anticipating impacts other than those that can be seen easily and measured. Environmental impact analysis in advance of development is increasingly utilized in developed nation contexts. Cost–benefit analysis is similarly a normal occurrence. In 1950 K.W. Kapp, an economist, pointed the way with his *The Social Costs of Business Enterprise* (Hodgson, 1997, pp. 56–57). Among other assessments before tourism development occurs, social cost–benefit analysis ought to be undertaken if avoidance of cultural conflict is to be planned for and managed. Evaluation needs to be inclusive and have a wide embrace. As Dixon and Sherman (1990, p. 27) in considering non-rival goods say: 'air is free, as are scenic views, but if no price is charged then no information on the true value of the good is generated'. They go on to warn, as part of their overall discussion on valuing benefits:

> When an area is designated as protected, many of the benefits provided are available to all, and one person's use does not detract from anyone else's (with the exception of overcrowding and congestion). For benefits that accrue only locally, the total amount of social benefits remains within national borders in most cases. When benefits are non rival and accrue globally, however, the country protecting the area is freely providing these benefits to the world at large.
>
> (Dixon and Sherman, 1990)

This, as well as highlighting the need for social cost–benefit analysis, points to the relevance concerning cultural conflict of where power and control reside. The World Decade round table introduction looks to the 'cultural heritage' as a basis for 'development that would be at once economic, social and cultural' (UNESCO, 1997, p. 5). For delivering such an ideal, a wide social cost–benefit evaluation needs to be the prerequisite.

Features of Attention and Expectation

The matters of control, power, ownership, authority, and the associated items of balance, equality, individuality and freedom permeate discussion about tourism and cultural conflict and are critically relevant. The pressing idea is that shifts in power appear to be an inevitable necessity towards bringing improvement and alteration. Partnership at all levels resulting in informed and suitable strategies and plans of 'on-the-ground' implementation is clearly recognized as a need. A good sign is that partnership is featured as a plank of the WTO (1997) White Paper *Adapting to Change: A World Tourism Organization for the 21st Century.* Given that conflicts in tourism are so often the product of power imbalances, lack of necessary dialogue and the existence of inappropriate priorities for providing social good, a particular recommendation was that the role of WTO Affiliate Membership (the operating sector) 'should be enhanced' (*WTO News*, Issue 4, October 1997, p. 5). In all, it is especially important that there should be changes at such a macro-level.

It seems that delivering enough and appropriate information and knowledge to the situation is critical overall to rendering improvement. Information needs first to be obtained; MOST (UNESCO, 1995, p. 1) defines a requirement for 'research which will improve the quality of the evaluation of existing social policies, and which subsequently will provide a useful knowledge base for the design of appropriate social integration policies that secure unity in diversity'. A specific aspect of research needed is defined by Sharpley (1994, p. 202), as being 'how local cultures and people may impact on visitors', serving as a reminder that impacts between host and tourist are not necessarily by the latter upon the former. Also, limits of acceptable change need to be demarcated, and knowledge is necessary to define where the boundaries should be.

A clear priority is also training, of an adequate amount and type, and of all necessary people. On the ground specifically, it is possible that, as de Kadt (1979, p. 57), promoting the ideas of McKean, suggests, guides could serve a role of cultural mediation and explanation, serving to link cultural gaps. Welgemoed (1996) depicts the vital and sensitive roles of guides in discussing the complex touristic and cultural situation that is contemporary South Africa. The encouragement of 'professional training in tourism' was one of the requirements identified in the World Decade round table introduction (UNESCO, 1997, p. 5). But also required is the induction of tourists and hosts into each other's cultural values, priorities and ways of operation. The IIPT tried to encourage the required attitude in the tourist in its 'Credo' which requires the 'peaceful traveller' to – among other duties – 'Accept with grace and gratitude ... diversity ... Appreciate all cultures ... Respect ... hosts' and so on (International Institute for Peace Through Tourism, 1994, p. 5). A very significant demand of the 'Credo' is 'Support travel services that share these [the Credo's] views and act upon them'. Here is a potentially strong influence because if tourists outlawed tourism agencies and operators who were not acting in line with the Credo's principles, then alteration and improvement in the matter of cultural conflict in tourism would certainly be seen. Tourists and hosts, whether consumers, resource owners or protectors, as participators generally do hold and wield power and they need to recognize it.

Ways of Protection, Amelioration or Avoidance

A pessimistic view is to say that the situation relating to tourism and culture is of such fixedness and complexity that the types of changes suggested and recommended are not possible to effect, and that situations leading to conflict cannot be removed. If this counsel of defeat is accepted, are there still ways of protection to minimize and reduce conflict or to produce diversions from it?

One option is to accept the inevitability and to develop the extreme, which globalization heralds and tourism as a global industry encourages, of consciously creating the whole of tourism as operating to the template of a single culture. This would have the outcome of removing cultural conflict because all tourism would be in tune, but of course it would remove all cultural diversity which is exactly what the tourism industry utilizes.

The opposite extreme, and the ultimate defeat strategy, would be not to travel at all so that cultures would not feel any impact of tourism at all. The idea is not only unrealistic, but because of tourism's projected positive impacts such as encouraging peace, it is undesirable also. There is also the view that if we move to a situation where more cultures are badly affected and upset by tourism, eventually a shift of power will be effected in that the unadulterated cultures will emerge into a strong position through their holding a depleting resource which tourism wants for use.

A main option of pessimism is to do what is done by many cultural representatives and groups who are not in control of the tourism which invades and imposes upon their cultures, and this is to create boundaries or shields by producing cultural myths for touristic consumption. In other words developing the 'back-country' – staged authenticity (MacCannell, 1976; Boissevain, 1996). The matter of staged authenticity with regard to its effect on hosts is addressed by Jafari in participating in the World Decade round table debate (Jafari, 1997, p. 46). He enquires, pointing to the main deficiency of the approach, 'what consequences would this process have on the legitimacy or sacredness of a culture and very fabric of it?' He continues to ask the critical question, and it refers to the issue of where power is divested: 'Who does decide what should remain "buried" and what resurrectedly staged?' He adds the major comment of question and wry, elegiac regret: 'Stepping away from the touristic forces, is tourism the only industry which commercializes, consumes, and destroys?'

Critical Matters: Right Balances and Levels of Attention

Although the matter of cultural conflict in tourism has attracted much recognition and involvement, whether this reflects sufficient urgency and intensity is questionable. So often cultural conflict is experienced on the demand side but arises through supply side activity, inactivity, and by the cause of economics as an overriding priority. As important, is that at the macro level adequate communication needs to take place between the public and private sector, between government departments, and between tourism operators and carriers, in order that suitable policies and cooperative action plans may emerge. In discussing heritage dissonance, Tunbridge and Ashworth (1996, p. 275) attribute supreme level responsibility for 'human heritage affairs' to such as the United Nations, UNESCO especially, and in Europe, the EU and Council of Europe. The discussion here has focused on the initiatives and viewpoints of such organizations in recognition of this influence. But the opinion here is too that the whole solution to cultural conflict is unlikely to emerge without further and different efforts and dialogues becoming established and deployed towards the objective. As Tunbridge and Ashworth (1996) distinguish, a eurocentric attitude is a likely characteristic of global agencies. For settling cultural conflict in a travelling world, in which more than those from developed Europeanized countries are participants – as hosts at least – such a neo-colonial viewpoint imposed without adequate and equal participation from others involved might be to exacerbate cultural conflict even as settlement is being sought. Beauclerk *et al.* (1988) cite paternalism as among the potentially disruptive attitudes directed at indigenous peoples by national government agencies. To emphasize the point is not to forget that cultural conflict is as likely to feature between tourism participants among the globe's industrialized portions as between those from the First World and the Third.

The aim here overall has been to describe certain situations and offer discussion for identifying a route of onward travel towards deflecting conflict among cultures in tourism, and for leading towards consensus. It has been shown that cultural conflict seems easier to resolve in each individual case than when many major participants are involved. For significant progress, and for the underlying factors of influence upon cultural conflict in the tourist–host encounter (which is, after all, a symptomatic response at the place of effect, but which may not represent the original conflict and main cause), attention needs to be given to widening the process of debate to include those who control the economic, political and social context from which cultures emerge. The present debate remains too limited.

Accepting that 'culture plays a central role in the well-being of society' (UNESCO press release, 24 February 1998), as part of the 1998 Intergovernmental Conference on Cultural Policies for Development, the President called for '"culturism" instead of "economism"' (UNESCO press release, 30 March 1998). Culture's important role was recognized, as would have been the expectation of a conference gathered to build upon the framework of the report *Our Creative Diversity* (de Cuéllar *et al.*, 1996). More startling, and representing an important appreciation now needing firm and wide dissemination to all participants of influence and involvement, was the attitude of portrayal of the Presidential remark which was suggesting that economics could not and should not continue to be such a major conditioner. The view of reinforcement and extension at the Conference came from Swedish Government minister Carl Tham with the viewpoint: 'culture is an economic and political force, a power factor in itself' (UNESCO press release, 30 March 1998). If culture becomes perceived as so high on the agenda as this, and seen as more vital than the economic objective by tourism involvees, then resolution of cultural conflict may come to be a priority. As was declared at the World Decade for Cultural Development round table:

> Tourism presents a considerable challenge for the future of humanity. At stake are the preservation and best use of cultural and natural resources and heritage, the possibility of a harmonious development based on these resources, and the contribution of tourism to world peace by promoting quality encounters between different cultures.
>
> (UNESCO, 1997, p. 8)

These are fine words of encapsulation and they hold out hope. Yet, without intervention – of information, of planning, of the creativity of fresh ideas and applications, of new participants, of suitable levels and types of partnerships, and of adequate and rewarding patterns of communication – an agenda for consensus between tourism and culture will remain distant.

References

Beauclerk, J., Narby, J. and Townsend, J. (1988) *Indigenous Peoples: A Fieldguide for Development*, Oxfam, Oxford.

Boissevain, J. (ed.) (1996) *Coping with Tourists: European Reactions to Mass Tourism*, Berghahn Books, Providence and Oxford.

Commission of the European Communities (1996) *Cohesion Policy and Culture: A Contribution to Employment*, Commission of the European Communities.

Council for Ethnic Accord of the Project on Ethnic Relations (1993), meeting in Kona, Hawaii.

Craik, J. (1997) The culture of tourism. In: Rojek, C. and Urry, J. (eds) *Touring Cultures: Transformation of Travel and Theory*, Routledge, London and New York.

de Cuéllar, J.P. *et al.* (1996) *Our Creative Diversity*, Report of the World Commission on Culture and Development, 2nd edn. UNESCO Publishing, Paris.

de Kadt, E. (ed.) (1979) *Tourism: Passport to Development*, Oxford University Press, Oxford.

Dixon, J.A. and Sherman, P.B. (1990) *Economics of Protected Areas: A New Look at Benefits and Costs*, Earthscan Publications Ltd, London.

Frangialli, F. (1997) Speech to the 19th Special Session of the UN General Assembly, 24 June.

Gee, C.Y., Makens, J.C. and Choy, D.J.L. (1997) *The Travel Industry*, 3rd edn., Van Nostrand Reinhold, New York.

Hall, C.M. (1994) *Tourism and Politics: Policy, Power and Place*, John Wiley, Chichester.

Hall, C.M. (1996) Environmental impact of tourism in the Pacific. In: Hall, C.M. and

Page, S. (eds) *Tourism in the Pacific: Issues and Cases,* International Thomson Business Press, London, pp. 65–80.

Hannerz, U. (1996) *Transnational Connections: Culture, People, Places,* Routledge, London and New York.

Hodgson, G. (1997) Economics, environmental policy and the transcendence of utilitarianism. In: Foster, J. (ed.) *Valuing Nature: Economics, Ethics and Environment,* Routledge, London and New York.

International Institute for Peace Through Tourism (1994) 2nd Global Conference Programme 'Building a Sustainable World Through Tourism', Canada.

IUCN (1997) *Indigenous Peoples and Sustainability: Cases and Actions,* International Books, Utrecht.

Jafari, J. (1997) Tourism and culture: an inquiry into paradoxes. In: Proceedings of a round table *Culture, Tourism, Development: Crucial Issues for the XXIst Century,* UNESCO, Paris, pp. 43–47.

Krippendorf, J. (1987) *The Holidaymakers: Understanding the Impact of Leisure and Travel,* Butterworth-Heinemann, Oxford.

Lukes, S. (1974) *Power: A Radical View,* Macmillan, London.

MacCannell, D. (1976) *The Tourist: A New Theory of the Leisure Class,* Schocken Books, New York.

McNulty, R. (1993) Cultural tourism and sustainable development. In: Brent Ritchie, J.R. and Hawkins, D.E. (eds) *World Travel and Tourism Review: Indicators, Trends and Issues,* Vol 3, CAB International, Wallingford.

Mowforth, M. and Munt, I. (1998) *Tourism and Sustainability: New Tourism in the Third World,* Routledge, London and New York.

Nash, D. (1996) *Anthropology of Tourism,* Pergamon/Elsevier, Kidlington, Oxford.

Nuñez, T. (1989) Touristic studies in anthropological perspective. In: Smith, V. (ed.) *Hosts and Guests: The Anthropology of Tourism,* 2nd edn, University of Pennsylvania Press, Philadelphia, pp. 265–274.

Parker, B. (1997) as reported in *The Sunday Times,* 28 September.

Queen Noor of Jordan (1994) in the International Institute for Peace Through Tourism 2nd Global Conference Programme 'Building a Sustainable World Through Tourism', Canada.

Reisinger, Y. (1994) Social contact between tourists and hosts of different cultural backgrounds. In: Seaton, A. *et al.* (eds) *Tourism: The State of the Art,* John Wiley, Chichester, pp. 742–754.

Ryan, C. (1991) *Recreational Tourism,* Routledge, London and New York.

Sharpley, R. (1994) *Tourism, Tourists and Society,* ELM Publications, Huntingdon.

Shaw, G and Williams, A.M. (1994) *Critical Issues in Tourism: A Geographical Perspective,* Blackwell, Oxford.

Smith, V. (1989) Introduction. In: Smith, V. (ed.) *Hosts and Guests: The Anthropology of Tourism,* 2nd edn, University of Pennsylvania Press, Philadelphia, pp. 1–17.

Tunbridge, J.E. and Ashworth, G.J. (1996) *Dissonant Heritage: The Management of the Past as a Resource in Conflict,* John Wiley, Chichester.

Turner, L. and Ash, J. (1975) *The Golden Hordes: International Tourism and the Pleasure Periphery,* Constable, London.

United Nations/UNESCO (1994) *Rethinking Development: World Decade for Cultural Development 1988–1997,* United Nations/UNESCO, Paris.

UNESCO (1995) *MOST Newsletter,* 3 June.

UNESCO (1995) *From Social Exclusion to Social Cohesion: A Policy Agenda*, MOST Policy Paper, No 2, UNESCO, Paris.
UNESCO (1996) *Multiculturalism: New Policy Responses to Diversity*, MOST Policy Paper, No 4, UNESCO, Paris.
UNESCO (1997) Proceedings of a round table *Culture, Tourism, Development: Crucial Issues for the XXIst century*, UNESCO, Paris.
UNESCO (24 February 1998) Office of Public Information, press release.
UNESCO (30 March 1998) Office of Public Information, press release.
Vukonic, B. (1996) *Tourism and Religion*, Pergamon/Elsevier Science Ltd, Kidlington, Oxford.
Welgemoed, M (1996) The tourist guide and culture broker: a South African scenario. In: Robinson, M. *et al.* (eds) *Tourism and Culture: Image, Identity and Marketing*, Centre for Travel and Tourism and Business Education Publishers, Sunderland.
WTO (1997) *National and Regional Tourism Planning*, Routledge, London and New York.
WTO News No 4, November 1996, WTO, Madrid.
WTO News Issue 4, October 1997, WTO, Madrid.
WTO (23 May 1997) press release.
WTO (1997) *Adapting to Change: A World Tourism Organization for the 21st Century*. White Paper.

Index